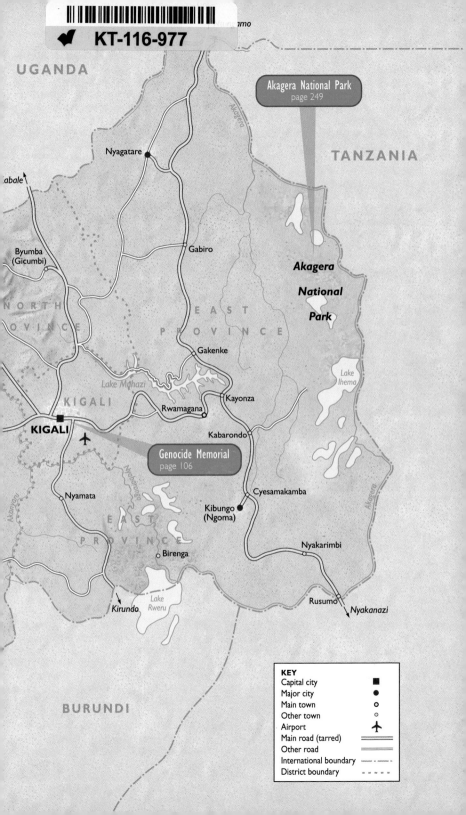

Rwanda
Don't
miss...

Intore dancing
Traditionally performances
consisted mainly of warlike
dances, such as the *ikuma*
(lance), *umeheto* (bow)
and *ingabo* (shield)
(AVZ) page 29

Gorilla tracking
Tracking mountain gorillas in the
Virungas is a peerless wildlife
experience, and one of Africa's
indisputable travel highlights
(AVZ) page 220

Exodus use
Amaharo turs fs Nei
Rwandain turs & JJ says
Nuyone good...

Rwanda

the Bradt Travel Guide

Philip Briggs　　**Janice Booth**

edition
4

www.bradtguides.com

Bradt Travel Guides Ltd, UK
The Globe Pequot Press Inc, USA

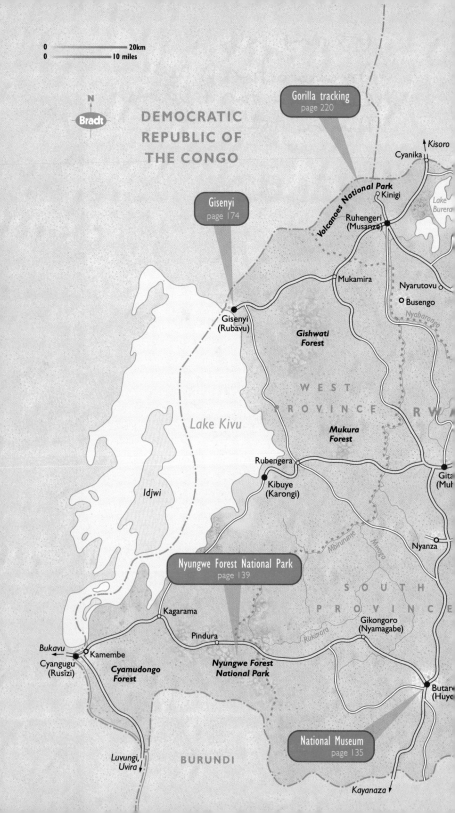

National parks
Akagera National Park is Rwanda's answer to the famous savanna reserves of Kenya, Tanzania and the like
(AVZ) page 249

People and culture
Batwa pottery – the Batwa use their feet to trample the clay into malleability and then their hands to shape it into a variety of items
(AVZ) page 30

Wildlife
Rwanda's conservation areas are home to several different ecosystems and a range of large mammals
(AVZ) page 3

The scenery around Lake Burera is enhanced by the outlines of the Virunga Mountains that provided the stunning backdrop to *Gorillas in the Mist* (AVZ) page 203 *right* All baby gorillas are given a name in the Kwita Izina naming ceremony, which is an annual event held in mid to late June (AVZ) page 217

below left The hike to Dian Fossey's tomb and the adjacent gorilla cemetery at the former Karisoke Research Camp makes a popular day hike (AVZ) page 228

below right Volcanoes National Park is an immensely scenic and ecologically diverse destination, spanning altitudes of 2,400m to 4,507m, and dominated by the string of volcanoes after which it is named (AVZ) page 211

bottom The Mountain gorilla (*Gorilla gorilla berengi*) is a highly sociable creature, moving in defined troops of anything from five to 50 animals (GE/MP/FLPA) page 222

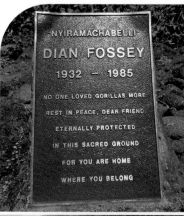

above Lake Muhazi — the birdlife here is highly rewarding, and the lake harbours an unusually dense population of spotted-necked otter (NF) page 237

left The Rusumo border with Tanzania is the site of Rwanda's most impressive waterfall (AVZ) page 245

bottom Rwanda's mountainous topography has earned it the nickname 'Land of a Thousand Hills' (AVZ) page 3

AUTHORS

Philip Briggs has been exploring the highways, byways and backwaters of Africa since 1986, when he spent several months backpacking on a shoestring from Nairobi to Cape Town. In 1991, he wrote the Bradt Guide to South Africa, the first such guidebook to be published internationally after the release of Nelson Mandela. Over the rest of the 1990s, Philip wrote a series of pioneering Bradt Guides to destinations that were then – and in some cases still are – otherwise practically uncharted by the travel publishing industry. These included the first dedicated guidebooks to Tanzania, Uganda, Ethiopia, Malawi, Mozambique,

Ghana and Rwanda (co-authored with Janice Booth), all now in their 4th–6th editions. Philip has visited more than two dozen African countries in total and written about most of them for specialist travel and wildlife magazines, including *Africa Birds & Birding, Africa Geographic, BBC Wildlife, Travel Africa* and *Wanderlust*. He still spends at least four months on the road every year, usually accompanied by his wife, the travel photographer Ariadne Van Zandbergen, and spends his rest of the time battering away at a keyboard in the sleepy village of Bergville, in the uKhahlamba-Drakensberg region of South Africa.

Janice Booth's career has included stage management, archaeology, charity work, writing, selling haberdashery in Harrods, translating documents about African agriculture, compiling puzzle magazines, editing Bradt guides, judging writing competitions and travelling whenever possible. Since co-authoring the first edition of this guide she has lectured and written about Rwanda and led tours there.

RWANDA UPDATES WEBSITE

For the latest travel news about Rwanda, please visit the new interactive Bradt Rwanda update website: http://updates.bradtguides.com/rwanda.

Administered by *Rwanda* author Philip Briggs, this website will supplement the printed Bradt guidebook, providing a forum whereby the latest travel news can be publicised online with immediate effect.

This update website is a free service for readers of Bradt's Rwanda – and for anybody else who cares to drop by and browse – but its success will depend greatly on the input of those selfsame readers, whose collective experience of Rwanda's tourist attractions and facilities will always be broader and more divergent than those of any individual author.

So if you have any comments, queries, grumbles, insights, news or other feedback, you're invited to post them directly on the website, or to email them to Philip at **e** philari@hixnet.co.za.

PUBLISHER'S FOREWORD   *Hilary Bradt*

The first Bradt travel guide was written in 1974 by George and Hilary Bradt on a river barge floating down a tributary of the Amazon. In the 1980s and '90s the focus shifted away from hiking to broader-based guides covering new destinations – usually the first to be published about these places. In the 21st century Bradt continues to publish such ground-breaking guides, as well as others to established holiday destinations, incorporating in-depth information on culture and natural history with the nuts and bolts of where to stay and what to see.

*   *   *

What a lot has changed in Rwanda since we launched the first edition in Kigali in 2001! During that visit I was the only tourist in the small group visiting the gorillas, the roads through the beguiling countryside were full of potholes, and accommodation outside Kigali was fairly basic. Now the new Rwanda has embraced tourism with the far-sighted view of the importance of sustainability and conservation that is a model for Africa. This remains *the* guidebook to the country and I am happy that it remains in the hands of the original authors whose enthusiasm for Rwanda is shared by all visitors.

Fourth edition December 2009
First published 2001

Bradt Travel Guides Ltd, 23 High Street, Chalfont St Peter, Bucks SL9 9QE, England
www.bradtguides.com
Published in the USA by The Globe Pequot Press Inc, 246 Goose Lane,
PO Box 480, Guilford, Connecticut 06475-0480

Text copyright © 2009 Philip Briggs
Maps copyright © 2009 Bradt Travel Guides Ltd
Illustrations copyright © 2009 Individual photographers and artists

ISBN-13: 978 1 84162 306 1
British Library Cataloguing in Publication Data
A catalogue record for this book is available from the British Library

Photographs Gerry Ellis/Minden Pictures/FLPA (GE/MP/FLPA), Nick Fraser (NF), Paul Hobson/FLPA (PH/FLPA), Frans Lanting/FLPA (FL/FLPA), Thomas Marent/Minden Pictures/FLPA (TM/MP/FLPA), Cyril Ruoso/Minden Pictures/FLPA (CR/MP/FLPA), Lindsay Stark (LS), Ariadne Van Zandbergen (AVZ)
Front cover Mountain gorilla (*Gorilla beringei beringei*) (AVZ)
Back cover Girl in market on Kigali–Butare road (LS), Lake Burera (AVZ)
Title page Woman in Gikongora (LS), Golden monkey (PH/FLPA), Fishermen on Lake Kivu (AVZ)
Illustrations Annabel Milne
Maps Redmoor Design, Tavistock, Devon; Steve Munns

Typeset from the authors' disc by Wakewing, High Wycombe
Printed and bound in Italy by Legoprint SpA, Trento

Acknowledgements

PHILIP BRIGGS AND ARIADNE VAN ZANDBERGEN The successful research of this fourth edition is largely thanks to the generous support of the following tourist-related individuals and institutions: Rosette Rugamba, Patrick Manzi Mbayiha and Emmanuel Werabe of ORTPN; Praveen Moman, Yusuf Mulima Mubiru and Boaz Tumwesigye of Volcanoes Safaris, as well as our enthusiastic drivers Kumugisha Kirenga and Paul Ruganintwali; Danny Bizimana of Bizidanny Tours; and Jimmy K Mugabo of Rwandair.

For various editorial contributions, updates and fact checking, thanks to Carlyla Dawson, Caroline Pomoroy, Chris Frean, Derek Schuurman, Elaine Gardner, Evelyn Karamagi-Kamau, Garron Hanson, Greg Bakunzi, Ian Munanura, Kenneth Barham, Damniel Lapidus, Luis Pinheiro, Lukas Austin-Page, Marcell Claassen, Mark Reiner, Melissa Peery, Michael Fuchs, Michael Grosspietsch, Rachel J Strohm, Rebecca White, Rica Rwigamba, Rosemary Mugambi, Ryan Plakonouris, Sarah Speake and the many readers of earlier editions whose updates are posted and acknowledged on our update website, http://updates.bradtguides.com/rwanda.

We remain indebted to the late Florence Nkera, who made sure our introduction to Rwanda in 2000 was such a positive experience, and to co-author Janice Booth for her hard work on earlier editions of this guide and ongoing 'behind the scenes' involvement in this one.

JANICE BOOTH As I won't be involved with subsequent editions of this guide, I'd like to remember some of the people in Rwanda who were so supportive of the first edition back in 2000, at a time when the media had nothing good to say about the country and tourists hesitated to return. The late Florence Nkera was an inspiration throughout, with her enthusiasm and energy, and Patricia Kanyiginya has been a steady source of help. Rosemary Museminali, then Rwandan Ambassador in London, patiently read and corrected the proofs of the first edition, working late into the night; Théogène Rudasingwa in the President's Office checked the History section; and Claver Gatete (now Ambassador in London) gave me additional information and encouragement. Rwanda's First Lady and the Minister for Tourism demonstrated their support by attending the guide's official launch in Kigali; and Zac Nsenga, now Rwandan Ambassador in Washington, reminded me – vitally! – on my first visit not to miss the mountain gorillas. They all had confidence in us, just as we had confidence in Rwanda. Beth Payne, Liz Williamson and Marie Chantal Uwimana all provided useful information, and many other Rwandans helped with smiles and friendship as I travelled round their country. Of course I also thank my co-author Philip, whose input has been essential and who is always a pleasure to work with. Finally, if Protais Rwihimba, who died in the genocide, had not written to me in 1978 and launched a friendship that lasted 16 years, I would never have come to Rwanda to look for his family and this book would not exist, so perhaps his has been the greatest contribution.

This should really be Philip's story, as the guide is now his, but he's allowing me a final word. When I first went to Rwanda, in February 2000, I had no thought whatever of writing a travel guide. I was hoping to find news of a Rwandan friend who'd been silent since the 1994 genocide; I assumed he was dead, and didn't expect to enjoy my visit. The media portrayed a grim, inhospitable country, deeply scarred, still volatile and dangerous.

In fact the beauty of Rwanda and the charm of its people captivated me. I jolted along twisty, pot-holed roads in battered public transport, feeling completely safe. The views were superb. People were still traumatised and grieving, but friendly. I even visited the mountain gorillas. From Kigali I faxed Hilary Bradt and convinced her that a guidebook was essential. Luckily Philip was available to co-author it – and you're now holding the fourth edition.

There's no doubt that it helped Rwanda greatly as the country struggled to recover. Before the genocide, tourism had been an important source of foreign exchange, and regaining this income was vital. The guide's existence reassured travellers and tour operators that the country was now safe and accessible. It was also read by aid workers, diplomats, investors – and even Rwandans, newly arrived from exile abroad.

Tourists returned, in rapidly growing numbers, and tourism is now the top earner of foreign exchange. But – how much impact has this had on villagers at grass-roots level? Have the 'small people', away from the tourist areas, benefited from this influx of dollars, sterling and euros? Did our guide's usefulness extend to them too? To find out, I went back to Rwanda in 2009.

Visiting remote hamlets deep in the green, hilly countryside, I saw the answers to my questions. From the fees paid by tourists visiting the national parks, 5% is used to finance small-scale development in the surrounding areas: water-tanks, classrooms, bridges, beekeeping, brick-making, market gardening, livestock, and dozens of other practical projects at the heart of rural life. Visitors are thus helping to fund activities they may never see, but which are a life-line for the local people. It's just the result I had hoped for.

My friend had indeed died in 1994, as did many of his family; but others survived and we're in regular contact. I'm proud of their friendship. Their children are part of the new, post-genocide generation that will carry Rwanda forward into the future. It is an astonishing – and humbling – country. I feel so fortunate to have been involved.

Foreword

It is a pleasure to write the foreword to this new edition of the Bradt Guide to Rwanda.

Back when the first edition was launched in Kigali in 2000, the shadow cast by the 1994 genocide was still making tourists reluctant to visit our country. The guide complemented government efforts to reassure them and, since then, there has been a steady increase in the numbers and nationalities of travellers crossing Rwanda's borders and arriving at our international airport.

The valuable foreign exchange that visitors bring is not the only benefit. Thanks to the guide, many tourists have been reaching Rwanda already aware of the progress that has been made over the last decade and a half, and the determination with which we are overcoming our challenges. Those drawn here by our rare mountain gorillas have seen that these are only one facet of the country. They have been able to read about Rwanda's complex history and learn about our people, then deepen this knowledge during their visit. In addition, the personal story behind the writing of the first edition has touched Rwandans and visitors alike, and gives the book a 'human face'; it has always been more than just a standard guidebook to the country.

The new, modern Rwanda charms tourists with the timeless warmth of its welcome and the beauty of its countryside. We invite friends and visitors from around the world to enjoy our rich culture, engaging story and amazing wildlife – this guide is an effective tool in helping them to experience our country and people.

Rt Honourable Bernard Makuza
Prime Minister, Republic of Rwanda

Contents

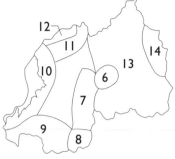

Introduction   IX

PART ONE   **GENERAL INFORMATION**   I

Chapter 1   **Background Information**   3
Geography 3, Natural history and conservation, 3,
History 6, People 23, Language 23, Religion 24,
Education 26, Culture 29

Chapter 2   **Practical information**   33
When to visit 33, Itinerary planning 33, Tourist
information and services 34, Tour operators 34, Red
tape 36, Embassies and consulates 36, Getting there and
away 37, Safety 40, What to take 44, Money 47,
Budgeting 49, Getting around 50, Accommodation 53,
Eating and drinking 54, Public holidays and events 57,
Shopping 58, Media and communications 58, Cultural
etiquette 60, Becoming involved 60, Investing in
Rwanda 63

Chapter 3   **Health**   64
Before you go 64, Common medical problems 68,
Ebola 73, Animals 73, Useful contacts in Kigali 74

PART TWO   **THE GUIDE**   75

Chapter 4   **Kigali**   77
Getting there and away 80, Getting around 81, Tourist
information 84, Tour operators 84, Where to stay 85,
Where to eat and drink 93, Nightlife 98, Arts and
entertainment 98, Sport 99, Shopping 100, Other
practicalities 105, What to see and do 106, Excursions
further afield 112

Chapter 5   **The road to Butare (Huye)**   115
Gitarama (Muhanga) 115, Ruhango 120, Nyanza 121

Chapter 6   **Butare (Huye)**   129
Getting there and away 129, Getting around 130,
Security 130, Where to stay 130, Where to eat and
drink 133, Nightlife 134, Shopping 134, Other
practicalities 134, What to see and do 135, Excursions
from Butare 136

Chapter 7	**Nyungwe Forest National Park**	139
	Natural history 141, Getting there and away 150, Park fees 150, Where to stay and eat 150, Trails and activities 151	
Chapter 8	**Lake Kivu**	161
	Cyangugu (Rusizi) 162, Kibuye (Karongi) 169, Gisenyi (Rubavu) 174	
Chapter 9	**Ruhengeri (Musanze) and Surrounds**	189
	Getting there and away 189, Tourist information 191, Tour operators 192, Where to stay 192, Where to eat and drink 196, Shopping 197, Other practicalities 199, Excursions from Ruhengeri 199	
Chapter 10	**Volcanoes National Park**	211
	History, conservation and ecotourism 213, Getting there and away 217, Where to stay and eat 218, Gorilla tracking 220, Golden monkey tracking 227, Other hikes 227, Iby'iwacu Cultural Village 232	
Chapter 11	**Eastern Rwanda**	233
	The Byumba (Gicumbi) road 233, The Nyagatare road 236, The Rusumo Road 241	
Chapter 12	**Akagera National Park**	249
	Natural history 250, Getting there and away 258, Park fees 258, Where to stay 259, Activities 259	
Appendix 1	**Language**	263
Appendix 2	**Further Information**	269

NOTE ABOUT MAPS

Several maps use grid lines to allow easy location of sites. Map grid references are listed in square brackets after listings in the text, with page number followed by grid number, eg: [156 C3].

LIST OF MAPS

Akagera National Park	248	Kigali environs	78–9
Butare (Huye) orientation	128	Kigali Nyamirambo & Nyakabanda	89
Butare (Huye) town centre	132	Lakes Burera & Ruhondo	206
Cyangugu (Rusizi) & Kamembe	164	Nyagatare	240
Eastern Midlands	234	Nyanza	122
Gisenyi (Rubavu)	176–7	Nyungwe Forest National Park	140
Gitarama (Muhanga)	116	Ruhengeri (Musanze)	194–5
Kibungo (Ngoma)	242	Rwanda	colour section ii–iii
Kibuye (Karongi)	170	Virunga Foothills	188
Kigali central area	82–3	Volcanoes National Park	212
Kigali city centre	86		

Introduction

Is there any other wildlife encounter to match tracking mountain gorillas through the thin moist air of Rwanda's Virunga Mountains? Ascending first through fertile volcanic slopes dense with cultivation, one crosses the boundary into Volcanoes National Park, to follow a narrow footpath into a hushed montane forest composed of impenetrable bamboo skyscrapers, broadleaved herbaceous shrubs and fragrant hagenia stands. This is nature in the raw: the muddy forest floor scattered with elephant and buffalo spoor while birds and monkeys chatter overhead and spiteful nettles lie waiting in the margins.

Deep in the misty forest, you finally come upon your quarry. It might be a young female attempting to climb a liana, soft black coat comically fluffed-up as it demonstrates the arboreal incompetence of this most sedentary of apes. Or perhaps a barrel-headed silverback, no taller than an average human, but thrice as bulky, delicately shredding a succulent stick of bamboo as it sits peaceably on the forest floor. Or a curious mother, taking two paces forward then raising its head in your direction to stare questioningly into your eyes, as if seeking a connection. Or maybe a young male putting on a chest-beating display for your benefit, safe in the knowledge that this naked ape won't challenge its dominance. No two gorilla encounters can be exactly the same but, as anybody who has looked into the liquid brown eyes of a wild mountain gorilla will confirm, it is always an awesome experience – inspirational, emotional, and profoundly satisfying.

Rwanda is the world's premier gorilla-tracking destination. It was here, on the southern slopes of the Virungas, that the late Dian Fossey studied gorilla behaviour for almost 20 years, and on these very same bamboo-covered slopes that the acclaimed movie *Gorillas in the Mist* was shot on location in 1988. At that time, Rwanda was entrenched as *the* place to see mountain gorillas, and tourism had emerged as one of its three main sources of foreign revenue. And all else being equal, that should have been the beginning of Rwanda's emergence as a truly great ecotourism destination. Instead, the country was destabilised by a protracted civil war that started in 1990 and reached its horrific climax four years later.

Today, Rwanda doesn't feature prominently on many people's holiday wish list. Like Uganda after Idi Amin, or Ethiopia after the 1985 famine, this small central African country is known to most outsiders for a solitary event: the 1994 genocide that claimed the lives of one-eighth of its population, and forced twice as many to flee into wretched makeshift refugee camps in Tanzania, Uganda or the Congo. The genocide subsided barely 100 days after it began, when the Rwanda Patriotic Front captured the capital Kigali, and forced the ringleaders into exile.

But one of the flaws inherent in viewing the world through the restless eyes of the mass media is that the likes of Rwanda are deemed newsworthy only when disaster strikes. The moment things calm down, the cameras shift their attention to the next breaking crisis. And so it was that the world largely ignored Rwanda as it embarked on the long and arduous road to normalisation – miraculously, a path from which it has barely deviated in 15 years. Indeed, Rwanda today is widely regarded as ranking among the most economically buoyant and politically enlightened African countries.

Few could travel through Rwanda and not be cognisant of the terrible events of 1994. Indeed, almost every town and village houses a genocide memorial paying respect to the massacred, whilst also highlighting the survivors' determination that such atrocities should neither be forgotten nor be repeated. But for potential visitors, it is more important to dwell on the future, and the capacity of tourism to stimulate economic growth and nurture political stability.

Some figures. In 1999, when Volcanoes National Park reopened for gorilla tracking, it attracted fewer than 2,000 visitors, most of them backpackers and overland trucks making a cross-border pit-stop visit from Uganda. By contrast, a full 38,350 people tracked Rwanda's gorillas in 2008, and tourism now ranks as the country's largest source of foreign revenue, contributing more than US$200 million to the annual GDP, and providing direct or indirect employment to around 350,000 people.

So if you've ever dreamed of tracking gorillas through the same misty slopes once trodden by Dian Fossey or Sigourney Weaver, visit Rwanda. And while you're about it, don't forget that there is much else to see here besides gorillas. The mountain-ringed inland sea that is Lake Kivu; the immense Nyungwe Forest National Park with its chimpanzees, monkeys and rare birds; the wild savanna of Akagera National Park – and above all, perhaps, the endless succession of steep cultivated mountains that have justifiably earned Rwanda the soubriquets 'the Land of a Thousand Hills' and 'The Switzerland of Africa'. It's a wonderful place to visit.

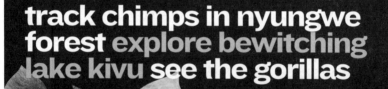

Part One

GENERAL INFORMATION

GEOGRAPHY
Land area 26,340km² (less than half that of Scotland)
Location 120km south of the Equator in the Tropic of Capricorn
Capital Kigali
Rainfall Annual average 900–1,600mm; rainy seasons March–May and October–December
Average temperature 24.6–27.6°C; hottest August and September
Altitude From 1,000 to 4,500m above sea level; highest point is Mt Kalisimbi (4,507m)
Terrain Mostly grassy uplands and hills; relief is mountainous with altitude declining from west to east
Vegetation Ranges from dense equatorial forest in the northwest to tropical savanna in the east
Land use 47% cropland, 22% forest, 18% pasture, 13% other
Natural resources Some tin, gold and natural gas
Main exports Coffee and tea
National parks Volcanoes (northwest); Nyungwe (southwest); Akagera (east)

HUMAN STATISTICS
Population 9.9 million (2007 estimate); 53.8% female, 46.2% male
Life expectancy at birth Women 45 years, men 42 years
Religion Roman Catholic (majority), Protestant, Muslim, traditional
Official languages Kinyarwanda and English. French and Swahili are also widely spoken.
Education Primary, secondary, technical/vocational, higher/university
GDP per capita US$1,000 (2007 estimate)

POLITICS/ADMINISTRATION
Government The broad-based Government of National Unity, with three branches: executive, legislative and judicial
Ruling party Rwanda Patriotic Front (RPF)
President Paul Kagame
Prime minister Bernard Makuza
National flag Blue, yellow and green, with a sun in the top right-hand corner
Administrative divisions 4 provinces plus Kigali City, subdivided into 30 districts and 416 sectors

PRACTICAL DETAILS
Time GMT +2 hours
Currency Rwandan franc
Main health risk Malaria
Electricity 230/240 volts at 50Hz
International telephone country code 250
Airport Kigali International Airport
Nearest seaports Mombasa (1,760km); Dar es Salaam (1,528km)

Background Information

Rwanda is a land-locked country in Central Africa. Also known as the 'Land of a Thousand Hills', Rwanda has five volcanoes, 23 lakes and numerous rivers. The country lies 1,270km west of the Indian Ocean and 2,000km east of the Atlantic – literally in the heart of Africa.

GEOGRAPHY

Rwanda's mountainous topography is a product of its position on the eastern rim of the Albertine Rift Valley, part of the Great Rift Valley which cuts through Africa from the Red Sea to Mozambique. The country's largest freshwater body, Lake Kivu, which forms the border with the Democratic Republic of the Congo (DRC), is effectively a large sump hemmed in by the Rift Valley walls, while its highest peaks – in the volcanic Virunga chain – are a result of the same geological process that formed the Rift Valley 20 million years ago. The Rift Valley escarpment running through western Rwanda also serves as a watershed between Africa's two largest drainage systems: the Nile and the Congo.

Western and central Rwanda are characterised by a seemingly endless vista of steep mountains, interspersed with several substantial lakes whose irregular shape follows the mountains that surround them. Much of this part of the country lies at elevations of between 1,500 and 2,500m. Only in the far east of the country, along the Tanzania border, do the steep mountains give way to the lower-lying, flatter terrain of the Lake Victoria Basin. The dominant geographical feature of this part of the country is the Kagera River and associated network of swamps and small lakes running along the Tanzania border, eventually to flow into Lake Victoria, making it the most remote source of the world's longest river, the Nile (see box *The Riddle of The Nile*, pages 4–5). Much of this ecosystem is protected within Akagera National Park.

NATURAL HISTORY AND CONSERVATION

VEGETATION In prehistoric times, as much as a third of what is now Rwanda was covered in montane rainforest, with the remainder of the highlands supporting open grassland. Since the advent of Iron-Age technology and agriculture some 2,000 years ago, much of Rwanda's natural vegetation has been replaced by agriculture, a process that has accelerated dramatically in the last 100 years. The only large stand of forest left in Rwanda today is Nyungwe, in the southwest, though several other small relic forest patches are dotted around the country, notably Cyamudongo and Mukura Forests. Patches of true forest still occur on the Virungas, though most of the natural vegetation on this range consists of bamboo forest and open moorland. Outside of Nyungwe (now designated a national park) and the Virungas, practically no montane grassland is left in

The first European to see Lake Victoria was John Hanning Speke, who marched from Tabora to the site of present-day Mwanza in 1858 following his joint 'discovery' of Lake Tanganyika with Richard Burton the previous year. Speke named the lake after Queen Victoria, but prior to that Arab slave traders called it Ukerewe (still the name of its largest island). It is unclear what name was in local use, since the only one used by Speke is Nyanza, which simply means lake.

A major goal of the Burton-Speke expedition had been to solve the great geographical enigma of the age, the source of the White Nile. Speke, based on his brief glimpse of the southeast corner of Lake Victoria, somewhat whimsically proclaimed his 'discovery' to be the answer to that riddle. Burton, with a comparable lack of compelling evidence, was convinced that the great river flowed out of Lake Tanganyika. The dispute between the former travelling companions erupted bitterly on their return to Britain, where Burton – the more persuasive writer and respected traveller – gained the backing of the scientific establishment.

Over 1862–63, Speke and Captain James Grant returned to Lake Victoria, hoping to prove Speke's theory correct. They looped inland around the western shore of the lake, arriving at the court of King Mutesa of Buganda, then continued east to the site of present-day Jinja, where a substantial river flowed out of the lake after tumbling over a cataract that Speke named Ripon Falls. From here, the two explorers headed north, sporadically crossing paths with the river until they reached Lake Albert, then following the Nile to Khartoum and Cairo. Speke's declaration that 'The Nile is settled' met with mixed support back home. Burton and other sceptics pointed out that Speke had bypassed the entire western shore of his purported great lake, had visited only a couple of points on the northern shore, and had not attempted to explore the east. Nor, for that matter, had he followed the course of the Nile in its entirety. Speke, claimed his detractors, had seen several different lakes and different stretches of river, connected only in his own deluded mind. The sceptics had a point, but Speke had nevertheless gathered sufficient geographical evidence to render his claim highly plausible. His notion of one great lake, far from being mere whimsy, was backed by anecdotal information gathered from local sources along the way.

Matters were scheduled to reach a head on 16 September 1864, when an eagerly awaited debate between Burton and Speke – in the words of the former, 'what silly tongues called the "Nile Duel"' – was due to take place at the Royal Geographical Society (RGS). And reach a head they did, but in circumstances more tragic than anybody could have anticipated. On the afternoon of the debate, Speke went out shooting with a cousin, only to stumble while crossing a wall and in the process discharging a barrel of his shotgun into his heart. The subsequent inquest recorded a verdict of accidental death, but it has often been suggested – purely on the basis of the curious timing – that Speke deliberately took his life rather than face up to Burton in public. Burton, who had seen Speke less than three hours earlier, was by all accounts deeply troubled by Speke's death, and years later he was quoted as stating 'the uncharitable [say] that I shot him' – an accusation that seems to have been aired only in Burton's imagination.

Speke was dead, but the 'Nile debate' would keep kicking for several years. In 1864, Sir Stanley and Lady Baker became the first Europeans to reach Lake Albert and the nearby Murchison Falls in present-day Uganda. The Bakers, much to the delight of the anti-Speke lobby, were convinced that this newly named lake was a source of the Nile,

Rwanda; the highlands are instead dominated by the terraced agriculture that gives the Rwandan countryside much of its distinctive character. The far east of Rwanda supports an altogether different vegetation: the characteristic African 'bush', a mosaic of savanna woodland and grassland dominated by thorny acacia trees.

though they openly admitted it might not be the only one. Following the Bakers' announcement, Burton put forward a revised theory, namely that the most remote source of the Nile was the Rusizi River, which he believed flowed out of the northern head of Lake Tanganyika and emptied into Lake Albert.

In 1865, the RGS followed up on Burton's theory by sending Dr David Livingstone to Lake Tanganyika. Livingstone, however, was of the opinion that the Nile's source lay further south than Burton supposed, and so he struck out towards the lake along a previously unexplored route. Leaving from Mikindani in the far south of present-day Tanzania, Livingstone followed the Rovuma River inland, continuing westward to the southern tip of Lake Tanganyika. From there, he ranged southward into present-day Zambia, where he came across a new candidate for the source of the Nile: the swampy Lake Bangweulu and its major outlet the Lualaba River. It was only after his famous meeting with Henry Stanley at Ujiji, in November 1871, that Livingstone (in the company of Stanley) visited the north of Lake Tanganyika and Burton's cherished Rusizi River, which, it transpired, flowed into the lake. Burton, nevertheless, still regarded Lake Tanganyika as the most likely source of the Nile, while Livingstone was convinced that the answer lay with the Lualaba River. In August 1872, Livingstone headed back to the Lake Bangweulu region, where he fell ill and died six months later, the great question still unanswered.

In August 1874, ten years after Speke's death, Stanley embarked on a three-year expedition every bit as remarkable and arduous as those undertaken by his predecessors, yet one whose significance is often overlooked. Partly, this is because Stanley cuts such an unsympathetic figure, the grim caricature of the murderous pre-colonial White Man blasting and blustering his way through territories where Burton, Speke and Livingstone had relied largely on diplomacy. It is also the case, however, that Stanley set out with no intention of seeking headline-making fresh discoveries. Instead, he determined to test methodically the theories advocated by Speke, Burton and Livingstone about the Nile's source. First, Stanley sailed around the circumference of Lake Victoria, establishing that it was indeed as vast as Speke had claimed (and, incidentally, crossing the so-called 'Alexandra Nile' (Kagera River) into what is now Akagera National Park, where he camped on the shore of Lake Ihema). Stanley's next step was to circumnavigate Lake Tanganyika, which, contrary to Burton's long-held theories, clearly boasted no outlet sufficiently large to be the source of the Nile. Finally, and most remarkably, Stanley took a boat along Livingstone's Lualaba River to its confluence with an even larger river, which he followed for months with no idea as to where he might end up.

When, exactly 999 days after he left Zanzibar, Stanley emerged at the Congo mouth, the shortlist of plausible theories relating to the source of the Nile had been reduced to one. Clearly, the Nile did flow out of Lake Victoria at Ripon Falls, before entering and exiting Lake Albert at its northern tip to start its long course through the sands of the Sahara. Stanley's achievement in putting to rest decades of speculation about how the main rivers and lakes of East Africa linked together is estimable indeed. He was nevertheless generous enough to concede that: 'Speke now has the full glory of having discovered the largest inland sea on the continent of Africa, also its principal affluent as well as its outlet. I must also give him credit for having understood the geography of the countries we travelled through far better than any of us who so persistently opposed his hypothesis'.

FAUNA Rwanda naturally supports a widely varied fauna, but the rapid human population growth in recent decades, with its by-products of habitat loss and poaching, has resulted in the extirpation of most large mammal species outside of a few designated conservation areas. Rwanda today has three main conservation areas: the Volcanoes Park, Akagera Park and Nyungwe Forest. Each of these protects a very different ecosystem and combination of large mammals, for which reason greater detail on the fauna of each reserve is given under the appropriate regional section. Broadly speaking, however, Akagera supports a typical savanna fauna dominated by a variety of antelope, other grazers such as zebra, buffalo and giraffe, the aquatic hippopotamus, and plains predators such as lion, leopard and spotted hyena (see also pages 250–8).

Nyungwe Forest and the Volcanoes Park probably supported a similar range of large mammals 500 years ago. Today, however, the faunas differ, mostly as a result of extensive deforestation on the lower slopes of the Virungas. The volcanoes today support bamboo specialists such as golden monkey and mountain gorilla, as well as relic populations of habitat-tolerant species such as buffalo and elephant (see also pages 211–13). The latter two species are probably extinct in Nyungwe (buffalo were hunted out 25 years ago, while elephant spoor has not been detected since a dead elephant was found in late 1999), but this vast forest still supports one of Africa's richest varieties of forest specialists, ranging from 13 types of primate to golden cat, duiker and giant forest hog (see also pages 141–50). Despite the retreat of most large mammals into reserves, Rwanda remains a rewarding destination for game viewing: the Volcanoes Park is the best place in the world to track mountain gorillas, while Nyungwe offers visitors a good chance of seeing chimpanzees and 400-strong troops of colobus monkeys – the largest arboreal primate troops in Africa today.

Rwanda is a wonderful destination for birdwatchers, with an incredible 670 species recorded in an area which is smaller than Belgium and has less than half the land surface of Scotland. Once again, greater detail is supplied in regional chapters, but prime birdwatching destinations include Nyungwe (280 species including numerous forest rarities and 26 Albertine Rift endemics) and Akagera (savanna birds, raptors and waterbirds). Almost anywhere in the country can, however, prove rewarding to birders: an hour in the garden of one of the capital's larger hotels is likely to throw up a variety of colourful robin-chats, weavers, finches, flycatchers and sunbirds.

HISTORY

EARLIEST TIMES Even back in the **ice age**, Rwanda was showing its typically green and fertile face; a part of the Nyungwe Forest remained uncovered by ice, so that animal and plant life could survive there. Excavations undertaken from the 1940s onwards identified several **early Iron-Age** sites in Rwanda and neighbouring Burundi, yielding fragments of typical 'dimpled' pottery (see *Africa in the Iron Age*, Roland Oliver & Brian M Fagan, Cambridge University Press, 1975). At Nyirankuba in what is now South province, a site of **late Stone-Age** occupation (without pottery) underlay a later occupation level containing both pottery and iron slag. Iron-smelting furnaces at two other sites in southern Rwanda (Ndora and Cyamakusa) gave radio-carbon datings of around AD200–300. Oliver and Fagan (above) describe these furnaces as being some 5ft in diameter, built of wedge-shaped bricks. Other sites in the area of Rwanda, Burundi and Kivu show late Stone-Age occupation sites underlying early Iron-Age occupation. The early Iron-Age pottery was later succeeded by a different and coarser type, apparently made by newcomers from the north who were cattle raisers – but archaeological investigation in Rwanda has been sparse, and there must be much still awaiting discovery. Some artefacts are displayed in the National Museum in Butare (formerly Huye).

Rwanda's earliest inhabitants were Pygmoid **hunter-gatherers**, ancestors of the *Twa* (the name means, roughly, 'indigenous hunter-gatherers'), who still form part of the population today and are still known for their skill as potters. Gradually

– the dates are uncertain, but probably before about 700BC – they were joined by Bantu-speaking **farmers**, who were spreading throughout Central Africa seeking good land on which to settle. Fertile Rwanda was a promising site. The arrival of these incomers, known as *Hutus*, was bad news for the Twa; now a minority, they saw some of their traditional hunting grounds cleared to make way for farming, and retreated further into the forests. Then Iron-Age technology developed tools – such as hoes – which enabled the farmers to grow more crops than were needed for subsistence and thus to trade.

Next came the **cattle raisers**, taller and lankier people than either the pygmoid Twa or the sturdy farmers, who may have come from either the north or the northeast. With only oral tradition to guide us, there's no hard historic evidence for the timing of their arrival – some say before the 10th century AD, others after the 14th. Gradually, whether by conquest or by natural assimilation, a hierarchy emerged in which the cattle raisers (known as *Tutsis*, meaning 'owners of cattle') were superior to the farmers and a master–client relationship known as *ubuhake* developed. Then most of Rwanda was a monarchy ruled by a Tutsi king or *mwami* – although there remained outlying areas where the farming groups did not accept his authority.

Note: The three groups are more correctly called Batwa, Bahutu and Batutsi, while individuals are a Mutwa, a Muhutu and a Mututsi. However, we have opted for the forms Twa, Hutu and Tutsi because outside Rwanda they are commonly used. The plural of Mwami (sometimes spelt Mwaami) is Bami. The language spoken by all three groups is Kinyarwanda.

THE KINGDOMS OF RWANDA Rwanda has a rich oral history, which was maintained primarily by members of the Rwandan royal court. According to this history the founder of Rwanda's ruling dynasty, Abanyiginya, was not born naturally like other humans, but was born from an earthenware jar of milk. The grandmother of Rwandans lived in heaven with Nkuba (thunder) who was given the secret of creating life. He made a small man out of clay, coated him with his saliva, and placed him in a wooden jar filled with milk and the heart of a slaughtered bull. The jar was constantly refilled with fresh milk. At the end of nine months the man took on the image of Sabizeze. When Sabizeze learned of his origin, he was angry that his mother had revealed the secret and decided to leave heaven and come to earth. He brought with him his sister Nyampundu, his brother Mututsi, and a couple of Batwa. Sabizeze was welcomed by Kabeja who was of the Abazigaba clan and king of the region (in the present-day Akagera National Park). Sabizeze then had a son named Gihanga who was to found the Kingdom of Rwanda. A Rwandan historian, Alexis Kagame, estimates that Gihanga ruled as King of Rwanda in the late 10th or early 11th century.

Before the arrival of Europeans, Rwandans believed they were the centre of the world, with the grandest monarchy, the greatest power and the highest civilisation. Their king or *mwami* was the supreme authority and was magically identified with Rwanda. There was a strong belief that if the ruling monarch was not the true king, the people of Rwanda would be in danger. The well-being of Rwanda was directly linked to the health of the king. When he grew old, Rwanda's prosperity was compromised. Only when the ageing ruler died and a new, stronger king was enthroned did the country re-stabilise.

The centralised control by the king was balanced by a very powerful queen mother and a group of dynastic ritualists: the *abiiru*. Queen mothers could never come from the same family clan as the king and rotated among four different family clans. The abiiru, who were also drawn from four different clans, could reverse the king's decisions if they conflicted with the magical Esoteric Code, protected and interpreted by the abiiru. They also governed the selection and installation of a new king. Any member of the abiiru who forgot any part of his assigned portion of the Esoteric Code was punished severely. Members of the abiiru and other custodians of state secrets who revealed the secrets of the royal court were forced to drink *igihango*, a mixture containing a magical power to kill traitors or anyone who failed in his duty. While the king could order the death of a disloyal member of the abiiru, he was required to replace the traitor with a member from the same family clan.

Rwanda's dynastic drums, which could be made only by members of one family clan from very specific trees with magical elements, had the same dignity as the king. The genitals of the enemies of Rwanda killed by the king hung from the drum. The capture of a dynastic drum from an enemy country normally signified annexation, with the group whose drum was stolen losing all faith in itself. This tradition is shared among all Bantu-speaking peoples in Africa. When Rwanda's royal drum Rwoga was lost to a neighbouring kingdom by King Ndahiro II Cyaamatare in the late 15th century, Rwanda was devastated. Rwoga was eventually replaced by Karinga, the last dynastic drum, when King Ruganzu II Ndori regained Rwanda's pride through his military exploits. The fate of Karinga is unknown. It is reported to have survived the colonial period, but disappeared soon after Rwanda's independence.

The origin of the division between Tutsis and Hutus is still being debated, but oral history portrays a feudal society with one group, the Tutsis or cattle herders, occupying a superior status within the social and political structure, and the other group, the Hutus or peasant farmers, serving as the serfs or clients of a Tutsi chief. The hunter-gatherer Twa were potters and had various functions at the royal court – for example, as dancers and music makers.

The complex system known as *ubuhake* provided for protection by the superior partner in exchange for services from the inferior: ubuhake agreements were made either between two Tutsis, or between a Tutsi and a Hutu. While ubuhake was a voluntary and revocable private contract between two individuals, with subjects able to switch loyalty from one chief to another, a peasant could not easily survive without a patron. Cattle could be acquired through ubuhake as well as by purchase, fighting in a war, or marriage. A Hutu who acquired enough cattle could thus become a Tutsi and might take a Tutsi wife, while a Tutsi who lost his herds or otherwise fell on hard times might become a Hutu and marry accordingly. A patron had no authority over a client who had gained cattle, whether Hutu, Tutsi or Twa. Whereas Hutus and Tutsis could and did sometimes switch status, a Twa seldom became a Tutsi or Hutu. In the rare instances when this did occur, it would be because the king rewarded a Twa for some act of bravery by granting him the status of a Tutsi. He would then be given a Tutsi wife and a political post within the royal court. Meanwhile the three groups spoke the same language (Kinyarwanda, a language in the Bantu group), lived within the same culture and shared the same recent history.

Rwandan nobles were experts in cattle breeding and an entire category of poetry was devoted to the praises of famous cows. Cattle were bred for their beauty, rather than utility. Between AD1000 and 1450 herders in the Great Lakes region invented no fewer than 19 words for the colourful patterns of their animals' hides. As elsewhere in Africa, cattle were closely associated with wealth and status.

AD1000–1894 Whatever the exact timespan may have been, Rwanda (or the larger part of it) was ruled over by a sequence of Tutsi monarchs, each with his various political skirmishes, battles and conquests. Oral tradition shows us a colourful bunch of characters: for example, Ndahiro II Cyaamatare who catastrophically lost the royal drum; Mibambwe II who organised a system of milk distribution to the poor, ordering his chiefs to provide jugs of milk three times a day; and Yuhi III Mazimpaka, the only king to compose poetry – and to go mad. From the 17th century onwards the rulers seem to have become more organised and ambitious, using their armies to subjugate fringe areas. The royal palace was by then at Nyanza – and can still be seen, carefully reconstructed, today.

The *mwami* was an absolute monarch, deeply revered and seen to embody Rwanda physically. The hierarchy beneath him was complex and tight-knit, with different categories of chief in charge of different aspects of administration. His power covered most of Rwanda, although some Hutu enclaves in the north, northwest and southwest of the country clung to their independence until the 20th century. The country was divided into a pyramid of administrative areas: in ascending order of size, from base to apex, these were the immediate neighbourhood, the hill, the district and the province. (These are echoed in today's administrative pyramid of Commune, Sector, District and Province.) And through this intricate structure ran the practice and spirit of ubuhake, the master–client relationship in which an inferior receives help and protection in return for services and allegiance to a superior.

Beneath the mwami, power was exercised by various chiefs, each with specific responsibilities: *land chiefs* (responsible for land allocation, agriculture and agricultural taxation), *cattle chiefs* (stock-raising and associated taxes), *army chiefs* (security) and so on. While Hutus might take charge at neighbourhood level, most of the power at higher administrative levels was in the hands of Tutsis.

Since our only source of information about these early days is oral tradition, which by its nature favours the holders of power, we cannot be certain to what extent the power structure was accepted by those lower down the ladder, to what extent they resented it and to what extent they were exploited by it. But, whether harsh, benevolent or exploitative (or possibly all three), it survived, and is what the Europeans found when they entered this previously unknown country.

Rwanda had remained untouched by events unfolding elsewhere in Africa. Tucked away in the centre of the continent, the tiny kingdom was ignored by slave traders; consequently Rwanda is one of the few African countries that never sold its people, or its enemies, into slavery. There is no record of Arab traders or Asian merchants, numerous in other parts of East and Central Africa, having penetrated its borders, with the result that no written language was introduced and oral tradition remained the norm until the very end of the 19th century.

The Kingdom of Rwanda was isolationist and closed to foreigners (also to many Africans) until the 1890s. The famous American explorer, Henry Stanley, attempted to enter several times and did penetrate as far as Lake Ihema in 1874, but was then forced to retreat under arrow attack. Trade with neighbouring countries was extremely limited and Rwanda had no monetary system.

GERMAN EAST AFRICA Unlike most African states, Rwanda and Burundi were not given artificial borders by their colonisers – they had both been established kingdoms for many centuries. At the Berlin Conference of 1885, they – under the name of Ruanda-Urundi – were assigned to Germany as a part of German East Africa, although at that stage no European had officially set foot there. The first to do so formally was the German Count Gustav Adolf von Götzen on May 4 1894 (an Austrian, Oscar Baumann, had previously entered privately from Burundi in 1892 and spent several days in the south of the country). Von Götzen entered Rwanda by the Rusumo Falls in the southeast and crossed the country to reach the eastern shore of Lake Kivu. *En route* he stopped off at Nyanza where he met the mwami, King Rwabugiri – apparently causing consternation among the watching nobles when he, a mere mortal, shook the sovereign by the hand. They feared that such an affront might cause disaster for the kingdom. At this stage the mwami had no idea that his country had officially been under German control for the past nine years.

Von Götzen subsequently became Governor of German East Africa, into which Ruanda-Urundi was formally absorbed in 1898; the same year that the mountain gorilla was first recorded by a European (see box below). At this time the kingdom was larger, stretching as far as Lake Edward in the north and beyond Lake Kivu in the west; it was reduced to its present area at the Conference of Brussels in 1910.

The Germans were surprised to find that their new colony was a highly organised country, with tight, effective power structures and administrative divisions. They left these in place and ruled through them, believing that support for the traditional chiefs would render them and their henchmen loyal to Germany. Meanwhile various religious missions, Roman Catholic at first and then Protestant, began setting up bases in Ruanda-Urundi and establishing schools, farms and medical centres. In 1907 the colonisers opened a 'School for the Sons of Chiefs' in Nyanza, as well as providing military training.

Allowing for the blurring caused by intermarriage and the switching of status between Tutsi and Hutu, the power structures encountered by the colonisers were linked – and this proved to be a matter of great anthropological fascination – to three very visibly different groups of inhabitants: the tall, lanky Tutsi chiefs and nobles; the shorter, stockier Hutu farmers (who formed the majority); and the very much smaller Twa. The Duke of Mecklenburg, visiting the country in 1907, noted:

> The population is divided into three classes – the Watussi, the Wahutu, and a pygmy tribe, the Batwa, who dwell chiefly in the bamboo forests of Bugoie, the swamps of Lake Bolero, and on the island of Kwidschwi on Lake Kiwu.

THE DISCOVERY OF THE MOUNTAIN GORILLA

The mountain gorilla was first discovered on 17 October 1902, on the ridges of the Virunga Mountains, by German explorer Captain Robert von Beringe, then aged 37. Captain von Beringe, together with a physician, Dr Engeland, Corporal Ehrhardt, 20 Askaris, a machine gun and necessary porters set off from Usumbura on August 19 1902 to visit the Sultan Msinga of Rwanda and then proceed north to reach a 'row of volcanoes'. The purpose of the trip was to visit the German outposts in what was then German East Africa in order to keep in touch with local chiefs and to confirm good relations, while strengthening the influence and power of the German Government in these regions. On arriving at the volcanoes, an attempt was made to climb Mount Sabinyo.

Captain von Beringe's report of the expedition (below) is adapted from *In the Heart of Africa* by Duke Adolphus Frederick of Mecklenburg (Cassell, 1910).

From October 16th to 18th, senior physician Dr. Engeland and I together with only a few Askaris and the absolutely necessary baggage attempted to climb the so far unknown Kirunga ya Sabyinyo which, according to my estimation, must have a height of 3,300 metres. At the end of the first day we camped on a plateau at a height of 2,500 metres; the natives climbed up to our campsite to generously supply us with food. We left our camp on October 17th taking with us a tent, eight loads of water, five Askaris and porters as necessary.

After four and a half hours of tracking we reached a height of 3,100 metres and tracked through bamboo forest; although using elephant trails for most of the way, we encountered much undergrowth which had to be cut before we could pass... After two hours we

The Watussi are a tall, well-made people. Heights of 1.80, 2.00 and even 2.20 metres are of quite common occurrence, yet the perfect proportion of their bodies is in no wise detracted from... The primitive inhabitants are the Wahutu, an agricultural Bantu tribe, who look after the digging and tilling and agricultural economy of the country in general. They are a medium-sized type of people...Ruanda is certainly the most interesting country in the German East African Protectorate – in fact in all Central Africa – chiefly on account of its ethnographical and geographical position. Its interest is further increased by the fact that it is one of the last negro kingdoms governed autocratically by a sovereign sultan, for German supremacy is only recognised to a very limited extent. Added to this, it is a land flowing with milk and honey, where the breeding of cattle and bee-culture flourish, and the cultivated soil bears rich crops of fruit. A hilly country, thickly populated, full of beautiful scenery, and possessing a climate incomparably fresh and healthy; a land of great fertility, with watercourses which might be termed perennial streams; a land which offers the brightest of prospects to the white settler.

In 1911–12 the Germans joined with the Tutsi monarchy to subjugate some independent Hutu principalities in the north of the country which had not previously been dominated. Their inhabitants, who had always been proud of their independence, resisted vigorously, overrunning much of what are now Ruhengeri and Byumba provinces before they were defeated and brought under the mwami's control. Their resentment and deep sense of grievance were to endure for the next half-century.

Germany had little time to make its mark in the colonies; in 1916 Belgium invaded Ruanda-Urundi and occupied the territories until the end of World War I; Belgium was subsequently officially entrusted with their administration under a League of Nations mandate in 1919, to be confirmed in 1923.

reached a stony area with vegetation consisting mainly of blackberry and blueberry bushes. Step by step we noticed the vegetation becoming poorer and poorer, the ascent became steeper and steeper, and climbing became more difficult – for the last one and a quarter hours we climbed only over rock. After covering the ground with moss we collected, we erected our tent on a ridge at a height of 3,100 metres. The ridge was extremely narrow so that the pegs of the tent had to be secured in the abyss. The Askaris and the porters found shelter in rock caverns, which provided protection against the biting cold wind.

From our campsite we were able to watch a herd of big, black monkeys which tried to climb the crest of the volcano. We succeeded in killing two of these animals, and with a rumbling noise of falling rocks they tumbled into a ravine, which had its opening in a north-easterly direction. After five hours of strenuous work we succeeded in retrieving one of these animals using a rope. It was a big, human-like male monkey of one and a half metres in height and a weight of more than 200 pounds. His chest had no hair, and his hands and feet were of enormous size. Unfortunately I was unable to determine its type; because of its size, it could not very well be a chimpanzee or a gorilla, and in any case the presence of gorillas had not been established in the area around the lakes.'

On the journey back to Usumbura, the skin and one of the hands of the animal that von Beringe collected were taken by a hyena but the rest (including the skull) finally arrived safely at the Zoological Museum in Berlin. It was classified as a new form of gorilla and named *Gorilla beringei* in honour of the Captain. Later it was considered rather to be a subspecies and renamed *Gorilla gorilla beringei*.

THE BELGIAN ERA In its adjoining colony of the Congo, Belgium had full control, but for Ruanda-Urundi it remained answerable first to the League of Nations and then (after 1945) to the United Nations Organisation. Annual reports had to be submitted and no important changes could be made without agreement from above. Despite these constraints, and despite the fact that Ruanda-Urundi had far less potential wealth than the Congo, Belgium took its charge seriously, and by the time of independence some 40 years later its material achievements (in terms of increased production; public services such as roads, schools and hospitals; and buildings and administrative infrastructures) were considerable. In terms of human beings it did far less well, as later events demonstrated.

Priorities Rwanda had always been subject to periodic famines, to such an extent that some were named and absorbed into history as milestones of time: such-and-such a child was born 'just after the Ruyaga famine' (1897), or a man died 'just before the Kimwaramwara famine' (1906). Most had climatic origins, but some which occurred around the time of the Belgian takeover (in 1916/17 and 1917/18) could also be blamed on World War I, as precious foodstuffs were shipped overseas to feed the troops. At the same time the new Belgian authorities commented that the local chiefs made little attempt to prevent the famines recurring, or to get emergency relief to the worst-hit areas. They therefore set about implementing a strict overall food strategy to make supplies less precarious.

The peasant farmers were first of all encouraged (by field workers) to maximise their production using traditional methods. They were then given help to improve their existing techniques, for example by using higher-yielding varieties of their normal crops. From 1924 the cultivation of food crops was made compulsory, including foreign species such as manioc and sweet potatoes. Next the distribution channels were upgraded, with a new road network and the development of markets and co-operatives. Storage facilities were set up; high-grade seed was distributed; the use of manure and fertiliser was promoted; the problem of erosion (caused by overuse of vulnerable land) was tackled; farmers were required to set aside a small emergency hoard of beans, peas or cereals each year; and various new types of stock breeding were initiated. Factories and processing plants were built. Finally, the farmers were encouraged to grow crops (especially coffee) for export, so that they could earn cash with which to buy extra food in times of hardship.

These measures – not easily implemented, because of the farmers' understandable initial resentment and resistance to change – proved more or less successful, helped by a regulated but controversial and sometimes harsh policy of forced labour (*uburetwa*). Famine did recur in 1942–44 and resulted in thousands of deaths, but this could be blamed partly on the appropriation of manpower and the lack of efficient machinery caused by World War II. By the time of independence, large areas of farmland had been better protected against erosion and per-hectare crop yields had risen substantially. The scale of the anti-erosion works was massive, and many remain in the terracing visible today. Horizontal ditches were dug on the hillsides, following the contours; directly below these, hedges were planted. Water running down the slope of the hillside was trapped by the ditch, and then seeped through it to irrigate the hedge on the lower side; while the roots of the hedge contributed by securing the soil and strengthening first the ditch and then the hillside.

The agricultural improvements, together with extensive physical provisions such as roads, schools, hospitals and all the associated construction work, were probably colonisation's most helpful input to Rwanda. Its contribution to the relationship between the country's long-term inhabitants was less positive.

Power structures Like the Germans before them, the Belgians decided to retain and use the existing power structures, but unlike their predecessors they then proceeded to undermine the authority of the mwami and his chiefs and to forbid some of their traditional practices, introducing their own Belgian experts and administrators at every level. This interference did not make for easy collaboration. In any case the mwami in power at the time of Belgian accession, Mwami Musinga, was hostile to colonisation and also resented the missionaries, since their innovations undermined the established order and worked against the subjugation of Hutus. In 1931 he was forced by the Belgians to abdicate in favour of his son, the more amenable and Westernised Mwami Mutara Rudahigwa. Until well into the 1950s, although the traditional structures keeping them in a subservient position were somewhat weakened, the Hutus still got a bad deal and remained 'second-class citizens' in almost all respects. So both Hutus and Tutsis – and indeed the minority Twas too, because they received virtually no recognition or privilege – reacted to colonisation with varying degrees of grievance.

Education The Germans had established a few government schools in Rwanda and the Belgians followed suit, but the main source of education was always the Church. In the 1930s, the Catholic Bishop Léon Classe, who had arrived in Rwanda almost 30 years earlier as a priest and worked his way up through the hierarchy, entered into an agreement with the Belgian administration by which the Catholic Church took over full responsibility for the educational system. He may not have been entirely without financial motive, since the government then subsidised the church to the tune of 47 francs per pupil and 600 francs per qualified teacher.

The Church broadened its curriculum to cover more secular subjects such as agronomy, medicine and administration; however, the main beneficiaries of the increased educational possibilities were still largely Tutsis, although Hutus were not entirely neglected and many attended primary school. Some did make good use of the limited educational openings available to them but could not easily progress beyond a certain level. Of those who trained in the Catholic seminaries (which they could enter more easily than secular educational institutions) some went on to become priests, while others switched back to secular careers. Less than one-fifth of the students attending the Groupe Scolaire in Butare from 1945 to 1957 – and emerging as agronomists, doctors, vets and administrators – were Hutus. The School for the Sons of Chiefs originally opened by the Germans in Nyanza had a minimum height requirement which effectively reserved it for Tutsis.

In 1955, there were some 2,400 schools of various types and levels (the majority were primary) in Rwanda, with around 215,000 pupils. Of the 5,500-odd teachers, over 5,000 were Rwandan.

Categorisation Size mattered. Like the Germans before them, the Belgians were intrigued by the sharply differing physical characteristics of their colony's inhabitants, and enthusiastically measured, recorded, compared and commented on the facial and bodily proportions of Rwanda's three indigenous groups. For the more timid of the Rwandans, this 'attack' with callipers, measuring tapes, scales and other paraphernalia proved a fearsome ordeal. So man dehumanises his brothers…

Most tellingly, in the early 1930s the Belgians embarked on a census to identify all indigenous inhabitants, on the basis of these physical characteristics, as either Hutu, Tutsi or Twa, and in 1935 issued them with identity cards on which these categories ('ethnic groups' or, in French, *'ethnies'*, although the accuracy of this term is debatable) were recorded. If, even after strenuous measuring, someone's *ethnie* was not immediately clear, having been blurred by intermarriage or a change of status, those who were reasonably wealthy and/or had more than ten cattle were generally recorded as Tutsis. Identity cards – and the habit of classification they engendered – were still in use at the time of the genocide in 1994, providing an extra pointer (if one were needed) as to who should or should not die.

In 1945 the United Nations Organisation was created, with its charter promising the colonised peoples of the world justice, protection and freedom. Formerly a League of Nations mandate, Ruanda-Urundi now became a UN Trust Territory and Belgium was responsible to the UN's trusteeship council, which was to preside over all colonies' transition to independence. In 1948 a UN mission visited Ruanda-Urundi, and its report was critical of the administration, particularly regarding the inferior status of the Hutus and Twa by comparison with the Tutsis. All too often, compulsory labour was harshly enforced, and the educational system remained heavily biased in favour of Tutsis, although many priests and missions were starting to veer more towards the Hutus.

At the same time, the observers were surprised by the completeness and intricacy of the social and political hierarchy which, if used properly, would offer a sound framework for democratic development. All the necessary command structures were in place, but badly oriented.

Subsequent visits gave rise to similarly critical reports. The Belgians introduced elections at local and administrative levels – which Tutsis won, except in the far north where resentment still smouldered after the 1912 defeat. Throughout Africa, colonies were becoming restless and the scent of independence was in the air, but in Ruanda-Urundi far too little preparation had yet been made, in terms both of political awareness and practical training. Nothing was ready.

THE RUN-UP TO INDEPENDENCE From about 1950, as the numbers of educated Hutus increased, the Hutu voice grew stronger. Hutu leaders such as Grégoire Kayibanda began to demand recognition for the majority. In 1954 the system of *ubuhake* was officially abolished, although in reality it lingered for a few more years. In 1957 the Superior Council of Rwanda (which had a huge Tutsi majority) called for independence preparations to be speeded up.

In 1956, Mwami Rudahigwa had called for total independence and an end to Belgian occupation. Just before another UN visit in 1957, a Hutu Manifesto drawn up by a group of Hutu intellectuals was presented to the Vice Governor General, Jean-Paul Harroy. It challenged the whole structure of Rwanda's administration, called for political power to be placed in the hands of the Hutu majority, pointed out injustices and inequalities, and proposed solutions. Little official action was taken.

The Catholic Church, now pro-Hutu, encouraged Grégoire Kayibanda and his associates to form political parties: APROSOMA (Association pour la Promotion Sociale des Masses) was openly sectarian, championing Hutu interests strongly, while RADER (Rassemblement Démocratique Rwandais) was more moderate. Whereas Tutsis, comfortably in a position of power, were calling for immediate independence without any changes to the system, Hutus wanted change first (to a more democratic system, recognising the fact that they were the majority) and then independence. For whatever reasons and after whatever deliberations, Belgium, having supported the powerful Tutsi minority throughout colonisation, now switched its allegiance to the Hutu majority, ostensibly in the name of fairness and democracy.

The wind of independence was blowing strongly in colonial Africa. More political parties sprang up. UNAR (Union Nationale Rwandaise) was formed by the proponents of immediate independence under the Rwandan monarchy, while PARMEHUTU (Parti du Mouvement de l'Emancipation Hutu) was established under the guidance of the Catholic Church by those favouring delayed independence. MSM (Mouvement Social Muhutu) was created by Grégoire Kayibanda to support Hutu interests, while UNAR was a pro-monarchy and anti-Belgium party.

In July 1959 the Mwami Rudahigwa died in hospital, in circumstances that may or may not have been suspicious. Rumours of Belgian involvement were rife and tension grew. He was succeeded by one of his brothers. There were arrests and some sporadic small-scale violence – which erupted on a larger scale on 1 November, when a Hutu sub-chief belonging to PARMEHUTU was attacked and beaten in Gitarama by young members of UNAR. Within 24 hours, highly organised Hutu gangs were out on the streets of towns and villages throughout the country, burning, looting and killing. Then Tutsis began to retaliate. Within about a fortnight things were calm again – around 300 had died, and 1,231 (919 Tutsis and 312 Hutus) were arrested by the Belgian authorities. The country was placed under military rule headed by the Belgian Colonel Guy Logiest, who quickly began replacing Tutsi chiefs with Hutus. He was strongly pro-Hutu, claiming to be righting the injustices of colonisation, and played a virtually unconcealed part in anti-Tutsi attacks.

It is worth remembering that this was the first organised violence between the two groups, and it happened little more than 40 years ago. Those who speak of a long-drawn-out feud originating before colonisation are mistaken. But the revolution had begun, Tutsis started to flee the country in large numbers, and outbursts of violence continued.

PARMEHUTU won hastily manipulated elections in 1960. Belgium, the reins of power slipping rapidly from its grasp, organised a referendum on the monarchy under the auspices of the United Nations. In January 1961, Rwanda's elected local administrators were called to a public meeting in Gitarama, Grégoire Kayibanda's birthplace. They and a massed crowd of some 25,000 declared Rwanda a republic – and the United Nations had little option but to accept this ultimatum. However, the 1960 elections were not recognised by the UN so more were held in September 1961, under UN supervision. Again they were won by PARMEHUTU, with Grégoire Kayibanda at its head. Later that year, some 150 Tutsis were killed in the Butare area, 5,000 homes were burned and 22,000 people were displaced. In July 1962 Rwanda's independence was finally confirmed with Kayibanda as its new president, heading a republican government. The university town of Astrida, so named after Queen Astrid of Belgium, reverted to its local name Butare. Violence against Tutsis continued; by now about 135,000 had fled as refugees to neighbouring countries and the number was growing. Among those who left in 1960 was a three-year-old child named Paul Kagame, of whom much more was to be heard later.

It is true that Belgium emerged from the fiasco with little credit. But it is equally true that, even without colonisation, some kind of revolution would inevitably have occurred sooner or later, for the tightly stratified hierarchy of the 19th century could not have held firm indefinitely against the pressures, promises and potentials of the modern world.

The trend today in Rwanda is to hold the colonisers – through their behaviour during colonisation – responsible for the eventual genocide. Indeed, without colonisation the explosion might well, as a Rwandan friend said to me, 'have happened differently', and perhaps after something as inexplicable as a genocide there is a need to apportion blame as part of the recovery process. But to claim – as is also the trend today – that before the arrival of the Europeans all was peace and harmony may simply reflect the fact that oral tradition tends to favour those in power.

1962–1994 The situation became yet more tangled and yet more sensitive. Since this is a guidebook rather than a historical treatise, readers who want a fuller picture than is given below will find several good sources in *Appendix 2*, pages

271–2. John Reader's *Africa* (Penguin, 1998) is particularly recommended, as is Gérard Prunier's *The Rwanda Crisis – History of a Genocide* (Hurst, 1998). They (among others) have been used as sources in this chapter.

Once in power, the government sought to reinforce its supremacy. 'Quotas' were introduced, giving the Tutsis (who were a minority of about 9% of the population) a right to only 9% of school places, 9% of jobs in the workforce and so on. Small groups of Tutsi exiles in neighbouring countries made sporadic commando-style raids into Rwanda, leading to severe reprisals. In late 1963, up to 10,000 Tutsis were killed. The pattern of violence continued.

In 1964 the Fabian Society (London) published a report entitled *Massacre in Rwanda*, commenting on events since 1959. Also – chillingly, in view of what happened 30 years later – a report entitled *Attempted Genocide in Rwanda* appeared in the March 1964 issue of *The World Today* (vol 20, no 3).

In 1965 Kayibanda was re-elected president and Juvenal Habyarimana was appointed Minister of Defence. In 1969 Kayibanda was again re-elected and PARMEHUTU was renamed the MDR (Mouvement Démocratique Républicain). But Kayibanda's regime was becoming increasingly dictatorial and corrupt. The 'quotas' and other 'cleansing' measures began to be enforced so rigidly that even Hutus became uneasy. In 1973, ostensibly to quell violence following a purge of Tutsis from virtually all educational establishments, Major General Juvenal Habyarimana toppled Grégoire Kayibanda in a military coup.

In 1975, a single party, the MRND (Mouvement Révolutionnaire et National pour le Développement), was formed. For a while, there were signs of improvement, although this tends to be forgotten in the light of subsequent events. Despite initial optimism and a period of relative stability, however, the regime eventually proved little better than its predecessor. Some educational reforms were undertaken, with the object of 'Rwandanisation' – revaluing Kinyarwanda and Rwandan culture. Habyarimana was reconfirmed as president in 1978, 1983 and 1988 – unsurprisingly, since he was the only candidate. The Hutu–Tutsi conflict was to some extent replaced by conflict between Hutus from the south and those from the north (Habyarimana was a northerner, so was accused of favouring 'his own'). Meanwhile, in the international sphere, rising oil prices and falling commodity prices were bringing the country's economy close to collapse and, among all but the privileged elite, dissatisfaction grew.

In 1979 a group of Rwandan exiles in Uganda established the RRWF (Rwandan Refugee Welfare Foundation) which in 1980 became RANU (Rwandan Alliance for National Unity), whose name explains its aim. In 1981, in Uganda, one Yoweri Museveni, later to become Uganda's president, started a guerrilla war against the oppressive regime of Dr Milton Obote – among his men were two Rwandan refugees, Paul Kagame and Fred Rwigyema. Obote was hostile to the Rwandan refugees in Uganda and political youth groups were encouraged to attack them and their property. As a result of such attacks in 1982–83, there was massive displacement of the refugees in southern Uganda and large numbers tried (or were forced) to return to Rwanda. The Rwandan government quickly closed its borders with Uganda and confined those who had already entered to a small and inhospitable area in the north, where many of the young and the old died of hunger and disease.

In 1986, in Uganda, Yoweri Museveni's National Resistance Army (which contained a number of Rwandan refugees) overthrew Obote, and Museveni assumed power. In 1987 RANU was renamed the RPF (Rwandan Patriotic Front), and was supported not only by exiled Tutsis but also by a few prominent Hutus opposed to Habyarimana's regime.

In 1987/8, a military coup in Burundi and consequent ethnic tensions caused a wave of Burundian refugees to flood into Rwanda. In 1989 the price of coffee,

Rwanda's main export, collapsed, causing severe economic problems. Censorship rules were flouted, new politically oriented publications emerged and reports of corruption and mismanagement appeared openly. In July 1990, under pressure from Western aid donors, Habyarimana conceded the principle of multi-party democracy and agreed to allow free debate on the country's future. In practice, little changed.

Then, on 1 October 1990, the RPF (led by Major General Fred Rwigyema), invaded the northeast of Rwanda from Uganda, with the stated objective of ending the political stalemate once and for all and restoring democracy. French, German and Zairean troops were called in to support the Rwandan national army and the incursion was soon suppressed; but the government now took the RPF threat seriously. Habyarimana enlarged the Rwandan army from around 5,000 in 1990 to about 24,000 in 1991 and 35,000 in 1993. Various overseas countries (France, South Africa, the US) provided arms. Additionally, the 1990 RPF invasion was followed by severe reprisals: thousands of Tutsis and southern Hutus were arrested and held in prison for some months. Several were tried and sentenced to death but the sentences were not carried out, although, as one of those arrested later wrote, 'many died of the hunger and the beatings'. Sporadic unrest continued throughout the country.

Political solutions were sought, both nationally and internationally, with several Western countries now involved. In November 1990 Habyarimana agreed to the introduction of multi-partyism and the abolition of 'ethnic' identity cards, but nothing was implemented. The Rwandan army began to train and arm civilian militias known as *interahamwe* ('those who stand together'). It was later estimated that up to 2,000 Rwandans (Tutsis or anti-government Hutus) were killed by their government between October 1990 and December 1992.

The RPF – now led by Major Paul Kagame, since the charismatic Rwigyema had died in the October 1990 invasion – continued its guerrilla raids, striking at targets countrywide. By the end of 1992 it had expanded to a force of almost 12,000 and was growing rapidly. Its stated aim was always to bring democracy to Rwanda rather than to claim supremacy. Meanwhile, French troops were supporting the government forces. In the face of increasing violence, international pressure was applied more strongly and the Arusha Agreement (so named because it was drawn up in Arusha, Tanzania) committed Habyarimana to a number of reforms, including the establishment of the rule of law, political power-sharing, the repatriation and resettlement of refugees, and the integration of the armed forces to include the RPF. A 70-member Transitional National Assembly was to be established. The Agreement was signed in August 1993 and should have been implemented within 37 days, overseen by a United Nations force. But the process, unpalatable to both Tutsi and Hutu hardliners, stalled. Hostilities deepened. Radio stations poured forth inflammatory propaganda. Rwanda's *Radio-Télévision Libre des Mille Collines*, in particular, insistently and viciously identified Tutsis as 'the enemy', in dehumanising and vilifying terms. Scattered outbursts of violence rumbled on.

On 21 October, the Hutu president of neighbouring Burundi, Melchior Ndadaye, elected only a few months previously, was killed in a military coup, fuelling ethnic tensions in Rwanda. The UN began sending UNAMIR (UN Assistance Mission for Rwanda) forces to the country. Politics were deadlocked. A sense of impending danger grew and, by March 1994, vulnerable (or well-informed) citizens were starting to evacuate their families from Kigali.

On 6 April 1994, a plane carrying Rwanda's President Habyarimana and Burundi's new President Cyprien Ntaryamira was shot down by rocket fire near Kigali airport. Both men died. The source of the attack has never been confirmed. Within hours, the killing began.

THE GENOCIDE It had been well planned, over a long period. Roadblocks were quickly erected and the army and *interahamwe* went into action, on a rampage of death, torture, looting and destruction. Tutsis and moderate Hutus were targeted. Weapons of every sort were used, from slick, military arms to rustic machetes. Orders were passed briskly downward from *préfecture* to *commune* to *secteur* to *cellule* – and the gist of every order was: 'These are the enemy. Kill.'

A painfully detailed account, which includes many eyewitness testimonies and brings home the full horror of the slaughter, is given in the 1,200 pages of *Rwanda – Death, Despair and Defiance* (African Rights, London, 1995). In *A People Betrayed*, L R Melvern analyses the political and international background (Zed Books, London & New York, 2000), as does Gérard Prunier in *The Rwanda Crisis* (see *Appendix 2*). A condensed overview of events is given below.

In three months, up to a million people were killed, violently and cruelly. Barely a family was untouched. The international media suddenly found Rwanda newsworthy. Chilling images filled our TV screens and the scale of the massacre was too great for many of us to grasp. Amid the immensity came tiny tales of heroism: villagers who flatly disobeyed the order to kill; Hutus who hid their Tutsi neighbours, at great (often fatal) risk to their own lives, or who, while feigning to round them up for the killers, furtively led some to safety. But these glimpses of humanity were engulfed and lost in the great, surging tide of slaughter that spread across the country.

On 8 April, just two days after the plane crash, the Rwandan Patriotic Front (RPF) launched a major offensive to end the genocide. As they advanced, they rescued and liberated Tutsis still hiding in terror from the killers. Meanwhile, however, a new Hutu government, based on the MRND and supporting parties, was formed in Kigali and later shifted to Gitarama.

The United Nations' UNAMIR force was around 2,500 strong at the time. They watched helplessly, technically unable to intervene as this would breach their 'monitoring' mandate. After the murder of ten Belgian soldiers the force was cut to 250. On 30 April the UN Security Council spent eight hours discussing the Rwandan crisis – without ever using the word 'genocide'. Had this term been used, they would have been legally obliged to 'prevent and punish' the perpetrators. Meanwhile tens of thousands of refugees were fleeing the country. In May the UN agreed to send 6,800 troops and police to Rwanda to defend civilians, but implementation was delayed by arguments over who would cover costs and provide equipment. The RPF army had taken control of Kigali airport and Kanombe barracks and was gaining ground elsewhere. In June, France announced that it would deploy 2,500 peacekeeping troops to Rwanda (Opération Turquoise) until the UN force arrived. These created a controversial 'safe zone' in the southwest.

On 4 July the RPF captured Kigali and set up an interim government. The remnants of the Hutu government fled to Zaire, followed by a further tide of refugees. The RPF continued its advance westward and northward. Many thousands of refugees streamed into the French 'safe zone' and still more headed towards Zaire, cramming into makeshift camps on the inhospitable terrain around Goma. The humanitarian crisis was acute, later to be exacerbated by disease and a cholera outbreak which claimed tens of thousands of lives.

On 18 July 1994, the RPF announced that the war had been won, declared a ceasefire, established a broad-based Government of National Unity and named Pasteur Bizimungu as president. Faustin Twagiramungu was appointed prime minister. The following day, the new president and prime minister were sworn in, and RPF commander Major General Paul Kagame was appointed defence minister and vice president. By the end of July, the UN Security Council had reached a final agreement about sending an international force to Rwanda. By the end of August

A report produced in July 2000 by the Statistics Department of Rwanda's Ministry of Finance and Economic Planning concluded that the horrors of the 1994 genocide had left large segments of the population with severe mental health problems that could not in fact be expressed in statistics. Many people had lost family members, and/or had witnessed, experienced (or participated in) massacres or rapes. A National Trauma Survey by UNICEF in 1995, quoted in the same report, estimated the percentages of children affected by the genocide as follows:

- 99.9% witnessed violence
- 79.6% experienced death in the family
- 69.5% witnessed someone being killed or injured
- 61.5% were threatened with death
- 90.6% believed they would die
- 57.7% witnessed killings or injuries with machete
- 31.4% witnessed rape or sexual assault
- 87.5% saw dead bodies or parts of bodies

Opération Turquoise was terminated and UN forces had replaced the French. Internationally, it had now been accepted that a 'genocide' had indeed taken place – and it was over. At sites of the worst massacres, memorials now commemorate the dead and remind the world that such an atrocity must never, never be allowed to occur again.

THE AFTERMATH The 70-member Transitional National Assembly provided for in the Arusha Agreement of 1993 finally became operational in December 1994. In November 1994, the UN Security Commission set up the International Criminal Tribunal for Rwanda (ICTR), whose brief is to prosecute those who were guilty, between 1 January and 31 December 1994, of genocide and other violations of international humanitarian law; by the end of 1996 suspects were being brought to trial.

Sporadic bursts of violence were to continue for a further three years or so, with killings on both sides, as tensions in and around refugee settlements persisted and hardline Hutus who had fled across the border mounted guerrilla raids. But the RPF army and the new government remained in control. UN forces left the country in March 1996. Refugees returned home, in massive numbers. Problems of insecurity posed by former Rwanda government forces and *interahamwe* troops caused Rwanda to become militarily involved with the Democratic Republic of the Congo (DRC).

In 1999, local elections were held at sector and cellule level, and the Lusaka Agreement, to end the war in the DRC, was signed.

In March 2000, President Pasteur Bizimungu resigned and in April Major General Paul Kagame was sworn in as the fifth president of Rwanda, exactly four decades after his flight as a three-year-old refugee.

In July 2000, the Organisation of African Unity (OAU) recommended that the international community should make payments to the government and people of Rwanda in reparation for the genocide. Later the same year, the Rwandan government launched a census to determine the true and total number of genocide victims – irrespective of whether they were Hutus, Tutsis, Twa or foreigners.

In June 2002, with some 115,000 genocide suspects still in gaol after eight years and the country's regular courts unable to clear the backlog, the Gacaca Judicial

Background Information **HISTORY**

The traditional system of 'Gacaca' courts was revived in Rwanda in order to clear the prisons of the throng of genocide suspects who had by then been held captive (awaiting trial) for up to eight years. It was estimated that the regular justice system, lacking adequate facilities and qualified personnel, could take almost 100 years to clear the backlog – clearly impossible – whereas Gacaca offers the hope of a faster solution. Around 250,000 local judges, men and women, were elected by and within their local communities in 2001, and in 2002 they were given brief training in such subjects as law, conflict resolution and judicial ethics. They receive no salaries but are entitled to free schooling and medical fees for their families. Throughout Rwanda up to 11,000 Gacaca courts have been set up (with a panel of 19 judges per court, and requiring the presence of at least 15 judges and 100 witnesses to be valid) in different administrative areas.

First, the courts identify victims of the genocide. Next, suspects are identified and categorised, according to the extent of their crime. They attend courts in their home areas, where local witnesses speak for or against them. Suspects who confess fully and plead guilty can expect lighter sentences, as can those who agree to community service in atonement for their crimes. The courts are authorised to try, and then to sentence, anyone suspected of carrying out (or being an accomplice to) killing, serious assault or property crimes during the genocide. The more serious 'Category 1' suspects, those who allegedly organised, instigated, led or played a particularly zealous part in the violence, continue to be tried and sentenced in the formal judicial system. Gacaca courts cannot impose the death penalty, nor can they try army personnel.

For the witnesses, confronting the *génocidaires* and re-living the events of 1994 can be both traumatic and cathartic. No-one claims that the Gacaca courts are a perfect solution, just that they are the best solution under the circumstances – and at least they offer a very visible form of justice in which the villagers have a voice. Observers monitor their progress and so far they seem to be mostly free of corruption, although there have increasingly been instances of witness intimidation. Once again, as they have done in so many ways since the genocide, Rwandans are playing a very personal role in solving their country's problems.

System was launched. Gacaca (pronounced Ga-cha-cha, with a hard g) means 'grass', and is based on the traditional form of Rwandan justice where villagers used to gather together on a patch of grass to resolve conflicts between families, with heads of household acting as judges. See box above.

In the first half of 2003, around 30,000 genocide suspects were released from prison and, after a spell of 're-education', returned to their villages, in an amnesty aimed at those who were aged 14–18 at the time of the genocide, the old and sick, those accused of lesser crimes and those who had already been in gaol for longer than the sentence they would have received. Further releases over the past six years have returned tens of thousands more prisoners to their home villages. Solving one problem (prison overcrowding) risks creating another, as survivors – many of them still suffering either physically or mentally – find themselves once again living close to the alleged *génocidaires*, and it's a tribute to the extraordinary strength, courage and forbearance of Rwanda's village communities that the situation has so far proved manageable.

In June 2003, Rwanda's new Constitution was signed, marking the end of the transition period that followed the genocide and replacing various documents referred to as the Fundamental Law. The presidential elections held – entirely peacefully – in August 2003 saw Paul Kagame returned as president for a term of seven years, with 3,544,777 votes or 95.05% of the total. Parliamentary elections followed in September 2003 in which women took 48.8% of the seats, making Rwanda the country with the highest number of women in its parliament. This statistic partly reflects a belief that women would never allow the sort of mass killing that has occurred in the past, and many others hold high positions in both state and private institutions.

Rwanda has qualified for debt relief under the Highly Indebted Poor Countries Initiative and had economic reform and development programmes supported by the IMF and the World Bank. Huge amounts of foreign aid have been provided – and the fact that these grants have been ongoing since the genocide demonstrates international satisfaction about how the money is used. Donors renew their contracts. As an example, in September 2003 US$30 million was granted by the World Bank for the HIV/AIDS programme; US$19.9 million by the EU Mission in Rwanda for the repair and rehabilitation of roads; and US$29.9 million by the African Development Bank for the improved supply of water and energy to Kigali, the management of natural resources and, again, HIV/AIDS. The UK's total 2005–06 budget for Rwanda was £47 million. Meanwhile, Rwanda's economy keeps growing, and more children are attending school than at any other time in the country's history.

Rwanda's international links are strengthening. In June 2005, Rwanda's President Paul Kagame took over from Ugandan President Yoweri Museveni as chairman of COMESA (Common Market for Eastern and Southern Africa) and in 2006 his tenure was extended. In July 2005, Rwanda's then finance minister, Dr Donald Kaberuka, was elected president of the African Development Bank group; and in September 2005 Rwanda's ambassador in Switzerland, Valentine Sendanyoye-Rugwabiza, was appointed one of four deputy directors-general of the World Trade Organization – the first woman to hold such a high position. A contingent from the Rwandan army formed part of the peace-keeping force in Sudan's troubled Darfur region. In December 2006, Rwanda was accepted into the East African Community by Kenya, Tanzania and Uganda, thereby strengthening its ties to the region's stronger economies, and encouraging the adoption of English as the main language of education in 2008.

The country's second round of democratic parliamentary elections was held in September 2008, with the RPF under Kagame gaining 79% of the vote, whilst the remainder was divided between the minority Social Democratic and Liberal Parties. By law, at least a third of parliamentary representatives must be female, but in 2008 a remarkable 45 of the 80 seats were won by women. Rwanda is now the only country in the world whose parliament contains fewer males than females (Sweden and Cuba are next, with 47% and 43% female parliamentarians respectively; the UK and USA both have fewer than 20%).

A guiding principle of current government strategy in Rwanda is Vision 2020, a progressive and consultative set of policies that aim to transform the country's economy to that of a middle-income country. Vision 2020 also places strong emphasis on gender equality, anti-corruption, sustainable management of natural resources, technological progress centred on the IT field, private sector-led economic and infrastructural development, and regional economic integration. An important development in this regard is the recent laying of fibre-optic cables throughout the country, which will make Rwanda the regional leader in internet technology.

It seems unlikely that Rwanda will attain the ambitious pro-poor targets set when Vision 2020 was first implemented: the reduction of poverty from 60% of the population to 25%, the increase of the per-capita income to US$900, raising life

In January 2006, the federal map of Rwanda was redrawn to merge the 12 former provinces, namely Butare, Byumba, Cyangugu, Gikongoro, Gisenyi, Gitarama, Kibungo, Kibuye, Kigali Rural, Kigali City, Ruhengeri and Umutara, into the larger and more neutrally named North, South, East, West and Kigali Provinces. The creation of these new provinces (*intari* in Kinyarwanda) was designed to have several benefits, among them the increased decentralisation of government, the blurring of old provincial ethnic distinctions, and the dissociation of the present-day administration with names that retained associations with the genocide.

At the same time, each province was divided up into several new administrative districts (*akarere*), and where the main municipality (*umujyi*) in that new district shared its name with one of the old provinces, it was decided that the district would not bear the old name. So the town of Butare, formerly capital of Butare Province, became capital of a new district called Huye. Ruhengeri, former capital of the eponymous province, became capital of a new district called Musanze. And so on, and (with the notable exception of Kigali) so on... as listed below:

'Old' town name	'New' district name
Butare	Huye
Byumba	Gicumbi
Cyangugu	Rusizi
Gikongoro	Nyamagabe
Gisenyi	Rubavu
Gitarama	Muhanga
Kibungo	Ngoma
Kibuye	Karongi
Ruhengeri	Musanze

Straightforward enough so far, but a quagmire of ambiguity seems to surround the correct names of the district capitals. The official government websites www.musanze.gov.rw and www.huye.gov.rw, both created *after* the new districts came into being, unambiguously refer to their respective capitals as Ruhengeri and Butare. And most other written and online sources indicate that these town names remain unchanged. On the other hand, several verbal sources and personal correspondence suggest the opposite, as does a government document created at the time of the change: the towns popularly referred as Ruhengeri and Butare now go by the official names of Musanze and Huye, or soon will do, and their old names are destined to fall into disuse.

This poses something of a dilemma for us. My best guess is that these new town names currently enjoy a kind of semi-official status, one that will almost certainly be formalised in due course. But I may be wrong on either count. And whatever the official situation, my guiding principle here has to be pragmatism. For potential visitors to Rwanda, the reality is that the established town names remain in wide use within the country, and are almost ubiquitous outside it, whether you are looking at maps, google results, tourist brochures, or whatever. So, at least for this edition, it seems most sensible to treat established town names as primary, whilst drawing the reader's attention to the new district name in the write-up for every affected town, in the index, and the table of 'old' and 'new' names above.

expectancy to 65 years, and literacy to 90%. And of course, on the political front, the country still has its tensions, the government inevitably has its critics, and there's still too wide a gap between the 'haves' and the 'have-nots' – indeed, many if not most Rwandans still live in economic conditions that are far from ideal.

But considering the size and resources of Rwanda, considering what happened there in 1994, and considering the inherent problems faced by almost all countries in sub-Saharan Africa, even without the aftermath of a genocide, the achievements of the past 15 years have been amazing, and based on a huge amount of energy, courage, goodwill and sheer hard work. Progress has been dramatic and durable. Rwanda today is a vibrant and forward-looking country, well able to cope with the demands and technologies of the 21st century.

It deserves respect.

PEOPLE

Rwanda today probably contains inhabitants raised in a greater number of countries than most other African nations, as long-term exiles returned after the genocide from Uganda, Kenya, Tanzania, Burundi, Europe, the USA and more. But of course Rwanda is their origin and their home.

Following the disruptive ethnic clashes of the post-colonial years, which culminated in the 1994 genocide, the currently accepted line is to stress Rwandan unity: the fact that before the arrival of the colonisers Rwandans were living together on the same hills, speaking the same language and practising the same culture.

In fact, matters may not be quite so clear-cut and the insistence on 'same-ness' should not be carried to the extent of concealing historical individuality. But there's no doubt that the people of Rwanda in general are committed to overcoming any awkward or damaging differences. There's a story, well known now, about a group of schoolgirls who, during the genocide, were told by the killers to divide up into Hutus and Tutsis (with the implication that the Hutus would be spared). The girls refused, saying that they were all Rwandans. So all of them died. In a different context, a genocide survivor wrote: 'Before the genocide, Hutus and Tutsis lived together. I remember we used to play with Hutu children and share everything. There were even intermarriages. The only time when we felt discriminated against was when a place at school, or a job, was given to a Hutu, even if there was a Tutsi more qualified for it. But this was no reason for hatred between the two groups.'

Of course individual attitudes may vary around the country and from person to person. Inevitably differences persist in some areas; sadly these have led to a few instances of bullying in schools, which are being firmly tackled. However, the energetic – and courageous – efforts at reconciliation and peaceful coexistence are visible nationwide, extending from government level down to small rural groups and individuals.

LANGUAGE

The local language is Kinyarwanda, but almost all Rwandans speak a little of at least one international language. In rural areas, this is most likely to be KiSwahili, a coastal Bantu language with strong Arabic influences which, thanks largely to the 19th-century slave caravans, has come to serve as the lingua franca of East Africa. Most educated Rwandans who were brought up within the country also speak passable to fluent French, but may not speak English. By contrast, many returned long-term exiles were educated in Uganda, Kenya or Tanzania or another Anglophone territory, and don't know any French, but do speak fluent English.

The upshot of this is that French speakers will have no difficulty getting by in the towns, and should always be able to find somebody who can speak French in rural areas. English speakers will struggle more, though particularly in Kigali and Ruhengeri they'll find that a fair number of people speak English. Travellers who know some Swahili will also find this very useful, particularly in rural areas. The potential for chaos is, of course, immense: in Ruhengeri, I regularly tried my faltering Swahili in a bar or hotel to no avail, followed up on this in my even more limited French, only to have the person I was addressing ask me whether perhaps I spoke English!

In 2008, English replaced French as the main language of education from primary school onwards, a move aimed to help Rwanda integrate into the (Anglophone) East Africa Community, and which should result in the spread of English at the expense of French. However, the national language, spoken by everyone, remains Kinyarwanda, and for the sake of friendliness and courtesy you should try to take on board a few words. At the very least aim for *yégo* (yes), *oya* (no), *murakozé* (thank you), *muraho* (hello, good morning/afternoon), *bitesé?* (how are you?) and *byiza* (good). For me, an essential phrase in any language is 'What's your name?', to be used on children; their faces light up and they start to take you seriously! Then point to yourself and say your own name, and the introduction is complete. In Kinyarwanda it's easy – *Witwandé?* The above words are written phonetically – the value of consonants may change a bit in different parts of the country; for example 'b' may sometimes sound more like 'v' or 'w'. If you're linguistically ambitious, turn to the more comprehensive vocabulary in *Appendix 1*.

PLACE NAMES In Kinyarwanda, as in most African languages, place names are more or less phonetic, so that the town of Base, for instance, is pronounced *Bah-say*. But the transcription of place names in Rwanda displays some other quirks that I've not encountered anywhere, namely the occasional pronunciation of 'g' as 'j' (Kinigi, for instance, is pronounced *Kiniji*), and of an initial 'k' as 'ch' and 'cy' as 'sh'(Kigali = Chigali, Cyangugu = Shangugu). Further complication is created by the African tendency to treat 'r' and 'l' as interchangeable, and the local custom of distinguishing certain towns from the synonymous region by adding the French word ville to the end of the town's name. Hence, when you hear a bus conductor yelling *Chigari-ville* at the top of his voice, he is in fact referring to the city of Kigali!

RELIGION

The Christian religions are a powerful force in Rwanda today, as witnessed by the great number of active churches throughout the country. Roman Catholicism leads the field with 65% adherence, followed by 9% for Protestantism. Pope John Paul II visited Rwanda in 1990. Some evangelical sects are now gaining ground. There is a small (1%) Muslim population, leaving a 25% following for minority and traditional beliefs, some of which may have absorbed traces of Christianity.

TRADITIONAL RELIGION AND BELIEFS Rwandans traditionally believe in a supreme being called Imana. While Imana's actions influence the whole world, Rwanda is his home where he comes to spend the night. Individuals hold informal ceremonies imploring Imana's blessing. There is a tradition that, before retiring, a woman may leave a pitcher of water for Imana in the hope he will make her fertile.

Since words can have a magical impact, the name of Imana is often used when naming children, also in words of comfort, warnings against complacency, blessings, salutations, and during rites associated with marriage and death. Oaths take the form of 'May Imana give me a stroke', or 'May I be killed by Imana'. In instances when a long-desired child is born, people say to the new mother, 'Imana has removed your shame.' Tales of Imana granting magical gifts to humans, who then lose these gifts through greed and disloyalty, are common.

There is a special creative act of Imana at the beginning of each person's life. Impregnation in itself would not be sufficient to produce a new human being. This is why the young wife, at evening, leaves a few drops of water in a jar. Imana, as a potter, needs some water to shape the clay into a child in her womb. Then after birth, Imana decides what life is to be for that individual: happy or unhappy. If, later on, a man is miserable, poverty-stricken or in bad health, it is said that he was created by Ruremakwaci, a name given to Imana when he does not create very successfully, when 'he is tired', or, for some inscrutable reason, decides that a certain destiny will be unhappy.

Rwandans traditionally believe that a life force exists in all men and animals. In animals this invisible soul disappears when the creature dies, but in humans it is transformed into *bazimu*, spirits of the dead who live in Ikuzimu, the underworld or the world below the soil. While the deceased kings of Rwanda constitute a kind of governing body in the underworld, there are no social distinctions. Life is

RWANDA'S NATIONAL SYMBOLS

Rwanda's new flag, coat of arms and national anthem were launched on 31 December 2001, to replace the old ones designed in 1962, at a time when Rwanda was shaken by ethnic violence, human-rights violations and bad governance.

The old flag contained red, symbolising the blood shed for independence, but in today's peaceful Rwanda this is seen as inappropriate. The new flag is blue, yellow and green: blue to signify peace and tranquillity; yellow to signify wealth as the country strives for economic growth; green to symbolise agriculture, productivity and prosperity. There is a sun in the top right-hand corner, against a blue background, representing new hope for the country and its people. The flag was designed by Alphonse Kirimobenecyo, a Rwandan artist and engineer.

The coat of arms consists of a green ring with a knot tied at the upper end, representing industrial development through hard work. Inscriptions read Repubulika Y'U Rwanda and the national motto Ubumwe, Umurimo, Gukunda Igihugu (Unity, Work, Patriotism). Other features are the sun, sorghum and coffee, a basket, a cog wheel – and two shields, representing defence of national sovereignty and integrity and justice.

The national anthem, *Rwanda Nziza*, has four verses and highlights heroism, the Rwandan culture and the people's patriotism. The words are by Faustin Murigo of Karubanda prison in South Province. The music is by Captain Jean-Bosco Hashkaimana of the army brass band.

neither pleasant nor unhappy. The bazimu continue the individuality of living persons and have the same names. Though non-material, they are localised by their activity. They do not drink, eat, or mate but their existence in other respects is similar to that in the world of the living. Bazimu return to the world, often to places where they used to live. Some may stay permanently in the hut where their descendants live or in the small huts made for them in the enclosure around the dwelling. Bazimu are generally bad. They bring misfortune, sickness, crop failure and cattle epidemics because they envy the living the cherished things they had to leave behind. Their power, actuated by the male spirits, or grandfathers, extends only over their own clan. The living members of a family must consult a diviner to discover the reason for the ancestor's anger. Respect to bazimu is shown principally by joining a secret cult group.

The cult of Ryangombe Ryangombe is said to be the chief of the *imandwa*, Rwandans who are initiated into the cult of Ryangombe. According to Rwandan legend, he was a great warrior who was accidentally killed by a buffalo during a hunting party. To share their hero's fate, his friends threw themselves on the bull's horns. Imana gave Ryangombe and his followers a special place, the Karisimbi volcano in the Virunga volcano chain, where they have a notably more agreeable afterlife than the other bazimu. The cult of Ryangombe became an important force of social cohesion, with Tutsi, Hutu and Twa being initiated into it. Ryangombe has said himself that he should be called upon by everybody. He is propitiated by the *babandwa*, a politico-religious fraternity, who perform rituals, chants and dances in his honour. They are not a permanent group and meet only once a year during July, at which time initiation takes place. During their festival the members of the fraternity paint themselves and decorate the spirit huts. A member of the group appears as the personification of the spirit of Ryangombe, carrying his sacred spear. After a ritual is performed, all members purify themselves at the stream. While involvement in the cult is not common today, Rwandans can recall when their grandfathers or fathers participated in the Ryangombe festival and a popular Rwandan song recounts Ryangombe's exploits as a warrior and lover. Also see box on page 202.

EDUCATION

More children are attending school in Rwanda today than at any time in the country's history. The education at state schools is free, but pupils from poorer families still find it hard to cover the additional costs of equipment, uniform etc; a number of NGOs and local charities are currently targeting this problem. Many private schools – primary and secondary, some of them church-run – also function throughout the country, but here fees must generally be paid. English has now become the language of education from primary school onwards, which has led to considerable training and re-training of teachers whose command of it was not previously good. French is also included in both the primary and the secondary curriculum, so that children should leave school with at least a working knowledge of the two languages. In addition, in October 2008 Rwanda became the eighth country to sign up to the 'One laptop per child' scheme (*http://laptop.org*), with the aim of providing internet access to all of its 2.3 million schoolchildren. As the first batch of simple, sturdy laptops reached schools across the country, there were reports of teachers struggling to keep pace with the new computing skills of their young pupils. This initiative should transform classroom learning and expand the children's horizons.

A further noticeable change over the past few years is that far more girls are now attending primary school and continuing to secondary education (see page 28).

The Rwanda chapter of the Forum for African Women Educationalists (*www.fawerwa.org.rw*) strongly supports this trend and runs its own girls' school with 800 pupils as well as working with schools throughout the country.

The death of so many professionals during the genocide left the country with a severe shortage of qualified teachers. Organisations such as VSO (Voluntary Service Overseas, *www.vso.org.uk*) helped to fill the gap and gradually the situation is improving.

Further education is also well catered for. Apart from the long-established National University in Butare, the Kigali Institute of Science and Technology (KIST), the Kigali Free University (Université Libre) and the Kigali Institute of Education, there are colleges and training schools throughout the country, several of which have opened or re-opened since the genocide. In some cases distance learning via the internet is possible, enabling students to study in their spare time while holding down a job and just to attend the institute in order to sit exams.

THE LIFE OF A STUDENT AT KIST *Akili Fidèle, October 2004*

KIST (the Kigali Institute of Science and Technology; *www.kist.ac.rw*) is a governmental body that was set up in 1997, three years after the 1994 genocide, in response to the serious lack of educational establishments at that time: the National University of Rwanda was then the only state body in either the capital or the country as a whole.

The institute offers both full-time and part-time courses. Grant-aided students study from 08.00 to 17.00; those without grants from 17.30 to 20.30. The official language of instruction is English. Previously French was Rwanda's main European language, because of the country's history as a Belgian (thus francophone) Trust Territory. However, in 2002, as a result of Rwanda's growing tendency to set up links with the anglophone countries of East Africa, KIST replaced the French language with English and the old French system of teaching with the English system. Any non-Rwandan lecturers come mostly from anglophone countries such as India, the USA, Uganda, Tanzania, Britain, Kenya etc. English-language classes are available for students who are stronger in French.

As a part-time student, I set off for KIST at 17.00 and arrive there at 17.20, so I've got ten minutes to settle down and get my breath back before the first lesson starts. The lecturer arrives at 17.30 and begins to teach; the students follow his words attentively. At the end of the session the students ask questions, and this develops into an exchange of ideas, so that when they finally leave the lecture room their heads are still buzzing with thoughts.

The lecturers are approachable and understanding. If a student has a problem in any course, he or she can easily discuss it with the lecturer, who will find time to sort out and explain the difficulty outside teaching hours.

Every two weeks, tests are set to check how well the students have assimilated their subject. After three or four months, examinations are held, and preparation for these starts from the very beginning of term. The timetable for the semester – giving the dates of the exams – is displayed on the notice board, as a warning to students to take their work seriously and be ready for them.

Two weeks after the exams, the results are announced. Students who have failed must re-sit the exam. A student who fails again at this second attempt is expelled, no matter how good his/her conduct may have been otherwise, so this is a strong incentive to study hard.

KIST's most important facility for its students is the library, open Monday to Friday from 08.00 to 20.00 and Saturday 08.00 to 13.00. It contains the books necessary for all the courses, and is available to every student who has a library card. It's on the second floor of KIST 2 building, in an airy and comfortable room where one can read and study peacefully. Students have access to a wide range of books, and during the examination period many choose to do their reading in the library.

There is also a cinema, which provides entertainment for students outside teaching hours or at weekends.

The institute's canteen is open to everyone; grant-aided students get their meals free, while others must pay.

Finally, many sporting activities are organised, for example football, basketball and tennis – these help with the physical growth of young students, the strengthening of their muscles and the avoidance of certain illnesses. Thus KIST caters for the body as well as for the mind.

WOMEN'S ACCESS TO EDUCATION *Marie Chantal Uwimana*

After the genocide, with up to a million of its people slaughtered, the political, social and economic structures of Rwanda were at rock bottom. To rehabilitate, reintegrate and reconcile the country was a colossal task for the Government of National Unity. In every sector, they were starting from scratch. Among the priorities, education initially took second place to the more urgent needs of food, clothing and health.

Historically, education – and particularly that of girls – had not been greatly developed in Rwanda before and even after independence. Missionaries did build schools, but they were mainly for the children of chiefs and those in power. The intake of girls was very low.

Before 1994, the low enrolment rate for girls at primary school (and the still lower rate at secondary school and college) was explained by the ignorance of the parents (a belief that girls should not study scientific subjects), by custom (that after primary school girls should stay in the family and work at home or on the land) and by enforced early marriage.

After 1994, their parents now dead, many of these girls had also become single 'parents', head of their household and caring for their younger siblings. Recognising the problem, the government began setting in place mechanisms to support Rwandan women, and particularly to motivate girls to go to school. The statistics began to change rapidly, and by 2003 the number of girls at primary school equalled that of boys. At secondary school, however, girls continued to be oriented towards the more 'feminine' subjects and the drop-out rate for girls was 10.8% versus 9.5% for boys.

Although primary schooling had theoretically been compulsory, the fees were beyond the reach of some parents. Under the new constitution, state primary schools are now free and thus available to all – as long as the law is enforced that defines 'free education' as 'students receiving without payment education provided by the teacher together with learning aids and basic textbooks needed by both the teacher and the students'.

Problems remain, and steps still needing to be taken include:

- Possible sanctions against parents who fail to send their children to school
- Elimination of discriminatory practices against schoolgirls who fall pregnant
- Non-discriminatory guidance for career selection
- Improved access for girls to non-traditional subjects
- Provision of literacy programmes and literacy trainers
- Grants and scholarships awarded with no bias towards gender
- Information and training about sexually transmissible diseases and HIV/AIDS
- Social integration measures for disadvantaged girls/women

Then, little by little, Rwanda's women can play their full part in rebuilding and running their country.

LITERATURE A written language was not introduced until the Europeans arrived in Rwanda at the end of the 19th century, so there is no great tradition of written literature. However, there is a wealth of oral literature in the form of myths, folk stories, legends, poetry and proverbs. These have passed on not only stories but also moral values and historical traditions from generation to generation. Before (and to some extent after) the arrival of the Europeans, the Mwami's court was a centre for training young nobles in various art forms, particularly the composition and performance of songs and poems dedicated to valour in warfare and the magnificence of their cattle.

The historian Alexis Kagame wrote extensively about oral poetry and recorded many poems in both Kinyarwanda and French. A display in the National Museum of Rwanda in Butare (see pages 135–6) gives an idea of the intricacy of some poetic structures.

MUSIC Music is of great importance to all Rwandans, with variations of style and subject among the three groups. Traditionally, Tutsi songs praised excellence and valour; Hutu songs were lighter, sometimes humorous and linked to social occasions; Twa songs related more directly to aspects of their original occupation, hunting. During the time of the monarchy, the court was dominated musically by the royal drummers, and drumming is still of great artistic importance.

A full drum ensemble typically consists of either seven or nine drums. The smallest of these, sometimes called the soprano, which is often (but not invariably) played by the director of the orchestra, sets the rhythm for each tune and is backed up by some or all of the following drums: a tenor, a harmonist alto, two baritones, two bass and two double bass. The other widely used musical instrument is the *lulunga*, an eight-stringed instrument somewhat resembling a harp. It is most often played solo, perhaps as the background to singing or dancing, but may also be used to provide a melodic interlude and/or as a counterpoint to drums.

DANCE Dance is as instinctive as music in Rwanda and its roots stretch back through the centuries. As with music, there are variations of style and subject among the three groups. Best known today are the Intore dancers, based in Nyanza and Butare, who perform both nationally and internationally. At the time of the monarchy and for centuries before the arrival of the Europeans, the Intore dancers at the royal court were selected young men who had received a privileged education and choreographic training in order to entertain their masters and to perform at special functions. The name intore means 'best', signifying that only the best of them were chosen for this honour.

Traditionally their performances consisted mainly of warlike dances, such as the *ikuma* (lance), *umeheto* (bow) and *ingabo* (shield), in which they carried authentic weapons. In the 20th century dummy weapons were substituted, the dances were given more peaceful names and rhythm and movement (rather than warfare) became their main feature. The Intore dancers were divided into two groups. The first group, the *indashyikirwa* or 'unsurpassables', were all Tutsi. The second, the *ishyaka* or 'those who challenge by effort', were Twa led by a Tutsi. A description nearly three-quarters of a century old leads us through a performance:

In the opening movement, the group of Twa advances with measured step. The musicians also are Twa. The dancers form a square or line up in double file. They perform the opening sequence and then a dance representing 'safety'. Next they stand at ease, chanting the exploits of real or imaginary Rwandan heroes. Then come

29

Sheer delight – and what is particularly appreciable, the authenticity... and to discover a whole aspect of Rwandan culture that I didn't know existed!

So commented a recent visitor at a display of traditional dance organised at a Twa pottery in Kigali – Batwa are, both currently and historically, Rwanda's favourite exponents of this particularly distinctive and highly reputed dance. In olden times, they were dancers and potters at the Royal court.

The Batwa (or Twa) are a pygmy people, comprising Rwanda's third 'ethnic' group – today numbering around 22,000–25,000. That they are indigenous Rwandans is surprisingly little known; even the recent film *A Hundred Days* mentioned only two groups as making up Rwanda's cultural diversity.

They lived originally as hunter-gatherers in the high mountain forests around Central Africa's Great Lakes. As the forests were felled and national parks established, the Batwa evolved another lifestyle, as potters, using the clay found in the marshes that lie between Rwanda's many hills. They left the forests with virtually no material possessions – and they process the clay with none. They use their feet to trample it into malleability and then their hands to shape cooking pots, stoves, decorative vases, traditional lamps, candle-holders and charming little replicas of local animals, from cattle to gorillas. The pots are fired without kilns, largely in a hollow in the ground, by burning grasses and natural debris, and sealed with earth.

Because of their pygmy origins the Batwa have suffered extreme prejudice over the years; they are socially and economically marginalised and extremely poor. Only 28% of Batwa children attend primary school (and far fewer start secondary school) compared with 88% in the population as a whole. Only 1.6% Batwa have enough land to feed their families. Most survive by begging, working on the land of others in return for food, or carrying loads. An estimated 30% of the Batwa population, as against 14% of the population overall, was lost during the 1994 genocide. So, income-generating schemes are vital – which is where the pottery and dance come into their own.

The UK-based charity, Forest Peoples' Project (*1c Fosseway Centre, Stratford Rd, Moreton-in-Marsh GL56 9NQ, UK;* ✆ *01608 652893;* e *info@fppwrm.gn.apc.org; www.forestpeoples.org*), works in Rwanda in partnership with CAURWA (*Communauté des Autochtones Rwandais* or Community of Indigenous Peoples in Rwanda), which FPP has supported since 1995. In December 2001, the UK Community Fund awarded FPP a three-year grant to start a Pottery Commercialisation Project with the Batwa potters.

movements representing 'tattooing', 'stability', 'the incomparable' and 'the most difficult case'. At this point the Tutsi dancers leap into the arena, armed, to mingle with the Twa and demonstrate that they deserve the name of 'unsurpassables'. The names of some of their dances translate into English as 'that which puts an end to all discussion', 'the crested crane', 'the exit dance' and 'thanks'.

The costume worn by the Tutsi dancers consists of either a short floral skirt or a leopard skin wound around their legs. Crossed straps decorated with coloured beads are generally worn across the chest. On their heads they wear a fringe of white colobus monkey fur. Depending on the theme of the dance and the region they may carry a bow, a spear or a stick decorated with a long tail of raffia. Around their ankles they wear bells, the sound of which adds to the rhythm of the dance.

The Intore dancers perform regularly today and it's a dramatic spectacle. You may come across them in Kigali, Nyanza, Butare – or abroad, on one of their tours. Ask ORTPN in Kigali (see page 84) for details of any scheduled performances.

Another striking performance of dance – equally traditional – is given by a group of Twa in Kigali – see page 98.

HANDICRAFTS As in other countries, most genuinely traditional handicrafts have a practical use or are decorated forms of everyday objects. An object which gives purely visual pleasure and is unrelated to any function has probably evolved for the tourist market – although it is none the worse for that. In Rwanda the weaving (of bowls, mats, baskets, storage containers, etc) from various natural fibres is particularly fine. The quality of wood-carving is variable, but at best it's excellent. Pottery made by the Twa community is plain but strong and its uncluttered style is attractive. See *Chapter 4* (pages 102–3) for details of where in Kigali to find handicrafts on sale.

SPORT
Football *Chris Frean and Philip Briggs*

Sport is a passion in Rwanda. Volleyball, rugby, swimming, cricket, tennis, golf and even karate are all there, and developing. But the most popular sport, as it is throughout most of Africa, is football, whose supporters number among them President Paul Kagame.

A few years ago, the future of Rwandan football looked very exciting, with the national side the Amavubi (which translates as 'wasps') qualifying ahead of Uganda and Ghana for the African Nations Cup, and APR reaching the Semi Finals of the African Cup Winners' Cup. Since then, unfortunately, Rwandan football has had limited cause for celebration.

The Amavubi finished last in their qualifying group for the Nations Cup and World Cup (one group for both) in 2006, with the only result of note being a 1–1 home draw to Nigeria. Rwanda's problems began when they lost their coach to Ghana and replaced him with Roger Palmgren, an unknown Swede. After an early win over Gabon, the side stumbled to the bottom of the group and stayed there.

Domestically at least, though, the national league (sponsored by brewer Primus, whose products are of course on sale at the National Stadium) has seen some changes, with the ATRACO club (sponsored/owned by the transport company of the same name) winning the league in 2008 and looking good for 2009. For the moment they seem to have risen above long-time champs APR (the army team – expect to see the president at home matches).

The former Dinamo Zagreb player Branko Tucak was appointed manager of the Rwandan national team in 2008. The Wasps fared better in the preliminary rounds of the 2008 Africa National Cup, coming third in their group of four, with two wins in six matches (including a 4–0 home drubbing of Liberia), but still failed to quality. Rwanda has enjoyed greater recent success in the CECAFA Cup, which involves 11 East African nations. True, its solitary championship win came way back in 1998, but Rwanda has emerged as runner-up three times since 2001, and also taken third place three times in that period.

Currently placed at 84 in the FIFA World Rankings, Rwanda has started strongly in the 2010 qualifiers for the Africa Nations Cup, winning three out of four matches in the first round - it's true that two were against Mauretania but one was over Morocco, which is not to be sniffed at. It is now placed in a strong qualifying group with Egypt, Algeria and Zambia, where anything better than last will ensure it is one of the 16 teams to make the Africa Nations Cup finals in Angola – and a top spot would secure it a berth in the 2010 World Cup in South Africa.

For details of how to attend a football match in Kigali, see *Chapter 4*, page 100.

Women's rugby Rwanda made history in February 2005 when the inaugural East African international women's rugby match was held against Uganda in the floodlit Amahoro Stadium. A return match was held in Kampala in December of the same year. Unfortunately, Rwanda was thrashed in both matches (0–92 and 81–0 home and away respectively). However, despite there being no dedicated rugby pitches in the country, there's huge enthusiasm nationwide and progress is being made. Rwanda was one of eight teams participating in the inaugural women's tournament staged by the Confederation of African Rugby (*www.carugby.com*) in Kampala in 2009. Young people in Rwanda (both girls and boys) are increasingly being coached and enabled to play; the UK-registered charity Friends of Rwandan Rugby (*www.friendsofrwandanrugby.org*) is strongly involved in this. See also page 62.

Cricket Cricket is gaining in popularity rapidly, particularly among the young. The Rwanda Cricket Association lists several teams in Kigali and Butare, and matches are played throughout the year at Kicukiro Secondary School in Kigali. In June 2009, international cricket icon Brian Lara played a brief three-ball innings at Kicukiro Oval, as part of a one-day visit to Rwanda. See also *Chapter 4*, page 101.

2

Practical Information

WHEN TO VISIT

Rwanda can be visited at any time of year. The long dry season, June to September, is the best time for tracking gorillas in the Volcanoes National Park and for hiking in Nyungwe Forest, since the ground should be dry underfoot and the odds of being drenched are minimal. This should not be a major consideration for any reasonably fit and agile travellers unless they are planning to hike to Virunga peaks such as Visoke or Karisimbi, in which case the rainy season should definitely be avoided. The dry season is also the best time for travelling on dirt roads, and it is when the risk of malaria should be lowest.

There are two annual rainy seasons: the big rains which last from mid-February to the beginning of June, and the small rains from mid-September to mid-December. Rainfall, especially over the mountains, can be heavy during these two periods – particularly from March to May, although it is still perfectly feasible to travel at these times of year, and, for those visiting at short notice, it is far easier to obtain a gorilla permit at the last minute.

As for the two dry seasons, the major one lasts from June to September and the shorter from December to February. However, the climate is not uniform throughout the country: it is generally dryer in the east than in the west and north. On occasion, the volcanoes of the north may be capped by snow, and evenings in Kigali can call for a sweater – as do days anywhere in the highlands should you happen to hit a cold snap! Nevertheless, every season is good for swimming and tanning on the banks of Lake Kivu.

An advantage of travelling during the rainy season is that the scenery is greener, and the sky less hazy (at least when it isn't overcast), a factor that will be of particular significance to photographers. The wet season is also the best time to track chimps in Nyungwe (in the dry season they may wander further off in search of scarce food), while the months of November to March will hold the greatest appeal for birders, as resident birds are supplemented by flocks of Palaearctic migrants.

ITINERARY PLANNING

Rwanda is so small, and all parts of it are so easily accessible from Kigali, that you needn't engage in any complicated planning. Your first port of call should be Kigali, to gather information and to get your gorilla-viewing permits from the ORTPN (see page 84). It's sensible not to rush off to the gorillas immediately; take a few days to get the feel of the country and to acclimatise, because the trek can be quite strenuous and the altitude can catch you unawares.

The best map available outside Rwanda is currently *Rwanda and Burundi*, scale 1:400,000, published in Canada by International Travel Maps (*www.itmb.com*). There is also *Tanzania, Rwanda and Burundi*, scale 1:1,500,000, published by

Nelles Guides & Maps (*www.nelles-verlag.de*). ORTPN sells a tourist map of Rwanda.

All GPS readings in this guide are taken with Map Datum set to 'Cape'.

Useful websites for information on Rwanda are www.rwandatourism.com, www.rwandaembassy.org (of the Rwandan Embassy in Washington), and www.ambarwanda.org.uk (of the Rwandan Embassy in London), all of which give relevant addresses and contact details and have numerous links. For all-purpose information there is www.rwandagateway.org; and good sites for current news are www.allafrica.com and www.newtimes.co.rw. Also useful is www.rwandaphonebook.com, a kind of condensed *Yellow Pages*, giving phone numbers for hotels, restaurants, businesses etc. Last, but hopefully not least, check out the updates, or contribute your own, on our website http://updates.bradtguides.com/rwanda.

Also see *Appendix 2*, page 269.

i TOURIST INFORMATION AND SERVICES

The **Office Rwandais du Tourisme et des Parcs Nationaux** (❂ *0252 576514 or 573396;* e *reservation@rwandatourism.com or info@rwandatourism.com; www.rwandatourism.com*), more commonly referred to as ORTPN (Or-ti-pen), doubles as both tourist office and national parks authority. Its tourist offices in the airport arrivals hall, central Kigali and the three national parks stock a fair range of booklets and maps. The office in central Kigali (⊕ *07.00–17.00 Mon–Fri, 08.00–14.00 w/ends & holidays*) also issues permits for gorilla tracking and certain other activities in the national parks (see box, *Booking a gorilla permit*, page 49). Permits can sometimes – depending on availability – also be bought at the ORTPN office in Ruhengeri, but check in Kigali first. Regular updates are posted on our website http://updates.bradtguides.com/rwanda.

TOUR OPERATORS

All those listed below will arrange gorilla visits plus international travel. Most offer both scheduled tours and tailor-made trips. More will start to cover the rest of Rwanda during the life of this guide. The many operators in neighbouring countries (Uganda etc) are deliberately not all listed, because readers in those countries are less likely to need them. Tour operators based in Rwanda are listed in the chapter on Kigali (see pages 84–5).

UK (*national code +44*)

Aim 4 Africa Ltd ❂ 0114 255 2533; e enquiries@aim4africa.com; www.aim4africa.com

Aardvark Safaris ❂ 01980 849160; e mail@aardvarksafaris.com; www.aardvarksafaris.co.uk

Abercrombie & Kent ❂ 0845 618 2200; www.abercrombiekent.co.uk

Absolute Africa ❂ 020 8742 0226; e absaf@absoluteafrica.com; www.absoluteafrica.com. Overland truck & camping safaris.

Africa Travel Centre ❂ 0845 450 1541; e info@africatravel.co.uk; www.africatravel.co.uk

Discovery Initiatives ❂ 01285 643333; f 01285 885888; e enquiry@discoveryinitiatives.com; www.discoveryinitiatives.co.uk. Part of the Steppes Travel Group.

Exodus ❂ 0845 869 9600; e sales@exodus.co.uk; www.exodus.co.uk

Expert Africa ❂ 020 8232 9777; e info@expertafrica; www.expertafrica.com

Footprint Adventures ❂ 01522 804929; e sales@footprint-adventures.co.uk; www.footprint-adventures.co.uk

Imagine Africa ❂ 020 7622 5114; e info@imagineafrica.co.uk; www.imagineafrica.co.uk

Naturetrek ❂ 01962 733051; e info@naturetrek.co.uk; www.naturetrek.co.uk

Rainbow Tours ☏ 020 7226 1004; f 020 7226 2621; e info@rainbowtours.co.uk; www.rainbowtours.co.uk
Reef & Rainforest Tours ☏ 01803 866965; f 01803 865916; e mail@reefandrainforest.co.uk; www.reefandrainforest.co.uk
The Zambezi Safari & Travel Company ☏ 01548 830059; f 0870 094 1881; e info@zambezi.co.uk; www.zambezi.co.uk
Tribes Travel ☏ 01728 685971; e bradt@tribes.co.uk; www.tribes.co.uk

USA *(national code +1)*
Aardvark Safaris ☏ 888 776 0888 (toll free); e info@aardvarksafaris.com; www.aardvarksafaris.com
Africa Adventure Company ☏ (toll free USA & Canada) 800 882 9453; e safari@africanadventure.com; www.africa-adventure.com
Churchill Safaris ☏ 909 427 1512/684 4701; e ether@churchillsafaris.com; www.churchillsafaris.com (see also under *Uganda* below)

EUROPE
Belgium *(national code +32)*
Continents Insolites ☏ 2218 2484; e info@insolites.be; www.continentsinsolites.be

Spain *(national code +34)*
Kananga Travel ☏ 93 268 7795; e info@kananga.com; www.kananga.com

AFRICA
Uganda *(national code +256)*
Adventure Trails Ltd ☏ 031 226 1930; f 0392 842044; e info@gorilla-safari.com; www.gorilla-safari.com
Alpha & Beta Investments Ltd ☏ 414 344332; f 414 232659; e info@alpharentals.co.ug; www.alpharentals.co.ug
Churchill Safaris ☏ 414 341 815/772 671 285; f 414 253976; e ether@churchillsafaris.com or caasafaris@africaonline.co.ug; www.churchillsafaris.com (see also under *USA* above)

Kenya *(national code +254)*
Origins Safaris ☏ 20 331191, 222075; e trade@originsafaris.info; www.originsafaris.info

South Africa *(national code +27)*
Unusual Destinations ☏ 11 706 1991; f 11 463 1469; e info@unusualdestinations.com; www.unusualdestinations.com

Vintage Africa Ltd UK office: ☏ 01451 850803; e vintagelon@vintageafrica.com; www.vintageafrica.com (offices also in South Africa, Tanzania & Kenya)
Volcanoes Safaris UK office: ☏ 0870 870 8480; f 0870 870 8481; e salesuk@volcanoessafaris.com; www.volcanoessafaris.com (offices in UK, USA, Uganda & Rwanda – also see details on page 85)
Wildlife Worldwide ☏ 0845 130 6982; f 0845 130 6984; e sales@wildlifeworldwide.com; www.wildlifeworldwide.com

Ker & Downey ☏ 281 371 2500, (toll free USA & Canada) 800 423 4236; e info@kerdowney.com; www.kerdowney.com
Volcanoes Safaris ☏ 866 599 2737 (toll free), 404 993 6116; e salesus@volcanoessafaris.com; www.volcanoessafaris.com (also see under *UK*, above)

Magic Safaris ☏ 717 342 926; e info@magic-safaris.com; www.magic-safaris.com
The Far Horizon ☏ 41 312 264 894; e info@thefarhorizons.com; www.thefarhorizons.com (also have an office in Rwanda)
Volcanoes Safaris ☏ 414 346464; e salesug@volcanoessafaris.com; www.volcanoessafaris.com (see also under *UK*, above)

Wild Frontiers ☏ 11 702 2035; e wildfront@icon.co.za; www.wildfrontiers.com (also have offices in Uganda & Tanzania)

XA! nini African Wildlife Safaris ↘ 21 434 7184;
f 21 434 7183; e limar@iafrica.com;
www.xasafaris.com

RED TAPE

Check well in advance that you have a valid **passport**, and that it won't expire within six months of the date you intend to leave Rwanda. Should your passport be lost or stolen, it will generally be easier to get a replacement if you travel with a photocopy of the important pages.

Bilateral agreements currently allow nationals of the following countries to visit Rwanda without a **visa** for a period of up to 90 days: Burundi, Canada, Democratic Republic of Congo (DRC), Germany, Hong Kong, Kenya, Mauritius, Singapore, South Africa, Sweden, Tanzania, Uganda, UK and USA. This might change, however, so check at the website below before you travel.

Visas are required by all other visitors and cost up to US$60, depending on the place of issue. Technically, they can no longer be bought upon arrival. Either arrange yours through the nearest Rwandan embassy or high commission, or apply online at www.migration.gov.rw (click on 'public forms' then 'single entry visa'). So far as we can ascertain, the visa issued online is valid for 15 days only, but can be extended for up to 90 days after you arrive. For further details contact the Directorate General of Immigration and Emigration in Rwanda (↘ *(+250) 0252 585430;* m *078 8899971;* e *info@migration.gov.rw).*

Immigration officials at Kigali Airport are now highly reluctant to issue a visa upon arrival. The best they will do – and this may require some tense negotiations – is give you a temporary visa, valid for up to two weeks, at a cost of US$60. If you intend to spend longer in the country, then you'll need to make several visits over several days to the immigration office in Kigali and spend another US$50 on a full visa.

If there is any possibility that you'll want to drive or hire a vehicle while you're in the country, do organise an **international driving licence** (via one of the main motoring associations in a country in which you're licensed to drive), which you may be asked to produce together with your original licence. You may be asked at borders for an international health certificate showing you've had a **yellow-fever shot**.

For security reasons, it's advisable to detail all your important information on one sheet of paper, photocopy it, and distribute a few copies in your luggage, your money-belt, and amongst relatives or friends at home: the sort of things you want to include on this are travellers' cheque numbers and refund information, travel insurance policy details and 24-hour emergency contact number, passport number, details of relatives or friends to be contacted in an emergency, bank and credit card details, camera and lens serial numbers, etc. You might also want to email this information to yourself immediately before you leave, so it is stored in your in-tray throughout your travels. It's also handy to carry a photo of your suitcase or other luggage, to save trying to describe it if it's misplaced by an airline.

Ⓔ EMBASSIES AND CONSULATES

RWANDAN EMBASSIES AND CONSULATES ABROAD

Belgium 1 Av des Fleurs, 1150 Brussels; ↘ (+32) 02 763 0738; e ambabruxelles@minaffet.gov.rw; www.ambarwanda.be

Burundi 24 Av de la République Démocratique du Congo, Bujumbura; ↘ (+257) 223255; e ambuja@minaffet.gov.rw

Canada 153 Gilmour St, Ottawa; ↘ (+1613) 569 5420/4; e ambaottawa@minaffet.gov.rw; www.ambarwaottawa.ca.

China Hsieu Shaouei Bei Yie, Beijing; ↘ (+861) 065 321820; f 065 322006; e ambabeijing@minaffet.gov.rw; www.embarwanda-china.com

Ethiopia Africa Av, H 17k-20 No 001, PO Box 5618 Addis Ababa; ☎ (+251) 661 0300; e ambaddis@minaffet.gov.rw

France 12 Rue Jadin, 75017 Paris; ☎ (+33) 1 476 65420; f +33 1 422 77469; e ambaparis@minaffet.gov.rw; www.ambarwanda.fr

Germany Beethovenallee 72, 53173 Bonn; ☎ (+49) 228 3670238; f 228 351922; e ambabonn@minaffet.gov.rw; www.rwanda-botschaft.de

India B 112 Neet Bash, New Delhi 110016; ☎ (+91) 11 51661604; e ambadelhi@minaffet.gov.rw

Kenya 2nd floor, International House, Mama Ngima Rd, Nairobi; ☎ (+254) 2 575975; e ambanairobi@minaffet.gov.rw; www.kenya.embassy.gov.rw

South Africa 35 Marais St, Brooklyn, Pretoria; ☎ (+27) 12 460 0709; e ambapretoria@minaffet.gov.rw

Switzerland Rue de la Serviette 93, CH-1202 Geneva; ☎ (+41) 22 919 1000; e ambageneve@minaffet.gov.rw

Tanzania 32 Ali Hassan Mwinyi Rd, PO Box 2918 Dar es Salaam; ☎ (+255) 211 7631; e ambadaresalam@minaffet.gov.rw

Uganda 2 Nakaima Rd, PO Box 2446 Kampala; ☎ (+256) 41 234 3662; e rwanda@swiftuganda.com

UK 120–122 Seymour Place, London W1H 1NR; ☎ (+44) 020 7224 9832; e uk@ambarwanda.org.uk; www.ambarwanda.org.uk

USA 124 East 39th St, New York, NY 10016; ☎ (+1) 212 679 9010; e ambanewyork@minaffet.gov.rw. Also 1724 New Hampshire Av NW, Washington, DC 20009; ☎ (+1) 202 232 2882; e ambawashington@minaffet.gov.rw; www.rwandaembassy.org

FOREIGN REPRESENTATION IN RWANDA Foreign embassies and consulates in Kigali (or in other East African countries, if there is none in Rwanda) are given below. International dialling codes are Rwanda: 250; Kenya: 254; Uganda: 256.

Austria (Kenya) City House, Wabera St, PO Box 30560 Nairobi; ☎ (2) 228281/2; f 331792

Belgium Rue de Nyarugenge, Kigali; ☎ 0252 575551–4; e kigali@diplobel.be; www.diplomatie.be/kigali

Burundi 4 Rue Ntaruka, Kigali ☎ 0252 517529, 575718, 573465

Canada 1534 Rue Akagera, Kigali ☎ 0252 573210; e kgali@international.gc.ca; www.dfait-maeci.gc.ca/africa/rwanda-contact-en.asp

China 44 Bd de la Révolution, Kigali; ☎ 0252 570843/5; e chinaemb_rw@mfa.gov.cn; www.rw.china-embassy.org

Denmark (Uganda) 3 Lumumba Av, PO Box 11234 Kampala; ☎ (41) 256687, 256783, 250938; f 254970; e denmark@emul.com

France Rue Nyarugenge, Kigali; ☎ 575551–3; e kigali@diplobel.org; www.ambafrance-lc.org

Germany 10 Av Paul VI, Kiyovu, Kigali; ☎ 0252 575141; www.kigali.diplo.de

Netherlands Bd de Kacyiru; ☎ 0252 510603/4; e kig@minbuza.nl

Norway (Uganda) Acacia Av Quarter, Kololo, PO Box 22770 Kampala; ☎ (41) 343621, 346733, 346757, 340848; f 343936

Russian Federation 19 Av de l'Armée, BP 40 Kigali; ☎ 575286; e ambruss@rwanda1.com

South Africa 1370 Bd de l'Umuganda, Kigali; ☎ 0252 583185-7; e saemkgl@rwanda1.com; www.saembassy-kigali.org.rw

Switzerland 38 Bd de la Révolution, BP 1257 Kigali; ☎ 0252 575534

Tanzania 15 Av Paul VI; ☎ 0252 505400; e tanmos@wm.west-call.com

Uganda Plot 9, Av de l'Akagera, ☎ 0252 576854; e ugaemb@rwanda1.com

United Kingdom Bd de l'Umuganda; ☎ 0252 584098/586072; e embassy.kigali@fco.gov.uk; www.ukinrwanda.fco.gov.uk

USA 2756 Av de la Gendarmerie, Kacyiru, Kigali; ☎ 0252 596400; e consularkigali@state.gov; http://rwanda.usembassy.gov

GETTING THERE AND AWAY

✈ **BY AIR** The national airline **Rwandair Express** (☎ *0252 575757/503691;* e *info@rwandair.com; www.rwandair.com*) flies directly between Kigali and Brussels (Belgium), Entebbe (Uganda), Johannesburg (South Africa), Nairobi (Kenya), Bujumbura (Burundi) and Dar es Salaam (Tanzania). It has a reservations office in the Union Trade Centre in central Kigali, as well as in all the countries to which it flies (see website for contact details), and bookings can also be made online.

Other operators that fly directly to Kigali include **Kenya Airways** (*www.kenya-airways.com*), **Brussels Airlines** (*www.brusselsairlines.com*), **Ethiopian Airlines** (*www.ethiopianairlines.com*), and **South African Airways** (*www.flysaa.com*). All of these carriers operate a good network of intra- and intercontinental flights – travellers coming from the Americas and Australasia will do best to aim for Johannesburg or Nairobi, while those from Europe are best off flying via Brussels, Nairobi and Addis Ababa. The Brussels Airlines daytime flight from Brussels, while generally not the cheapest, gets you to Kigali in time for dinner and a good night's sleep before you embark on sightseeing or business. For those tagging a visit to Rwanda on to a safari in northern Tanzania, it is worth knowing that **Coastal Aviation** (*www.coastal.cc*) operates a flight between Kigali and Arusha, Manyara or the Serengeti by inducement.

The international airport lies less than 10km from central Kigali, and taxis are available to/from the city centre (see *Chapter 4*, page 80), though it's possible that the existing airport will be replaced by the planned Bugesera International Airport about 40km south of the city during the lifespan of this edition. The departure tax that used to be payable at the airport is now included in your ticket – but check when you book, in case this changes again.

On no account neglect to confirm your return flight at least three days in advance, via an airline office or travel agent in Kigali. Unless you do this, there is – at least with some airlines – a serious risk of being 'bumped' at the last minute, or of finding that the schedule changed unexpectedly and your flight left early.

Air tickets A number of travel companies are good sources of cut-price tickets, as well as offering various other services. London is the best place for cheap fares, hence the bias of the list below! It isn't exhaustive but should give you a start. As shown on their websites, most of the companies listed also have offices in other countries.

UK (London)

Africa Travel Centre New Premier House, 3rd Floor, 150 Southampton Row, Bloomsbury, London WC1B 5AL; ☎ 0845 450 1520; e info@africatravel.co.uk; www.africatravel.co.uk

Flight Centre ☎ (booking) 0870 499 0040; www.flightcentre.com. Flight Centre has several offices in London & elsewhere in UK. It offers cut-price airfares & insurance services. Also in Australia, New Zealand, South Africa & USA.

STA Travel ☎ 0871 230 0040; e enquiries@ statravel.co.uk; web (very comprehensive): www.statravel.co.uk. Has 65 branches in UK & over 450 worldwide.

Trailfinders 194 Kensington High St, London W8 7RG (one-stop travel shop); ☎ 020 7938 3939; web (very comprehensive): www.trailfinders.com. Also in Ireland, Australia, etc.

WEXAS 45–49 Brompton Rd, Knightsbridge, London SW3 1DE; ☎ 0845 643 6568; www.wexas.com. There is an annual subscription to WEXAS (*for current details:* ☎ 020 7581 8768; e mship@wexas.com) but membership gives access to a whole range of useful services (good rates for hotels & airport parking, use of airport lounges, travel insurance, visas...) as well as an excellent travel magazine, *Traveller*.

OVERLAND Four countries border Rwanda: Burundi to the south, the Democratic Republic of the Congo (DRC) to the west, Uganda to the north and Tanzania to the east. Assuming peaceful conditions, frontier formalities aren't too much of a hassle – but nor are they standardised. Most frontier offices open at 08.00; they may close at 17.00 or 18.00. At the time of writing, there's a plan to open the DRC crossings 24 hours, but double-check this. See page 36 for details of which nationalities don't require visas; for others, to buy a visa at the border costs around US$60. (But, for safety, check with your nearest embassy beforehand that it's still possible.) Don't count on official exchange facilities being available; there are likely to be 'black-market' money-changers around, but you should decide in advance what rate you're prepared to accept.

At the time of writing, there are still buses running between Kigali and Bujumbura in Burundi and bus travel is reckoned to be safe. However, historically it's a volatile area, and the situation could change at any time. If in doubt, air travel is safer. Onatracom (\ *0252 575404/575411/501302; www.onatracom.rw*) runs a daily bus service from Kigali to Bujumbura. This departs at 08.00 in either direction, takes around seven hours, and costs Rfr4,000.

Despite the ongoing civil war in the DRC, it is normally safe to travel in the immediate Rwanda border area, though you're strongly advised to check the current situation first. Regular minibus services run between Kigali and Goma/Bukavu. On both sides of each border there is accommodation reasonably close by – in the case of Cyangugu and Gisenyi, only a few minutes away, but further for Bukavu. Travelling further into the DRC remains highly risky.

Crossing to and from Uganda is simple. Direct buses and minibus-taxis connect Kampala and Kigali. Onatracom (contact details above) runs two daily services from Kigali to Kampala via Mbarara. These depart from Kigali at 05.30 and 06.00, and from Kampala at 06.30 and 07.00, take around nine hours, and cost Rfr4,500. Of the more expensive private operators, one of the best buses is Regional Coach Services (\ *0252 575963, 078 8866792 or (+256) 41 256862/3 in Kampala*), which departs Kampala for Kigali at 09.00 daily and has connections on to Nairobi and Dar es Salaam. There are plenty of local minibus-taxis along the roughly 50km road between Kisoro in southwest Uganda and Ruhengeri in northwest Rwanda (an hour's trip, not allowing for changing vehicles and other delays at the Cyanika border post, which might add another hour to the journey). It is also easy to travel by minibus-taxi between Kabale, the largest town in southwest Uganda, and Kigali, though once again you might have to change vehicles at the border – this trip should take about four hours in total. Entering from Uganda in your own vehicle is relatively hassle-free.

Crossing between Rwanda and Tanzania is something of a slog, due to the poor state of roads and lack of large towns in northwest Tanzania. The Rusumo border post lies about 160km from Kigali, roughly a four-hour trip by minibus-taxi, with the possibility of staying the night *en route* at the town of Kibungo (see page 241), 60km from the border. Or there is a restaurant with basic accommodation at Rusumo itself, on the Rwandan side (page 247). The closest Tanzanian town to the border is Ngara, which is connected to Rusumo by occasional minibus-taxis taking about six hours, and has a few small guesthouses. From Ngara, daily buses to Mwanza on Lake Victoria take 12–18 hours depending on the condition of the road. Mwanza is a large port with a full range of accommodation and other facilities, including thrice-weekly rail links to Dar es Salaam on the coast and daily buses to Arusha in northeast Tanzania. A rail link between Rwanda and Tanzania is planned, but don't count on it being up and running in the near future. See also the box *Travelling from Kigali to Mwanza* on page 243.

SAFETY

THEFT So far as tourists need be concerned, Rwanda is among the most crime-free of African countries. Kigali is a very safe city, even at night, though it would probably be courting trouble to stumble around dark alleys with all your valuables on your person. Be aware, too, that this sort of thing can change very quickly: all too often, as tourism volumes increase, so too does opportunistic and petty crime.

The following security hints are applicable anywhere in Africa:

NOTES FOR DISABLED TRAVELLERS
Gordon Rattray

Renowned as the 'Land of a Thousand Hills', Rwanda might sound like one to avoid if mobility is an issue for you. Furthermore, the country's tourism industry is relatively new and there are few provisions foreseen for the local disabled population. Despite all that, my advice is to go, making sure your itinerary is not rushed and being prepared to compromise to some degree. Africans are usually delighted to offer help and are often, through necessity, experts in improvisation.

ACCOMMODATION In general, it is not easy to find disabled-friendly accommodation. Only top of the range hotels and lodges have 'accessible' rooms while budget guesthouses and campsites are more basic. Occasionally (more by accident than through design) bathrooms are step-free and spacious, but they usually contain standard fittings only.

TRANSPORT
By road Most tour companies use 4x4s and minibuses, which are higher than normal cars and therefore might make entry more difficult. Similarly, buses and minibuses have no facilities for wheelchairs, and getting off and on can be a hectic affair. Drivers, guides and fellow passengers are usually prepared to assist but they are not trained in this skill so you must thoroughly explain your needs and stay in control of the situation.

By air If you need assistance then let the airline know in advance and arrive early for your departure. During the flight, anyone who uses a pressure-relieving wheelchair cushion should consider using it instead of or on top of the fitted seat cushion. There is no guarantee that aisle chairs will be present at airports in Rwanda, so expect to be manhandled if you cannot transfer unaided.

ACTIVITIES Gorilla tracking is literally a stumble in the jungle, even for able-bodied people. You don't need to be super-fit, but check with your tour operator if you think your disability may exclude you. I have heard of non-ambulant people being physically carried, though this would obviously require extra planning and payment. Museums and other public places rarely have disability access but are unlikely to be completely inaccessible.

HEALTH AND INSURANCE Rwandan hospitals and pharmacies are often basic so, if possible, take all essential medication and equipment with you. It is advisable to pack this in your hand luggage during flights in case your main bags don't arrive immediately. Doctors will

- Most casual thieves operate in busy markets and bus stations. Keep a close watch on your possessions in such places, and avoid having valuables or large amounts of money loose in your daypack or pocket.
- Keep all your valuables and the bulk of your money in a hidden money belt. Never show this money belt in public. Keep any spare cash you need elsewhere on your person – a button-up pocket on the front of the shirt is a good place as money cannot be snatched from it without the thief coming into your view. It is also advisable to keep a small amount of hard currency (ideally cash) hidden in your luggage in case you lose your money belt.
- Where the choice exists between carrying valuables on your person or leaving them in a locked room I would favour the latter option (thefts from locked hotel rooms are relatively rare in Africa). Obviously you should use your judgement on this and be sure the room is absolutely secure. Bear in mind that some travellers' cheque companies will not refund cheques which were stolen from a room.
- Leave any jewellery of financial or sentimental value at home.

know about 'everyday' illnesses, but you must understand and be able to explain your own particular medical requirements. It can also be hot; if this is a problem for you then try to book accommodation and vehicles with fans or air-conditioning, and a plant-spray bottle can be a useful cooling aid.

Travel insurance can be purchased from Age Concern (0800 169 2700; www.ageconcern.org.uk), who have no upper age limit, and Free Spirit (0845 230 5000; www.free-spirit.com), who cater for people with pre-existing medical conditions. Most insurance companies will insure disabled travellers, but it is essential that they are made aware of your disability.

SECURITY For anyone following the usual security precautions (see above) the chances of robbery are greatly reduced. In fact, as a disabled person I personally feel more 'noticed', and therefore a less attractive target for thieves. But the opposite may also apply, so do stay aware of where your bags are and who is around you, especially during car transfers and similar activities.

SPECIALIST OPERATORS There are currently no disability-specialised operators running trips to Rwanda. Having said that, most travel companies will listen to your needs and try to create an itinerary suitable for you.

FURTHER INFORMATION
Books Bradt Travel Guides' new title *Access Africa – Safaris for People with Limited Mobility* doesn't deal with Rwanda specifically but is packed with useful advice and resources for disabled adventure travellers.

Online
www.able-travel.com A regularly updated website with both worldwide and country-specific info.
www.globalaccessnews.com A searchable database of disability travel information.
www.rollingrains.com A searchable website advocating disability travel.
www.youreable.com A UK-based general resource for disability information, with an active forum.
www.apparelyzed.com A site dedicated to spinal injury, but containing information that other disabilities will also find useful. It also hosts a hugely popular forum.

Janice Booth

As a lone female traveller, I have experienced far less hassle and anxiety in Rwanda during my several visits than I have in many other countries. I travelled all over the country by public transport feeling completely safe. There was a refreshing absence of 'smart Alecs' trying to engage me in dubious conversation.

In one town, a young man (Congolese, as it turned out) overheard me asking directions to the guesthouse and spontaneously walked with me, chatting occasionally, to make sure I found it safely. Then he shook my hand and went off. Another day I gave my driver, who had had a long hard morning, Rfr2,000 to go and buy a good lunch, and he spontaneously handed me Rfr1,000 change when he returned. Once I left my unlockable duffel bag with a smiling girl in a small wooden drinks kiosk near a minibus stop while I explored a village; when I returned to collect it, it had been stowed safely in a corner and the girl's baby was gurgling happily on top. I felt a kind of 'sisterhood', particularly with village women – if I smiled it was always reciprocated, although often shyly, and I always asked a woman first if I needed help or directions.

In Kigali I've spent a lot of time walking both in and outside the city centre and never felt threatened, although there are some poorer areas which (and a Rwandan woman friend agrees with me) become scarier after dark. This applies to men too, of course, but women are generally seen – rightly or wrongly! – as a target less likely to put up resistance. The rule here is to take the same sensible precautions you'd take in any capital city, and then relax.

As a matter of courtesy, watch what the local women wear and don't expose parts of yourself that they leave covered, particularly in village areas. In business areas people are smartly dressed; I've been glad of bringing a skirt and some crumple-free tops. Be sensitive to the fact that people here have suffered a great deal; if someone is reluctant to talk or to answer questions, don't push it.

You may not be as fortunate as I've been. Nor do I suggest that you drop your guard and behave over-confidently. There can be bad apples in any barrel. Would-be Lotharios exist in any country and they tend to home in on female travellers. In fact, one night in Kigali a strange man did knock on my bedroom door at 11pm, but it turned out that he needed money to take a sick street kid to hospital (yes, honestly!).

I place Rwanda very high on the list of relatively hassle-free countries where good manners, honesty and trust are the order of the day – and of course this should be a two-way process.

Useful contact
Police ✆ 08311117

OTHER HAZARDS People new to exotic travel often worry about tropical diseases, but it is accidents which are most likely to carry you off. Road travel isn't as dangerous in Rwanda as in some other African countries but still accidents aren't uncommon, and the number of vehicles is increasing; so be aware and do what you can to reduce risks. For example, try to travel during daylight hours and refuse to be driven by anyone who is drunk. Always heed local advice about where you should (or should not) travel, or about areas where you should take particular care. At the time of writing, Rwanda is a relatively safe country – but, sadly, it has been seen elsewhere that an increase in tourism can lead to an increase in opportunistic crime. Be as sensible in Rwanda as (I hope!) you would be in any other strange country about carrying your cash discreetly and not flaunting jewellery, and (particularly in towns) about where you walk after dark. Also be sensible in hotels and guesthouses: don't leave tempting items too readily accessible.

HASSLES

Overcharging and bargaining Tourists may sometimes need to bargain over prices, but this need is often exaggerated by guidebooks and other travellers. Hotels, restaurants and supermarkets generally charge fixed prices, and deliberate overcharging is so rare that it's not worth challenging a price unless it is blatantly ridiculous. In other situations – mostly markets or in the street – you're bound to be asked a higher price than the vendor will expect, and a certain degree of bargaining is considered normal. It is, however, important to keep this in perspective. Some travellers, after a couple of bad experiences, start to haggle with everyone from hotel owners to old women selling fruit by the side of the road, often accompanying their negotiations with aggressive accusations of dishonesty. This may be the easiest way to find out whether you are being overcharged, but it is unfair on the majority of Rwandans who are forthright and honest in their dealings with tourists.

Minibus conductors may occasionally ask tourists for higher fares than normal. The way to counter this is to watch what other people are paying, or to ask a fellow passenger what the fare should be. The main instance where bargaining is essential is when buying handicrafts or curios. However, the fact that a curio seller is open to negotiation does not mean that he or she was initially trying to rip you off. Vendors will generally quote a starting-price knowing full well that you are going to bargain it down – they'd probably be startled if you didn't – and it is not necessary to respond aggressively. It is impossible to say what size of reduction you should expect (some people say that you should offer half the asking price and be prepared to settle at around two-thirds, but my experience is that curio sellers are far more whimsical than such advice allows for). The sensible approach is to ask the price of similar items at a few different stalls before you actually contemplate buying anything.

In fruit and vegetable markets and stalls, bargaining is often the norm, even between Africans, and the healthiest approach to this sort of haggling is to view it as an enjoyable part of the travel experience. There will normally be an accepted price-band for any particular commodity. To find out what it is, listen to what other people pay (it helps if you know some Kinyarwanda) and try a few stalls – a ludicrously inflated price will drop the moment you walk away. When buying fruit and vegetables, a good way to feel out the situation is to ask for a bulk discount or a few extra items thrown in. And bear in mind that the reason why somebody is reluctant to bargain may be that they asked a fair price in the first place.

Above all, don't lose your sense of proportion. No matter how poor you may feel, it is your choice to travel on a tight budget. Most Rwandans are much poorer than you will ever be, and they do not have the luxury of choosing to travel. If you find yourself quibbling with an old lady selling a few piles of fruit by the roadside, stand back and look at the bigger picture. There is nothing wrong with occasionally erring on the side of generosity.

Begging To anyone who knows Africa it should come as no surprise to see beggars on the streets; the surprise, in view of Rwanda's recent past, is that they aren't more numerous. Nor are they often aggressive. For a charity (one of several) helping Kigali's street kids, see *rYico* on page 61. The maimed, handicapped and very old tell an obvious story. I can't advise you what to do about them. It's true that if you give to one you risk being surrounded by a dozen – but sometimes it's hard to walk on by. Rwandans themselves often recommend that you give something; they and the country's budget have little enough to spare. I set aside a 'ration' of small notes each day – when they're used up, that's it. If you don't believe in giving cash, see *Becoming involved*, pages 60–3, which lists some charities where your money will be well used.

Bribery and bureaucracy For all you read about the subject, bribery is not the problem to travellers in Africa that it is often made out to be. Those who are most often asked for bribes are the ones with private transport; and even they only have a major problem at some borders and from traffic police in some countries (notably Mozambique and Kenya). If you are travelling in Rwanda on public transport or as part of a tour, or even if you are driving yourself, I doubt whether you need to give the question of bribery serious thought, although if you make a day trip into the DRC you may encounter someone inventively explaining why you should part with a few thousand francs.

There is a tendency to portray African bureaucrats as difficult and inefficient in their dealings with tourists. As a rule, this reputation says more about Western prejudices than it does about Africa. Sure, you come across the odd unhelpful official, but then such is the nature of the beast everywhere. The vast majority of officials in the African countries I've visited – Rwanda included – have been courteous and helpful in their dealings with tourists, often to a degree that is almost embarrassing.

A factor in determining the response you receive from African officials – and those in Rwanda are unlikely to be an exception – will be your own attitude. If you walk into every official encounter with an aggressive, paranoid approach, you are quite likely to kindle the feeling held by many Africans that Europeans are arrogant and offhand in their dealings with other races. Instead, try to be friendly and patient, and remember that the person to whom you are talking does not speak English (or French) as a first language and may thus have difficulty understanding you. Treat people with respect rather than disdain, in Rwanda as elsewhere, and they'll tend to treat you in the same way.

WHAT TO TAKE

In 1907, when the Duke of Mecklenburg set off on an expedition through Rwanda with a group of scientific researchers, he carried (or rather his team of bearers carried) numerous cases of soap, candles, rope and cigars, as well as such items as salt, wire, beads and woollen blankets to barter with the natives. You could probably cut down on this a little.

In fact Rwanda is a relatively well-stocked little country, in terms of clothing, toiletries, stationery, batteries and so forth. Unless you have particularly exotic tastes (or your schedule is too crowded to allow you time for shopping), you should be able to find most of the everyday items a traveller needs, even if the brands are unfamiliar. Obviously you should bring a supply of any personal medication (and some extra, in case your return home is delayed); as well as enough sunscreen. Otherwise, unless you plan to go way off the beaten track (or you need camping/trekking gear, which is in shorter supply), don't feel that you must fill your bag up with a lot of semi-useful items 'just in case'. Buying things locally helps Rwanda's economy!

The comments below apply as much to any neighbouring African countries you may pass through or visit as they do to Rwanda.

CARRYING YOUR LUGGAGE Visitors who are unlikely to be carrying their luggage for any significant distance will probably want to pack most of it in a conventional suitcase. Make sure it is tough and durable, and that it seals well, so that its contents will survive bumpy drives and boisterous baggage handlers at airports. Travellers carrying a lot of valuable items should look for a bag that can be easily padlocked. A locked bag can, of course, be slashed open, but that would be highly unusual in Rwanda – you are more likely to be exposed to casual theft of the sort to which a lock would be real deterrent.

If you are likely to use public transport, then a backpack is the most practical solution. An internal frame is more flexible than an external one. Again, ensure your pack is durable and that it has several pockets. If you intend doing a lot of hiking, you definitely want a backpack designed for this purpose. On the other hand, if you'll be staying at places where it might be a good idea to shake off the sometimes negative image attached to backpackers, then there would be advantages in using a suitcase that converts into a backpack.

However you travel, a small daypack will be useful for gorilla tracking and other walks, and to stow any breakable goods on your lap during long drives – anything like an mp3 player or camera will suffer heavily from vibrations on rutted roads.

CAMPING EQUIPMENT There are only a few opportunities for camping in Rwanda, and the financial advantages are limited since affordable accommodation is generally available. Balanced against that, for those without transport the campsite at Nyungwe is a far more convenient base for walks than the resthouse, and a tent is essential for hiking in off-the-beaten-track areas. Also, although there is now accommodation in Akagera Park, camping there gets you closest to the wildlife.

For backpackers who decide to carry camping equipment, the key is to look for the lightest available gear. It is now possible to buy a lightweight tent weighing little more than 2kg, but make sure that the one you choose is mosquito-proof. Other essentials for camping include a sleeping bag and a roll-mat, which will serve as both insulation and padding. You might want to carry a stove and Camping Gas cylinders (not readily available in Rwanda). A box of firelighter blocks will get a fire going in the most unpromising conditions. It would also be advisable to carry a pot, plate, cup and cutlery.

CLOTHES Try to keep your clothes to a minimum, especially if you are travelling with everything on your back. Bear in mind that you can easily and cheaply replace worn items in markets. In my opinion, the minimum is one or possibly two pairs of trousers and/or skirts, one pair of shorts, three shirts or T-shirts, one light sweater or similar, one heavy sweater or similar, a waterproof jacket during the rainy season, enough socks and underwear to last five to seven days, one solid pair of shoes or boots for walking, and one pair of sandals, flip-flops or other light shoes.

It's widely held that jeans are not ideal for African travel, since they are bulky to carry, hot to wear and take ages to dry. In their favour, however, jeans do have the advantages of durability and comfort, and of hiding the dust and dirt that tend to accumulate during public transport rides – and they are excellent for gorilla tracking and other forest walks. A good alternative is light cotton trousers, which dry more quickly and weigh less, but try to avoid light colours, as they show dirt more easily. Skirts are best made of a light natural fabric such as cotton. T-shirts are lighter and less bulky than proper shirts, though the top pocket of a shirt (particularly if it buttons up) is a good place to carry spending money in markets and bus stations, since it's easier to keep an eye on than a trouser pocket. A couple of sweaters or sweatshirts will be necessary in places such as Nyungwe, which get chilly at night.

Socks and underwear *must* be made from natural fabrics. Bear in mind that re-using sweaty undergarments will encourage fungal infections such as athlete's foot, as well as prickly heat in the groin region. Socks and underpants are light and compact enough to make it worth bringing a week's supply. As for footwear, only if you're a serious off-road hiker should you consider genuine hiking boots, since they are very heavy whether on your feet or in your pack. A good pair of walking shoes, preferably made of leather with good ankle support, is a good compromise. For gorilla-tracking, a pair of old gardening gloves can be handy when you're grabbing for handholds in thorny vegetation.

Another factor in selecting your travel wardrobe is local sensibilities. In Rwanda, which is predominantly Christian, this isn't the concern it would be in several other parts of Africa, but travellers are nevertheless advised to dress relatively modestly. For women, the ideal garment is a knee-length skirt, though long trousers – while unconventional female wear in rural Rwanda – are most unlikely to give offence. For men, shorts are not unacceptable, but few local men wear them and it is considered more respectable to wear trousers. Walking around in a public place without a shirt is dodgy.

Many Africans think it is insulting for Westerners to wear scruffy or dirty clothes in their country, reasoning that we wouldn't dress like that at home. It is difficult to explain that at home you also wouldn't spend a morning slithering around the muddy Virungas in your last clean outfit! If you're travelling rough, you're bound to look a mess at times, but it's worth trying to look as spruce as possible, particularly since many Rwandans dress well.

OTHER USEFUL ITEMS Most backpackers, even those with no intention of camping, carry a **sleeping bag**. I've never seen the necessity for this, particularly in Rwanda. You might meet travellers who, when they stay in local lodgings, habitually place their own sleeping bag on top of the bedding provided. Nutters, in my opinion: I'd imagine that a sleeping bag placed on a flea-ridden bed would be unlikely to provide significant protection – it would be more likely to become flea-infested itself.

I wouldn't leave home without **binoculars**, which some might say makes me the nutter. Seriously, though, if you're interested in natural history, it's difficult to imagine anything that will give you such value-for-weight entertainment as a pair of light, compact binoculars, which these days needn't be much heavier or bulkier than a pack of cards. Binoculars are essential if you want to get a good look at birds (Africa boasts a remarkably colourful avifauna even if you've no desire to put a name to everything that flaps) or to watch distant mammals in game reserves. For most purposes, 7x21 compact binoculars will be fine, though some might prefer 7x35 traditional binoculars for their larger field of vision. Serious birdwatchers will find a 10x magnification more useful.

A **padlock** is useful if you have a pack that is lockable. Combination locks are reputedly easier to pick than conventional padlocks, but you're probably safer with a combination lock in Rwanda, because potential thieves will have far more experience of breaking through locks with keys.

Your toilet bag should at the very minimum include **soap** (secured in a plastic bag or soap holder unless you enjoy a soapy toothbrush!), **shampoo**, **toothbrush** and **toothpaste**. This sort of stuff is easy to replace as you go along, so there's no need to bring family-sized packs. Men will probably want a **razor**. Women should carry enough **tampons** and/or **sanitary pads** to see them through at least one heavy period, since these items may not always be immediately available. If you wear **contact lenses**, be aware that the various fluids are not readily available in Rwanda, and, since many people find the intense sun and dust irritate their eyes, you might consider reverting to glasses. Nobody should forget to bring a **towel**, or to keep handy a roll of **loo paper**, which although widely available at shops and kiosks cannot always be relied upon to be present where it's most urgently needed. A lot of washbasins in Rwanda lack **plugs**, so one of those 'universal' rubber plugs that fit all sizes of plughole can be useful.

Other essentials include a **torch (flashlight)**, a **penknife** and a compact **alarm clock** for those early morning starts. If you're interested in what's happening in the world, you might also think about taking a short-wave **radio**, though these days the ubiquity of internet access probably makes it redundant. Some travellers carry **games** – most commonly a pack of cards, less often chess, draughts or travel Scrabble.

You should carry a small **medical kit**, the contents of which are discussed in chapter on health, as are **mosquito nets**. For those who wear **glasses**, it's worth bringing a spare pair, though in an emergency a new pair can be made up cheaply and quickly in most Rwandan towns, provided that you have your prescription available.

$ MONEY

The unit of currency is the **Rwandan franc** (Rfr), which comes in Rfr5,000, 2,000, 1,000 and 500 notes and Rfr100, 50, 20, 10, 5 and 1 coins. The October 2009 exchange rate was around Rfr567 to the US dollar, Rfr835 to the euro and Rfr895 to the British pound, depending on whether the transaction involved cash or travellers' cheques, and where it took place. Most local services are best paid in local currency, but there are exceptions, such as gorilla-tracking fees and some upmarket hotels, which require payment in US dollars or another hard currency. Throughout this guide, prices are quoted in local currency except where the institution in question quotes rates in another currency such as US dollars or euros, in which case we follow their lead. Prices are correct for 2009, but will almost certainly be subject to inflation during the lifespan of this edition.

CHANGING MONEY AT BORDERS

The black markets that once thrived in East Africa were killed off some years ago, but you might still need to exchange money on the street at some international borders, so that you have enough local currency to pay for transport to the next town, for a room when you get there, and – should you expect to arrive outside banking hours or over the weekend – to cover other expenses until the next banking day. As a rule you won't get the greatest rate of exchange at any border, which is fair enough, considering that moneychangers, like banks, profit by offering different rates of exchange in either direction. So there's no sense in exchanging significantly more money than you'll require before you reach a bank or forex bureau. The only exception is when you have a surfeit of cash from the country you're leaving and no intention of returning there – the border may be the last place you can unload it.

Many private moneychangers are incidental con artists, so be prepared. Check the exchange rate in advance and calculate roughly what sum of local currency you should expect. Put whatever bills you intend to change in a pocket discrete from your main stash of foreign currency before you arrive at the border. And don't stress too much if you are offered a slightly lower rate than might be expected, since pushing too hard for a good rate carries the risk of weeding out the honest guys so you end up dealing with a con artist. And be wary of a quick-talking moneychanger trying to exploit the mind-boggling decimal shifts involved in many African currency transactions.

Should you be surrounded by a mob of yelling moneychangers, pick any one of them and tell him that you will only discuss rates when his pals back off. Having agreed a rate, insist on taking the money and counting it before you hand over, or expose the location of, your own money. Should the amount be incorrect, it is almost certainly phase one of an elaborate con trick, so safest to hand it back and refuse to have anything further to do with that person. Alternatively, if you do decide to continue, then re-count the money after it is handed back to you and keep doing so until you have the correct amount counted in your hand – some crooked moneychangers possess such sleight of hand they can seemingly add notes to a wad right in front of your eyes while actually removing a far greater number of notes. Only when you are sure you have the right amount should you hand over your money.

ORGANISING YOUR FINANCES Normally there are three ways of carrying money: hard cash, travellers' cheques and credit cards. However, at the time of writing credit cards and travellers' cheques are both of limited use in Rwanda.

Unusually for this part of Africa, MasterCard used to be more widely accepted than Visa, but this is rapidly changing and Visa is probably the more useful option today. Even so, the use of credit cards extends only to certain upmarket hotels in Kigali and a very few places outside the capital. If you are relying on using a card, then it's best to check what cards your hotel accepts when you make your booking. Worth noting here too that the ORTPN head office in Kigali now accepts Visa but not MasterCard – see box *Booking a gorilla permit* opposite.

It is also possible to draw up to US$1,500 per day (or the equivalent in Rwandan francs or any other hard currency to hand) against Visa or MasterCard in the Access Bank in the UTC in Kigali. This is a remarkably straightforward procedure but be warned that it does depend on the bank having access to a specific website – if the electricity is down, or the computers or the internet server or the website itself, then this service will be unavailable and you may have to wait a day or two for it to come back online.

As for travellers' cheques (it's best if they're in euros or US dollars) – again, theoretically they can be cashed up to a value of US$200 daily at the Banque Commerciale du Rwanda (BCR) and a few other banks in central Kigali, but in practice this can fall apart, or be quite a slow procedure. You'll get a poorer exchange rate for travellers' cheques than for cash. When cashing them, you must generally show the sales advice slip that you got when you obtained them – that's the slip of paper that one is supposed never to keep in proximity to the cheques!

That leaves cash. The US dollar is the most widely accepted foreign currency, but all main currencies should be exchangeable in Kigali, whether in banks or in official or private forex bureaux. If you do bring US dollars, be aware that US$100 and US$50 bills attract a significantly better rate than smaller-denomination bills, and few if any institutions will accept notes issued before 2003. After the US dollar, the euro and pound sterling are the most widely recognised currencies in Kigali, with the advantage that there are no problems related to changing older notes. Except in Kigali, US dollars cash is the only foreign currency easily exchangeable outside of banks.

Bear in mind that this is a changing scene. Conditions regarding credit cards and travellers' cheques may be different – and better – by the time you travel. Until that happens, best carry enough cash to allow for glitches. If you don't want to carry too much, or your budgeting has fallen apart and you need to be bailed out, there are Western Union facilities all over the place. This isn't cheap – the cost depends on the amount being transferred – but it's quick and secure. Any Rwandan francs left over at the end of your trip can be changed back into dollars, euro or whatever by banks, forex bureaux or money-changers.

FOREIGN EXCHANGE All Rwandan banks have branches in Kigali and there's at least one bank in each other main town. There are also several private bureaux de change (known locally as forex bureaux) in the capital, which generally offer slightly better rates than banks against cash (especially if you bargain), not to mention a quicker service, but don't handle travellers' cheques. Banking hours are from approximately 08.00 to 12.00 and 14.00 to 17.00 Monday to Friday (some banks stay open longer), and 08.00 to 12.00 Saturday. Private forex bureaux keep slightly longer hours than banks. Both are closed on Sundays and public holidays.

There are private forex bureaux in several other large towns, particularly those that lie close to a border crossing (eg: Ruhengeri, Gisenyi and Cyangugu) and they are usually as efficient as their counterparts in Kigali. Where no forex bureaux exist, there are banks in the likes of Butare and Gitarama, but they generally deal in cash only and rates tend to be poorer than in the capital.

BUDGETING

Any budget will depend so greatly on how and where you travel that it is almost impossible to give sensible advice in a general travel guide. As a rule, readers who are travelling at the middle to upper end of the price range will have pre-booked most of their trip, which means that they will have a good idea of what the holiday will cost them before they set foot in the country. Pre-booked packages do vary in terms of what is included in the price, and you are advised to check the exact

BOOKING A GORILLA PERMIT

The one thing that almost all tourists to Rwanda want to do is track gorillas in Volcanoes National Park, and – unlike when the first edition of this book was researched, in 2000 – it is no longer the case that you can just pitch up in Kigali and be almost certain of obtaining a permit for the next day, or failing that, the day after. Particularly during the peak season of June to September, and again over the Christmas and New Year holiday period, it is now often the case that all 56 gorilla permits available daily are booked up months in advance for several days running – a scenario that is likely to become increasingly normal as greater volumes of tourists visit Rwanda.

What this means is that any visitors with a tight schedule should book their permits as far in advance as possible. If a tour operator arranges your trip, they will also arrange your gorilla permit and will normally include it in the cost of the trip (or specify it as an extra). But if you are travelling independently, you will need to arrange it yourself. There are two approaches to doing this. The first is to get a reliable local tour operator to act as a go-between and buy the permit on your behalf, which can save a lot of hassle, though the operator will add a small service charge – typically around US$25 – to the normal cost of US$500.

The alternative is to book directly through the ORTPN (see page 84 for contact details), which is normally a fairly straightforward procedure, though the booking office has a reputation for ignoring email queries, so better perhaps to phone. In order to secure the booking, you will be required to transfer a deposit of at least US$100 per permit a month prior to your tracking date, with the outstanding balance to be paid upon your arrival in Kigali. The best way to pay this is in US dollars cash, but ORTPN accepts cash in most other hard currencies (including sterling and euro) calculated at the official US$ bank rate for the day. Visa cards can also be used to pay for your gorilla permit at the booking office in Kigali, though a 4% levy may be added. Or you can transfer the full amount upfront, and save yourself the hassle of paying in Rwanda. It is possible to book (and if you like pay for) any other activities and park entrance fees associated with Volcanoes National Park at the same time.

If you are prepared to take the risk, it does remain possible to pitch up at the ORTPN office in Kigali until 17.00 on the day before you want to track, and – assuming availability – to buy a permit on the spot. And if you are coming from across the Uganda border and want to skip Kigali altogether, you can also buy a permit at the ORTPN office in Ruhengeri or the Volcanoes National Park headquarters at Kinigi the day before you want to track. There is of course no guarantee that a permit will be available at such short notice, particularly at busy times when there may already be a waiting list, but the odds are pretty good in the main rainy season of March to May. The offices in Kinigi and Ruhengeri accept cash only.

conditions in advance, but generally the price quoted will cover everything but drinks, tips and perhaps some meals.

For budget travellers, Rwanda is no longer one of the cheaper countries in Africa. Genuine budget accommodation is thin on the ground; in many towns it can be difficult to find a basic room for much under Rfr10,000 (around US$20) and you'll often need to spend two or three times that amount for something less basic. Throughout the country, a soft drink will cost you around Rfr200 and a 700ml beer around Rfr600–800 in a local bar, but these things cost a lot more in a hotel or restaurant that caters primarily to Westerners. Outside of Kigali, a simple meal in a local restaurant might cost around Rfr800–1,500, a main course in a restaurant catering more to Western palates seldom costs less than Rfr4,000, while snacks such as brochette and chips fall somewhere in between. Public transport is cheap – typically about US$1 per 50km – and distances are relatively small. Taking the above figures into account, the most scrupulous budget travellers should bank on spending around US$30 daily (a bit less for couples, as accommodation costs less per person than for single travellers) and more like US$60–100 if you plan on staying in moderate hotels and eating in proper restaurants. This doesn't include expensive one-off activities such as gorilla tracking or visiting other national parks.

GETTING AROUND

BY AIR Rwandair Express (see page 274) operates regular thrice-weekly flights between Kigali and Cyangugu. There has been talk of privately run helicopter links from Kigali to Akagera and Ruhengeri, but nothing is up and running at the time of writing.

SELF-DRIVE Several travel agencies in Kigali rent out saloons and 4x4s, with or without drivers. For their contact details see page 85. Further up-to-date listings are given in the tourism section of the Rwanda website www.rwandatourism.com. Rates vary according to whether you'll be driving outside Kigali, and whether fuel is

APPROXIMATE DISTANCES BETWEEN MAIN TOWNS

	Kigali	Butare	Byumba	Gitarama	Kibungo	Kibuye	Gisenyi	Gikongoro	Musanze	Cyangugu
Kigali		135	60	53	112	144	187	164	118	293
Butare	135		210	82	247	129	237	29	190	158
Byumba	60	210		128	187	219	173	240	104	349
Gitarama	53	82	128		165	91	177	112	108	221
Kibungo	112	247	187	165		256	299	277	230	386
Kibuye	144	129	219	91	256		108	258	199	130
Gisenyi	187	237	173	177	299	108		366	69	238
Gikongoro	164	29	240	112	277	258	366		220	128
Ruhengeri	118	190	104	108	230	199	69	220		307
Cyangugu	293	158	349	221	386	130	248	128	307	

included. A 4x4 can cost from US$100 to US$150 per day including driver, depending on its type/size. If the deal excludes fuel, bear in mind that this is not cheap – more than US$1 per litre – and that most 4x4s have a heavy consumption.

If you rent a self-drive vehicle, be aware that Rwanda follows the continental and American custom of driving on the right side of the road. Check the vehicle over carefully and ask to take it for a test drive. Even if you're not knowledgeable about the working of engines, a few minutes on the road should be sufficient to establish whether it has any seriously disturbing creaks, rattles or other noises. Check the condition of the tyres and that there is at least one spare tyre, better two, both in a condition to be used should the need present itself. Ask to be shown the wheel spanner and jack, check that all parts of the latter are present, and ensure that the licence is valid for the duration of your trip. Ask also to be shown filling points for oil, water and petrol and check that all the keys do what they are supposed to do. Once on the road, check oil and water regularly in the early stages of the trip to ensure that there are no existing leaks. See also the *Driving into Rwanda* box, page 39, for further survival tips.

Most trunk roads in Rwanda are surfaced and in reasonable condition, including the main road from Kigali to Cyangugu via Butare; to Gisenyi and Kinigi via Ruhengeri; to Rusumo via Kibungo; to Kibuye via Gitarama; and to the Uganda border via Byumba or Umutara. A big programme of road improvement is under way; meanwhile there are still some pot-holed sections along all these routes which, together with the winding terrain and the tendency for Rwandans to drive at breakneck speeds and particularly to overtake on sharp or blind corners, necessitate a more cautious approach than one might take at home.

The unsurfaced roads most likely to be used by tourists include the long stretch running parallel to Lake Kivu between Gisenyi, Kibuye and Cyangugu, the approach roads to Akagera National Park (and roads within the park), the approach roads to Volcanoes National Park from Kinigi, and the roads around Lakes Burera and Ruhondo from Ruhengeri. In all cases, these roads are in variable condition, and should be passable in a saloon car, though a 4x4 would certainly be preferable. And do bear in mind that unsurfaced roads tend to vary seasonally, with conditions most difficult during the rains and least so towards the end of the dry season. Even within this generalisation, an isolated downpour can do major damage to a road that was in perfectly good nick a day earlier, while the arrival of a grader can transform a pot-holed 4x4 track into one navigable by any saloon car.

The main hazard on Rwandan roads, aside from unexpected pot-holes, is the road-hog mentality of most drivers. Minibus-taxis in particular regularly overtake on blind corners, and speed limits (60–80km/h) are universally ignored except when enforced by road conditions. On all routes, be alert to banana-laden cyclists swaying from the verge, and livestock and pedestrians wandering blithely into the middle of the road. Putting one's foot to the floor and hooting like a maniac is the customary Rwandan approach to driving through crowded areas; driving rather more defensively than you would at home is the safer one!

A peculiarly African road hazard – one frequently taken to unnecessary extremes in Rwanda – is the giant sleeping policeman, which might be signposted in advance, might be painted in black-and-white strips, or might simply rear up without warning like a 30cm-tall macadamised wave. It's to be assumed that the odd stray bump will exist on any stretch of road that passes through a town or village, so slow down at any looming hint of urbanisation.

Rwandans, like many Africans, display an inexplicable aversion to switching on their headlights except in genuine darkness – switch them on at any other time and every passing vehicle will blink its lights back at you in bemusement. In rainy, misty or twilight conditions, it would be optimistic to think that you'll be alerted to oncoming traffic by headlights, or for that matter to expect the more demented element among Rwandan drivers to avoid overtaking or speeding simply because they cannot see more than 10m ahead. It's best to avoid driving at night, since a significant proportion of vehicles lack functional headlights, whilst others go around with their lights permanently on blinding full beam!

MOUNTAIN BIKING OR CYCLING
The relatively short distances between tourist centres and the consistently attractive scenery should make Rwanda ideal for travelling by mountain bike. These cannot easily be bought locally, so you would have to bring one with you (some airlines are more flexible than others about carrying bicycles; you should discuss this with them in advance). More and more Rwandans are using cycles now, and if you ask around you should be able to find some for hire – but check the brakes carefully and carry a repair kit. Minibuses will allow you to take your bike on the roof, though expect to be charged extra for this. Minor roads vary in condition, but in the dry season you're unlikely to encounter any problems. Several of the more off-the-beaten-track destinations mentioned in this book would be particularly attractive to cyclists. In Kigali, Mercator Assistance (m *078 8834800; www.mercatorassistance.rw*) rents out bikes and arranges guided cycling tours.

HITCHING
This is an option on main routes, though you should expect to pay for lifts offered by Rwandans. Some minor roads carry little traffic so you could face a long wait.

PUBLIC TRANSPORT
Boat and rail
There are no rail services in Rwanda (although a rail link with Tanzania has been under discussion for some time), nor is there at present a public ferry service on Lake Kivu, although private links operate between Cyangugu, Kibuye, Gisenyi and Goma. It's possible to rent local dugouts for short excursions on the lake. Motor boats are also available for hire at Kibuye, Cyangugu and Gisenyi. Small boats can be used to get around the smaller lakes, such as Burera and Ruhondo, by making an informal arrangement with the boat owner.

Road
The main mode of road transport is shared **minibuses**, generally known as taxis (and referred to in this book as minibus-taxis to distinguish them from cabs). These connect all major centres (and most minor ones) and leave from the town's minibus station (*gare taxi/minibus*) when they are full. No smoking inside is the rule, as it is on all public transport. Departures continue throughout the day but it's best not to wait until too late, in case the last one proves to be full. Fares generally work out at around Rfr500 (US$1) per 50km. Travel times along main surfaced roads typically average about 50km/h, with frequent pauses to drop off passengers balanced against driving that verges on the manic between the stops.

If you're carrying luggage, either keep it on your lap (if it's small enough) or else ask for it to be stuffed in at the back or put on the roof. If you have anything fragile, keep it with you. Overloading is not the problem it is in many African countries, nor are tourists routinely overcharged, though the latter does happen from time to time, so check the fare with other passengers if it feels too high. Fares are collected just before you alight rather than when you board; you'll see other passengers getting their money ready as their destinations approach. If you're not sure of the fare, ask another passenger.

On some routes **buses** are also available. These are mostly run by the state-owned company Onatracom (*www.onatracom.rw*) and leave at fixed times. There are also several private companies running regular express services to fixed timetables with bookable seats between Kigali and other main towns. These start and finish at the company's offices rather than at the public minibus stations. The price is generally much the same as for public minibuses. Details appear under the relevant towns in *Part Two*.

Two-wheeled taxis In and around minibus-taxi stations you may find 'taxis' in the form of motorbikes (motos) or bicycles. They're handy for short distances – but be aware that your travel insurance may not cover you for accidents when on either of them, and you certainly won't be offered a safety helmet. Agree a price beforehand, and check with a passer-by if it seems excessive. If you've got a heavy bag, a comfortable alternative is to stick it on the saddle of the bicycle and walk alongside.

Taxis In some larger towns you'll also find normal taxis – identifiable by a yellow or orange stripe round the side – known as *taxi-voitures* to distinguish them from taxi-minibuses. The same rules apply as in most African countries – agree a price in advance and haggle if it seems extortionate. Fares in Kigali are fixed according to distance.

ACCOMMODATION

Accommodation options in Rwanda range from five-star international hotels to dingy local guesthouses, and prices vary accordingly. The main concentration of high-quality accommodation is in Kigali, but there are also facilities to international standards in and around Volcanoes and Akagera National Parks and the Lake Kivu resorts of Kibuye and Gisenyi, with Nyungwe National Park soon to follow. Elsewhere, there are usually mid-range hotels geared to local businesspeople as much as to tourists, and cheaper local guesthouses favoured by genuine budget travellers.

Most accommodation establishments are recognisably signposted as a hotel, *logement*, guesthouse or similar, but some local places are signposted as *Amacumbi* (pronounced 'amachoombi') – which literally means 'Place with rooms' in Kinyarwanda. Note, too, that in the Swahili language – not indigenous to Rwanda but more widely spoken by locals than any other exotic tongue – a *hoteli* is a restaurant, which can create confusion when asking a non-French speaker for a hotel.

All accommodation listings in this guidebook are placed in one of five categories: exclusive/luxury, upmarket, moderate, budget, and shoestring. The purpose of this categorisation is twofold: to break up long hotel listings that span a wide price range, and to help readers isolate the range of hotels that will best suit their budget and taste. The application of categories is not rigid. Aside from an inevitable element of subjectivity, it is based as much on the feel of a hotel as its rates (which are quoted anyway) and placement is also sometimes influenced by the standard of other accommodation options in the same location.

EXCLUSIVE/LUXURY This category embraces a handful of international four- and five-star luxury hotels, as well as a few select smaller lodges and resorts notable less for their luxury than for offering a genuinely exclusive experience. Rates are typically upwards of US$300 dbl, but many cost twice as much as that. This is the category to look at if you want the best and/or most characterful accommodation and have few financial restrictions.

UPMARKET This category includes most Western-style hotels, lodges and resorts that cater mainly to international tourist or business travellers but lack the special something that might elevate them into the luxury or exclusive category. Hotels in this range would typically be accorded a two- to three-star ranking elsewhere, and they offer smart en-suite accommodation with a good selection of facilities. Rates are typically around US$100–250 for a double, dependent on quality and location. Most package tours and privately booked safaris use accommodation in this range.

MODERATE In Rwanda, as in many African countries, there is often a wide gap in price and standard between the cheapest hotels geared primarily towards tourists and the best hotels geared primarily towards local and budget travellers. For this reason, the moderate bracket is rather more nebulous than other accommodation categories, essentially consisting of hotels which, for one or other reason, couldn't really be classified as upmarket, but are also a notch or two above the budget category in terms of price and/or quality. Expect unpretentious en-suite accommodation with hot water and possibly television, a decent restaurant and some English-speaking staff. Prices for moderate city and beach hotels are generally in the US$50–80 range (more in Kigali). This is the category to look at if you are travelling privately on a limited or low budget and expect a reasonably high but not luxurious standard of accommodation.

BUDGET Hotels in this category are aimed largely at the local market and definitely don't approach international standards, but are still reasonably clean and comfortable, and a definite cut above the basic guesthouses that proliferate in most towns. More often than not, a decent restaurant is attached, there are English-speaking staff, and rooms have en-suite facilities with running cold or possibly hot water, and netting. Expect to pay around US$25–50 for a double, less away from major tourist centres. This is the category to look at if you are on a limited budget, but want to avoid total squalor!

SHOESTRING This is the very bottom end of the market, usually small local guesthouses with simple rooms and common showers and toilets. Running the gamut from pleasantly clean to decidedly squalid, hotels in the category typically cost around US$10–20 for a room. It is the category for those to whom keeping down costs is the main imperative.

CAMPING Few formal campsites exist in Rwanda. Some hotels will permit camping in the gardens, but at little saving over the price of a budget room. There are campsites at the Volcanoes and Akagera national parks and in Nyungwe Forest. At Nyungwe, the campsite is far more attractively located than the resthouse for travellers without a vehicle. A tent may also come in handy for travellers backpacking or cycling through relatively non-touristed rural areas, where you are strongly advised to ask permission of the local village official before setting up camp.

✖ EATING AND DRINKING

EATING OUT Kigali boasts a good range of restaurants representing international cuisines such as Indian, Italian, Chinese and French. In most other towns, a couple of hotels or restaurants serve uncomplicated Western meals – chicken, fish or steak with chips or rice. Possibly as a result of the Belgian influence, restaurant standards seem to be far higher than in most East African countries, and Rwandan chips are among the best on the continent. Servings tend to be dauntingly large, and prices very reasonable – around Rfr1,000–1,500 (US$2) for a *mélange* (mixed plate) at local eateries and Rfr4,000–7,000 (US$6–10) for a main course at a smarter restaurant.

Buffet or self-service meals are also on offer, often at very inexpensive rates (as little as Rfr1,000 in local restaurants) – and are said to originate from a period in the 1980s when the government decreed that civil servants should have shorter lunch breaks. As a result, enterprising restaurants dreamed up this way of enabling them to eat faster. Smarter restaurants, especially in Kigali, may be closed or take a while to rustle up food outside of normal mealtimes.

Wherever you travel, local restaurants serve Rwandan favourites such as goat kebabs (brochettes), grilled or fried tilapia (a type of lake fish), bean or meat stews. These are normally eaten with one of a few staples: *ugali* (a stiff porridge made with maize meal), *matoke* (cooking banana/plantain), *chapatti* (flat bread), and boiled potatoes (as in Uganda, these are somewhat mysteriously referred to as Irish potatoes) – not to mention rice and the ubiquitous chips.

Unless you have an insatiable appetite for greasy omelettes or stale *mandazi* (deep-fried dough balls not dissimilar to doughnuts), breakfast outside of Kigali (where good French bread and croissants are available) or the larger hotels can be a problematic meal. One area in which Rwanda is definitely influenced more by its anglophone neighbours than by its former coloniser is baking: in common with the rest of East Africa, the bread is almost always sweetish and goes stale quickly. In such cases a bunch of bananas, supplemented by other fresh fruit, is about the best breakfast option: cheap, nutritious and filling.

COOKING FOR YOURSELF The alternative to eating at restaurants is to put together your own meals at markets and supermarkets. The variety of foodstuffs you can buy varies from season to season and from town to town, but in most major centres you can rely on finding a supermarket that stocks frozen meat, a few tinned goods, biscuits, pasta, rice and chocolate bars. If you're that way inclined, and will be staying in hotels rather than camping, bring a small electric immersion heater for use in your bedroom (sockets take standard continental two-pin plugs), plus some teabags or instant coffee, so you can supplement your picnic with a hot drink.

Fruit and vegetables are best bought at markets, where they are very cheap. Potatoes, sweet potatoes, onions, tomatoes, bananas, sugar cane, avocados, paw-paws, mangoes, coconuts, oranges and pineapples are seasonally available in most towns.

For hikers, about the only dehydrated meals available are packet soups. If you have specialised requirements, you're best doing your shopping in Kigali, where a wider selection of goods (cheese, local yoghurt…) is available in the supermarkets; there are also a handful of excellent bakeries, with mouth-watering goodies hot from the oven.

DRINKS Brand-name soft drinks such as Pepsi, Coca-Cola and Fanta are widely available, and cheap by international standards. Tap water is debatably safe to drink in Kigali, although the smell of chlorine may put you off; bottled mineral water is widely available if you sensibly prefer not to take the risk. Locally bottled fruit juice (passion fruit, orange, pineapple…) isn't bad and comes in concentrated versions too.

The most widely drunk hot beverage is tea (*chai* or *icyayi* in Swahili/Kinyarwanda). In rural areas, the ingredients are often boiled together in a pot: a sticky, sweet, milky concoction that definitely falls into the category of acquired tastes. Most Westernised restaurants serve tea as we know it, but if you want to be certain, specify that you want black tea. The milk served separately with it is almost always powdered, but of a type that dissolves well and doesn't taste too bad. Coffee is one of Rwanda's main cash crops, but you'd hardly know it judging by the insipid slop that passes for coffee in most restaurants and hotels – unless they are serving Maraba coffee (see box in *Chapter 6*, page 138). You're on safe if unexciting ground with instant coffee (ask for Nescafé); after a few days in the country we made a policy of checking whether coffee was of the brewed or instant variety before we ordered – if the former, we settled for tea.

The most popular alcoholic drink is beer, brewed locally near Gisenyi. The cheaper of the two local brands is Primus, which comes in 700ml bottles which cost Rfr600–800 in local bars and as much as Rfr3,000 in Kigali's swankiest hotels. The alternatives are Mutzig, which tastes little different, costs about 30% more and comes in 700ml or 350ml bottles, and the more expensive premier brand Amstel.

South African and French wines are sold at outrageously inflated prices in a few upmarket bars and restaurants. Far more sensibly priced are the boxes of Spanish or Italian wine sold in some supermarkets. If you want to check out your capacity for locally brewed banana wine (also called *urwagwa*) before ordering it with a meal, most supermarkets and some small grocers/snack bars have bottles on sale. It comes in many varieties – some have honey added, and I've heard of a kind made in the northeast that contains hibiscus flowers. There's also a banana liqueur.

As for the harder stuff, *waragi*, a millet-based clear alcohol from Uganda, is available everywhere; either knock it back neat or mix it as you would gin. (In its undistilled form it could strip away a few layers of skin!) The illegal Rwandan firewater, *kanyanga*, is also available widely: treat with care.

PHOTOGRAPHIC TIPS   *Ariadne Van Zandbergen*

EQUIPMENT Although with some thought and an eye for composition you can take reasonable photos with a 'point and shoot' camera, you need an SLR camera with one or more lenses if you are at all serious about photography. The most important component in a digital SLR is the sensor. There are two types of sensor: DX and FX. The FX is a full size sensor identical to the old film size (36mm). The DX sensor is half size and produces less quality. Your choice of lenses will be determined whether you have a DX or FX sensor in your camera as the DX sensor introduces a 0.5x multiplication to the focal length. So a 300mm lens becomes in effect a 450mm lens. FX ('full frame') sensors are the future, so I will further refer to focal lengths appropriate to the FX sensor.

Always buy the best lens you can afford. Fixed fast lenses are ideal, but very costly. Zoom lenses make it easier to change composition without changing lenses the whole time. If you carry only one lens a 24–70mm or similar zoom should be ideal. For a second lens, a lightweight 80–200mm or 70–300mm or similar will be excellent for candid shots and varying your composition. Wildlife photography will be very frustrating if you don't have at least a 300mm lens. For a small loss of quality, teleconverters are a cheap and compact way to increase magnification: a 300mm lens with a 1.4x converter becomes 420mm, and with a 2x it becomes 600mm. NB: 1.4x and 2x teleconverters reduce the speed of your lens by 1.4 and 2 stops respectively.

The resolution of digital cameras is improving the whole time. For ordinary prints a 6-megapixel camera is fine. For better results and the possibility to enlarge images and for professional reproduction, higher resolution is available up to 21 megapixels.

It is important to have enough memory space when photographing on your holiday. The number of pictures you can fit on a card depends on the quality you choose. You should calculate how many pictures you can fit on a card and either take enough cards or take a storage drive onto which you can download the card's content. You can obviously take a laptop which gives the advantage that you can see your pictures properly at the end of each day and edit and delete rejects. If you don't want the extra bulk and weight you can buy a storage device which can read memory cards. These drives come in different capacities.

Keep in mind that digital camera batteries, computers and other storage devices need charging. Make sure you have all the chargers, cables, converters with you. Most hotels/lodges have charging points, but it will be best to enquire about this in advance. When camping you might have to rely on charging from the car battery.

In addition to the following fixed public holidays, Rwanda recognises Good Friday and Easter Monday.

1 January	New Year's Day
1 February	Heroes' Day
7 April	Genocide Memorial Day
1 May	Labour Day
1 July	Independence Day
4 July	Liberation Day
15 August	Assumption Day
1 October	Patriots' Day
25 December	Christmas Day
26 December	Boxing Day

The week around Genocide Memorial Day is an official week of mourning during which commemorative ceremonies are held and some activities may be reduced.

DUST AND HEAT Dust and heat are often a problem. Keep your equipment in a sealed bag, and avoid exposing equipment to the sun when possible. Digital cameras are prone to collecting dust particles on the sensor which results in spots on the image. The dirt mostly enters the camera when changing lenses, so you should be careful when doing this. To some extent photos can be 'cleaned' up afterwards in Photoshop, but this is time-consuming. You can have your camera sensor professionally cleaned, or you can do this yourself with special brushes and swabs made for this purpose, but note that touching the sensor might cause damage and should only be done with the greatest care.

LIGHT The most striking outdoor photographs are often taken during the hour or two of 'golden light' after dawn and before sunset. Shooting in low light may enforce the use of very low shutter speeds, in which case a tripod/beanbag will be required to avoid camera shake. The most advanced digital SLRs have very little loss of quality on higher ISO settings, which allows you to shoot at lower light conditions. It is still recommended not to increase the ISO unless necessary.

With careful handling, side lighting and back lighting can produce stunning effects, especially in soft light and at sunrise or sunset. Generally, however, it is best to shoot with the sun behind you. When photographing animals or people in the harsh midday sun, images taken in light but even shade are likely to look nicer than those taken in direct sunlight or patchy shade, since the latter conditions create too much contrast.

PROTOCOL In some countries, it is unacceptable to photograph local people without permission, and many people will refuse to pose or will ask for a donation. In such circumstances, don't try to sneak photographs as you might get yourself into trouble. Even the most willing subject will often pose stiffly when a camera is pointed at them; relax them by making a joke, and take a few shots in quick succession to improve the odds of capturing a natural pose.

Ariadne Van Zandbergen is a professional travel and wildlife photographer specialised in Africa. She runs 'The Africa Image Library'. For photo requests, visit the website www.africaimagelibrary.co.za or contact her direct on e ariadne@hixnet.co.za

Practical Information **PUBLIC HOLIDAYS AND EVENTS**

2

Two public events may draw crowds large enough to affect the availability of accommodation in some areas: the International Peace Marathon and Fun Run held annually in and around Kigali in May (see *www.kigalimarathon.com* and page 102), and the Gorilla Naming Ceremony held near the Volcanoes National Park in June (details from the ORTPN and on page 217).

The last Saturday of any given month is Umuganda (Public Cleaning) Day. Between 08.00 and 11.00 there is a countrywide ban on road traffic, as the whole country embarks on communal work for the public good. This might consist of anything from local street cleaning to road repairs, tree planting, land clearance and building homes for genocide survivors – and can result in sizable proportions of the workforce being too busy to attend to travellers! Generally, tour operators' vehicles are permitted to carry on as normal on Umuganda Day, but it is worth checking with your tour operator. If you need to be at the airport to catch a flight, a passport and valid travel ticket should be enough to secure dispensation in a taxi.

🛒 SHOPPING

All basic requirements (toiletries, stationery, batteries and so forth) are available in Kigali, and, away from the capital, most towns of any size have a pharmacy as well as a reasonable supermarket or general store. In Kigali, the pharmacy in Boulevard de la Révolution is open 24 hours, as is the superb Nakumatt Supermarket in the gleaming new Union Trade Centre.

For handicrafts you've a very wide range – wood-carvings, weaving, pottery, baskets, clay statues, beadwork, jewellery, masks, musical instruments, banana-leaf products, batik – see *Handicrafts* in the Kigali chapter (pages 102–3) and the Butare chapter (page 134) for more details. CDs or cassettes of Rwandan music make good gifts, as does local honey: buy it in a market and decant it into a screw-top soft-drinks bottle for travelling. (Some countries prohibit the import of foodstuffs, so check local regulations before you take any home.) Some markets stock candles made of local beeswax. Locally made wines, spirits and liqueurs are heavier to carry but generally appreciated! For traditional musical instruments, you need a well-informed local advisor to help you to pick the best and most authentic.

Women can buy lengths of brightly dyed fabric in the market and have street dressmakers make up a garment on the spot; men can similarly kit themselves out with hand-tailored shirts. And just browsing in any large street market will give you dozens more ideas…

✆ MEDIA AND COMMUNICATIONS

NEWSPAPERS AND MAGAZINES The main English-language newspaper is the daily *New Times* (*www.newtimes.co.rw*) which provides reasonably balanced coverage with a pro-government slant. Imported dailies and weeklies from Uganda and Kenya are also available on the streets of Kigali and Butare. A very limited range of international papers can be bought at the kiosks of upmarket hotels such as the Mille Collines in Kigali. News magazines such as *Time* and *Newsweek* are available from street vendors and some bookshops. The Ikirezi bookshops in both central Kigali and Remera have a good stock, and Ikirezi also sells them at the airport.

INTERNET, EMAIL AND FAX The electronic communications age has fast gained a foothold in Rwanda, with increasing use of email. Outside of Kigali, local servers tend to be slower and subject to breakdowns, and there are still a few towns (eg: Kibuye) that have no public internet facilities at all. However, this is set to change dramatically when a high-capacity national fibre-optic cable network worth US$50 million comes online, something that is almost certain to happen before the 2010 World Cup. Most hotels of mid-range and upwards have email and fax facilities.

TELEPHONE Rwanda's telephone system is reasonably efficient, and it will improve further once the fibre-optic cable project referred to above comes online. From overseas, it is definitely one of the easier African countries to get through to first time. The international code is 250. Because of the small size of the country, and limited number of phones, no area codes are in use. Note, however, that in 2009 the old six-digit land lines were extended to 10 digits. Numbers in this book have been modified to reflect these changes, but in case we missed any, or you come across old numbers elsewhere, just add the prefix 0252.

In Kigali, international phone calls can be made from the central post office in Avenue de la Paix and from various other shops and kiosks in the city. For calls within Rwanda the street kiosks and shops with public phones work well – calls are metered and you pay when you've finished, so there's no fussing with coins or tokens. Some of these can handle international calls too. To make an international call out of Rwanda, dial 000 then the country code, area code and local number.

Cell phones (mobiles) have caught on in a big way in Rwanda. Cell-phone numbers used to be recognisable as an eight-digit number starting with '03' or '08' (eg: 08 123456). In 2009 these numbers gained a '78' after the leading zero (eg: 078 123456). Again, we have changed all numbers accordingly, but they're easy enough to convert if there are any we missed. Mobile-phone owners can buy a local SIM card giving them a local number using the local satellite network for the equivalent of US$1 (as part of an Rfr3,000 'starter pack' with Rfr2,500 of airtime included) – but check, if you need them, that it allows you voice-mail and international texting, because not all do. International text messages work out at Rfr100 each and international phone calls are also very cheap from local mobile phones.

The ubiquity and relative efficiency of mobile phones means that many hotels and other organisations in Rwanda no longer bother with landlines. Unfortunately, when it comes to hotels, this means that contact telephone details tend to change more regularly than is the case with fixed lines. For this reason we have included both numbers where they exist – the mobile will usually be easier to get through to, but there's a far greater chance a landline will still be in place in two or three years' time. Readers are welcome to alert us to any such changes by posting on our website http://updates.bradtguides.com/rwanda.

POST Post from Rwanda is cheap and reasonably reliable, but can be slow. Yellow post-buses with *Iposita* on the side shuttle mail around Rwanda. Letterboxes outside post offices have a variety of appellations – sometimes *Boîte aux Lettres*, sometimes (eg: in Butare) *Box of Letters* and sometimes (a Belgian/Flemish relic in Kibuye) *Brievenbus*.

RADIO AND TELEVISION The BBC World Service comes across loud and clear, on different frequencies according to the time of day. Local radio stations broadcast in Kinyarwanda, French, English and Swahili. TV is largely piped in from elsewhere, notably by the South African company DSTV, whose bouquet of channels includes CNN, Sky, BBC News et al. For football fans, the Supersport Channel operated by the DSTV shows most international and English Premiership matches and can be seen at bars all around the country.

CULTURAL ETIQUETTE

As in most African countries, Rwandans tend to be tolerant of Westerners' ways and won't easily take offence at mildly inappropriate behaviour. All the same, it is a relatively conservative and by-and-large highly religious society, and visitors should bear in mind that certain behaviours are very unacceptable. This would include public affection between members of the opposite sex (even if they are married), overt drunkenness, skimpy attire (particularly for women), proclamations of atheism, and in some circles smoking. In conversation, extended greetings are normal, and it is considered rude to ask somebody directions or ask for something in a shop or restaurant without first greeting the person and asking after their health. Probably the biggest social gaffe you could make in Rwanda, however, is insensitive probing into matters of ethnicity or perceived ethnicity – in the aftermath of the genocide people understandably avoid referring to themselves or others as Hutu and Tutsi, and it would be wise for visitors to follow suit.

BECOMING INVOLVED

You may leave Rwanda without a backward glance, or you may find that it has affected you more than you realised. It's an amazing country. If you do want to become further involved with its people and its culture, a few suggestions are given below, to add to those already mentioned. There are many more: ask around when you're in Rwanda, or do an internet search for whatever aspect of development interests you. For gorilla conservation charities, see pages 214–15.

RWANDA UNITED KINGDOM GOODWILL ORGANISATION (RUGO) Mike Hughes
(*UK Registered Charity No 1074088; 86 Dover Rd, London E12 5EA; www.rugo.org*)
RUGO was formally launched on July 4 1997. Its aim is to provide a means for the people of the UK to support the people of Rwanda as they rebuild after the 1994 Genocide. RUGO received charitable status in February 1999, with Baroness Chalker of Wallasey as its Patron.

Objectives RUGO's stated mission is the advancement of education and training of the people of Rwanda, and the relief of poverty, sickness and distress, through the provision and support of community-based projects designed to improve the conditions of life for those in need.

Vocational training One of the consequences of the genocide was that most of Rwanda's artisans with skills were lost. With that in mind, two of the institutions RUGO has assisted are a new vocational school at Nyamata (see *Chapter 4*, page 113) and the Amizero Vocational Training Centre at Kayonza (see *Chapter 11*, page 237). Both enable young people who do not achieve places at secondary school to acquire important skills, so they can make a living for themselves and their families and assist in the reconstruction of their country.

Nyamata, one of the areas worst affected by the genocide, is in the Bugesera, a region of Rwanda previously undeveloped because the presence of the tsetse fly makes it unsuitable for pastoralists and its dry climate hampers cultivation. RUGO collected about £120,000 worth of tools and equipment for the technical school, where courses include masonry and construction, carpentry, plumbing and appropriate technology, information technology, and tailoring. At Amizero VTC in Kayonza, where RUGO has donated computers for use in its computer courses, many students come from disadvantaged backgrounds; for example they may be genocide survivors, demobilised soldiers, released prisoners or from extremely poor families. Also in Kayonza, RUGO has raised funds for the construction of a Parish Community Centre, in partnership with St Andrew's Parish in Harrow.

Additional activities RUGO has also:

- Shipped to Rwanda 20 specialist hospital beds, mattresses, and other equipment such as wheelchairs and zimmer frames for use by Kigali Health Institute in a polyclinic
- Issued newsletters to inform people about the situation in Rwanda
- Received donations of computers and books for the National University of Rwanda and other educational establishments
- Supported centres such as Kigali Junior Academy; Kigali Parents' School; Village of Hope (part of the Rwanda Women's Network); Village d'Orphelins (orphanage in Kibuye) and Uyisenga N'Imanzi (which supports child-headed households)
- Held memorial services in remembrance of the victims of genocide
- Held social events to fundraise and promote Rwandan culture, most recently an annual Open Garden event hosted in Esher (UK)

Income RUGO's income derives from members' subscriptions, donations and fundraising. The organisation employs no-one and is administered by volunteers; thus almost every penny goes towards RUGO's objectives. Annual membership is currently £20 for an individual, £30 for a family and £100 for corporate bodies.

Contacts
Mike Hughes (Chairman) ☎ 01252 861059;
e mikehughesuk@gmail.com

Alex Morton (Secretary) ☎ 0797 0119793;
e alegisi2004@yahoo.co.uk

SEND A COW (*Registered Charity No 299717;* ☎ *01225 874222; e info@sendacow.org.uk; www.sendacow.org.uk*) The UK-based charity Send a Cow works with the people of Africa to overcome poverty and malnutrition through the sustainable development of livestock farming systems and self-reliant local groups. Current programmes are in Lesotho, Kenya, Tanzania, Uganda, Zambia and Ethiopia – as well as Rwanda, where Send a Cow mainly provides livestock plus training in animal care and natural manure/compost-based organic farming. The beneficiaries are as many as their backgrounds are varied.

RWANDAN YOUTH INFORMATION COMMUNITY ORGANISATION (RYICO) (☎ *Brighton (UK) office (+44) 01273 234836; e info@rYico.org; www.rYico.org*) RYico is both a UK-registered charity (no 1004274) and a locally registered Rwandan NGO based in Kigali.

About RYICO In 2005 rYico established Centre Marembo (e *marembo@ryico.org*), a youth centre that provides a space for young people to meet, access information and engage in training and education. It also provides accommodation for former street children. In the UK rYico seeks partnerships and support for Centre Marembo whilst also raising awareness and challenging perceptions of Rwanda in the UK.

Centre Marembo Centre Marembo offers young people free access to its library, computing facilities and team of dedicated staff and volunteers that counsel, train, educate, supervise and care for them. Since opening in September 2005, the centre has offered food, shelter and a place in school to 32 boys aged 7–18 who previously lived and worked on the street. It opens its gates weekly to other street children for showering and washing their clothes, sharing lunch together, and a programme of training and educational games.

Vulnerable young people also have the opportunity to follow a transitional programme that encourages them to give up their street habits for the classroom. The centre has welcomed the help and involvement of volunteers from the Kigali Institute of Education, Kigali Health Institute, secondary schools and local businesses, all offering their skills and time to support and challenge the youngsters at the centre. Marembo runs informal school classes where possible, offering the chance for young people to study at the centre. Furthermore there are now a variety of activities on offer such as an AIDS awareness club, a youth journal, mechanics training and crafts workshops.

Gradually the centre is reaching out to more and more young people – mostly boys at present, but more activities are being developed to encourage girls to join. The centre also aims to work with organisations that can support its residents' families, providing the required holistic approach to reintegrate the young people into their families and the community. Specifically rYico has set up www.shop4rwanda.com through which it markets crafts from the centre and from women's cooperatives online.

At the end of your visit, if you've any clothing or other practical items that you don't want to take back home with you, please do contact the Centre Marembo. They have a monthly bring and buy sale to raise funds to help sustain the centre, so could definitely put them to good use.

SURVIVORS FUND (*10 Rickett St, West Brompton, London SW6 1RU;* ☏ *020 7610 2589;* e *info@survivors-fund.org.uk; www.survivors-fund.org.uk*) Since 1997, UK-based Survivors Fund (SURF) has helped survivors of the Rwandan genocide deal with and recover from the tragedies of 1994, supporting a wide range of services for victims in Rwanda and assisting survivors in the UK. Funded by a variety of public and private organisations and individuals, SURF acts as a channel to distribute financial assistance to groups, individuals and charitable organisations in the day-to-day operations of bringing the people of Rwanda hope, safety, and a decent standard of living.

Current activities are focused on: HIV/AIDS, psychosocial support projects, education/vocational training, income-generating activities, shelter, and legal assistance/advocacy.

FRIENDS OF RWANDAN RUGBY (☏ *07861 296736;* e *info@friendsofrwandanrugby.org; www.friendsofrwandanrugby.org*) This may seem an unusual choice of charity, but sport is what binds people – particularly young people – together and is vital to

Rwanda's post-genocide reconciliation process. FORR is a UK-registered charity supporting school and community participation in rugby, providing coaching and encouraging young people (girls as well as boys) to play. For example, in 2009 one of its activities was to coach around 400 youngsters in four government schools in the Butare area, including their teachers and local players. There is huge enthusiasm to learn and to join the teams. Rugby-minded tourists could join in a game or two while they're in Rwanda and offer a bit of coaching, donate some old balls, provide some kit, or just make a donation to the cost of the work.

ENGALYNX (*35 Birch Drive, Brantham, Manningtree, Essex CO11 1TG;* ﹨ *01206 393022;* e *lantern@cpwpost.com; www.engalynx.org.uk; founder & director: Maralyn Bambridge*) This is a small UK-registered charity operating from Manningtree in Essex and set up after the genocide to help Rwanda rebuild. Its name, Engalynx, meaning 'England links with…', was chosen by the children of a local school which also became involved. Since then, with the help of local friends and businesses and even a football club, Engalynx has sent not only funds but also packages and a container with computers, tools, clothes, shoes, stationery, sewing machines, hairdressing equipment, photocopiers, bicycles, seeds, etc. It has given microscopes to students, and goats to child-headed families. The charity supports l'Ecole Sciences et Santé in Gisenyi, a school specialising in teaching the sciences; in addition a new school in Gikondo, a very poor suburb of Kigali, is benefiting from some aid. In the same area Engalynx is offering widows and orphans training in sewing skills, woodwork and some computer skills, as well as operating a micro-credit scheme to aid widows to start up their own businesses. Young street orphans in the area are benefiting from some sports and social involvement; Engalynx provides supplies and guidance, working with the local community officers. Local craft products made by widows/orphans in Rwanda can be purchased; see contact details above.

CARDS FROM AFRICA (m (+250) 078 8413770; e *info@cardsfromafrica.com; www.cardsfromafrica.com;* ◷ *09.00–15.00 Mon–Fri*) This is a small business that was started in November 2004 to provide employment to vulnerable orphaned youths who are responsible for their younger brothers and sisters. They make paper by hand (from office waste), and then use that to make greeting cards, etc. CfA practises fair-trade principles, ensuring a fair wage to the card makers. Order the cards online or call to arrange a visit. They are a 10-minute bumpy-road drive from Remera, near the airport (a downloadable map is on the website).

INVESTING IN RWANDA

The ultimate involvement in Rwanda is to invest in one of the many opportunities that the country's rapid development has created. The Rwanda Development Board or RDP, formerly the Rwanda Investment and Export Promotion Agency (﹨ (+250) 0252 585179; e *info@rwandainvest.com; www.rwandainvest.com*), can provide full information, including the generous incentives and concessions available. The mechanisms are straightforward and investor-friendly, with a minimum of red tape.

Openings exist in many sectors; for example food processing (tea, coffee, fruit, vegetables…), flower production, tourism (hotels, restaurants, watersports, training, hospitality services, handicrafts, transport…), livestock, solar installations, medical services, telecommunications, power, ICT, construction, transportation and finance. It's an Aladdin's cave of opportunity.

If any of the above raises even a tiny flicker of interest, do check it out. The website is very comprehensive. If you don't, you may miss a life-changing opportunity. And Rwanda needs you!

3

Health

with Dr Felicity Nicholson

Rwanda itself isn't a particularly unhealthy country for tourists and you'll never be far from some kind of medical help. The main towns have hospitals (for anything serious you'll be more comfortable in Kigali) and all towns of any size have a pharmacy, although the range of medicines on sale may be limited. In Kigali, the pharmacy in Boulevard de la Révolution is open 24 hours.

Outside of Kigali, district hospitals and health centres are spread all around the country. A health centre is generally staffed by one or two nurses, supported by medical assistants. In rural areas traditional medicine is also widely used.

The severe shortage of qualified medical personnel – particularly doctors – caused by the targeting of professionals during the genocide has not yet been remedied: there are around 1,690 inhabitants per nurse and 18,000 per doctor. However, the private medical sector is developing fast around the country (particularly in Kigali), and now includes more than 300 private clinics and dispensaries.

The incidence of HIV/AIDS is hard to estimate accurately. The national infection rate has reportedly dropped from 9% to 3% since 1998, but Dr Richard Sezibera, the Minister of Health, announced that 34% of adult deaths in Rwanda are AIDS-related in 2009.

The guidelines below relate to tropical Africa in general, since travellers may well want to spend time in more than one country.

BEFORE YOU GO

IMMUNISATIONS Preparations to ensure a healthy trip to Rwanda require checks on your immunisation status: it is wise to be up to date on tetanus, polio and diphtheria (now given as an all-in-one vaccine, Revaxis, that lasts for ten years), and hepatitis A. Immunisations against meningococcus and rabies may also be recommended. Proof of vaccination against yellow fever is needed for entry into Rwanda for all travellers over one year of age, regardless of where you are coming from. If the vaccine is not suitable for you then obtain an exemption certificate from your GP or a travel clinic. However, the implications of travelling to an at-risk area without protection against yellow fever must be considered and discussed with a travel health expert. Immunisation against cholera is recommended for Rwanda.

Hepatitis A vaccine (Havrix Monodose or Avaxim) comprises two injections given about a year apart. The course costs about £100, but may be available on the NHS; it protects for 25 years and can be administered even close to the time of departure. Hepatitis B vaccination should be considered for longer trips (two months or more) or for those working with children or in situations where contact with blood is likely. Three injections are needed for the best protection and can be given over a three-week period if time is short. Longer schedules give more sustained protection and are therefore preferred if time allows. Hepatitis A vaccine can also be given as a combination with hepatitis B as 'Twinrix', though two doses are needed at least seven days apart to be effective for the hepatitis A component, and three doses are needed for the hepatitis B.

The newer injectable typhoid vaccines (eg: Typhim Vi) last for three years and are about 85% effective. Oral capsules (Vivotif) are currently available in the US (and soon in the UK); if four capsules are taken over seven days it will last for five years. They should be encouraged unless the traveller is leaving within a few days for a trip of a week or less, when the vaccine would not be effective in time. Meningitis vaccine containing strains A, C, W and Y is recommended for all travellers, especially for trips of more than four weeks (see *Meningitis*, page 73). Vaccinations for rabies are ideally advised for everyone, but are especially important for travellers visiting more remote areas, especially if you are more than 24 hours from medical help and definitely if you will be working with animals (see *Rabies* page 73).

Experts differ over whether a BCG vaccination against tuberculosis (TB) is useful in adults: discuss this with your travel clinic.

In addition to the various vaccinations recommended above, it is important that travellers should be properly protected against malaria. For detailed advice, see below.

Ideally you should visit your own doctor or a specialist travel clinic (see pages 66–8) to discuss your requirements if possible at least eight weeks before you plan to travel.

MALARIA PREVENTION Malaria is probably the greatest health risk to travellers in Rwanda, although it is less prevalent there than in some other African countries. There is no vaccine against malaria, but using prophylactic drugs and preventing mosquito bites will considerably reduce the risk of contracting it. Seek professional advice to ascertain the preferred anti-malarial drugs for Rwanda at the time you travel. If mefloquine (Lariam) is suggested, start this 2½ weeks (three doses) before departure to check that it suits you; stop it immediately if it seems to cause depression or anxiety, visual or hearing disturbances, severe headaches, fits or changes in heart rhythm. Side effects such as nightmares or dizziness are not medical reasons for stopping unless they are sufficiently debilitating or annoying. Anyone who has been treated for depression or psychiatric problems, has diabetes controlled by oral therapy or who is epileptic (or who has suffered fits in the past) or has a close blood relative who is epileptic, should probably avoid mefloquine.

In the past doctors were nervous about prescribing mefloquine to pregnant women, but experience has shown that it is relatively safe and certainly safer than the risk of malaria. That said, there are other issues, so if you are travelling to Rwanda whilst pregnant, seek expert advice before departure.

Malarone (proguanil and atovaquone) is as effective as mefloquine. It has the advantage of having few side effects and need only be continued for one week after returning. However, it is expensive and because of this tends to be reserved for shorter trips. Malarone may not be suitable for everybody, so advice should be taken from a doctor. The licence in the UK has been extended for up to three months' use and a paediatric form of tablet is also available, prescribed on a weight basis.

Another alternative is the antibiotic doxycycline (100mg daily). Like Malarone it can be started one day before arrival. Unlike mefloquine, it may also be used in travellers with epilepsy, although certain anti-epileptic medication may make it less effective. In perhaps 1–3% of people there is the possibility of allergic skin reactions developing in sunlight; the drug should be stopped if this happens. Women using the oral contraceptive should use an additional method of protection for the first four weeks when using doxycycline. It is also unsuitable in pregnancy or for children under 12 years.

Chloroquine and proguanil are no longer considered to be effective enough for Rwanda but may be considered as a last resort if nothing else is deemed suitable.

All tablets should be taken with or after the evening meal, washed down with plenty of fluid and, with the exception of Malarone (see above), continued for four weeks after leaving.

Some travellers like to take a treatment for malaria, as well as prophylaxis if they are travelling for more than six months. Whatever you decide, you should seek up-to-date advice to find out the most appropriate medication.

There is no malaria transmission above 3,000m; at intermediate altitudes (1,800–3,000m) the risk exists but is low.

In addition to taking anti-malarial medicines, it is important to avoid mosquito bites between dusk and dawn, which is when the anopheles (malaria-carrying) mosquito is most active. Pack a DEET-based insect repellent, such as one of the Repel range, and take either a permethrin-impregnated bednet or a permethrin spray so that you can treat bednets in hotels. Permethrin treatment makes even very tatty nets protective and mosquitoes are also unable to bite through the impregnated net when you roll against it. Putting on long clothes (including long-sleeved shirts or blouses) at dusk means you can reduce the amount of repellent needed; but be aware that malaria mosquitoes hunt at ankle level and will penetrate through socks, so apply repellent to your feet and ankles too. Travel clinics usually sell a good range of nets, treatment kits and repellents.

Important: While you are away, assume that any high fever lasting more than a few hours is malaria, regardless of any other symptoms. Always seek medical help. And remember that malaria may occur anything from seven days into your trip to up to one year after leaving Africa. If symptoms appear after you have returned home, visit your doctor immediately, and mention that you have been travelling in a malarial area.

✚ TRAVEL CLINICS AND HEALTH INFORMATION A full list of current travel clinic websites worldwide is available on www.istm.org/. For other journey preparation information, consult www.nathnac.org/ds/map_world.aspx. Information about various medications may be found on www.netdoctor.co.uk/travel.

UK

Berkeley Travel Clinic 32 Berkeley St, London W1J 8EL (near Green Park tube station); ☏ 020 7629 6233; ⊕ 10.00–18.00 Mon–Fri, 10.00–15.00 Sat
Cambridge Travel Clinic 41 Hills Rd, Cambridge, CB2 1NT; ☏ 01223 367362; f 01223 368021; e enquiries@travelcliniccambridge.co.uk; www.travelcliniccambridge.co.uk; ⊕ 10.00–16.00 Mon, Tue & Sat, 12.00–19.00 Wed & Thu, 11.00–18.00 Fri
Edinburgh Travel Health Clinic 14 East Preston St, Newington, Edinburgh EH8 9QA; ☏ 0131 667 1030; www.edinburghtravelhealthclinic.co.uk; ⊕ 09.00–19.00 Mon–Wed, 9.00–18.00 Thu & Fri. Travel vaccinations & advice on all aspects of malaria prevention. All current UK prescribed anti-malaria tablets in stock.
Fleet Street Travel Clinic 29 Fleet St, London EC4Y 1AA; ☏ 020 7353 5678; www.fleetstreetclinic.com;

⊕ 08.45–17.30 Mon–Fri. Injections, travel products & latest advice.
Hospital for Tropical Diseases Travel Clinic Mortimer Market Centre, 2nd Flr, Capper St (off Tottenham Ct Rd), London WC1E 6AU; ☏ 020 7388 9600; www.thehtd.org; ⊕ 09.00–16.00. Offers consultations & advice, & is able to provide all necessary drugs & vaccines for travellers. Runs a healthline (☏ 020 7950 7799) for country-specific information & health hazards. Also stocks nets, water purification equipment & personal protection measures. Travellers who have returned from the tropics & are unwell, with fever or bloody diarrhoea, can attend the walk-in emergency clinic at the hospital without an appointment.
MASTA (Medical Advisory Service for Travellers Abroad), at the London School of Hygiene & Tropical Medicine, Keppel St, London WC1 7HT; ☏ 09068 224100;

e enquiries@masta.org; www.masta-travel-health.com. This is a premium-line number, charged at 60p per minute. For a fee, they will provide an individually tailored health brief, with up-to-date information on how to stay healthy, inoculations & what to take. **MASTA pre-travel clinics** ✆ 01276 685040. Call or check http://www.masta-travel-health.com/travel-clinic.aspx for the nearest; there are currently 30 in Britain. They also sell malaria prophylaxis, memory cards, treatment kits, bednets, net treatment kits, etc.

NHS travel website www.fitfortravel.nhs.uk. Provides country-by-country advice on immunisation & malaria prevention, plus details of recent developments, & a list of relevant health organisations.

Nomad Travel Stores Flagship store: 3–4 Wellington Terrace, Turnpike Lane, London N8 0PX; ✆ 020 8889 7014; f 020 8889 9528; e turnpike@nomadtravel.co.uk; www.nomadtravel.co.uk; walk in or

appointments ⊕ 09.15–17.00 every day with late night Thu. 6 stores in total country wide: 3 in London, 1 in Bristol, Southampton & Manchester. As well as dispensing health advice, Nomad stocks mosquito nets & other anti-bug devices, & an excellent range of adventure travel gear.

InterHealth Travel Clinic 111 Westminster Bridge Rd, London, SE1 7HR, ✆ 020 7902 9000; e info@interhealth.org.uk; www.interhealth.org.uk; ⊕ 08.30–17.30 Mon–Fri. Competitively priced, one-stop travel health service by appointment only.

Trailfinders Immunisation Centre 194 Kensington High St, London W8 7RG; ✆ 020 7938 3999; www.trailfinders.com/travelessentials/travelclinic.htm; ⊕ 09.00–17.00 Mon, Tue, Wed & Fri, 09.00–18.00 Thu, 10.00–17.15 Sat. No appointment necessary.

Travelpharm www.travelpharm.com. The Travelpharm website offers up-to-date guidance on travel-related health & has a range of medications available

Irish Republic

Tropical Medical Bureau Grafton St Medical Centre, Grafton Buildings, 34 Grafton St, Dublin 2; ✆ 1 671

9200. Has a useful website specific to tropical destinations: www.tmb.ie.

USA

Centers for Disease Control 1600 Clifton Rd, Atlanta, GA 30333; ✆ (800) 232 4636 or (800) 232 6348; e cdcinfo@cdc.gov; www.cdc.gov/travel. The central source of travel information in the USA. Each summer they publish the invaluable *Health Information for International Travel*.

IAMAT (International Association for Medical Assistance to Travelers) 1623 Military Rd, #279 Niagara Falls, NY 14304-1745; ✆ 716 754 4883; e info@iamat.org; www.iamat.org. A non-profit organisation with free membership that provides lists of English-speaking doctors abroad.

Canada

IAMAT (International Association for Medical Assistance to Travellers) Suite 1, 1287 St Clair Av W, Toronto, Ontario M6E 1B8; ✆ 416 652 0137; www.iamat.org

TMVC (Travel Doctors Group) Suite 314, 1030 W Georgia Street, Vancouver, BC V6E 2Y3; ✆ 905 648 1112; e info@tmvc.com; www.tmvc.com. One-stop medical clinic for all your international travel medicine & vaccination needs.

Australia, New Zealand, Thailand

TMVC ✆ 1300 65 88 44; www.tmvc.com.au. 22 clinics in Australia, New Zealand & Thailand, including: *Auckland* Canterbury Arcade, 170 Queen St, Auckland; ✆ 9 373 3531; *Brisbane* 75a Astor Terrace, Spring Hill, Brisbane, QLD 4000; ✆ (07) 3815 6900; e brisbane@traveldoctor.com.au; *Melbourne* Dr Sonny Lau, 393 Little Bourke St, 2nd floor,

Melbourne, VIC 3000; ✆ (03) 9935 8100; melbourne@traveldoctor.com.au; *Sydney* Dr Mandy Hu, Dymocks Building, 7th Flr, 428 George St, Sydney, NSW 2000; ✆ 2 9221 7133; f 2 9221 8401 **IAMAT** PO Box 5049, Christchurch 5, New Zealand; www.iamat.org

South Africa

SAA-Netcare Travel Clinics e travelinfo@netcare.co.za; www.travelclinic.co.za. 12 clinics throughout South Africa.

TMVC NHC Health Centre, Cnr Beyers Naude & Waugh Northcliff; ✆ 0 11 214 9030; e traveldoctor@wtmconline.com; www.traveldoctor.co.za. Consult the website for details of clinics.

Switzerland

IAMAT 57 Chemin des Voirets, 1212 Grand-Lancy, Geneva; e info@iamat.org; www.iamat.org

TRAVEL INSURANCE Before you travel, make sure that you have adequate medical insurance – choose a policy with comprehensive cover for hospitalisation as well as for repatriation in an emergency. Nowadays the range of cover available is very wide – choose whatever suits your method of travel. Be aware, if you plan to use motorbike taxis in Rwanda, that not all policies cover you for this form of transport. Remember to take all the details with you, particularly your policy number and the telephone number that you have to contact in the event of a claim.

PERSONAL FIRST-AID KIT A minimal kit contains:

- A good drying antiseptic, eg: iodine or potassium permanganate (don't take antiseptic cream)
- A few small dressings (Band-Aids)
- Suncream
- Insect repellent; anti-malarial tablets; impregnated bed-net or permethrin spray
- Aspirin or paracetamol
- Antifungal cream (eg: Canesten)
- Ciprofloxacin or norfloxacin, for severe diarrhoea
- Tinidazole for giardia or amoebic dysentery (see below for regime)
- Antibiotic eye drops, for sore, 'gritty', stuck-together eyes (conjunctivitis)
- A pair of fine pointed tweezers (to remove hairy caterpillar hairs, thorns, splinters, coral, etc)
- Alcohol-based hand rub or bar of soap in plastic box
- Condoms or femidoms
- Malaria diagnostic kits (5) and a digital thermometer (for those going to remote areas)

COMMON MEDICAL PROBLEMS

TRAVELLER'S DIARRHOEA At least half of those travelling to the tropics/developing world will experience a bout of travellers' diarrhoea during their trip; the newer you are to exotic travel, the more likely you will be to suffer. By taking precautions against travellers' diarrhoea you will also avoid typhoid, cholera, hepatitis, dysentery, worms, etc.

From food Travellers' diarrhoea and the other faecal-oral diseases come from getting other peoples' faeces in your mouth. This most often happens from cooks not washing their hands after a trip to the toilet, but even if the restaurant cook does not understand basic hygiene you will be safe if your food has been properly cooked and arrives piping hot. The maxim to remind you what you can safely eat is:

PEEL IT, BOIL IT, COOK IT OR FORGET IT.

This means that fruit you have washed and peeled yourself, and hot foods, should be safe, but raw foods, cold cooked foods, salads, fruit salads prepared by others, ice cream and ice are all risky, as are foods kept lukewarm in restaurant or hotel buffets. Self-service or buffet meals are popular in Rwanda, so try to eat these when the food is hot and freshly cooked – for example a late buffet lunch eaten in the

Dr Jane Wilson-Howarth

It is dehydration which makes you feel awful during a bout of diarrhoea and the most important part of treatment is drinking lots of clear fluids. Sachets of oral rehydration salts give the perfect biochemical mix to replace all that is pouring out of your bottom but they do not taste nice. Any dilute mixture of sugar and salt in water will do you good, so if you like Coke or orange squash, drink that with a three-finger pinch of salt added to each glass. Otherwise make a solution of a four-finger scoop of sugar with a three-finger pinch of salt in a glass of water. Or add eight level teaspoons of sugar (18g) and one level teaspoon of salt (3g) to one litre (five cups) of safe water. A squeeze of lemon or orange juice improves the taste and adds potassium, which is also lost during a bout of diarrhoea. Drink two large glasses after every bowel action, and more if you are thirsty. If you are not eating, then you need to drink three litres a day plus the equivalent of whatever is pouring into the toilet. If you feel like eating, take a bland, high-carbohydrate diet. Heavy, greasy foods will probably give you cramps.

If the diarrhoea is bad, or you are passing blood or slime, or you have a fever, you will probably need antibiotics in addition to fluid replacement. A three-day course of Ciprofloxacin 500mg twice daily (or Norfloxacin) is appropriate treatment for dysentery and bad diarrhoea. If the diarrhoea is greasy and bulky and is accompanied by 'eggy' burps, the likely cause is giardia. This is best treated with Tinidazole (2g in one dose repeated seven days later if symptoms persist).

mid-afternoon will have been sitting around a long while. If you do get travellers' diarrhoea, see box above for treatment.

From water It is also possible to get sick from drinking contaminated water, so try to drink from safe sources. You must assume that tap water is risky wherever you are in Rwanda. To make risky water safe it should be brought to the boil (even at altitude it only needs to be brought to the boil), passed through a good bacteriological filter or purified with iodine; chlorine tablets (eg: Puritabs) are also adequate although theoretically less effective, and they taste nastier. Micropur tablets are tasteless but take at least two hours to become effective. If you buy bottled water (which is widely available in Rwanda) make sure the seal is intact. Iodine is not recommended in pregnancy so you should ask a doctor what you should do.

DENGUE FEVER This mosquito-borne disease resembles malaria but there is no prophylactic available to deal with it. The mosquitoes which carry this virus bite during the daytime, so it is worth applying repellent if you see them around. Symptoms include strong headaches, rashes and excruciating joint and muscle pains with high fever. Dengue fever lasts for only a week or so and is not usually fatal if you have not previously been infected. Complete rest and paracetamol are the usual treatment. Plenty of fluids also help. Some patients are given an intravenous drip to keep them from dehydrating.

INSECT BITES It is crucial to avoid mosquito bites between dusk and dawn; as the sun is going down, don long clothes and apply repellent on any exposed flesh. This will protect you from malaria, elephantiasis and a range of nasty insect-borne viruses. Malaria mosquitoes are voracious, hunt at ankle-level, and can penetrate through socks. Sleep under a permethrin-treated bednet or in an air-conditioned room. During the day it is wise to wear long, loose (preferably 100% cotton) clothes if you are pushing through scrubby country; this will deter ticks as well as tsetse flies and day-biting Aedes mosquitoes which may spread dengue and yellow fever. Tsetse flies hurt when they bite and are attracted to the colour blue; locals will advise on where they are a problem and where they transmit sleeping sickness.

Minute pestilential biting blackflies spread river blindness in some parts of Africa between 90°N and 170°S; the disease is caught close to fast-flowing rivers since flies breed there and the larvae live in rapids. The flies bite during the day but long trousers tucked into socks will help keep them off. Citronella-based natural repellents do not work against them.

Tumbu flies or *putsi* are a problem in areas of eastern, western and southern Africa where the climate is hot and humid. The adult fly lays her eggs on the soil or on drying laundry and when the eggs come in contact with human flesh (when you put on clothes or lie on a bed) they hatch and bury themselves under the skin. Here they form a crop of 'boils' each of which hatches a grub after about eight days, when the inflammation will settle down. In putsi areas either dry your clothes and sheets within a screened house, or dry them in direct sunshine until they are crisp, or iron them.

Jiggers or sandfleas are another kind of flesh-feaster. They latch on if you walk barefoot in contaminated places, and set up home under the skin of the foot, usually at the side of a toenail where they cause a painful, boil-like swelling. These need picking out by a local expert; if the distended flea bursts during eviction the wound should be dowsed in spirit, alcohol or kerosene, otherwise more jiggers will infest you.

BILHARZIA OR SCHISTOSOMIASIS with thanks to Dr Vaughan Southgate of the Natural History Museum, London, and Dr Dick Stockley, The Surgery, Kampala

Bilharzia or schistosomiasis is a disease that commonly afflicts the rural poor of the tropics. Two types exist in sub-Saharan Africa – *Schistosoma mansoni* and *Schistosoma haematobium*. It is an unpleasant problem that is worth avoiding, though can be treated if you do get it. This parasite is common in almost all water sources in Rwanda – even places advertised as 'bilharzia-free', such as Lake Kivu. The most risky shores will be close to places where infected people use water, wash clothes, etc.

It is easier to understand how to diagnose it, treat it and prevent it if you know a little about the life cycle. Contaminated faeces are washed into the lake, the eggs hatch and the larva infects certain species of snail. The snails then produce about

---

QUICK TICK REMOVAL   Dr Jane Wilson-Howarth

African ticks are not the prolific disease transmitters they are in the Americas, but they may occasionally spread disease. Lyme disease, which can have unpleasant after-effects, has now been recorded in Africa, and tick-bite fever also occurs. The latter is a mild, flu-like illness, but still worth avoiding. If you get the tick off whole and promptly the chances of disease transmission are reduced to a minimum.

Manoeuvre your finger and thumb so that you can pinch the tick's mouthparts, as close to your skin as possible, and slowly and steadily pull away at right angles to your skin. This often hurts. Jerking or twisting will increase the chances of damaging the tick which in turn increases the chances of disease transmission, as well as leaving the mouthparts behind.

Once the tick is off, dowse the little wound with alcohol (local spirit, whisky or similar is excellent) or iodine. An area of spreading redness around the bite site, or a rash or fever coming on a few days or more after the bite, should stimulate a trip to a doctor.

Any prolonged immobility including travel by land or air can result in deep vein thrombosis (DVT) with the risk of embolus to the lungs. Certain factors can increase the risk and these include:

- Previous clot or close relative with a history
- People over 40 but > risk over 80 years
- Recent major operation or varicose veins surgery
- Cancer
- Stroke
- Heart disease
- Obesity
- Pregnancy
- Hormone therapy
- Heavy smokers
- Severe varicose veins
- People who are very tall (over 6ft/1.8m) or short (under 5ft/1.5m)

A deep vein thrombosis (DVT) causes painful swelling and redness of the calf or sometimes the thigh. It is only dangerous if a clot travels to the lungs (pulmonary embolus). Symptoms of a pulmonary embolus (PE) include chest pain, shortness of breath, and sometimes coughing up small amounts of blood and commonly start three to ten days after a long flight. Anyone who thinks that they might have a DVT needs to see a doctor immediately.

PREVENTION OF DVT
- Keep mobile before and during the flight; move around every couple of hours
- Drink plenty of fluids during the flight
- Avoid taking sleeping pills and excessive tea, coffee and alcohol
- Consider wearing flight socks or support stockings (see *www.legshealth.com*)

If you think you are at increased risk of a clot, ask your doctor if it is safe to travel.

10,000 *cercariae* a day for the rest of their lives. The parasites can digest their way through your skin when you wade, or bathe in infested fresh water.

Winds disperse the snails and cercariae. The snails in particular can drift a long way, especially on windblown weed, so nowhere is really safe. However, deep water and running water are safer, while shallow water presents the greatest risk. The cercariae penetrate intact skin, and find their way to the liver. There male and female meet and spend the rest of their lives in permanent copulation. No wonder you feel tired! Most finish up in the wall of the lower bowel, but others can get lost and can cause damage to many different organs. *Schistosoma haematobium* goes mostly to the bladder.

Although the adults do not cause any harm in themselves, after about 4–6 weeks they start to lay eggs, which cause an intense but usually ineffective immune reaction, including fever, cough, abdominal pain, and a fleeting, itching rash called 'safari itch'. The absence of early symptoms does not necessarily mean there is no infection. Later symptoms can be more localised and more severe, but the general symptoms settle down fairly quickly and eventually you are just tired. 'Tired all the time' is one of the most common symptoms among expats in Africa, and bilharzia, giardia, amoeba and intestinal yeast are the most common culprits.

Health **COMMON MEDICAL PROBLEMS**

3

Although bilharzia is difficult to diagnose, it can be tested at specialist travel clinics. Ideally tests need to be done at least six weeks after likely exposure and will determine whether you need treatment. Fortunately it is easy to treat at present.

Avoiding bilharzia If you are bathing, swimming, paddling or wading in fresh water which you think may carry a bilharzia risk, try to get out of the water within ten minutes.

- Avoid bathing or paddling on shores within 200m of villages or places where people use the water a great deal, especially reedy shores or where there is lots of water weed.
- Dry off thoroughly with a towel; rub vigorously.
- If your bathing water comes from a risky source try to ensure that the water is taken from the lake in the early morning and stored snail-free; otherwise it should be filtered or Dettol or Cresol should be added.
- Bathing early in the morning is safer than bathing in the last half of the day.
- Cover yourself with DEET insect repellent before swimming: it may offer some protection.

SKIN INFECTIONS Any mosquito bite or small nick in the skin provides an opportunity for bacteria to foil the body's usually excellent defences; it will surprise many travellers how quickly skin infections start in warm humid climates and it is essential to clean and cover even the slightest wound. Creams are not as effective as a good drying antiseptic such as dilute iodine, potassium permanganate (a few crystals in half a cup of water), or crystal (or gentian) violet. One of these should be available in most towns. If the wound starts to throb, or becomes red and the redness starts to spread, or the wound oozes, and especially if you develop a fever, antibiotics will probably be needed: flucloxacillin (250mg four times a day) or cloxacillin (500mg four times a day). For those allergic to penicillin, erythromycin (500mg twice a day) for five days should help. See a doctor if the symptoms do not start to improve in 48 hours.

Fungal infections also get a hold easily in hot moist climates, so wear 100% cotton socks and underwear and shower frequently. An itchy rash in the groin or flaking between the toes is likely to be a fungal infection. This needs treatment with an antifungal cream such as Canesten (clotrimazole); if this is not available try Whitfield's ointment (compound enzoic acid ointment) or crystal violet (although this will turn you purple!).

PRICKLY HEAT A fine pimply rash on the torso is likely to be heat rash; cool showers, dabbing (not rubbing) dry, and talc will help; if it's bad you may need to check into an air-conditioned hotel room for a while. Slowing down to a relaxed schedule, wearing only loose, baggy 100% cotton clothes and sleeping naked under a fan reduce the problem.

SUN DAMAGE Give some thought to packing suncream. The incidence of skin cancer is rocketing as Caucasians are travelling more and spending more time exposing themselves to the sun. Keep out of the sun during the middle of the day and, if you must expose yourself to the sun, build up gradually from 20 minutes per day. Be especially careful of exposure in the middle of the day and of sun reflected off water, and wear a T-shirt and lots of waterproof suncream (at least SPF20) when swimming. Sun exposure ages the skin, makes people prematurely wrinkly and increases the risk of skin cancer. Cover up with long, loose clothes and wear a hat when you can. The glare and the dust can be hard on the eyes, too, so bring UV-protecting sunglasses and, perhaps, a soothing eyebath.

MENINGITIS This is a particularly nasty disease as it can kill within hours of the first symptoms appearing. The telltale symptoms are a combination of a blinding headache (light sensitivity), a blotchy rash and a high fever. Immunisation with the newer tetravalent vaccine ACWY protects against the most serious bacterial form of meningitis and is usually recommended for longer-stay trips to Rwanda or if you are working closely with the local population – in particular with children. A single injection gives good protection for three years. Other forms of meningitis exist (usually viral) but there are no vaccines for these. Local papers normally report outbreaks. If you show symptoms go to a doctor immediately.

SEXUAL RISKS Travel is a time when we may enjoy sexual adventures, especially when alcohol reduces inhibitions. Remember the risks of sexually transmitted infection are high, whether you sleep with fellow travellers or with locals. More than half of HIV infections in British heterosexuals are acquired abroad and AIDS is a serious problem in Rwanda. Use condoms or femidoms, preferably bearing the British kite mark and ideally bought before travel. If you notice any genital ulcers or discharge get treatment promptly.

EBOLA

So far this has never occurred in Rwanda, but it has claimed some lives in Uganda. It is a rare, but deadly, highly contagious, virally induced disease which causes haemorrhagic fever. In the unlikely event of an outbreak, protective measures will be taken and you should follow whatever local advice is given.

ANIMALS

RABIES Rabies can be carried by all mammals (beware the village dogs and small monkeys in the parks) and is passed on to man through a bite, scratch or a lick of an open wound. You must always assume any animal is rabid, and seek medical help as soon as possible. Meanwhile scrub the wound with soap under a running tap or while pouring water from a jug. Find a reasonably clear-looking source of water (but at this stage the quality of the water is not important), then pour on a strong iodine or alcohol solution of gin, whisky or rum. This helps stop the rabies virus entering the body and will guard against wound infections, including tetanus.

Pre-exposure vaccinations for rabies are ideally advised for everyone, but are particularly important if you intend to have contact with animals and/or are likely to be more than 24 hours away from medical help. Ideally three doses should be taken over a minimum of 21 days, though even taking one or two doses of vaccine is better than none at all. Contrary to popular belief these vaccinations are relatively painless.

If you are bitten, scratched or licked over an open wound by a sick animal, then post-exposure prophylaxis should be given as soon as possible, though it is never too late to seek help, as the incubation period for rabies can be very long. Those who have not been immunised will need a full course of injections. The vast majority of travel health advisors including WHO recommend rabies immunoglobulin (RIG), but this product is expensive (around US$800) and may be hard to come by – another reason why pre-exposure vaccination should be encouraged.

Tell the doctor if you have had pre-exposure vaccine, as this should change the treatment you receive. And remember that, if you do contract rabies, mortality is 100% and death from rabies is probably one of the worst ways to go.

SNAKEBITE Snakes rarely attack unless provoked and bites to travellers are unusual. You are less likely to get bitten if you wear stout shoes and long trousers when in the bush. Most snakes are harmless and even venomous species will only dispense venom in about half of their bites. If bitten, then, you are unlikely to have received venom; keeping this fact in mind may help you to stay calm. Many so-called first-aid techniques do more harm than good: cutting into the wound is harmful; tourniquets are dangerous; suction and electrical inactivation devices do not work. The only treatment is antivenom. In case of a bite which you fear may have been from a venomous snake:

- Try to keep calm – it is likely that no venom has been dispensed.
- Prevent movement of the bitten limb by applying a splint.
- Keep the bitten limb BELOW heart height to slow the spread of any venom.
- If you have a crepe bandage, bind up as much of the bitten limb as you can, but release the bandage every half hour.
- Evacuate to a hospital which has antivenom. At the time of writing this is only known to be available in Kampala. Many centres have an Indian antivenom that does not include the most common biting snakes in Rwanda

And remember:

- NEVER give aspirin; you may offer paracetamol, which is safe.
- NEVER cut or suck the wound.
- DO NOT apply ice packs.
- DO NOT apply potassium permanganate.

If the offending snake can be captured without risk of someone else being bitten, take it to show to the doctor – but beware, since even a decapitated head is able to dispense venom in a reflex bite.

USEFUL CONTACTS IN KIGALI

Central Hospital of Kigali ✎ 0252 575555
King Faycal Hospital (Kigali) ✎ 0252 582421
Sun City Pharmacy Bd de la Révolution; ⊕ 24hrs

Pharmacie Conseil Av des Mille Collines (opposite Belgian School); ⊕ 08.00–21.00 Mon–Sat, 10.00–15.00 Sun

Part Two

THE GUIDE

4

Kigali

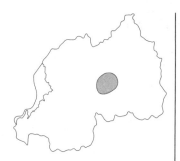

The low-key but attractive Rwandan capital city of Kigali stands in the centre of the country, where it straggles over several hills and valleys, spanning altitudes of around 1,300m to 1,600m. The city was founded in 1907 at a location chosen by Dr Richard Kandt, who built an administrative residence close to the present-day Gakinjiro Market. Two years later, 20 houses were built close to the present-day prison (one of which has been restored as a natural history museum) on the eastern slopes of Nyarugenge Hill, which now forms the commercial city centre.

Kigali remained a small and isolated colonial outpost prior to 1916, when Belgium captured it from Germany. Under Belgian rule, Kigali retained an important administrative role, but urban growth was very slow and confined mainly to Nyarugenge. Indeed, when Rwanda gained independence in 1962, the population of Kigali stood at no more than 6,000. When Ruanda-Urundi (the capital of which was Usumbura, now Bujumbura) split into Rwanda and Burundi, the strongest contender to become Rwanda's new capital seemed to be Butare, which had been the more important administrative centre during colonisation.

However, Kigali's central position and good road links to the rest of the country won out. As a result, while Butare has avoided capital-city brashness and remains relatively calm, Kigali has grown dramatically, with a population that had risen to 240,000 by 1991 and is likely to pass the one-million mark during the lifespan of this edition. The commercial city centre is still centred on Nyarugenge Hill, while the government and administrative quarter is further east on Kacyiru Hill. In between and around these elevated twin centres, empty spaces on the hillsides are filling with new housing, and pollution in the valleys (from the increasing volume of traffic) could soon be a problem.

The centre of Kigali is bustling, colourful and noisy, but (for an African city) surprisingly clean and safe (indeed, in 2008, Kigali was effectively pronounced the cleanest city on the continent, when it became the first African urban centre to be presented with the Habitat Scroll of Honour award, an annual award launched by the UN Human Settlements Programme in 1989). Kigali's occupants, from smart-suited businesspeople to scruffy kids hawking newspapers or pirated cassettes, go purposefully about their activities, only lessening tempo briefly in the middle of the day. Occasional traffic lights, roundabouts, a strictly enforced one-way road system and a cacophony of car horns manage (more or less) to regulate the traffic, although it's heavy and congested at peak times. Peaceful, tree-lined residential streets stretch outwards and generally downwards from the city's heart, and give visitors scope for strolling.

The government and administrative area in Kacyiru quarter is newer and quieter, with wide streets and some striking modern architecture. Kigali was the centre of much fighting during the genocide and offices were ransacked; when workers returned after the end of the war they had virtually no usable typewriters,

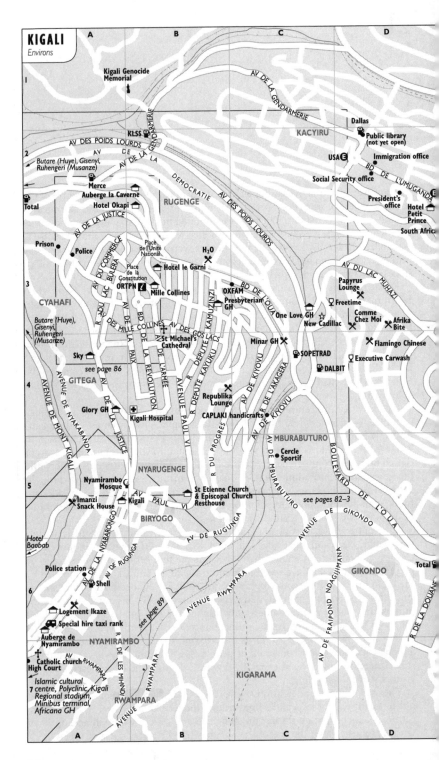

KIGALI
Environs

I

Kigali Genocide
Memorial

AV DE LA GENDARMERIE

KACYIRU

Dallas
Public library
(not yet open)

KLSS

AV DES POIDS LOURDS

USA

Immigration office

AV DE
DE LA LA

BD DE L'UMUGANDA

Butare (Huye), Gisenyi,
Ruhengeri (Musanze)

Social Security office

DEMOCRATIE

2

Merce
Auberge la Caverne
Hotel Okapi

AV DES POIDS LOURDS

President's
office

Hotel
Petit
Prince

Total

RUGENGE

South Africa

AV DE LA JUSTICE

Prison

Police

R DU COMMERCE
R DU LAC BULERA

Place
de l'Unité
National

H₂O

AV DU LAC MUHAZI

Papyrus
Lounge

Freetime

ORTPN

Place
de la
Constitution

Hotel le Garni

3

CYAHAFI

Mille Collines

OXFAM

BD DE L'OUA

Presbyterian
GH

One Love GH

New Cadillac

Comme
Chez Moi

Afrika
Bite

Butare (Huye),
Gisenyi,
Ruhengeri
(Musanze)

R DE LA PAIX

BD DE LA COLLINES

AV DES GDS LACS

R DEPUTE KAYUKU

Minar GH

Flamingo Chinese

Sky

St Michael's
Cathedral

SOPETRAD

Executive Carwash

4

see page 86

GITEGA

AVENUE PAUL VI

AV DE KIYOVU

DALBIT

AVENUE DE MONT KIGALI

DE LA JUSTICE

Glory GH

Kigali Hospital

Republika
Lounge

CAPLAKI handicrafts

R DU PROGRES

AV DE L'AKAGERA

AV DE KIYOVU

MBURABUTURO

Cercle
Sportif

BOULEVARD DE L'OUA

5

NYARUGENGE

Nyamirambo
Mosque

Imanzi
Snack House

Kigali

AV PAUL

St Etienne Church
& Episcopal Church
Resthouse

see pages 82–3

AV DE MBURABUTURO

AVENUE DE GIKONDO

AV DE RUGUNGA

Hotel
Baobab

BIRYOGO

R DE NYABARONGO

N DE RUGUNGA

6

Police station

Shell

GIKONDO

Total

Logement Ikaze

AVENUE RWAMPARA

AVENUE DE FRAIPOND NDAGIJIMANA

R DE LA DOUANE

Special hire taxi rank

Auberge de
Nyamirambo

see page 89

NYAMIRAMBO

Catholic church

High Court

R RWAMPARA

AV DE LES MIHINDI

7

Islamic cultural
centre, Polyclinic, Kigali
Regional stadium,
Minibus terminal,
Africana GH

RWAMPARA

AVENUE

RWAMPARA

KIGARAMA

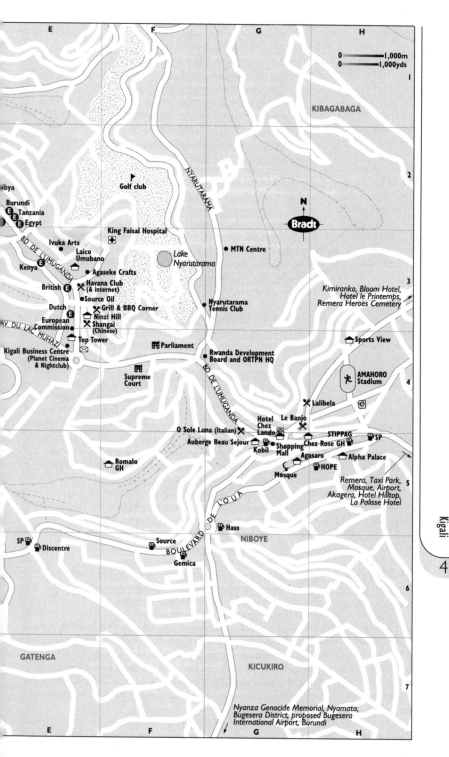

E   F   G   H

0 ━━━━━ 1,000m
0 ━━━━━ 1,000yds
I

KIBAGABAGA

2

Golf club

NYARUTARAMA

N

Bradt

ibya
Burundi
Tanzania
Egypt

BD DE L'UMUGANDA

King Faisal Hospital

● MTN Centre

Ivuka Arts
Laico
Umubano

Lake
Nyarutarama

Kimiranko, Bloom Hotel,
Hotel le Printemps,
Remera Heroes Cemetery

Kenya

Agaseke Crafts

3

British

Havana Club
(& internet)
Source Oil
Grill & BBQ Corner
Ninzi Hill
Shangai
(Chinese)
Top Tower

Nyarutarama
Tennis Club

Dutch

European
Commission

Sports View

Kigali Business Centre
(Planet Cinema
& Nightclub)

V DU LAC MUHAZI

Parliament

Rwanda Development
Board and ORTPN HQ

AMAHORO
Stadium

4

Supreme
Court

BD DE L'UMUGANDA

Lalibela

Le Banjo

Hotel
Chez
Lando

O Sole Luna (Italian)

Auberge Beau Sejour

Chez Rose GH

STIPPAG
SP

Kobil

Shopping
Mall

Agasaro

Alpha Palace

Romalo
GH

Mosque

HOPE

Remera, Taxi Park,
Mosque, Airport,
Akagera, Hotel Hilltop,
La Palisse Hotel

5

BOULEVARD DE L'OUA

Hass

NIBOYE

SP
Discentre

Source

Gemica

6

Kigali

4

GATENGA

KICUKIRO

7

Nyanza Genocide Memorial, Nyamata,
Bugesera District, proposed Bugesera
International Airport, Burundi

E   F   G   H

79

phones, stationery or furniture and had to start again from scratch. Also files, archives and other documentation had been destroyed.

There aren't many tourist attractions in Kigali itself and you're unlikely to want to spend many full days there, but there are some good hotels, the services (shops, banks, etc) are plentiful and the ambience is pleasant, making it an excellent base for exploring the rest of Rwanda, all parts of which are easily accessible by road in less than a day. Car-hire is easily arranged via one of the many tour operators and travel agencies – see pages 84–5.

GETTING THERE AND AWAY

BY AIR See pages 37–8 for details of flights to and from Rwanda – which means to and from Kigali, since the country's only international airport is situated about 5km from the city centre. There are firm plans to replace this with the larger and more modern Bugesera International Airport near Nyamata, about 40km south of Kigali, which would free the land for further development and bring jobs and opportunities to an underused area. Latest news is that construction will commence in 2010, so it could be functional within the lifetime of this edition.

In the arrivals hall of the airport you'll find foreign exchange and telephone facilities, various shops and a branch of ORTPN (Office Rwandais du Tourisme et des Parcs Nationaux) which is Rwanda's tourist office, where you can get a preliminary stock of maps, guides and so forth. (The main ORTPN office is in the city centre.) At present there is no pestering from porters – there aren't any – just grab a trolley from the stack in the baggage reclaim area and deal with your own bags.

To get into Kigali town you've three options. (Or four, if you're prepared to beg a lift from some fellow traveller who has a vehicle.) If your hotel does airport pick-ups, you'll have arranged this at the time of booking; give them a ring if no-one has turned up to collect you. If you've very little luggage and some small change in Rwandan francs, you can pick up a minibus-taxi in the road outside the airport and it'll take you to central Kigali. Otherwise take a *taxi-voiture* (a normal taxi, as opposed to a minibus-taxi). Agree a price with the driver in advance. At the time of writing the going rate is about Rfr10,000 or US$20, but rates do legitimately rise over time. If the exchange bureau in the airport is closed, taxi-drivers generally accept US dollars, but check the exchange rate on the list in the window of the bureau.

Whatever airline you've used, you MUST confirm your return flight at least three days in advance of departure – airline offices or travel agents in Kigali will deal with this for you. If you don't, you risk being 'bumped' or having your reservation cancelled.

BY ROAD Kigali is a well-connected little city – literally. Good roads and bus services link it to all the main border crossings with neighbouring countries: Uganda, Tanzania, Burundi and the Democratic Republic of Congo.

In addition, almost all towns within Rwanda are connected to Kigali by regular public minibus-taxis, most of which leave from Nyabugogo minibus-taxi station (*gare routière* Nyabugogo), 2km from the city centre along the Byumba Road. Minibus-taxis from the city centre to Nyabugogo station leave from the south end of Rue Lac Ihema opposite the market [86 B4]. Or you can take a taxi-voiture. Once there, it's a huge taxi park and the minibuses are lined up in ranks, some signposted with destinations, others not – if in doubt, just ask someone and you'll be shown where to wait.

The minibuses leave as soon as they've a full complement of passengers – and that does mean *full* as in can of sardines – but everyone gets a seat and there's a non-smoking policy on board. While you're waiting for your minibus to leave, vendors of all sorts will be trying to catch your eye and sell you something – including bottled drinks and fruit, as well as fresh bread and cakes, which are handy if you've a long journey ahead. You can even buy hard-boiled eggs, and season them from the salt and pepper pots conveniently provided!

Sample fares at the time of writing are Rfr1,500 to Butare, Rfr4,000 to Cyangugu, Rfr1,700 to Kibuye, Rfr1,800 to Gisenyi and Rfr1,000 to Ruhengeri.

In addition to standard minibus-taxis, many private companies run similarly priced express services that go directly between cities without stopping to drop or pick up passengers at points in between. These generally run hourly or more often between most major cities. The most reliable operator for the northwest is generally regarded to be Virunga Ponctuel [82 A2] (m *078 8510873; www.virungatravel.com*), whose minibuses depart from their office opposite Nyabugogo station every 30 minutes in either direction between Kigali and Ruhengeri, and hourly to/from Gisenyi.

For other parts of the country, Atraco, based on Rue Mont Kabuye in the city centre [86 C3], covers most routes, including hourly minibuses to Byumba, Nyagatare, Ruhengeri and Gisenyi (all on the hour from 06.00 to 16.00 or 17.00), Kibuye (quarter past the hour from 06.15 to 13.15), Nyanza (ten past the hour from 06.10 to 17.10), Kibungo (quarter to the hour from 06.45 to 17.45) and Butare (on the hour from 07.00 to 17.00) as well as regular departures to Kayonza via Rwamagana (18 daily from 06.10 to 18.00), Gitarama (20 daily between 06.00 and 17.30) and Cyangugu (four daily from 06.30 to 13.30). Other reliable operators include Stella and Sotra [86 C3], also both based on Rue Mont Kabuye.

Another good minibus company is Belvedere [86 D3] (m *078 8565081; e karefely@yahoo.fr*), which operates services to Bujumbura and Goma, as well as several Rwandan towns. Its office is opposite the UTC next to Amy's Fast Food. The buses seat about 30 people, and are clean and comfortable as these things go, and toilet stops are provided.

Smart green-and-white government-run buses, under the government department Onatracom (*0252 575404/575411/501302; e onatraco@rwanda1.com; www.onatracom.rw*) rattle about to all parts of Rwanda, including some rough roads which must tax their springs severely. You may see them parked in Nyamirambo, near the mosque, but that's not where you catch them; they leave from the Nyabugogo minibus station [82 A2]. Fares are slightly cheaper (about 20%) than minibuses and a full timetable of express and ordinary services is posted on their user-friendly website.

GETTING AROUND

The centre of Kigali – for shopping, banks, airline offices, tour operators, etc – is tiny, so once you're there, you'll never be far from what you're looking for. It's based around two streets, Boulevard de la Révolution and Avenue de la Paix, and the various roads branching off them. However, if you ask directions you'll soon become aware that people don't go much on street names, rather on well-known landmarks.

A good foldout map covering the whole of Kigali (as opposed to just the centre) is available from ORTPN (see page 84) for Rfr8,500, and also from some tour operators and hotels. There's a network of urban **minibuses** (minibus-taxis, commonly called taxis) serving all areas of the city, and plenty of **taxis** (saloons, commonly called *taxi-voitures* and recognisable by the yellow/orange stripe along the side) – they park, among other places, in Boulevard de la Révolution and at the top of Place de la Constitution, and also cruise the streets waiting to be flagged down.

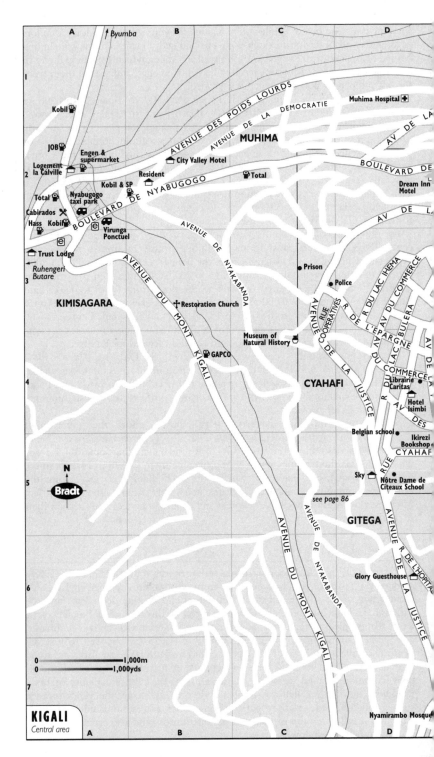

KIGALI
Central area

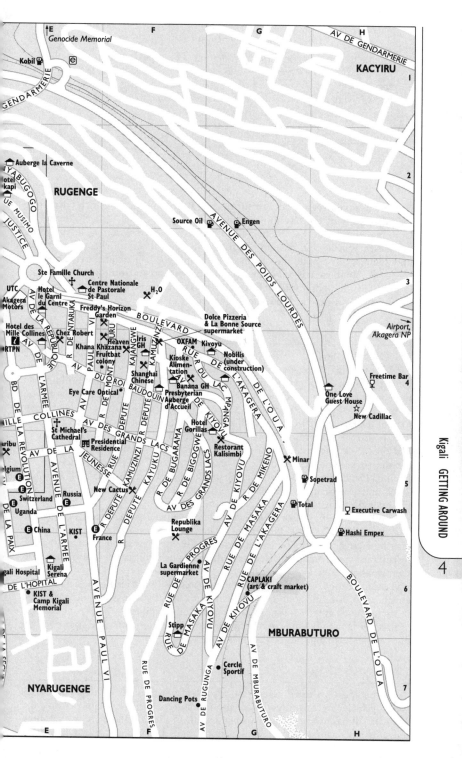

Caroline Pomeroy

If you get lost in Kigali, or it starts to rain, you will never be far from a moto – the local name for a motorbike taxi. Always agree the price for a moto ride in advance, and check the helmet – they are often good for decorative purposes only, as the buckles and straps are broken or far too loose. If you protest, the driver will usually try tp readjust the strap for you, or as likely as not offer you his own, usually rather hot and greasy…! Most drivers speak a smattering of French or English, so if you know the name of your destination they will get you there. But don't be fooled by the maps – road names are non-existent and rarely used. People navigate by buildings and local landmarks, so try using these instead.

There is no longer a central **minibus-taxi station** in Kigali. Vehicles departing for other parts of the city mostly leave from Avenue de la Justice, Avenue du Commerce and Rue Lac Ihema, all of which are lined with gaggles of white minibuses waiting for custom. Despite the general air of chaos, there's an underlying level of sanity and, if you ask someone, you'll be pointed to the bus that you need. Minibus-taxis to **Nyabugogo minibus-taxi station** [82 A2], the main terminus starting point for public transport to other parts of Rwanda, leave from the junction of Rues Lac Ihema and l'Epargne.

TOURIST INFORMATION

The **ORTPN** [86 D5] (*Office Rwandais du Tourisme et des Parcs Nationaux;* ☎ *0252 576514 or 573396;* e *reservation@rwandatourism.com; www.rwandatourism.com*) tourist information and booking office is situated in a one-storey building on the southeast side of Place de la Constitution. The staff here can inform you about current events in Kigali, and you can also buy a useful single-sheet street map of the city for Rfr8,500 as well as a good selection of books about Rwanda. This is also the main reservations office for permits to track gorillas in Volcanoes National Park (more details on page 49), which is best done before you set off for the park. Note that the administrative staff of ORTPN relocated to the Rwanda Development Board building on Boulevard de l'Umuganda [79 G4] in 2008, and it remains to be seen whether the tourist information office will follow them there.

Another excellent source of information is the quarterly magazine called *The Eye* (m *078 8496897/8570353;* e *theeye@theeye.co.rw; www.theeye.co.rw*), which is distributed free at several outlets in Kigali, and includes extensive listings of hotels, restaurants, shops and other facilities. Much of this information is also posted on their website.

A useful source of information for expatriates in Rwanda is *Kigali Life* , a yahoo email group that sends out daily bulletins with questions, answers, ads and news. It can be joined at http://groups.yahoo.com/group/kigalilife.

Last but hopefully not least, check out the updates, or contribute your own, on our website http://updates.bradtguides.com/rwanda.

TOUR OPERATORS

All of the operators listed below can organise day excursions or longer safaris, as well as vehicle hire, accommodation, airport transfers, gorilla-tracking permits, and so forth. All have some English-speaking staff. In addition there are several more travel agents, who can deal with national and international travel but don't necessarily obtain gorilla permits (which are issued by ORTPN). The three below offer particularly varied services.

Volcanoes Safaris [86 D5] Hotel des Mille Collines; ☎ 0252 502452, 576530; m 078 8302069; e salesrw@volcanoessafaris.com; www.volcanoessafaris.com. A recommended first stop, this well-established company is widely regarded as the leading tour company in Rwanda, & it is also specialised in Uganda (& included under international operators on pages 34–6). It can arrange gorilla trips (including fly-in visits) as well as tours to most other corners of the country, & its Virunga Lodge near Volcanoes National Park is one of the most beautifully located & best run in Rwanda.

Bizidanny Tours & Safaris [86 B5] Cnr Av du Commerce/Lac Bulera; m 078 8501461; e infobizidanny@yahoo.fr; www.bizidanny.com & http://bizidanny.over-blog.com. Praised by several

readers of the last edition, this small operator offers relatively budget-friendly tailor-made trips. As well as all the standard trips he also offers visits to schools, orphanages, women's cooperatives, local development projects, etc.

New Dawn Associates [86 D4] UTC Building; m 078 8513652; e info@newdawnassociates.com; www.newdawnassociates.com. This dynamic new company can arrange all the usual excursions – gorilla tracking, visits to Nyungwe & Akagera et al – but its real focus is more on interactive community-based tourism. It has developed 5 day-excursions: the Millennium Village Tour (Nyamata area), This is Africa (Nyamirambo), Humure (refugee community near Akagera National Park), Lake Kivu Coffee Experience, & Dancing Pots (life & culture of the Batwa in Gisenyi area).

Other established operators include:

Abacus Rwanda Safaris Hotel des Mille Collines, Annex Kigali; ☎ +256 414 232 657 (Uganda); e info@rwanda-safari.com; www.rwanda-safari.com
Concord Rwanda Chadel Building, Bd des Mille Collines; ☎ 0252 575988; m 078 8457272; e info@magic-safaris.com; www.magic-safaris.com
International Tours & Travel SORAS building, Bd de la Révolution; ☎ 0252 578831/2; e itt@rwanda1.com; www.itt.co.rw
Kiboko Tours & Travel BP 6628 Kigali; ☎ 0252 520118, 520119; e kiboko@rwanda1.com; www.kibokotravels.org.rw

Primate Safaris [86 C6] Av de la Paix; ☎ 0252 511718; e office@primatesafaris-rwanda.com; www.primatesafaris-rwanda.com
Rwanda Eco-tours ☎ 0252 500331; m 078 8352009; e info@rwandaecotours.com; www.rwandaecotours.com
Thousand Hills Expeditions ☎ 0252 504330; e info@thousandhills.rw; www.thousandhills.rw
Wildlife Tours – Rwanda Opp Banque Populaire du Kimironko; m 078 8527049; e info@wildlifetours-rwanda.com; www.wildlifetours-rwanda.com

There are several others around the city – too many to list here – and more are opening at the time of writing. Check the current position on www.rwandatourism.com. Their non-inclusion in this guide doesn't mean there's anything wrong with them, so by all means give them a go – and send in recommendations for the next edition!

WHERE TO STAY

Virtually all of the Kigali hotels in the 'Luxury' to 'Middle' categories can arrange airport pick-ups – just ask (and check the cost, if any) at the time of booking. Unless otherwise specified, bedrooms in all of the Kigali hotels listed here have en-suite facilities with either bath or shower. Hotels in Remera suburb are closer to the airport than are those in the centre.

LUXURY (*over $200 double*) Kigali is served by two city hotels that confirm to international standards at every level. Both are large, bland and somewhat impersonal, and they cater mainly to business travellers, offering the sort of facilities one would

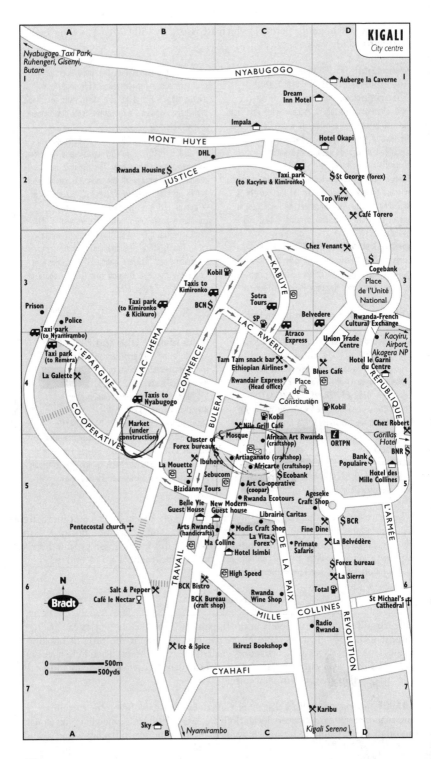

KIGALI
City centre

Nyabugogo Taxi Park,
Ruhengeri, Gisenyi,
Butare

NYABUGOGO

Auberge la Caverne

Dream
Inn Motel

Impala

MONT HUYE

Hotel Okapi

DHL

JUSTICE

Rwanda Housing

St George (forex)

Taxi park
(to Kacyiru & Kimironko)

Top View

Café Torero

Chez Venant

KABUYE

Cogebank

Place
de l'Unité
National

Kobil

Taxis to
Kimironko

Taxi park
(to Kimironko
& Kicikuro)

BCN

Sotra
Tours

LAC RWERU

Belvedere

Rwanda-French
Cultural Exchange

Prison

Police

SP

Atraco
Express

Union Trade
Centre

Kacyiru,
Airport,
Akagera NP

Taxi park
(to Nyamirambo)

L'EPARGNE

Taxi park
(to Remera)

LAC IHEMA

COMMERCE

Tam Tam snack bar
Ethiopian Airlines

Hotel le Garni
du Centre

La Galette

Blues Café

CO-OPERATIVE

Taxis to
Nyabugogo

BULERA

Rwandair Express
(Head office)

Place
de la
Constitution

RÉPUBLIQUE

Kobil

Kobil

Chez Robert

Market
(under
construction)

Nile Grill Café

Mosque

African Art Rwanda
(craftshop)

ORTPN

Gorillas
Hotel

Cluster of
Forex bureaux

Artiaganato (craftshop)

Bank
Populaire

BNR

La Mouette

Ibuhoro

Africarte (craftshop)

Hotel des
Mille Collines

Sebucom

Ecobank

Bizidanny Tours

Art Co-operative
(coopar)

Rwanda Ecotours

Ageseke
Craft Shop

Belle Vie
Guest House

New Modern
Guest house

Librairie Caritas

Pentecostal church

Arts Rwanda
(handicrafts)

Modis Craft Shop

Fine Dine

BCR

DE LA PAIX

Ma Colline

La Vita
Forex

Primate
Safaris

La Belvédère

Hotel Isimbi

Forex bureau

High Speed

La Sierra

L'ARMÉE

Salt & Pepper

BCK Bistro

Total

St Michael's
Cathedral

N

Bradt

Café le Nectar

BCK Bureau
(craft shop)

Rwanda
Wine Shop

MILLE

COLLINES

REVOLUTION

Radio
Rwanda

0   500m
0   500yds

Ice & Spice

Ikirezi Bookshop

TRAVAIL

CYAHAFI

Karibu

Sky

Nyamirambo

Kigali Serena

expect of any four- to five-star address in an African capital. In terms of quality of service and facilities, the **Serena** is undoubtedly the pick – indeed, it's the smartest hotel anywhere in Rwanda – and it is priced accordingly. The more established **Laico Umubano** doesn't lag far behind in quality, and is significantly cheaper, with a more convenient location for those whose business is centred on the administrative district of Kacyiru rather than the commercial city centre of Nyarugenge.

Kigali Serena Hotel [83 E6] (104 rooms)
0252 597100; m 078 8184500;
e reservations@serena.co.rw; www.serenahotels.com.
This top-notch 5-star hotel opened as the InterContinental in 2003 on the site of the former Diplomates, & it was bought & renamed by the Kenya-based Serena Group in 2007. It lies on the tree-lined Bd de la Révolution, a flat 10-min stroll from the city centre. The large carpeted rooms are the best on offer in Kigali, & come with king-size beds, DSTV, WiFi, mini-bar, tea/coffee-making facilities, safe, hairdryer, combined tub/shower, & 24hr room service. Other facilities include a 550-seat conference centre, gym, spa, several boutiques, top-class cuisine at 2 restaurants, 24hr business services & free air-conditioned airport shuttle. The compact green grounds are centred on a large swimming pool & the relaxed poolside Banana Jam Café. Credit cards are accepted. Extensive (& somewhat disruptive) renovations were under way in early 2009 but should be complete by the time you read this. *US$273/303 sgl/dbl; US$295/325 superior; US$400 upwards for suites; all rates inc a superb buffet b/fast.*

Laico Umubano Kigali [79 E3] (100 rooms)
0252 593500; e reservations.umubano@
laicohotels.com; www.laicohotels.com. Formerly part of the Novotel chain (& still frequently referred to by that name), this large 4-star hotel has a quiet & attractive location in well tended leafy 4ha gardens in the administrative quarter of Kacyiru, between central Kigali & the airport, & linked to both by plenty of transport, whether minibus-taxis or *taxi-voitures*. It's an efficient but relaxed place, very popular with local people for functions, & the personnel are friendly. The rooms are large & have good facilities, including king-size beds, DSTV, safe, fan, combined tub/shower & mini-bar, though the faded blue carpets make them look rather shabby & old-fashioned compared with the Serena. There's a post office nearby & banking facilities in the hotel, which also has a good restaurant & bar, swimming pool, mini-golf, tennis courts, conference facilities, fitness centre, WiFi & various boutiques. The patisserie in the foyer serves the best coffee in Rwanda, along with a tempting selection of freshly baked mini-pizzas, pastries & filled baguettes. Visa is accepted. *US$180/220 sgl/dbl; US$220-260 suite.*

UPMARKET (*US$130–180 double*) This header covers a wide variety of hotels offering high-quality accommodation at rates more likely to be affordable to non-business travellers. It's difficult to pick favourites, but the **Hotel le Garni du Centre** stands out as a smaller owner-managed hotel with a useful location and likeable character, while the blander multi-storey **Hotel des Mille Collines** is suited to those who place a high premium on in-house facilities.

Hotel des Mille Collines [86 D5] (112 rooms)
0252 576530/3; f 0252 576541;
e millecollines@millecollines.net;
www.millecollines.net. Taken over by a local company called Mikcor in 2005 & currently in the midst of major renovations, this Kigali institution was founded in 1973 & gained recent international fame as the subject of the film *Hotel Rwanda*. Despite its convenient location, a 5-min moderately sloping walk from the city centre, it lies in attractive grounds that offer some enjoyable urban birdwatching, dominated by a large swimming pool (under renovation at the time of writing) & a massive fig tree that looks as if it's been there since time began, but is only 40 years old. As things stand, the rooms, dominated by

floral fabrics, look rather timeworn & old-fashioned, but this is bound to change once the renovated wing reopens. In-room facilities include DSTV, mini-bar & WiFi access, & the hotel also has a good restaurant, a pricey bar, tennis court, conference & business facilities & various boutiques. Credit cards are accepted. The current room rates are lower than when the last edition was researched, making them very good value, but a substantial increase seems likely once renovations have been completed. *US$121/136 sgl/dbl; US$157 suite.*

Hotel le Garni du Centre [86 D4] (11 rooms)
0252 572652; e garni@rwanda1.com;
www.garni.co.rw. This commendable small hotel, tucked away down a side street near the better-known Hotel

des Milles Collines, is an unqualified gem. The quiet, comfortable rooms, which come with TV, free WiFi, phone & mini-bar, are simply but stylishly decorated, & overlook the garden & small swimming pool. Lunch & dinner are available by request; the Restaurant Chez Robert & Mille Collines are only a few mins' walk away. There's a log fire in the lounge for chilly evenings, & the Swiss owner-manager — who lives on the premises — is very obliging. It's deservedly popular so book in advance (this can be done online). *US$120/141 sgl/dbl for 1 night, inc a superb buffet b/fast, with discounts for longer stays.*

🏠 **Hotel Gorillas** [83 G4] (31 rooms) ☎ 0252 501717/8; m 078 8300473; e book@ hotelgorillas.com; www.gorillashotel.com. This smart, calm & efficient hotel, about 1km east of the city centre, has small but comfortable rooms & one of Kigali's most highly rated continental restaurants, with indoor & outdoor seating, & large draft beer on tap. Facilities include WiFi access in the restaurant & TV in all rooms, some of which have tubs & others showers, so state your preference if you have one. The downhill walk to the hotel from the centre of town is manageable but the upward walk into town is quite steep; however plenty of taxi-voitures ply the route & minibus-taxis run nearby. *US$110/130 standard sgl/dbl, US$120/140 deluxe rooms, inc b/fast.*

🏠 **Stipp Hotel Kiyovu** [83 F6] (50 rooms) ☎ 0252 500275/7; m 078 8305682; e stipphotels@rwanda1.com & management@stipphotelrwanda.com; www.stipphotelrwanda.com. The large new hotel has a suburban setting about 2km east of the city centre & excellent facilities including a large swimming pool, a continental restaurant with an Italian- & French-influenced menu, a health & fitness centre with gym, sauna & massage, & WiFi & DSTV in all rooms. The carpeted rooms are spacious & smartly decorated, with en-suite combined tub/shower, & suites have AC, sofa & safe. It's very

smart but a bit soulless. Visa, MasterCard & Amex accepted. *Rfr84,800/90,100 sgl/dbl B&B; Rfr106,000 dbl suite.*

🏠 **Top Tower Hotel** [79 E4] (48 rooms) ☎ 0252 592600; e info@toptowerhotel.com; www.toptowerhotel.com. This slick new 8-storey hotel in Kacyiru has made its name locally as the site of Kigali's first casino, which is on the 2nd floor & opens 20.00–05.00 daily. It also aspires to be one of the city's leading upmarket hotels, & the accommodation certainly impresses, consisting of spacious well-lit carpeted en-suite rooms with twin or king-size beds, large flat screen DSTV, writing desk, & combined tub/shower, as well as larger suites with a sitting area. It's also well placed for nightlife, with its in-house casino & bar with a view, & proximity to the lively Kigali Business Centre. That said, it suffers from something of a character deficit, lacks any outdoor seating or garden worth talking about, & the asking price seems steep for what it is. *US$150/170 sgl/dbl B&B; US$220–270 suite.*

🏠 **Hotel le Petit Prince Orange Court** [78 D2] (14 rooms) ☎ 0252 580181; m 078 8861479; e oracourts@yahoo.com. This smart new hotel in Kacyiru has sgl rooms with ¾ bed, netting, DSTV, fridge, balcony & tiled bathrooms, similar dbl rooms with king-size beds, & immense suites with a large sitting room, 2 TVs, a kitchen & a dining area. The ordinary rooms seem indifferent value, but the suites are pretty attractive at the price, especially for self-caterers. *US$80/120 sgl/dbl room; US$120/140 sgl/dbl suite.*

🏠 **Banana Guesthouse** [83 F4] (8 rooms) ☎ 0252 500154; m 078 8826777; e fbananaguesthouse@ yahoo.com. The small but stylish boutique guesthouse opened in Sep 2008 & offers very comfortable accommodation in small but nicely decorated en-suite rooms with terracotta tiles, DSTV, fan, writing desk & dbl beds. An excellent thatched restaurant is attached. It's a likeable set-up, but not exactly a bargain. *US$130–150 dbl, depending on room size.*

MODERATE (*US$60–120 double*) Cheaper and generally of lower quality than the upmarket options listed above, hotels listed in the moderate category mostly still cater routinely to bona fide tourists. That said, it's difficult to draw a clear qualitative line between some hotels listed as upmarket and the best of those in the moderate bracket, so we've settled on a cut-off price of US$120 for a standard double, which means that the best hotels in the moderate category – strikingly, **La Palisse** and the **Iris Guesthouse** – represent some of the best value in town.

🏠 **La Palisse Hotel** [79 H5] (79 rooms) m 078 8305505/8434390; e palisseho@yahoo.fr; www.hotel-lapalisse.com. Situated 2km from the airport along the

Akagera Rd, the new La Palisse is the least urban hotel in Kigali, set in sprawling wooded grounds that harbour a varied birdlife, & also host a swimming

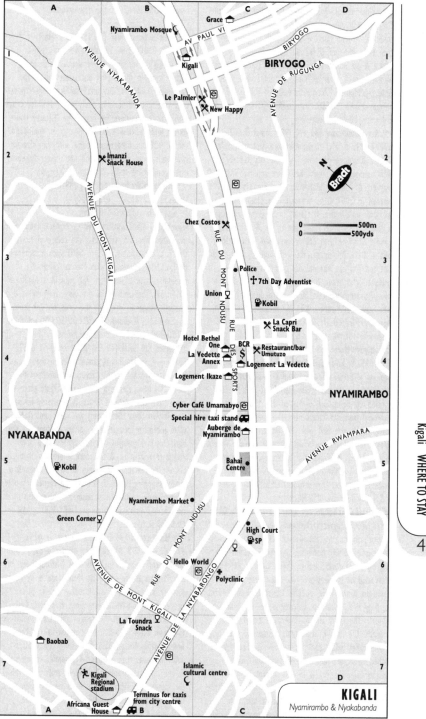

Grace

Nyamirambo Mosque

AV. PAUL VI

Kigali

BIRYOGO

BIRYOGO

AVENUE DE RUGUNGA

Le Palmier

New Happy

AVENUE NYAKABANDA

Imanzi
Snack House

N

Bradt

AVENUE DU MONT KIGALI

Chez Costos

0   500m
0   500yds

RUE DU MONT NDUSU

Police

† 7th Day Adventist

Union

Kobil

La Capri
Snack Bar

Hotel Bethel
One

BCR
$

Restaurant/bar
Umutuzo

La Vedette
Annex

Logement La Vedette

NYAMIRAMBO

Logement Ikaze

RUE DES SPORTS

Cyber Café Umamabyo

Special hire taxi stand

Auberge de
Nyamirambo

NYAKABANDA

Kobil

Bahai
Centre

AVENUE RWAMPARA

Nyamirambo Market

Green Corner

RUE DU MONT NDUSU

High Court

SP

Hello World

AVENUE DE MONT KIGALI

Polyclinic

AVENUE DE LA NYABARONGO

La Toundra
Snack

Baobab

Kigali
Regional
stadium

Islamic
cultural centre

Africana Guest
House

Terminus for taxis
from city centre

KIGALI
Nyamirambo & Nyakabanda

89

pool, children's playground, & outdoor bar & barbecue. The best accommodation is in spacious standalone rondawels (round huts), & comes with king-size or twin beds with net, DSTV, mini-bar, writing desk, phone & en-suite shower. The cheaper standard rooms in the main 4-storey building are similar but smaller & less outdoorsy. *Exceptional value at US$50/65 standard sgl/dbl, US$80 twin, US$60/70 sgl/dbl bungalow, US$100 suite.*

🏠 **Iris Guesthouse** [83 F4] (19 rooms) 📞 0252 501172/81; e iris1@rwanda1.com. Situated in Rue Député Kajangwe downhill from the city centre, this well-managed guesthouse has been popular with NGO workers & other regular visitors to Kigali since it opened in 2001, & as a result it is often full, so try to book in advance. It stands in pleasant grounds in a shady street away from the traffic, & the neat rooms all come with dbl or twin bed with netting, phone, DSTV, private terrace with seating, & en-suite hot tub. You can eat indoors or al fresco at the attached restaurant, which serves a varied selection of grills, sandwiches, salads & pasta dishes in the Rfr2,000–6,000 range. WiFi is available at Rfr3,000 per day. *Rfr40,000/50,000 sgl/dbl; Rfr80,000 2-bedroom apt; all rates B&B.*

🏠 **Kiyovu Motel** [83 G4] (6 rooms) m 078 8503695; e kiyomotel@yahoo.fr. Ideal for those seeking a personalised touch, this small guesthouse is essentially a converted homestead set in a pretty garden in the suburb of Kiyovu, 10–15mins' walk downhill from the city centre. The spacious rooms have a king-size bed with net, fan, fridge, DSTV, plenty of lockable cupboard space, & en-suite shower & tub. Lunch & dinner can be cooked by request, but several of the city's top eateries lie within easy walking distance. *Larger rooms US$80/90 sgl/dbl B&B, smaller ones US$70/80.*

🏠 **Hotel Chez Lando** [79 G5] (82 rooms) 📞 0252 582050; e contact@chezlando.com; www.chezlando.com. Founded in the 1980s, this well-established family hotel lies in green grounds just off the main road through the suburb of Remera, an easy taxi or minibus-taxi ride from town. The spacious rooms have satellite TV, international direct dialling, WiFi, a private balcony, & en-suite tub & shower. The Zoom nightclub/disco is popular at w/ends. The indoor La Fringale restaurant does a good buffet b/fast but can be slow & cheerless for other meals; for these the outdoor, downstairs restaurant is brisker & livelier. Several good restaurants & shops lie within easy walking distance of the hotel, as does a fast internet café & a sauna/massage centre. *US$60/70 sgl/dbl in the old*

building; US$90/120 in the new extension; US$100/130 bungalow.

🏠 **Romalo Guesthouse** [79 F5] (10 rooms) m 078 8301353; e romalo1@hotmail.com or kamazil@yahoo.com; www.romaloguesthouse.com. Tucked away in the sloping backstreets below the Parliament Buildings, this small family-run guesthouse is a little isolated so only really convenient for those with private transport. Set in a large 2-storey house with a wide balcony overlooking a green compound, the large, clean, tiled rooms come with king-size or twin beds, fridge, TV & en-suite hot shower. *It seems quite good value at Rfr25,000/40,000 sgl/dbl.*

🏠 **Alpha Palace Hotel** [79 H5] (38 rooms) 📞 0252 582981; m 078 8304947; e alphapalace@rwanda1.com; www.alpha-palace.com. Situated in Remera, about 1km from the airport & 4km from the centre of town, this is a comfortable, modern hotel with a swimming pool, a 24hr restaurant with French, African & oriental cuisine, a snack-bar for grills, & a nightclub on Fri/Sat. The tiled rooms are very comfortable & spacious, & come with king-size beds, DSTV, balcony & en-suite bath & shower. *Rfr38,000/50,000 sgl/dbl or Rfr80,000 suite, inc continental b/fast.*

🏠 **Ninzi Hill Hotel** [79 E3] (15 rooms) 📞 0252 587711–4; e ninzihill@yahoo.fr. Set in the administrative quarter of Kacyiru not far from the Laico Umubano, this is a quiet, comfortable place well away from city bustle, & it has a pleasantly laidback feel. The spacious tiled rooms are very comfortable, with queen-size bed, DSTV & balcony, & those at the back overlook gardens & greenery. There's a good mid-price restaurant, & the more interesting Shangai Chinese Restaurant, with swings for the children & a family shopping centre, is around the corner. It's only 10mins' walk to the Kigali Business Centre, with its cinema, bar-restaurant & shops. *US$70/90 sgl/dbl or US$120 semi-suite.*

🏠 **Hotel Okapi** [86 D2] (39 rooms) 📞 0252 571667; m 078 8359877; e okapihotel@ hotmail.com; www.okapi.co.rw. This 5-storey hotel on Rue Musima (between Bd de Nyabugogo & Av de la Justice) is a popular central choice in this price range, & it's convenient for public transport. Best pay extra for one of the comfortable tiled rooms in the main building, which have queen-size or twin beds, netting, fridge, DSTV & en-suite combination tub/shower, as their cheaper & gloomier counterparts in the downstairs annexe represent truly poor value for money. The restaurant offers a decent selection of Indian, Rwandan & continental dishes in the Rfr2,000–4,000 range, & vegetarians are well catered for. It also has a panoramic view across the Kigali landscape. *US$70/90 in the main building; US$50/70 in the annexe.*

🏠 **Impala Hotel** [86 C2] (20 rooms) ✆ 0252 571667; e impalahotelrw@yahoo.fr. Situated a few doors down from the Okapi, this 3-storey place opened in 2007 & can be recognised by the garish statues of gazelles (rather than impalas) that adorn the front parking. The tiled rooms have king-size or twin beds, DSTV, phone, en-suite hot shower & a nice little balcony offering great views on the non-street side. There is free computer usage at reception & WiFi for those with laptops. *Nothing special, but conveniently central & decent value at US$70/90 sgl/dbl or US$150 suite.*

🏠 **Hotel le Printemps** [79 H3] (20 rooms) ✆ 0252 582142; m 078 8307133;

e info@leprintempshotel.com; www.leprintempshotel.com. Set in pleasant gardens opposite Kimironko Taxi Park, this small suburban hotel offers a variety of spotlessly clean accommodation, ranging from tiled singles with ¾ bed, TV, phone & en-suite hot shower to larger suites & apartments. Facilities include an internet café, WiFi & restaurant. *Acceptable value at Rfr20,000/35,000 sgl/dbl to Rfr70,800 for an apartment.*

🏠 **Bloom Hotel** [79 H3] (26 rooms) m 078 8355014. Also situated in Kimironko, this likeable new hotel lies in large grassy gardens dotted with plastic tables & benches. The bright & spacious en-suite rooms have queen-size or twin beds, DSTV & combined tub/shower, & there is free internet access & WiFi. *Rfr25,000/35,000 sgl/dbl B&B.*

BUDGET The hotels listed below are more basic and in some cases a little seedy by comparison with those placed in higher brackets, but they will meet the requirements of reasonably undemanding cost-conscious travellers. Top choices include the central **Dream Inn Motel** and **Hotel Isimbi**, and the suburban **Hotel Baobab**, **Agasaro Motel** and **Hotel Hilltop**, while the **Grace Hotel** is worth a look for those seeking affordable longer-term accommodation.

🏠 **Dream Inn Motel** [86 D2] (17 rooms) ✆ 0252 503988/502477; e dreaminn7@yahoo.fr. This smart new hotel opposite the venerable Auberge la Caverne is arguably the pick of the budget options. The tiled rooms & dorms are clean, comfortable & modern-looking, with nets, TV, WiFi & fridge, & there are internet facilities on the ground floor, along with a good-value restaurant & bar. It's also very central, within walking distance of several restaurants, & plenty of public transport passes right by the door. Recommended. *Rfr15,000/20,000 sgl/dbl; Rfr30,000 suite; Rfr25,000 4-bed dorm.*

🏠 **Hotel Isimbi** [86 C6] (20 rooms) ✆ 0252 572578/81; e isimbi@hotmail.com or isimbi@rwanda1.com; www.hotelisimbi.co.rw. The most central hotel in this range, situated on Rue Kalisimbi just a few mins' walk from the market, post office & shops, this is an efficient, clean, business-type hotel. The unpretentious en-suite rooms with hot water are very good value (the back ones are quietest), & there's a non-smoking snack-bar & restaurant for main meals (up to around Rfr5,000), as well as room service. *US$30/35 sgl/dbl exc b/fast.*

🏠 **Presbyterian Auberge d'Accueil** [83 F4] (30 rooms) ✆ 0252 578915; e eprauberge@yahoo.fr. Close to the Gorillas Hotel, a 10-min walk downhill from the city centre, this church hostel is a clean, relaxing place with cheerful rooms, a good-value

dining room, & a computer room offering free internet access to residents. It can get busy with church guests so book in advance. Good monthly rates are available. *Rfr20,000/30,000 sgl/dbl B&B.*

🏠 **Hotel Baobab** [89 A7] (9 rooms) ✆ 0252 575633; e baobab@inbox.rw. This great place is full of character but some distance from the city centre, down in Nyakabanda suburb in the southwest near Mount Kigali & the Stade Régional de Kigali. If you have your own transport (or don't mind taking taxis), do consider it. The area is peaceful, with widespread views across the valley & to Mount Kigali, & the possibility of quite rural walks. The restaurant (mostly outdoor) has a good reputation locally. Rooms are en-suite with hot water, phone & TV. *Rfr20,000 dbl; b/fast not inc.*

🏠 **Agasaro Motel** [79 G5] (15 rooms) ✆ 0252 583293; m 078 8500182; e agasaromotel@yahoo.fr; www.agasaromotel.itgo.com. Set in leafy gardens a few mins from the Alpha Palace, on the opposite side of the same road, this small hotel offers good-value accommodation in simple but bright en-suite rooms with queen-size bed, TV & hot water. If you're arriving late by air & just want a straightforward night's sleep near the airport before moving on the next day, give it a try — reception is open 24hrs & it seems a well-cared-for place. *Rfr20,000 dbl B&B.*

Hotel Hilltop [79 H5] (38 rooms) m 078 8622522/8541409; e hilltopcountryclub@yahoo.fr. Conveniently located about 1km from the airport alongside the main road towards the city centre, this unpretentious & reasonably priced hotel lies in large green grounds with a good garden bar & restaurant. The rooms are simple but clean, with nets, DSTV, phone, lockable wardrobe & en-suite hot shower, & sgl (¾ bed), dbl & twin are all available. *Rfr15,000/20,000 sgl/dbl B&B.*

Hotel Bethel One [89 C4] (20 rooms) ☎ 0252 571404; m 078 8842261/8229833; e bethelhotelone@yahoo.co.uk. Situated in the lively suburb of Nyamirambo, south of the city centre, this new 3-storey hotel has comfortable accommodation in the form of singles (1 dbl bed) & doubles (2 ¾ beds) with net, DSTV & en-suite shower or tub. A restaurant & sauna/massage are attached. *Rfr20,000/25,000 sgl/dbl B&B; Rfr30,000 suite.*

Auberge Beau Séjour [89 G5] (19 rooms) ☎ 0252 582527; e beausejourhotel@yahoo.com. This homely lodge lies just off the main road to the airport & has a good reputation locally. The rooms are very pleasant, & come with TV & hot bath. Dinner is served by request. The owner supervises personally & takes a pride in the place – there are thoughtful touches like drinking-water in the bedrooms, & all rooms lead out to the well-cared-for garden. *Rfr20,000/30,000 sgl/dbl B&B.*

Sky Hotel [86 B7] (25 rooms) ☎ 0252 503882; e skyhotel1@yahoo.fr; www.skyhotelrw.net. This multi-storey hotel on Av de la Justice at the southern edge of the city centre has comfortable albeit rather tired-looking en-suite rooms with TV, queen-size bed, balcony, hot water, 24hr internet access, & a lovely view over the valley from the back. The room rates are very reasonable, as is the restaurant, & there's an affordable nightclub at w/ends, as well as a few other bars & restaurants within 5mins' walk, & plenty of public transport running straight past the door. However, it can also be very noisy when the nightclub is on song, & readers have expressed some concerns about security. *Rfr20,000/25,000 sgl/dbl B&B; Rfr40,000 suite.*

Auberge la Caverne [86 D1] (14 rooms) ☎ 0252 574549; m 078 8754110; e aubecav@yahoo.fr. This long-serving lodge receives mixed reports from travellers, but there's no doubt it is about the most affordable option in central Kigali. Spacious & mostly en-suite rooms with hot water are set away from the traffic around a central courtyard in Bd de Nyabugogo. Back windows have a good view out over the valley. The restaurant does a standard range of meals. It's a steepish but short walk up into the town centre, but the hotel lies along the main road used by minibus-taxis to/from the intercity Nyabugogo Taxi Park. *Rfr10,000/15,000 sgl/dbl.*

One Love Guesthouse [83 H4] (10 rooms) ☎ 0252 575412, 513154; e onelove@rwanda1.com. This welcoming place is run by an NGO (the Mulindi Japan One Love Project) that supports the disabled & works practically to help them – all profits are ploughed back into the NGO. There are simple but spacious twin rooms with balconies, & an OK restaurant serves a range of snacks/meals. It's a secure place, with good parking, in the valley between Kiyovu & Kacyiru, close to minibus-taxis. *The rate of Rfr20,000/25,000sgl/dbl is difficult to justify.*

City Valley Motel [82 B2] (19 rooms) m 078 3050775. Situated on Av des Poids Lourds a few hundred metres from Nyabugogo Taxi Park, this is a pleasant hotel with a decent-looking garden bar & restaurant attached, as well as a nightclub. The location, on a road used by heavy trucks, is potentially noisy, so best to ask for a room facing away from the traffic. The large rooms all have fan, net, TV & a balcony. *Rfr12,000 dbl using common showers; Rfr20,000 en-suite with hot water.*

Glory Guesthouse [82 D6] (8 rooms) m 078 8735341. Situated to the south of the city centre not far from the Sky Hotel, this prominently signposted place offers adequate but seriously overpriced accommodation in drab en-suite rooms. *US$50 dbl.*

Grace Hotel [89 C1] (60 rooms) m 078 85524101. This 4-storey building a block east of Nyamirambo Mosque has somehow contrived to deteriorate from being 'under construction' to 'looking rather rundown' in the space of an edition. That said, if the aura of abandonment doesn't put you off, the en-suite rooms with dbl bed, net, TV & phone are fair value at the daily rate. For those seeking no-frills longer term accommodation, the monthly rate looks to be a genuine bargain. There's no restaurant but it's well placed for eating out. *Rfr15,000 per night; Rfr80,000 per month.*

SHOESTRING (*below US$20 double*) The lodgings listed below are all on the basic side, with rooms using common showers or cold water only – or both! Most cater primarily to the local market, though they are also suitable for backpackers and other travellers on a rock bottom budget. Unusually for an African capital, there are very few real cheapies in the city centre. Instead, they're mostly clustered south of the city centre in the lively and characterful quarters of Nyamirambo and Nyakabanda, between Nyamirambo Mosque [89 B1] and the Kigali Regional Stadium [89 B7]. Probably the best choice in this category is the **Auberge de Nyamirambo**, which has the added advantage of being close to a cluster of similarly-priced options you could fall back on if it's full. To reach Nyamirambo and Nyakabanda on foot from the city centre, continue walking southwards (downhill) from the Sky Hotel [78 A4] about 15 minutes. Alternatively, a steady stream of minibus-taxis runs towards the stadium from the city centre (you can pick them up in front of the Sky Hotel or Kigali Prison), charging Rfr100 per person and passing within 100m of most of the listed hotels.

Centre National de Pastorale St Paul [83 E3] 0252 576371; m 078 8644468. Situated alongside the Eglise Saint-Famille about 200m east of the Place de l'Unité Nationale, this is the most central shoestring option in Kigali, offering decent accommodation in twin rooms with nets, electricity, a desk, towels & soap. The shared showers sometimes have hot water & the pretty gardens are very relaxing to sit in. Although it is a religious institution, people staying here can come home any time in the night. *Rfr6,000 twin with shared facilities, Rfr10,000 en-suite twin.*

Auberge de Nyamirambo [89 C5] (9 rooms) 0252 572879; m 078 8324079; e auberge.nyamirambo@yahoo.fr. This homely 2-storey lodge is one of the best-value options in Kigali, with clean en-suite rooms & a convenient location on the main road out of town towards the Islamic Centre. 6 rooms are in the main building, some en-suite & some using common showers, & the other 3, all en-suite, are in a little street-side annexe. The rooms in the annexe are marginally nicer but look slightly less secure, as you don't have to pass through reception to reach them. There's no in-house restaurant or bar, but there are 2 decent options within 500 metres. There's a good internet café next door. *All rooms Rfr7,000 dbl.*

Nyamirambo Women's Centre (2 rooms) m 078 8909063/8417790; e murungi.jackie@gmail.com or jmuhwezikaberuka02@gmail.com; www.nwc-kigali.org. Part of a self-help women's centre near Biryogo market that hosts the Nyamirambo day tours offered by New Dawn Associates, this offers accommodation in 2 en-suite dbl rooms & has a wireless internet

connection. *Rfr5,000 pp (or Rfr7,000 B&B). FB also offered.*

Logement La Vedette [89 C4] (14 rooms) 0252 573575. Situated around the corner from the Auberge de Nyamirambo, this unpretentious guesthouse, which now incorporates the former Home St Bernard, has comfortable large rooms, some en-suite, others with sinks & clean common showers – nothing special but fine at the price. *Rfr5,000–8,000 depending on room type & sgl/dbl occupancy.*

Kigali Hotel [89 B1] (16 rooms) 0252 571384/574542. Situated a block past the mosque on a one-way stretch of Av de la Justice, this is a good-value hotel, offering accommodation in small en-suite rooms with cold water, phone & TV. There's no restaurant or bar, so it's pretty quiet – if you can ignore the passing traffic & early morning mosque calls! There are plenty of other eateries & bars in the area. Minibus-taxis from central Kigali stop right opposite – ask for 'Chez Mayaka' or the mosque. *Rfr7,000/9,000/10,000 sgl/dbl/twin.*

Logement Ikaze [89 C4] (8 rooms) 0252 573655. The least inviting of the lodges in Nyamirambo, this place has spacious rooms, but the overall feel is rather dingy. *Rfr4,000 sgl using common shower; Rfr7,000 en-suite dbl.*

Episcopal Church Resthouse [78 B5] (13 rooms) m 078 8847592. Part of the St Etienne Church on Av Paul VI in Biryogo (aka Bilyogo) district some 500m east of Nyamirambo Mosque, this church guesthouse is not that convenient, though the clean but rundown rooms with nets are fair value. Inexpensive meals are available. *Rfr7,000 twin B&B or Rfr2,500 per dorm bed exc b/fast.*

WHERE TO EAT AND DRINK

For this section we remain indebted to André Verbruggen, the author of *Guide André: my 100 best Restaurants in Kigali*, last updated in 2008, who lived and worked in Kigali for well over a decade and contributed much of the content of this section for the third edition of this guidebook. What follows is a cross-section of the city's better eateries in various price categories, aimed mainly at short-term visitors, and organised according to suburb rather than price, with the top few picks for each area generally listed first. Most hotels offer acceptable food so, if you prefer to eat wherever you're staying, you won't necessarily miss out.

CITY CENTRE The city centre boasts an excellent selection of cafés, snack bars and coffee shops, of which the new **Café Torero** stands out for its funky and friendly atmosphere. More established favourites include **La Galette**, still arguably the best place in the city centre for a coffee, snack or filled baguette, though the upstart and somewhat pricier **Blues and Bourbon Café** provides it with some trendier competition. Formal restaurants are thin on the ground; the best options are in the upmarket **Serena** and **Mille Collines** hotels, but both are very pricey and there's a far more interesting selection of dedicated eateries within easy walking distance in Kiyovu, the suburb sloping eastward from the city centre.

✗ **Café Torero** [86 D2] m 078 8856637; e torerocafe@gmail.com; www.torerocafe.com; ⏰ 09.00–24.00 daily. The trendiest rendezvous in downtown Kigali is this 'artistic café', tucked away unsignposted in a basement on Av de la Justice (look out for a green Heineken, next to a dry cleaners). The ambience is casual, almost Bohemian, with orange & green walls lined with bookshelves, tables stacked with imported magazines, WiFi access, & regular theatre & music performances, art exhibitions, movie screenings, amateur photo contests & other cultural activities. The imaginative nachos-style menu, dominated by vegetarian dishes, is emphatically not aimed at the ravenous, but it's all very tasty & decent value at around Rfr2,500–3,500. Coffee & the usual alcoholic drinks are served. However, we heard unconfirmed rumours it had closed shortly before going to press.
✗ **La Galette** [86 A4] ☎ 0252 575434; ⏰ 07.30–19.30 Mon-Sat, 07.30–14.30 Sun. To combine sustenance with shopping, try the snack-bar attached to this excellent supermarket at the bottom of Rue du Marché just after it turns sharply to join Rue de l'Epargne. This is a popular meeting place for ex-pats & aid workers, & there are notice boards listing various items (cars, dogs, homes, motorbikes, TVs, garden hoses...) wanted or for sale. The supermarket stocks a good selection of fresh & imported groceries; the snack-bar serves fresh filled baguettes for Rfr700–850, salads in the Rfr1,200–2,400 range, light meals for Rfr2,000–3,000 & draft beer, as well as pastries (including croissants) & good coffee – b/fast nirvana!
✗ **La Sierra** [86 D6] ☎ 0252 575486; ⏰ from 07.30. Founded in 1968, this is a more low-key & central equivalent to La Galette, combining a good supermarket with a pleasant terrace snack-bar on Bd

de la Révolution. At other times, burgers, sandwiches & light meals are mostly in the Rfr1,200–2,500 range; it also serves samosas, burritos, pancakes & waffles, & is a good spot for b/fast. Somewhat pricier is the Indian-influenced lunchtime buffet, which costs Rfr6,500 & runs over 12.00–14.30.
✗ **Ice & Spice** [86 B7] ☎ 0252 570608; ⏰ 10.30–13.30 & 18.00–22.30 daily except Tue. This little Indian restaurant in Rue du Lac Bulera is one of the more interesting options in the city centre, & all dishes on the extensive menu are available mild, medium or hot. A good selection of vegetarian mains are mostly around Rfr2,800, while meat & fish dishes cost Rfr4,000–6,000 (add Rfr1,800 for plain rice or Rfr400–800 for Indian bread. The 'ice' part means just that – a colourful range of ices. The English-speaking staff is attentive & service is relatively quick.
✗ **Blues Café** [86 D4] m 078 8323666; e bluescafe@gmail.com; ⏰ 07.00–20.00 daily. Situated next to the Union Trade Centre, this trendy little coffee shop has WiFi access & an adjoining internet café. The coffee, as is so often the case in Rwanda, can be disappointing, but it also serves a selection of sandwiches & salads for around Rfr2,000 & light meals for Rfr3,500.
✗ **Café Bourbon** [86 D4] ☎ 0252 505307; ⏰ 08.00–19.00 daily. The most central branch of this popular coffee chain is in the central Union Trade Centre. The coffee is pretty good (though it doesn't beat the coffee shop in the lobby of the Laico Umubano Hotel) & a fair selection of snacks & sandwiches are available, mostly around Rfr1,000–2,000. It has free WiFi access. There are smaller branches in the suburban MTN Centre, & at the airport.

✗ **Panorama Restaurant** [86 D5] ☎ 0252 576530; ⌚ 06.00–10.30 (b/fast) & 19.00–23.00 (dinner). On the top floor of the Hotel des Mille Collines, this exclusive place has an appropriately panoramic view over the city, & background music is supplied by a pianist & saxophonist. Official dinners & banquets are held here & there are regular 'themed evenings'. The 'suggestion of the day' plus dessert is around Rfr10,000 but it's easy to spend more. The wine list is comprehensive.

✗ **Diplomat Restaurant** [83 E6] ☎ 0252 597100. This highly rated restaurant in the Serena Hotel serves a good selection of mostly continental-style dishes at similar prices to the above. It was closed during renovations in early 2009 but should have reopened by the time you read this.

✗ **La Belvédère** [86 D6] m 078 8562226; ⌚ for lunch & dinner daily. Situated on Bd de la Révolution, this is perhaps the only reasonably smart restaurant in the city centre, & one of the few central eateries in any category to open for lunch & dinner 7 days a week. Continental dishes & grills are in the Rfr5,000–7,000 range.

✗ **Karibu Restaurant** [86 C7] ☎ 0252 501793; ⌚ for b/fast & lunch. At the edge of the city centre on Av de la Paix, this is a shady place to stop for a cool drink or snack if you're in central Kigali, & it also has a convenient & varied lunchtime buffet; this is deservedly popular, so try to get there before 13.00 when it tends to fill up with business people. It closes in the evening.

✗ **Fine Dine** [86 D5] ☎ 0252 501564. Situated on Bd de la Révolution, this is a good spot for a buffet lunch in the city centre – just Rfr1,500 for a plateful including a small serving of meat.

✗ **Le Palmier** [89 C1] One of several good local eateries dotted along the one-way roads around Nyamirambo Mosque – also worth trying, should you be staying in this area, are the New Happy Restaurant & Chez Costos, both of which serve buffets & meals for around Rfr1,500.

✗ **Chez Venant** [86 D3] ⌚ daily from lunchtime until late. This is an agreeable & inexpensive local drinking hole with outdoor seating on Av de la Justice, about 100m south of Torero Café.

KIYOVU This leafy suburb on the eastern verge of the city centre is blessed with a fine selection of top-quality restaurants, a fortunate situation given that many of the city's most popular tourist hotels also lie in the area. Coming from the city centre, the closest restaurant is the rather unremarkable Chez Robert, but if you are prepared to walk a bit further – or to take a taxi – top recommendations are **Heaven Restaurant** and **Republika Lounge** for ambience, **Khana Khäzana** and **Shanghai Chinese** for exotic variety, and **Dolce** and **Iris** for affordability.

✗ **Heaven Restaurant & Bar** [83 F4] ☎ 0252 500235; m 078 8486581; e heavenrwanda@gmail.com; www.heavenrwanda.com; ⌚ 11.00–14.00 & 18.00–22.30 daily. This popular new restaurant in Kiyovu consists of a massive wooden deck scattered with wooden tables & chairs, set below a cane roof & offering good views over suburban Kigali. The main restaurant has a pleasant al fresco ambience, while the bar at the back is a good place to watch major sporting events on large-screen DSTV. It also shows recent movies at 18.30 & 20.30 on Sat nights. The continental fusion cuisine, created by a California-trained chef, is mostly in the Rfr6,000–8,000 range, but a bar menu has burgers & other light meals for Rfr2,000–3,500. Check the website for special events.

✗ **Republika Lounge** [83 F6] ☎ 0252 504051; m 078 8303030; ⌚ 17.00–late Mon–Sat. Tucked away along a dirt side road branching downhill from Av des Grand Lacs about 15mins' walk from the city centre, this vies with Café Torero as the most good-looking eatery in Kigali, boasting earthy adobe architecture that makes it blissfully cool inside on a humid day. The funky décor contrasts attractively with the more stolid appearance of most other Kigali restaurants, & there's a large wooden deck with views across to a eucalyptus-clad hill. Reliably busy even on weekday nights, it serves a selection of grills & brochettes in the Rfr4,000–6,000 range. There's a good handicraft shop under the restaurant.

✗ **Khana Khäzana Restaurant** [83 F4] m 078 8772087; e khazanarwanda@yahoo.com; ⌚ 12.00–15.00 & 18.00–23.00 daily. Reopened in April 2009 after a period of closure, this superb Indian restaurant is situated on Kajangwe Av, 10mins' walk downhill from the Mille Collines & the city centre. Most main courses are in the Rfr5,000–7,000 range & the Indian bread is excellent.

✗ **Shokola Café** [83 E4] m 078 8350265/8301293; e soniant@googlemail.com; ⌚ lunch & dinner daily. The newest eatery in Kigali has an

Arabian Nights atmosphere & serves a refreshing pan-African cuisine including filled pita bread, Moroccan tagines, freshly made hummus, salads, fresh fruit smoothies & premium Rwandan coffee & tea. Mains are in the Rfr4,500–5,500 range, & it is situated on Rue de Ntaruka just before the vehicle entrance to Chez Robert.

✕ **Iris Restaurant** [83 F4] ☎ 0252 501172; ⏰ 07.00–21.00 daily. Situated in the same part of town as the Indian Khāzana, the terrace restaurant at this popular guesthouse has a giddying choice of (mainly) continental dishes & grills. The superb pasta dishes are mostly around Rfr3,000, while salads & sandwiches cost Rfr2,000–3,500 & more substantial meat & fish dishes are in the Rfr4,500–6,000 range.

✕ **Shanghai Chinese Restaurant** [83 F4] m 078 8599995; ⏰ 11.00–20.00 daily. Not to be confused with its namesake in Kacyiru spelt Shangai, this pleasant garden restaurant is about 10mins' walk from the city centre, a couple of gates down from the Iris Guesthouse. The superb & inexpensive soups are a meal in themselves, while the pick of the other dishes are the sizzler plates of meat or chicken. Main dishes are Rfr4,000–5,000, soups are cheaper.

✕ **Dolce Bar-Resto-Pizzeria** [83 F4] m 078 8625108; ⏰ 12.00–24.00 daily. Unsignposted & hidden behind a wall, this easily missed bar & eatery stands next to the La Bonne Source Supermarket on Rue Député Kayuku, close to several popular hotels. If you're not looking for something fancy, it's a good spot for an inexpensive outdoor beer, & it also serves a good selection of grills & meals in the Rfr4,000–5,000 range, most notably pizzas, & salads in the Rfr1,500–2,000 range.

✕ **Restaurant Le Dos Argenté** [83 G4] ☎ 0252 501717; ⏰ 07.00–22.00 (bar stays open late). On the ground floor of the Hotel Gorillas, this smaller restaurant – whose name translates as silverback – is a member of the Chaîne des Rôtisseurs & the

food usually lives up to its reputation. Main dishes (French cuisine) go up to around Rfr10,000, desserts to Rfr4,000. There's indoor & outdoor seating, draft beer, & a good wine list. Service is relaxed.

✕ **Banana Restaurant** [83 F4] ☎ 0252 500154; m 078 8826777; ⏰ daily for dinner. Situated in the grounds of the eponymous guesthouse, this small restaurant is set on an open-sided wooden platform with thatch roof & attractive ethnic décor. The highly rated cuisine has a strong French influence, with most dishes falling in the Rfr5,000–10,000 range, & there's a good wine list.

✕ **Restaurant Chez Robert** [83 E4] ☎ 0252 501305; ⏰ for lunch & dinner daily. Situated on Av de la République, on the eastern border of the city centre opposite Hotel des Mille Collines, this is easily distinguished by the 2 elephantine statues marking its walk-in entrance (the drive-in entrance is actually a block east, on Rue de Ntaruka). It serves a good selection of continental dishes for around Rfr8,000, & brochettes, pasta & other light meals from Rfr4,000 upwards. You can eat indoors or in a large garden with several niches.

✕ **New Cactus Restaurant** [83 F5] ☎ 0252 572572; m 078 8678798; ⏰ 12.00–14.00 & 18.00–22.30 daily. Situated in Rue Député Kayuku (near the Hotel Gorillas) this is a super place, particularly for pizza-lovers – it's very welcoming, with a pleasant outdoor terrace giving a beautiful view over Kigali, good food (French cuisine as well as pizzas), & free WiFi access. Steak & fish main dishes up to Rfr7,000. There's also a take-away pizza service – phone beforehand & it'll be ready for you to collect.

✕ **Kioske Alimentation** [83 F4] Situated opposite the Banana Guesthouse, this welcoming but no-frills local drinking hole serves the cheapest drinks in Kiyovu – around Rfr800 for a large Primus, which is a third of the price charged by most of the restaurants & hotels in this posh suburb.

KIMIHURURA A variety of new restaurants has mushroomed in this sedate residential suburb to the east of Kiyovu, but many are quite difficult to find and somewhat isolated unless you have a private vehicle or take a taxi. There are no duds listed below, but the lunchtime buffet at **Afrika Bite** stands out for those wanting to sample Rwandan food at its finest, while **Papyrus Lounge** has a likeable chilled atmosphere, good honest Italian grub, and a 'last man standing' door policy conducive to partying into the wee hours.

✕ **Afrika Bite** [78 D3] m 078 8685184; ⏰ 12.00–15.00 daily except Sun & 18.00–22.30 daily except Wed & Sun. Widely regarded as the city's leading purveyor of Rwandan cuisine, this

homely restaurant on a side road in Kimihurura has indoor & outdoor garden seating & oodles of character. Aside from a legendary lunchtime buffet costing Rfr3,000, it serves a good selection of à la carte dishes in the Rfr2,500–3,500 range in the evening.

✘ **Papyrus Lounge** [78 D3] m 078 8220671; ⏰ food 11.00–24.00 daily. Tucked away in suburban Kimihurura, this likeable terrace restaurant serves a varied selection of mostly Italian dishes – salads Rfr1,700–4,100, pasta dishes Rfr3,000–5,000, pizzas Rfr4,500–5,500, meat & fish Rfr4,000–7,000 – & the owners make their own yoghurts & cheeses from a dairy farm. Kitchen hours are 11.00–24.00, but the bar stays open until the last straggler decides to go home, making it something of a hotspot at w/ends.

✘ **Comme Chez Moi** [78 D3] m 078 8454162; ⏰ lunch & dinner. As poorly signposted as it is highly rated, this small restaurant lies in a lush suburban garden in Kimihurura, along a dirt road branching south opposite the Papyrus Lounge. It specialises in Thai cuisine, but there's also an extensive selection of French dishes, & great desserts. Mains cost around Rfr5,000–7,000.

✘ **Restaurant Hellenique** ☎ 0252 583731; ⏰ lunch & dinner. This is tucked away in a residential part of Kimihurura not far from the Cadillac Club, in the valley between Kiyovu & Kacyiru – taxi-drivers will know it & it's signposted. The food is Greek/International with some unusual dishes & a good wine-list, the ambience is relaxed & there's a pleasant terrace. Service is attentive but may be slow. Government VIPs & ambassadors come here. Mains around Rfr5,000 upwards.

✘ **Flamingo Chinese Restaurant** [78 D4] ☎ 0252 501944; m 078 8300333; ⏰ lunch & dinner Mon–Sat. Generally rated as the best Chinese in Kigali, but also perhaps the priciest, this veteran restaurant is now installed in a suburban property in Kimihurura, diagonally opposite Afrika Bite. Mains are in the Rfr5,000–7,000 range.

✘ **L'Atelier** Set in a suburban house in Kimihurura, within walking distance of the Papyrus Lounge, this top-notch French restaurant has an intimate setting & sumptuous cuisine – try the Steak au Roquefort! There's a stock of games, so you'll often find people playing scrabble or chess as they wait for their food.

KACYIRU & REMERA
The restaurants here are a bit of a mixed bag, but if you are looking for somewhere for a sit-down meal, you can't go far wrong with the poolside **Côte Jardin** at the Laico Umubano Hotel. Elsewhere, **O Sole Luna** and **Shangai Restaurant** serve good Italian and Chinese respectively, while more adventurous palates are pointed to the Ethiopian fare at the **Lalibela**.

✘ **Côté Jardin Restaurant** [79 E3] ☎ 0252 593500; ⏰ 07.00–22.00 daily. The poolside restaurant at the Laico Umubano Kigali has a good & varied midday & evening buffet (sizzling main dishes, salads, calorific desserts...) as well as the type of general menu you'd expect from a hotel of this standard & special menus for functions or celebrations. Service is attentive & the atmosphere is relaxed. It's deservedly one of Kigali's most popular meeting places, & the coffee shop in the lobby of the same hotel is truly excellent.

✘ **O Sole Luna** [79 G4] ☎ 0252 583062; ⏰ lunch & dinner. Slightly cheaper than most upmarket eateries in Kigali, out along the airport road at the edge of Remera, this long-serving Italian restaurant has a good range of pizzas & pasta, well presented – & a beautiful view over the city from its terraces. Service is friendly & reasonably brisk.

✘ **Lalibela Ethiopia Restaurant** [79 G4] m 078 8505293; e nyala_trad@yahoo.com; ⏰ 12.00–23.30 daily. Recently relocated to Remera, along the road running north from Chez Lando, this singular eatery supplements the usual Rwandan selection of brochettes & grills with spicy Ethiopian *wat* stews, best eaten with that country's trademark staple of pancake-on-steroids *injera*. Mains cost around Rfr4,000.

✘ **Shangai Restaurant** [79 E3] m 078 8503111; ⏰ lunch & dinner. Near the Ninzi Hill Hotel & within walking distance of the Laico Umubano, this popular Chinese restaurant is friendly & good value; if you have children you can let them loose on the swings & other play equipment. The name board had vanished at the time of writing but it's easy to spot.

✘ **Planet Cinéma** [79 E4] Situated in the Kigali Business Centre or KBC &, you've guessed it, right at the door of Kigali's cinema, this café-bar serves sandwiches, snacks, salads etc, so is a convenient place to get food if you're going to a movie.

✘ **Havana Club** [79 E3] ☎ 0252 510440/1. Between the Laico Umubano & Ninzi Hill, this rather misleadingly named place isn't the sleazy cigar-stained bar you might expect, but a bright & modern pizzeria & general restaurant, serving good takeaways as well as sit-down meals.

4

✕ **Le Banjo Resto-Bar** [79 G4] This is a smart local eatery in Remera, diagonally opposite the nearby Hotel Chez Lando, & it serves a good & inexpensive African buffet.

✕ **Grill & BBQ Corner** [79 E3] m 078 3115554/ 5071648; e info@grillbbqcorner.com; www.grillbbqcorner.com; ⏲ 08.00–22.00 Sun–Thu, 08.00–17.00 Fri & 18.00–22.00 Sat. This new restaurant, tucked away around the corner from the Ninzi Hill Hotel, has indoor & outdoor seating, serves a huge variety of western, Asian & African dishes, & has facilities for online ordering & delivery.

NIGHTLIFE

For a capital city, Kigali isn't over-rich in nightclubs and discos. The biggest and best known is the **New Cadillac** [83 H4] (*0252 511622*) in Kimihurura, of which there are two parts: one for VIPs and the smart set and one for more relaxed and younger people. The VIP part, which charges a rather steep entrance fee, consists of a good Thai restaurant, piano bar, live band and disco, and opens 11.00–15.00 and 18.00–midnight Tuesday to Sunday. Drinks aren't exorbitant. If a group of visitors wants traditional music or dancers, this can be arranged. For young people, the New Cadillac Night Club functions Wednesday to Sunday, 21.00 to dawn.

Smaller than the New Cadillac but the same price is the smart **Planète Club** [79 E4] (m *078 8683043*) in the Kigali Business Centre. Hotel nightclubs are at the **Hotel Chez Lando** [79 G5] and the **Sky Hotel** [86 B7]. Finally, the **Alpha Palace Hotel** [79 H5] also has one on Fridays/Saturdays.

For a more chilled outdoor drink, the rather oddly named **Executive Carwash** [83 H5] around the corner from the New Cadillac is recommended, as is the bar at the **Papyrus Lounge** [78 D3], a few hundred metres uphill. A popular out-of-town drinking hole is the **Green Corner Bar**, a lofty outdoor set-up in Nyakabanda offering cheap chilled beers and great views towards Mount Kigali. In Kiyovu, trendier drinking spots include **Republika Lounge** [83 F6] and **Heaven** [83 F4], the latter being a good spot for live sporting action on large-screen TV, while the more down-to-earth **Kioske Alimentation** [83 F4] opposite the Banana Guesthouse is a great place to enjoy a few cheap beers in company with local Rwandans. In the city centre, **La Mouette** [86 B5] (*078 8514365/8421450*) on Rue du Lac Bulera has occasional live music at weekends.

ARTS AND ENTERTAINMENT

CINEMA The **Planet Cinema** [79 E4] is in the Kigali Business Centre in Avenue du Lac Muhazi. There are afternoon performances and evening performances of international movies (often in English with French sub-titles), children's performances, special screenings, etc. Tickets are inexpensive and with the Planet Cinéma snack-bar and Planète Club in the same block, a long and full evening of entertainment is possible! Saturday night is movie night at **Heaven** [83 F4] (see *Where to eat* page 95), which is also a good place to catch live sporting events on a giant screen satellite TV. The rather more downmarket **cinema** opposite the Kigali Hotel [89 B1] in Nyamirambo shows somewhat dated Western films as well as screening live international and Premiership football fixtures.

MUSIC AND DANCE Performances of traditional dancing and music take place from time to time in various venues around the city – these are publicised on local radio and in the local press. ORTPN should also have a list. One worth trying is the **RwaMakondera** (Rwandan Horns) Children's Dance Troupe, which was formed by **Ivuka Arts Studios** [79 E3] (see page 103) founded by Collin Sekajugo to provide skills, income and a sense of belonging to orphans and other children from disadvantaged backgrounds.

In 1999, the Rotary Club of Kigali-Virunga decided to build a public library, its first major project as a chartered Rotary Club, to counter the serious shortage of books in Rwanda and the consequent lack of a culture of reading. Also, a key path to ending violence and preventing another genocide is to make knowledge and ideas – from books – freely available to all Rwandans, regardless of social and economic status.

Rwanda's first public library is not just for adults. Its young people's section will play a major role in opening children's minds, helping to transport them from the commonplace to the extraordinary. Finally, it will help to build a sense of community, and will preserve the past, with special collections on subjects such as Rwandan history and literature.

This is no daydream! The library has received generous financial support both from overseas and from local Rwandan companies. It is supported by the American Friends of the Kigali Public Library (AFKPL) – via whom the international literary association, PEN, pledged US$45,000 in April 2002. The Government of Rwanda has pledged US$500,000 of which US$100,000 was released in July 2003. Construction work started on the foundations in 2002, but later stalled through lack of funds.

However, by 2009 the Kigali Public Library campaign had received donations and pledges of approximately US$2 million from individuals, businesses and corporations, foundations, governments, and intergovernmental organizations. The library will open in the near future, but an additional $500,000 will be necessary to ensure its long-term sustainability. So funds are still urgently needed and fundraising has taken place at all levels, in and outside Rwanda, from large companies to small schools and individuals. Secondhand book sales (another 'first' for Kigali) have been held.

In 2002, a young Rwandan boy named Sam called into the office of the Chairman of the Kigali Public Library Project – who initially thought he had come to ask for school fees, a common practice among Rwanda's youth who struggle every year to find the necessary amount. However, what Sam wanted was to donate 200 Rwandan francs (less than 50 US cents, but for him a large sum). He'd discovered the project through one of the secondhand book sales, and wanted to contribute in order to make sure the library would be completed.

By the time you read this, the buildings should be coming on well. Then it will be just a matter of time before they can be used and filled with books, so that Sam and his friends can read to their hearts' content.

To check out the progress of the library, or make a donation, call ✆ 0252 514338 or m 078 8312888, or visit www.kigalilibrary.org.

The **Centre Culturel d'Echanges Franco-Rwandaises** [86 D4] near the Hotel des Mille Collines used to have a small theatre that presented theatre, films, music, dance and other cultural events, but it is closed at the time of writing. The best bet for this sort of thing now is **Café Torero** [86 D2] (see *Where to eat*, page 94).

LIBRARIES Depending on how soon you visit, Kigali may have its own, brand-new, specially designed public library, built with funds raised both nationally and internationally in an initiative by the Rotary Club of Kigali-Virunga. See above for more details.

SPORT

Kigali caters for both golfers and cricketers! For **cricket**, see the box on page 101. The 18-hole **Nyarutarama Golf Club** [79 F2] (m *078 8524619; www.rwanda-golf.com*) is in an attractively green corner of northeastern Kigali and non-members are welcome to play for a reasonable fee. Nearby is the **Nyarutarama Tennis Club** [79 F3] (❨ *0252 587009;* e *cnorw@rwanda1.com*). The more central **Cercle Sportif** [83 G7] in Lower Kiyovu has facilities for tennis, table tennis, basketball, volleyball, badminton, darts, swimming, etc. Also check out the current **football** fixtures – enthusiast Chris Frean explains how:

> Going to a football match in Kigali is simple as long as you know that it's on. Matches generally take place at the Amahoro Stadium on Sunday afternoons at 4pm, sometimes preceded by each side's reserves' match on the same pitch. Fixtures are generally advertised in the New Times during the week beforehand. It is, however, pretty simple to find out if something is about to happen at Amahoro. Just go up to Kisimenti crossroads – the one by Chez Lando – and check the activity. If you see matatus with fans, and police on the crossroads holding up ordinary traffic for dignitaries, then something is on. Domestically the Kigali teams APR, Atraco and Rayon dominate. You can tell by the colours who is playing. Black and white means APR; blue and white Rayon; green and white Kiyovu.
>
> Inside the ground, you shouldn't expect anything like a programme or team info; although with the Rwanda Premier League now sponsored by the brewer Primus, you can actually buy a drink in the ground. For the World Cup qualifiers, tents were set up outside the stands, and a barbeque too.
>
> International match tickets are easy enough to come by too, and priced towards the local market, so not expensive, especially for the terraces. Just go up to the main Amahoro stadium in the hours before kick-off. But beware: you're not allowed to take a mobile phone into the main stand for an international. For one Angola match, I had to submit to a metal detector and was told my phone was not allowed. This, the police later told me, was because people might use phones in the ground to contact hooligans outside and cause problems. However, this policy is only in place when the President is likely to attend a match.

There's more on football (and rugby) in *Chapter 1*, pages 31–2.

SHOPPING

The biggest development in Kigali shopping-wise is the spanking new **Union Trade Centre (UTC)** [86 D4], which dominates the eastern side of Boulevard de la Révolution between Place de l'Unité Nationale and Place de la Constitution. The centrepiece of this two-storey mall is an immense 24-hour branch of the Kenyan Nakumatt supermarket chain, by far the best stocked shop of its type in Kigali (urban legend has it that more than one expatriate wept for joy outside when it opened, a story which, even if untrue, demonstrates the supermarket's impact on resident shoppers). In addition to a wide range of imported goods and electrical and other household items, the supermarket has an excellent bakery (freshly baked bread, croissants and other pastries) and meat-and-cheese counter. Sometimes referred to as the Nakumatt Centre, the UTC also hosts several fast-food outlets, a Bourbon Café for fresh coffee and light meals, an efficient forex bureau, a fast internet cafe, an MTN shop, the Rwandair Express booking office, several boutique shops, and a branch of Access Bank where you can draw currency against a Visa or MasterCard. The public toilets here are very clean and a nominal fee is charged to use them.

Otherwise, most of the shops that are of interest to tourists lie within a rough rectangle formed by Boulevard de la Révolution, Avenue du Commerce,

Cricket continues to flourish in Kigali. Matches of 40 overs a side are played on Sundays almost throughout the year, several tournaments have been held, and the national side participates in International Cricket Council competitions. Pitch availability, early sunsets, the superiority of ball over bat and the weather all combine to mean that 20/20 has often been the best format – long before it caught on elsewhere.

Although the country only really seems to have shifted to a pro-English bent since 1994, cricket has been played for several years in Rwanda. In Butare, the University boys, under Professor Singh, had been playing for quite some time before then. There was a match on a volcanic field in Gisenyi in the 1990s, which finally received appropriate recognition in *Wisden Cricketers' Almanack 2004*. Further reports have been recorded in the *Cricket Round the World* sections of *Wisden*.

By 2003 the RCA managed to get the ground at the Ecole Technique Officielle in the Kicukiro district of Kigali into a good enough condition for regular matches. The ground is basically the school's sports field, so is not exclusive to the Rwanda Cricket Association. Games are subject to regular interruptions, some of the more unusual having been unannounced athletics meetings and the 2004 filming of the BBC feature film *Shooting Dogs*.

Early attempts to bring in kit proved a headache, as Lillywhites has yet to open a branch in Kigali. The Rwanda Revenue Authority, anxious to squeeze whatever they could from persons perceived to have money to burn, decided that a rubber matting pitch supplied free of charge by the ICC was in fact a carpet, and should be subject to duty. Months of wrangling and negotiation failed to convince them. We could only assume a member of RRA staff wanted it to carpet her home.

After achieving ICC membership, Rwanda came 7th in the African Affiliates Championships in 2004 and in 2006 came 6th in Division Three of the African region of the ICC World Cricket League. In 2009, the RCA entered an U13 team in a regional ICC tournament in Uganda. In the event the team could not travel, but it's the desire that matters.

Avenue des Mille Collines and Rue de l'Epargne. In **Boulevard de la Révolution**, south of the UTC, the large Banque Commerciale du Rwanda is on the eastern side [86 D5], almost on Place de l'Indépendance (where the fountain is). Looking across the road from the bank you have, among other small shops/offices, the Agaseke handicrafts kiosk [86 D5], a small supermarket, the Belvedere Restaurant [86 D6], internet facilities, a 24-hour pharmacy, an MTN phone shop, the Sierra Café and Supermarket [86 D6], and a filling station [86 D6].

Turn right at the petrol station into Avenue des Mille Collines, then right again into **Avenue de la Paix**. On the opposite side of Avenue de la Paix before it reaches Avenue du Commerce you have (not necessarily in order) a florist, an excellent wine shop [86 C6], a forex bureau [86 C6], various clothing and stationery shops, phone/internet facilities, and a few tour operators and travel agents. The very good Ikirezi Bookshop [86 C7] is also on Avenue de la Paix, but just south of Avenue des Mille Collines

The first road running west from here is **Avenue du Commerce**, where the Librairie Caritas [86 C5] stands a little way down on the left. The next junction is with **Rue de l'Epargne**, which is the site of the main post office [86 C5], a good internet café, and a cluster of excellent handicraft shops, including Africarte [86 C5] and Artiaganato [86 C5]. Another block down Rue de l'Epargne you'll find

Kigali's main cluster of forex bureaux [86 B5], most of which will change cash in any hard currency. Further west is the central market [86 B4], which has been closed for redevelopment for several years now, and La Galette [86 A4], which hosts the city's best delicatessen and butchery, as well as a great café serving fresh coffee, filled baguettes and light meals – a good place to refuel after a morning's shopping.

The biggest suburban mall in Kigali is the **MTN Centre** [79 G3] on the Nyarutarama Road about 1km north of its junction with Boulevard de l'Umuganda. Though not as well equipped as the UTC, it has a good bookshop, a butcher and delicatessen affiliated to La Galette in the city centre (and of a similar quality), a branch of Bourbon Café, an MTN Shop, and a sports bar.

Be aware that plastic bags have been banned in Rwanda since 2005, following a city clean-up in which almost a million old bags or remnants were discovered. This ban is strictly enforced, so it's best to carry your own (non-plastic!) shopping bag if you plan to make many purchases.

HANDICRAFTS AND ART A wide range of handicrafts are sold in Kigali and there's great scope for browsing.

A successful newcomer on the handicrafts scene is the **Caplaki handicrafts co-operative** [83 G6] (☎ 078 8568596; e gerardmuhizi@yahoo.fr), also near the Cercle Sportif. As part of the recent Kigali clean-up, the clutter of craft stalls and pavement vendors in the city centre (for example along the edge of Avenue de l'Armée) had to move. A group of about 35 craftspeople approached the Kigali City Council asking for a piece of land where they could relocate. In line with the government's policy of encouraging small-scale income-generating projects, land was allocated. The craftspeople contributed by building the 30-odd wooden huts and stalls.

INTERNATIONAL PEACE MARATHON

This colourful and energetic event is an initiative of the European Federation of Soroptimists (www.soroptimisteurope.org), aimed at giving people from other countries the chance to run shoulder to shoulder with Rwandans in the name of peace. After long and careful preparations by the Soroptimists and Rwanda's Ministry of Youth, Sports and Culture, the first International Peace Marathon took place in Kigali on 15 May 2005. On that bright, hot Sunday morning, 2,000 runners from 20 different nations flocked into the Amahoro Stadium. Among them were 500 children, who set off with the less athletic participants on the accompanying 5km Fun Run.

As you might expect in the 'Land of a Thousand Hills', the marathon itself was, inevitably, hilly! And Kigali's altitude of 1,500m caused breathlessness among some runners from lower countries. It was a day of huge good humour, energy, enthusiasm and fellowship.

The most recent marathon was held on 24 May 2009, with participants from the USA, UK, Italy, France, Finland, Belgium, Germany, Austria, Netherlands, Greece, Luxembourg, Malta, Morocco, Kenya, Ethiopia and other African countries. Again there were many children, selected from schools all over Rwanda to take part in the fun run. Many are from underprivileged backgrounds, and the Soroptimists have raised funds to provide each with a commemorative T-shirt, a contribution to his/her school fees for a year, and a backpack with some school equipment. The Ministry of Sport looks after their transport and accommodation.

The Peace Marathon has become now an annual event, to be held in May each year. Check out the details on www.kigalimarathon.com. And start training now…

The complex isn't too far from the city centre, on the Gikondo/\ minibus-taxi route. There's parking space inside and outside for a few cars. stallholders, men and women of all ages, between them sell a huge variety goods. Carvings, weaving, sculpture, batik, pottery, metalwork, semi-precious stones, palm-fibre items, musical instruments, leather, fabrics, toys, stationery, small furniture, novelties … there's every chance you'll find it at Caplaki. You can visit as part of the Kigali City Tour (see page 106), catch a minibus-taxi or take a taxi-voiture.

Founded by Collin Sekajugo, **Ivuka Arts** [79 E3] (m *078 8620560; e ivukaartskigali@yahoo.com or info@ivukaarts.com; www.ivukaarts.com*) provides a workshop and showcase for more than a dozen up-and-coming Rwandan artists whose innovative work typically blends tradition and contemporary styles. *Ivuka* is the Kinyarwanda word for birth. The workshop is tucked away behind the Laico Umubano Hotel and visitors are welcome.

Weaving is one of the specialities of Rwanda – baskets, mats, hangings and pots appear in a variety of shapes and sizes, with carefully interwoven traditional patterns. They are sold by some street vendors, and there's a good selection (including woven hammocks) in the craft shop called **ASAR** (*Association des Artistes Rwandais; Rue Karisimbi, BP 939 Kigali;* ✆ *0252 571139*). This is an excellent little shop, combining the work of several craft-making co-ops; some items are very touristy but others are traditional and all make good gifts. As well as the weaving there are carvings, musical instruments, pottery, beadwork, palm-leaf crafts (including decorated notepaper and cards) and even stuffed toys. Prices are marked, so you needn't worry about bargaining – but a reduction for quantity would be legitimate.

Amahoro ava Hejuru is a peace-building women's sewing cooperative, whose goal is to provide sustainable income generation to women. They make a variety of high-quality fabric items such as purses, backpacks, laptop bags, aprons, place mats, quilts and children's toys. If you have two or three days they can make any custom item you like, from clothing to draperies. The cooperative is located in Gikondo; look for their blue gate and sign on the left of the road about 100 metres uphill from the roundabout, or call the manager Grace on m 078 8751878 for directions. On Fridays and Saturdays, they sell their wares in the lobby of the Laico Umubano Hotel [79 E3].

You'll also find street vendors selling most kinds of small handicrafts – carvings, jewellery, woven baskets, masks, musical instruments, notepaper and postcards decorated with palm fibres – and so on.

BOOKSHOPS Two good bookshops in central Kigali, both of them stocking a wide range of books on the history and culture of Rwanda, the background to the genocide and an assortment of other relevant themes, are the Librairie Caritas [86 C5] (✆ *0252 574295/576503; e librcar@rwanda1.com; www.caritasrwanda.org*) in Rue du Commerce just downhill from its junction with Avenue de la Paix, and the Ikirezi Bookshop [86 C7] (✆ *0252 571314;* m *078 8560358; e info@ikirezi.biz; www.ikirezi.biz*) in Avenue de la Paix. The Ikirezi, which sometimes holds book signings and other events, is open 09.00–12.30 and 14.00–18.00 (closes at 13.00 on Saturday) as well as 10.30–13.00 on Sunday; while Caritas keeps normal shop hours. A second branch of Ikirezi is in Remera suburb, about 200m from the Hotel Chez Lando [79 G5]. The ORTPN tourist office [86 D5] also stocks a good selection of books relating to Rwanda.

MARKETS In all market areas, take care – crowds are popular with pickpockets and opportunistic thieves, and instances of crime, though far from common, have

Patrick S

tourism in Rwanda lie mainly in the safe haven offered to the
in gorillas in our Volcanoes National Park, other various flora and
ra National Park and Nyungwe Forest, and physical features like the
border with the DRC, the Rusumo Falls in southern Rwanda, etc.
dan people also have an important part to play. Among other
talents, we are skilled at carving, sculpture and weaving. Most of this is done by the
ordinary Rwandan. Weaving is particular to women and girls while wood-carving is
done mostly by men.

Most importantly, the work is created according to various themes: mother
nature, beauty, achievement and virtues such as valour etc, as well as everyday
scenes. A woman carrying a baby on her back, a pot of milk on her head and a
bundle of firewood under her arm is a common sight around here. An old man
sitting on a traditional stool with a long straw dipped in a pot is also familiar.

However, it is sad when in some cases such talent is wasted through poor sales,
bad storage and poor preservation. Many pieces are sold on roadsides where they
gather so much dust, washed away by rains, that even an occasional tourist who
passes by can hardly notice their beauty!

A lot can be done to keep this heritage alive through publicity abroad: Rwandan
embassies setting up sales-points for such goods, modest though they may be, and
interested individuals taking it upon themselves to sell Rwandan handicrafts for the
good of it. But most of all, local government can help by giving assistance to these
craftspeople and tourists can help by purchasing their products.

The price of such items is quite small and affordable. The Caplaki centre near the
Cercle Sportif in Kigali is one place to find them on display. Even at the Kigali
International Airport there is a stall, and another near the Rwanda Revenue
Authority offices. Also independent vendors display and sell their wares in the street.

Come and buy 'at your eye's pleasure'! And help to promote traditional
craftsmanship in Rwanda as you explore the beauties of our Republic of a
Thousand Hills.

been reported. Also be tactful about taking photos; for every dozen people who
don't object to being in a picture, there'll be someone who does. Respect their
privacy.

The main market area [86 B4], off and around the Avenue du Commerce, is a
victim of the recent Kigali clean-up. Currently it is being redeveloped as a multi-
storey indoor market. It used to be wonderful: stacks of mattresses in floral cotton
covers; roughly made wooden furniture; ancient, dented kitchen utensils being
recycled; clothing imported from far-off countries; cassettes blaring out of ghetto-
blasters; eggs teetering precariously on shaky tables; rows of multicoloured
vegetables with their damp, earthy smell; footwear; shiny watches; creamy candles
made of local beeswax; chunky farm cheeses; tools, cushions, mirrors... it remains
to be seen how it will be when eventually it reopens.

You can still find good markets elsewhere in Kigali. The little stalls and
pavement vendors around the central minibus station have been cleared away too
– but the frenetic market across the road from the Nyabugogo bus station still
exists, at the bottom of Rue du Lac Hago. It's like a human kaleidoscope – a
changing, shifting mass of colours and noise. A few minutes being jostled by these
brisk crowds, determinedly going about their own business, may be enough for
you – but it's a typical and non-touristy experience which it would be a pity to miss
completely. See the walk *To Nyabugogo market* on page 110.

COMMUNICATIONS The main **post office** [86 C5] in Avenue de la Paix has a counter for international phone calls and an efficient fax office. If you want someone to send a fax to you there, the number is (+250) 0252 576574. There's also a philatelic counter.

Internet Cyber cafés are springing up fast and you'll see them all over the city. One hour online typically costs around Rfr400–600, with faster facilities such as the excellent Blues Café [86 D4] next to the UTC generally charging slightly higher rates. The main hotels (and some smaller ones) also offer internet access, but usually at an inflated cost. Public business facilities generally close on Sundays.

Telephone You can find **public telephones** in shops and kiosks all over Kigali – they are metered, so you pay when you've finished and don't need handfuls of small change. Calls to mobile phones from these are more expensive than those to normal phones, although calls from mobile to mobile are cheaper. Rwanda is now said to have one of the most modern telephone systems in East Africa.

You can buy a local SIM card to convert most imported **mobiles** for use in Rwanda; these cost around Rfr1,000 from any MTN (Mobile Telephone Networks) shop – there's one in the UTC [86 D4] and another in Boulevard de la Révolution near the Sierra Restaurant [86 D6], and various others around the city. If you need voicemail and international texting, check that your card includes this; some don't. Then it's a pay-as-you-go system: you buy cards in denominations of Rfr500 upwards to top up the balance in your account.

MEDICAL FACILITIES The largest hospitals are:

✚ **King Faisal** (or Faycal) [79 F3] ✆ 0252 582421/585397; emergency ✆ 0252 588888; e faisal@rwanda1.com; www.kfh.rw

✚ **Central Hospital of the University of Kigali** [83 E6] ✆ 0252 575406/575555; e chk@rwanda1.com; www.chk.org.rw

Clinics and laboratories include:

✚ **Faith Clinic** ✆ 0252 570296
✚ **Plateau Polyclinic** ✆ 0252 578767; m 078 8301630; e pcp@rwanda1.com

✚ **Central Kigali Polyclinic** ✆ 0252 576377
✚ **Polyfam** ✆ 0252 573477

For emergency dental treatment, contact the Adventist Dental Clinic (✆ *0252 582431*), while optometric services are available at Eye Care Optical [83 F4] (m *078 8867121;* e *eyecareoptical.rwanda@yahoo.com*). For further medical listings, see www.theeye.co.rw.

MONEY Assuming you arrive with hard currency cash (ideally, US Dollars, euros or UK pounds sterling), the easiest option is to change at one of the many private **bureaux de change** (known locally as **forex bureaux**) scattered around the city centre. These are mostly clustered along the east end of Rue de l'Epargne near the main post office [86 C5], and have current exchange rates chalked up on blackboards outside. You might want to shop around a bit, and bargain, if you're changing large amounts, and you should keep your wits about you. If the touts that hang out here seem intimidating, there is also an efficient forex bureau nearby in Avenue de la Paix as well as on the top floor of the Union Trade Centre (UTC) [86 D4]. There are counters in most hotels and banks, and at Kigali International

Airport. Forex bureaux offer a significantly lower rate of exchange for US dollar bills smaller than US$50, and the same applies to low-denomination bills in other currencies. US dollars printed before 2003 are unlikely to be accepted without a major fuss, if they are accepted at all.

Travellers' cheques are practically useless in Kigali. The Banque Commerciale du Rwanda (BCR) in Boulevard de la Révolution [86 D5] may change up to US$200 worth per day, but this is a tedious procedure and you may be required to produce proof of purchase. The Banque Continentale Africaine Rwanda (BACAR) has a **Moneygram** service and the BCR a **Western Union** service via which funds can be transferred quickly from abroad. In fact Western Union has hit Rwanda in a big way – there are several other offices in Kigali, and at least one in each of the other main towns, but bear in mind that these transfers attract a hefty charge.

It is now possible to draw local currency from **ATMs** (auto-tellers) in most East African cities. Unfortunately, however, Kigali still lags behind in this respect (as does every other town in Rwanda), though that might well change during the lifespan of this edition. In the meantime, the only way that money can be drawn against a credit card is by a manual transaction at the Access Bank (*formerly Bancor;* ⊕ *08.00–18.00 Mon–Fri & 09.00–16.00 Sat*) in the UTC [86 D4]. You can draw up to US$1,500 daily, but only against a Visa or MasterCard (other cards are not accepted), and the transaction attracts a commission of 3%.

WHAT TO SEE AND DO

For a capital city, Kigali doesn't offer a great deal in terms of buildings, museums and historical/cultural sites, but it is a pleasant place for strolling and people-watching. If you want to see the best of the city in an organised manner, this can be arranged through ORTPN [86 D5] (contact details on page 84), which runs **guided bus tours** of Kigali from Monday to Saturday at US$20 per person (minimum four persons). The tour takes in several places covered below, including the Museum of Natural History, Nyamirambo (the oldest quarter of Kigali), Caplaki Handicrafts Co-operative, Gisozi Genocide Memorial and the Heroes' Cemetery, as well as the Parliament Building and Kigali Institute of Science and Technology.

For those more interested in day-to-day African life than in landmarks, the **'This is Africa' experience** offered by New Dawn Associates [86 D4] (contact details on page 85) is run in collaboration with the Nyamirambo Women's Centre. It introduces visitors to the vibrant culture of contemporary urban Rwanda in Nyamirambo, the city's oldest and arguably most multi-cultural suburb. The women of Nyamirambo take visitors to a local hair salon and tailor, as well as the Muslim quarter and market, and finally a private home for a cooking lesson and traditional lunch. Rates range from US$60 to US$80 per person, depending on group size (minimum two), 70% of which goes straight to the community.

Note that it is forbidden to take photos near Kigali Prison, which lies on Avenue de la Justice opposite Rue de l'Epargne.

MEMORIALS
Kigali Genocide Memorial [78 B1] (*www.kigalimemorialcentre.org*) This dignified memorial has been constructed in the Gisozi area of Kigali and opened fully for the tenth anniversary of the genocide in April 2004. You can see it across the valley – a large, white, modern building with terraces in front – on the right as you go downhill on Boulevard de Nyabugogo. To drive there is easy as it's in sight for much of the way – take a right turn halfway down Boulevard de Nyabugogo, continue downwards into the valley, and when you're a little way past the

memorial take a left turn across the valley, then (at a T-junction) go sharp left along a short dirt road and you'll come to the gate.

A rose garden has been planted around the outside of the centre, in memory of the dead, and there's an open view out across Kigali. Inside, among other exhibits, is a Children's Memorial dedicated to the many thousands of children who lost their lives; each of its 14 windows details the life and death of a single child. There's also a Wall of Names under construction, which will eventually display the names of thousands of victims.

A guide takes visitors around the memorial, telling the story and showing the skulls and bones of victims, as well as graves. The idea behind displaying bones in this and other genocide memorials is to prevent anyone, ever, from claiming 'there was no genocide in Rwanda'. There are photos and information panels. The description in the box below is taken from an information leaflet currently available at the Memorial.

Importantly, the memorial centre is not just a mass grave and exhibition. In collaboration with the UK based Aegis Trust (a non-sectarian, non-governmental UK organisation mentioned in the box below; *www.aegistrust.org*), it operates a social programme to help widows and orphans of the genocide and it is also starting an education programme for students and a mobile exhibition that will visit schools and work on grassroots genocide education.

GISOZI GENOCIDE MEMORIAL AND EDUCATION CENTRE

There will be no humanity without forgiveness, there will be no forgiveness without justice, but justice will be impossible without humanity.

Yolande Mukagasana

Gisozi, in Kigali, is the burial site of over 250,000 people killed in a three-month period during Rwanda's 1994 genocide. Years later, victims are still being located in and around Kigali as new evidence emerges from trials of those accused of genocide. They are taken to Gisozi as their final resting place. Founded by the mayor of Kigali, the memorial building at Gisozi was designed by a local architect. So far, the construction undertaken here has been financed largely from Kigali City Council Revenue. This means that the citizens of one of the world's poorest countries pay through their taxes to give dignity to their murdered families, whom the rest of the world abandoned.

The international community failed Rwanda. It could have prevented the loss of a million men, women and children, but the United Nations viewed the killings as an internal matter and pulled out. Now that a million people have been murdered, we need to learn how and why such tragedies happen, so we can prevent them in the future.

The UK Holocaust Centre was invited by the Kigali City Council to work with its sister organisation Aegis, and survivors, to help complete the site by telling the story of the genocide in this building. It will assist Gisozi to function as an education centre.

The challenge facing Rwanda and the Great Lakes region is how to build a society free from the threat of dangerous ideology. Building stability starts by acknowledging the truth. Providing survivors with a place where their voice can be heard strengthens efforts towards unity. Schoolchildren can come to Gisozi and learn about the consequences of hatred and division. The environment of Gisozi will not accuse, but rather challenge.

Adapted from a leaflet produced by Aegis Rwanda.

The memorial centre runs an event called 'One Life in a Million' every Thursday and Saturday, starting at 18.00. It consists of a testimony from a genocide survivor and a film screening (either *Shooting Dogs*, *Sometimes in April* or *Journey into Darkness*), followed by a facilitated discussion on the causes and consequences of genocide, and the way forward. Entry is Rfr10,000, and all proceeds go towards the upkeep of the mass graves and the exhibitions. There is also a book shop that sells films, music and books with a Rwandan theme.

Nyanza Genocide Memorial [79 G7] In April 2009, this stark memorial overlooking the new Bugesera Road in the suburb of Kicukiro was the site of the official Genocide Memorial Day ceremony on the 15th anniversary of the Rwandan genocide. An estimated 10,000 victims of the genocide are buried in mass graves here, covered in large slabs of concrete. Many of these victims were Tutsis who, when the killing started, took refuge in the Ecole Technique Officielle (ETO), which fell under the protection of Belgian troops from the United Nations Assistance Mission for Rwanda (UNAMIR). Tragically, UNAMIR withdrew the Belgians from Rwanda, and the Interahamwe descended on the ETO to massacre the thousands of refugees gathered there. Constructed in 2008, but not yet open, a museum at the site will document the massacre at the ETO, and chart the abandonment of Rwanda by the International Community.

Remera Heroes' Cemetery [79 H3] Situated on Kimironko Road a few hundred metres past Amahoro Stadium, Heroes' Cemetery is another site associated with the 1994 genocide. Three graves here are of particular significance. The first is the grave of **Fred Gisa Rwigyema**, the co-founder and leader of the RPF, who was killed in battle on 2 October 1990 during a failed invasion of Rwanda. The second is the grave of **Agathe Uwilingiyimana**, the first (and thus far only) female prime minister of Rwanda, who was less than a year into her term when she was assassinated by the Interahamwe on 7 April 1994, within hours of the plane crash that killed President Habyarimana. The third is the **Tomb of the Unknown Soldier**, whose anonymous occupant symbolises all those who died in the civil war.

Camp Kigali Memorial [83 E6] Now the Kigali Institute of Science and Technology (KIST), Camp Kigali is where ten Belgian UNAMIR peacekeepers, deployed to guard the house of Prime Minister Agathe Uwilingiyimana, were executed brutally by the Presidential Guard on the first day of the genocide. The former military camp now hosts a memorial and small museum that still bears the scars of grenade shrapnel. In the garden, ten stone obelisks have been erected, each with the initials of one of the soldiers carved into the base, and horizontal slashes indicating his age.

For memorials outside Kigali, see *Ntarama and Nyamata genocide memorials* on page 113.

MUSEUMS
State House Museum The former state house of President Juvenal Habyarimana, situated about 4km from the Kigali International Airport, is currently being developed as a museum, and should open during the lifespan of this edition (for the latest progress, check *www.museum.gov.rw*). A multi-purpose museum, it is planned to serve as a centre for documentation, education and research related to the years preceding the 1994 genocide, but it will also host displays relating to traditional Rwandan culture and crafts. Other plans include the development of a small zoological park and botanical garden, a cafeteria, and a viewing structure area for the wreckage of the presidential aeroplane. The museum will include an

Caroline Pomeroy

One way to start to understand Rwandans and their culture is to go to church! On Sundays a huge proportion of the population head off in their Sunday best for what will often be many hours of joyful worship. As well as the traditional denominations, there are numerous newer church groups in the country. Since the genocide, churches and Christian groups have had a significant role in bringing reconciliation, forgiveness and healing to communities, as well as offering practical skills and hope though training and development projects.

If you walk though the door of any church, you can be assured of a warm welcome, and a very different church experience from Western cultures. If you're in the town centre at lunchtime and hear lively singing, why not drop in to the daily service at Nkuru Nziza (on Rue de l'Epargne)?

If you would prefer to understand and participate in what is going on, the following churches have English-language services. The list starts from the centre of town and works out.

St Michael's Catholic Cathedral [86 D6] Av de l'Armée, Kiyovu; ⊕ service 09.00–10.30
Kigali Anglican Cathedral (St Etienne) Av Paul VI, Biryogo (near KIST); ⊕ service 08.15–10.00
Presbyterian Church Av du Roi Badouin 1, Kiyovu; ⊕ service 11.00–12.00
Eglise Vivante Mburabutoro (in the industrial park near the roundabout on Bd de L'OAU; large blue lettering 'Jesus Christ' on the roof; m 078 8312899; ⊕ service 08.00–10.00
Global Missions Church Kimihurura (near Cadillac Nightclub); m 075 5100718; ⊕ service 08.15–10.15
The Door Christian Fellowship Church Gisozi (1km east of the National Genocide Memorial); m 078 8300788; ⊕ service 10.00–12.00
Christian Life Assembly Nyarutarama (between 'Tele10' junction & MTN Centre); m 078 8232699; ⊕ service 10.00–12.00
Christ Church Gacuriro (at centre of Caisse Sociale Estate); ⊕ service 10.00–11.30
St Peter's Anglican Church Remera (Giporoso junction on Airport Rd, on the opposite corner to SAR Motors); ⊕ service 08.15–10.00
New Life Bible Church Kicukiro (about 2km uphill past market); ⊕ service 09.00–10.45 & 11.00–12.45

overview of all other museums in Rwanda for those who don't have time to visit them.

Museum of Natural History [82 C4] (m *078 8463909; www.museum.gov.rw*) Standing alongside a small dirt road leading west from Avenue de la Justice, this new museum is set in Kandt House, which was built by Richard Kandt in 1907, restored with German aid over 2004–05, and opened as a museum in 2007. Effectively the founder of Kigali, Kandt embarked on his first journey to Rwanda in 1897 in search of the most remote source of the Nile, and he was appointed first Resident Governor of Rwanda upon his return in 1907. An ardent naturalist, he was the first westerner to visit Nyungwe Forest, and he also discovered several plant and animal species, among them the localised golden monkey.

Kandt House, probably the oldest in Kigali, is a moderately interesting example of German colonial architecture, set in pretty gardens with a lovely view over the valleys. Unfortunately, however, its contents fall into the 'mildly diverting' rather than 'must see' category, with captions in German and Kinyarwanda only (no French or English). Most interesting, in this writer's opinion, is a collection of monochrome photographs of the settlement on

Nyarugenge Hill in the early days of Kigali, but other displays cover minerals, hydrology, fossils, wildlife and volcanism in Rwanda. Also present is a motley collection stuffed animals and mounted butterflies from the various national parks, and (rather bizarrely) a collection of plastic toy dinosaurs. Whether the sum of these rather meagre parts justifies an entrance fee of Rfr3,000 (or Rfr2,000 for residents) is questionable.

NYARUTARAMA LAKE [79 F3] Situated at the south end of the Kigali Golf Club, in the valley between Nyarutarama and Kacyiru Hills, this small artificial lake and surrounding patchwork of exotic and indigenous woodland offers the best nature walk and birdwatching opportunity within Kigali city limits. The open water and its margins frequently support a variety of ducks, pelicans, herons and egrets, along with black crake, African jacana and pied and malachite kingfisher. The handsome long-crested eagle also appears to be resident, and the rank grasslands around the lake host widow birds, weavers, waxbills and seedeaters such as African citril.

The lake can be approached from two directions, either by following a rough dirt road downhill from King Faisal Hospital (a short way northeast of the Laico Umubano), or by following Nyarutarama Road north from the junction with Boulevard de l'Umuganda, then taking the first major intersection left and continuing northwards past the Nyarutarama Tennis Club for about 1.5km. These two main roads are connected by a vehicle-width track that runs through the woodland south of the lake, a promising area for barbets, cuckoos and other acacia-associated species.

STROLLING ROUND KIGALI If you don't mind the unavoidable hills, Kigali offers some good strolls. There are plenty of places where you can stop for a snack or a drink if you need to cool off. Two walks which could each fill up a morning, depending on how often you stop *en route*, are given below; but just look at a map of the whole city and you'll see that there are plenty more.

To the mosque and Nyamirambo district One way of getting to the big mosque in the Muslim quarter is to walk southwards along Avenue de la Justice, with views out across the valley to your right; the mosque is at the junction where Rue de la Sécurité joins from the left [78 A5]. Continue for a few minutes and you're in a lively, busy district (Nyamirambo) of small streets and colourful little local shops. The atmosphere has a touch of London's Soho about it. This is said to be the part of the present-day city where people first settled, long ago. There's a lot of small-scale activity going on here, and small bar/cafés where you can stop for a drink.

To return to the centre, you can either catch a minibus-taxi (they serve Avenue de la Justice; look out for the yellow signs indicating bus stops) or flag down a taxi. (A short stretch of Avenue de la Justice is one-way and minibuses only travel outward from the centre; to get one going back you'll need to be in the two-way part.) Or else retrace your steps towards the mosque and look out for Avenue Paul VI on your right – follow this upwards and it'll bring you on to the area covered by the map on page 86. Or – be adventurous and find your own variations!

To Nyabugogo market This takes you through an area of many small shops and market stalls, finishing at the busy market opposite Nyabugogo minibus-taxi stand [82 A2]. If you can cope with seething crowds and a lot of jostling, try it (but don't take photos without the permission of the subjects).

Walk down Rue de l'Epargne or along Avenue de la Justice until you come to the prison [82 C3]. As you face it from the road, the first road beside it to your right, turning off at a sharp angle, is Rue du Mont Huye, an unsurfaced road running downhill. Take this and follow it – you'll pass homes, small shops, an enclosed market area off it to your right, and then you arrive at the bottom – and the lively Nyabugogo market. Just look at the variety of people here – you'll see so many different bone structures, shades of colour, styles of clothing...

If you cross over into the minibus-taxi station (which is a 'market area' all of its own, with vendors offering everything from leather shoes and hi-fi equipment to – improbably – plastic hair curlers and freshly baked bread) you can get a minibus-taxi back to the central minibus station or else take a taxi-voiture; they park just by the main gate. Or turn right up the main road as you leave the market; this upward hill is Boulevard de Nyabugogo and will take you back to Place de l'Unité Nationale and the centre of town.

WALKING AND CYCLING AROUND KIGALI
Caroline Pomeroy

Sprawling over numerous hills and valleys, with roads that wind crazily around and across the contours, Kigali can be a confusing city to navigate. Just when you think you know where you are going, your destination appears on the horizon in another direction! However, it's a fairly compact city and assuming that you aren't put off by the idea of steep slopes, over-friendly children and changeable weather, walking is a fantastic way to get about. If you have just arrived, don't forget that Kigali lies at an altitude of around 1,600m, so take it easy on the hills!

Although the geography of the city is confusing, you can nearly always spot a landmark to help you find your way to your destination. Many buildings offer great views across Kigali, so if you plan to explore on foot you will do well to start by getting to grips with the geography, map in hand, from one of these: the panoramic top-floor bar of the Top Towers Hotel in Kacyiru; Bourbon Café in the MTN building, Nyarutarama; the upper floors of the Bank of Kigali; the terrace of the Museum of Natural History; and Bourbon Café in the UTC. If you don't have a map, there's a good one on the foyer wall of the Laico Umubano Hotel.

As well as walking as a means of getting about town, there are plenty of good hikes on the hills which ring the city. These offer spectacular views and can be surprisingly peaceful away from the constant calls of 'mazungu'. You could start your walk by taking a minibus taxi from the centre of town – these are very cheap and are all labelled with their eventual destination.

At 1,850m, Mount Kigali is the highest peak around the city, and it can be climbed from Nyamirambo. Catch a minibus-taxi as far as the terminus opposite the stadium, then keep walking along the main cobbled road until it eventually peters out to dirt. There are many routes up the mountain – follow your nose or ask locals to direct you. At the top, there's a path along a wooded ridge, with very few people about. Beware that as you head north, you will encounter a military camp and be asked to turn back.

The hills above Gikondo and Kicukiro can be reached by taking a taxi to Gikondo 'Stade'. Get off at the last stop, and then keep walking uphill. When you reach the ridge, veering left will bring you to Park Juru, a laid-back outdoor restaurant with pleasant gardens and views over the city. There are numerous roads and tracks all over this ridge, many with spectacular views in all directions. One leads to Kicukiro, where you can find transport back to the city centre.

While the heat, the hills and the traffic mean that cycling in Kigali is not for the faint-hearted, it can be an exhilarating and rewarding experience. Heading out of town in any direction will soon lead you to a huge network of dirt tracks and paths, offering a great insight into rural Rwandan life. A good direction to start is to the east and south of the city (head for Kibagabaga, Kimironko, Remera, Kicukiro or the airport, and keep going) where the terrain is a little flatter. Mercator Assistance (m *078 8834800; www.mercatorassistance.rw*) rents out bikes and arranges guided cycling tours.

Rwanda is such a small country that almost any of the towns and other attractions covered in this guidebook make for a feasible day or overnight trip from the capital. This is certainly true for **Butare** and the National Museum of Rwanda (*Chapter 6*), as well as the former royal capital of **Nyanza** along the same road (*Chapter 5*), though it would be a push to squeeze both sites into a one-day outing from Kigali. If you were to go to Butare by public minibus-taxi, you could ask to be dropped at the museum, and walk from there to the town centre to catch a minibus back. If you leave early and check the return times, you should be able to visit the attractive little lakeside town of **Kibuye** (*Chapter 8*) as a round trip from Kigali.

Of the national parks, **Akagera** (*Chapter 12*) can technically be visited from Kigali in a day, but you'll need your own transport, a very early start, and would get a lot more from the exercise by overnighting in or near the park. The mountain gorillas in **Volcanoes National Park** (*Chapter 10*) can also be visited as a day trip from Kigali, but you'd need a very early start (before 05.00) in a private vehicle to reach the park headquarters by 07.00. **Nyungwe** (*Chapter 7*) really is too far away for a day trip, but it could be visited as an overnight trip, though two nights would be more realistic.

The following suggestions are closer to Kigali.

BUGESERA DISTRICT The relatively hot and low-lying part of Rwanda running directly south from Kigali to the Burundi border now forms the administrative district of Bugesera, which is centred upon the town of Nyamata, some 35km south of the capital. Bugesera was severely affected by the genocide. At least 80% of the local Tutsi population was killed (actual numbers are unknown), and many of the victims were thrown into the Nyabarongo River, eventually to wash up on the Uganda shore of Lake Victoria. Two of the most brutal massacres in Bugesera are commemorated at the genocide memorials at Ntarama and Nyamata (see opposite).

Although Bugesera receives a relatively low rainfall and is prone to periodic droughts, its dominant geographic feature is the Nyabarongo River, the country's longest, a tributary of the Akagera that rises in Nyungwe and feeds a wetland area comprising at least a dozen lakes and several large areas of swampland. Listed as one of Rwanda's seven Important Bird Areas, these vast wetlands are of special interest for waterbirds, including localised papyrus-associated species such as papyrus gonolek, Carruthers cisticola, white-winged scrub-warbler, papyrus yellow warbler, northern brown-throated weaver, papyrus canary and possibly even shoebill. In addition to boasting immense potential for birding tourism, several of the lakes also host hippos and crocodiles (indeed, wild elephants still roamed the area until 1975, when the last 26 elephants were rounded up and transported to Akagera National Park).

Until recently, road access to Bugesera was poor, and few tourists visited the area. But this has changed following the construction of an excellent surfaced road from Kigali to the Burundi border in 2008, and the area is likely to gain greater prominence as and when the proposed Bugesera International Airport opens outside Nyamata to replace the current international airport in Kigali. Already, an attractive hotel has opened on the shore of Lake Rumira, to the east of Nyamata, a promising start for future tourist development in this underrated part of Rwanda.

Nyabarongo Bridge The nippy new bridge that spans the Nyabarongo River less than halfway from Kigali to Nyamata forms the northern boundary of Bugesera. It also offers a superb viewpoint over the river and associated patches of papyrus swamp and acacia woodland, which it fringes for about 1km to form probably the best birding spot in the immediate vicinity of Kigali (only 15 minutes' drive away).

You might easily record a few dozen species in the space of two hours with an early-morning start – among the more interesting species we picked up were pink-backed pelican, common moorhen, African jacana, three types of weaver, marsh flycatcher and black-headed gonolek – and it looks like good potential territory for the eagerly sought papyrus gonolek.

Nyamata and Ntarama genocide memorials *Co-written with Rachel J Strohm*

The Catholic Church at **Nyamata**, about 35km from Kigali, was the scene of a horrific massacre during the genocide. Many people from the town and surrounding areas took refuge in the church, thinking that they were safe there. But on 10 April 1994, members of the Interahamwe and army attacked the church compound and killed the 10,000 people who had gathered there. Today, the victims' clothing and personal belongings are piled up on every single pew in the church, and the altar has a machete on it, as well as a rosary in a glass box, which is said to have been blessed by John Paul II and given to the memorial a few years ago. Two underground crypts hold the bodies of 41,000 people who died in the church massacre and elsewhere in Nyamata. Visitors can enter both of the crypts with a guide, though many will prefer not to be underground in an unlit chamber with skulls piled on four layers of shelves all around them. The remains of genocide victims are still being exhumed around the country today, and on most days there's a bag or two of bones in a corner of the church right next to the door (under the wall where babies were smashed to death), waiting to be added to the piles in the crypts. The three guides that work at the site now (two Francophone, one Anglophone) all lost family members in the attacks there.

There is another genocide memorial at **Ntarama**, about 1km down a right-hand fork that branches off the Nyamata road at Kuri Arete 20km outside Kigali. As was the case at Nyamata, people fled to the church here seeking safety. A sign outside the gate records that around 5,000 victims died there. The church interior is now piled with the clothes of victims, similar to Nyamata, although it's even eerier because a good deal of the clothing is hanging from the rafters near the doorways. Two sets of large metal shelves, at the front and back of the church, hold the skeletons and personal belongings (ID cards, jewellery, toys, etc) of a number of victims from the site. Outside, a memorial garden is slowly being created, with all the flowers now planted and a wall of names being inscribed whenever they find money to do it. The single guide at Ntarama now is English-speaking.

Both memorials are grim, and go some way to conveying the appalling scale of the tragedy. There's no charge for entry to the sites and the guides do a difficult job with dignity. A donation is requested (a few thousand Rwandan francs or US$5–10 would be appropriate), as the memorials are almost entirely dependent on such contributions for their basic operations and salaries. Further information is available at www.museum.gov.rw.

Getting there and away It is easy to visit either site, or both, as a day trip from Kigali. Now that the road is paved, the drive takes about 30 minutes. For visitors who didn't rent a car or don't wish to hire a private taxi at a cost of about Rfr25,000 for the round trip, minibus-taxis bound for Nyamata leave from the Kicukiro stand in Kigali every hour on the hour. Easier still, Sotra Tours has very nice buses that leave for Nyamata every half hour from their station on Rue Mont Kabuye in central Kigali. The trip costs Rfr500 one way, and buses stop directly in central Nyamata, less than 500m from the memorial, which is signposted. The easiest way to get to Ntarama from Nyamata is by moto-taxi.

Another option for visiting the Nyamata memorial is the Millennium Village tour offered by New Dawn Associates (see *Tour Operators* on page 85). This offers a multifaceted look at the district, starting with the memorial and then continuing to a school, a farm, a health centre, and a basket-weaving cooperative. It costs US$100 per person, including transportation and food for the day-long tour; they'll pick up participants from wherever they're staying in Kigali and drop them back at the end of the day.

Gashora and environs The small and rather nondescript town of Gashora lies at the heart of the Nyabarongo Wetlands, where it is flanked by Lake Rumira to the north and Lake Mirayi to the south. The La Palisse Hotel, 2km from the town centre, is a superb location in its own right, set on the reed-lined shore of Lake Rumira, and it also forms the ideal base for exploring the surrounding wetlands. This one hotel aside, the area is poorly developed for tourism, but the possibilities are boundless. Plenty of local footpaths surround Lake Rumira itself, and it's also possible to walk to Lake Mirayi, which lies about 1km north of the town centre.

Further afield, follow the Kibungo road out of Gashora for about 2km, and you'll find yourself on an elevated causeway running through the dense papyrus swamp that divides the two lakes – potentially a superb spot for papyrus endemics. Once roadworks along the 65km to Kibungo are complete, it would be possible to follow this road in its entirety, passing through several areas of swamp and within eyeshot of a trio of lakes: Birara, Mugesera and Sake.

Further south, Rweru (also known as Rugweru) is the largest lake in the Nyabarongo Wetlands, extending over some 100km², of which four-fifths lies within Burundi. A shallow sump set at an altitude of around 1,350m, it is nowhere more than 4m deep, and much of its marshy shoreline is difficult to access. A motorable track to the Rwandan part of the lakeshore branches left from the surfaced road to the Burundi border about 57km south of Kigali (and 3km before the border post). It's a rather circuitous 18km drive, and after 7km you need to turn right (downhill) in a small trading centre called Mayuboro. You reach the lakeshore at a village called Nyiragiseke, where it is easy enough to arrange to be taken out in a local dugout, and there's even a motorboat available if you can supply the fuel.

Getting there and away The town lies 55km from Kigali along a dirt side road to the left signposted 48km along the surfaced road to the Burundi border. The drive shouldn't take longer than 45 minutes in a private vehicle, though you might want to stop at the Nyabarongo Bridge and Nyamata on the way. A regular minibus-taxi service from Kigali to Gashora is operated by Rugali Travel Agency and costs Rfr1,000. From the town, you can get a motorbike taxi or walk the 2km to La Palisse.

Where to stay

La Palisse Hotel & Clubhouse (46 rooms) m 078 8300505; e palisseho@yahoo.fr; www.lapalisse.com. This lovely resort, which opened on the south shore of Lake Rumira in early 2009, is one of the most attractive spots to stay near Kigali, & its popularity is likely to soar as & when the country's international airport relocates to Bugesera. (Don't confuse it with La Palisse Hotel 2km from the current airport, listed on page 88.) Spread across large green gardens rattling with birdlife, the comfortable tiled rooms have king-size or twin beds with netting, satellite TV, fridge, wardrobes & a large en-suite bathroom with shower & tub. There are also larger suites designed in the shape of a traditional royal palace. A lakeside restaurant with indoor & outdoor seating serves a varied selection of mains in the Rfr4,000–5,000 range. But the setting is the real attraction here: the lake supports hippos, crocs & a varied birdlife, including the magnificent African fish eagle & an array of colourful weavers & bishops. *US$65/80 sgl/dbl B&B; US$100 suite.*

5

The Road to Butare (Huye)

The surfaced 136km road between Kigali and Butare can usually be covered in about two hours, depending to some extent on how often you get stuck behind trucks on the steeper slopes, and how aggressively your driver attempts to overtake such obstacles. The largest town *en route*, Gitarama, sprawls alongside the main road for several kilometres either side of the junction westward to Kibuye, while nearby tourist attractions include the Kabgayi Cathedral and an associated museum, as well as the former royal compound at Nyanza, also now a museum. Either can be visited as a day trip out of Kigali or *en route* to Butare.

GITARAMA (MUHANGA)

The somewhat scattered and unmemorable capital of Muhanga District comes across as an improbable contender for the honour of second-largest town in Rwanda. And yet that is exactly what Gitarama is, with a population of 85,000 in the 2002 census now likely to have passed the 100,000 mark. Thanks to its strategic location at the junction of the roads running southward to Butare and westward to Lake Kivu, Gitarama is passed through by a great many tourists, but explored by few. And, with the exception of the cathedral and associated museum at nearby Kabgayi (more details below), there really is very little to do or see in this workaday town, though the everyday hustle and bustle of ordinary Rwandans going about their lives can be a change from more intensive tourism.

Despite its unassuming appearance, Gitarama has often been involved in Rwanda's recent history. It is famous as the location of the historic gathering on 28 January 1961 at which the people first declared Rwanda a republic, and it was the probable starting point for the violence that led to the imposition of martial law under Colonel Guy Logiest in November 1959. Gitarama was the birthplace of Rwanda's first president Grégoire Kayibanda, whose modest tomb now stands in the town centre alongside a disused open-air auditorium built during his rule. On 12 April 1994, it replaced Kigali as the seat of the Provisional Government that presided over the genocide, prior to its capture by the RDF on 13 June 1994.

If you do opt to explore Gitarama, helpfully a Banque de Kigali stands opposite the main taxi-minibus park in the town centre [116 E3], as do a handful of small shops, and the bar/restaurants Tranquillité [116 F2] and Le Palmier [116 F2]. The post office [116 B1] is about 1km away: turn right as you leave the minibus stand and keep straight on; you'll come to it on the left just after the Rwanda Revenue Authority. There are motorbike-taxis at the minibus stand – but you won't be given a helmet, so be sure that your insurance includes this form of transport.

Over recent years, Gitarama has experienced a tangible drift in development from the old town centre to the recently built main Kigali–Butare Road, which is

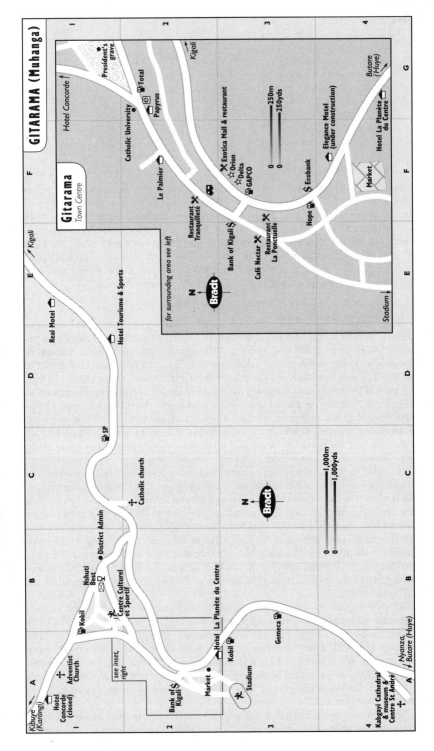

GITARAMA (Muhanga)

Gitarama
Town Centre

for surrounding area see left

lined with tall modern buildings, most notably – at least so far as tourists are concerned – the Exotica Mall [116 F3], which houses a good restaurant, pharmacy, dry cleaner, sports salon, a supermarket that stays open at night, a sauna/massage centre, and a nightclub.

GETTING THERE AND AWAY Gitarama lies about 50km south of Kigali, a drive that shouldn't take longer than an hour except in very heavy traffic. Regular minibus-taxis connect the centrally located taxi park [116 F2] to Kigali (Rfr700), Kibuye (Rfr1,200), Butare (Rfr800) and smaller towns *en route*.

WHERE TO STAY
Moderate

Real Motel [116 E1] (7 rooms) m 078 8403424/8610354; e realmotel@gmail.com. This small new hotel stands in neat gardens alongside the main Kigali Rd about 4km from the town centre. There are 3 large en-suite rooms with hot tub & shower, TV, built-in cupboard, balcony & dbl bed with netting, & 4 smaller twins & dbls using shared showers. A ground-floor bar & restaurant serves a typical selection of snacks & meals in the Rfr1,200–3,000 range. *Rfr20,000 B&B en-suite; Rfr12,000–15,000 sharing facilities.*

Budget

Centre St André [116 A4] (89 rooms) ✆ 0252 562812/562450; m 078 8421378; e saintandrekabgayi@yahoo.fr; ✧ S 02°05.896, E 029°45.147, 1,867m. Situated alongside Kabgayi Cathedral about 3km south of central Gitarama & some 200m or so off the Butare road, this large & reasonably priced church-run guesthouse is undoubtedly the best place to stay in the area, assuming that you don't mind the non-central location. Rooms range from basic dbls using common showers to comfortable mini-suites, while facilities include a restaurant, a bar (serving beer as well as soft drinks), an internet café, & a well-equipped business centre. It can fill up if there's a religious convention, so you might want to book in advance. *Rfr4,000/6,000 sgl/dbl using common showers; Rfr8,000 en-suite dbl; Rfr15,000 mini-suite, b/fast an additional Rfr1,500 pp, other meals Rfr2,500.*

Le Palmier [116 F2] (6 rooms) m 078 842 0632; ✧ S 02°04.788, E 029°45.123, 1,884m. This is the pick of 3 small guesthouses in Gitarama, & very conveniently located more or less opposite the main taxi park. The clean spacious rooms are centred around a pleasant courtyard, shaded by the namesake palm tree, & basic meals & drinks are served. The entrance is rather poorly signposted & well hidden behind a photo studio. *Dbl with common shower Rfr5,000; en-suite dbl Rfr8,000–10,000.*

Hotel Tourisme et Sports [116 D1] (12 rooms) ✆ 0252 562269; ✧ S 02°04.551, E 029°46.1679, 1,880m. Situated about 3km from the town centre alongside the main road to Kigali, this is a newish hotel, & probably the best-value secular option in Gitarama, the outlying location notwithstanding. It's a pleasant, peaceful place with large but slightly rundown rooms & concrete-dominated grounds. There's a bar but no formal restaurant, though it does serve evening meals by request. *En-suite rooms with net & hot water Rfr7,000 with ¾ bed or Rfr9,000 twin.*

Hotel La Planète du Centre [116 G4] (20 rooms) ✆ 0252 562905; ✧ S 02°05.111, E 029°45.246, 1,891m. This quirky 3-storey building is clearly signposted alongside the main Butare road just outside central Gitarama. The rooms are large but rather rundown & the location is potentially noisy, making it rather poor value at the asking price. *Rfr10,000 en-suite dbl, Rfr8,000 sgl using common showers, Rfr3,000 for a bed in a 4-berth dorm.*

WHERE TO EAT AND DRINK Most of the hotels offer meals of a sort, with the Real Motel probably forming the most attractive option, though it's not madly convenient if you are staying elsewhere. Other options include the following:

Exotica Classic Restaurant [116 F3] m 078 8420632; ◷ 12.00–24.00 daily. Opened in early 2009, this is easily the smartest restaurant in town, set in a large open-sided thatch building that forms an extension to the Exotica Mall on the Kigali Rd. A varied selection of curries, stews &

grills costs around Rfr2,000–3,000 per main course, & snacks such as omelettes, brochettes & sandwiches are in the Rfr1,000–1,500 range. There's a TV & a decent sound system, supplemented by live music from 19.00 to 23.00 on Fri & Sat. The attached Orion Nightclub opens its doors at around 23.00 on the same days, & keeps going throughout the night.

✗ **Restaurant-Bar Café Nectar** [116 E3] A popular lunchtime rendezvous for local office workers, this small but busy eatery serves a good selection of snacks & meals in the Rfr500–1,500 range. You can

BANANA REPUBLIC

With its distinctive tall green stem topped by a luxuriant clump of thick, wide leaves, the banana (or plantain, known locally as *insina*) is an integral feature of the Rwandan landscape, occupying a full 35% of the country's cultivated land. Grown at a wide range of altitudes – from as low as 800m to above 2,000m – the banana thrives in Rwanda's characteristically moist climate, and is unquestionably the most important cash crop countrywide, accounting for 60–80% of the income of most subsistence-level households.

So it might come as a surprise to many visitors to learn that the banana is not indigenous to Rwanda – or anywhere else in Africa for that matter. One Ugandan legend has it that the first banana plant was brought to the region by Kintu, whose shrine lies on a hill called Magonga (almost certainly a derivative of a local Ugandan name for the banana) alongside a tree said to have grown from the root of the plant he originally imported. If this legend is true, it would place the banana's arrival in east-central Africa in perhaps the 13–15th century, probably from the Ethiopian highlands. Most botanists argue, however, that the immense number of distinct varieties grown in the region could not have been cultivated within so short a period – a time span of at least 1,000 years would be required.

Only one species of banana, *Musa ensete*, is indigenous to Africa, and it doesn't bear edible fruit. The more familiar cultivated varieties have all been propagated from two wild Asian species, *M. acuminata* and *M. balbisiana* and hybrids thereof. Wild bananas are almost inedible and riddled with hard pits, and it is thought that the first edible variety was cultivated from a rare mutant of one of the above species about 10,000 years ago – making the banana one of the oldest cultivated plants in existence. Edible bananas were most likely cultivated in Egypt before the time of Christ, presumably having arrived there via Arabia or the Indian Ocean. The Greek sailor and explorer Cosmas Indicopleustes recorded that edible bananas grew around the port of Adulis, in present-day Eritrea, circa AD525 – describing them as 'moza, the wild-date of India'.

The route via which the banana reached modern-day Rwanda is open to conjecture. The most obvious point of origin is Ethiopia, the source of several southward migrations in the past two millennia. But it is intriguing that while the banana is known by a name approximating the generic Latin *Musa* throughout Asia, Arabia and northeast Africa – 'moz' in Arabic and Persian, for instance, or 'mus' or 'musa' in various Ethiopian languages and Somali – no such linguistic resemblance occurs in East Africa, where it is known variously as 'ndizi', 'gonja', 'matoke', 'insina' et al. This peculiarity has been cited to support a hypothesis that the banana travelled between Asia and the East African coast either as a result of direct trade or else via Madagascar, and that it was entrenched there before regular trade was established with Arabia. A third possibility is that the banana reached east-central Africa via the Congolese Basin, possibly in association with the arrival of Bantu-speakers from West Africa.

However it arrived, the banana has certainly flourished there, forming the main subsistence crop for most people in the region – indeed, Rwanda's mean banana consumption of almost 2kg per person per week ranks among the highest in the world. Some 50 varieties are grown in the region, divided into four broad categories based on their primary use – most familiar are sweet bananas, eaten raw as a snack or dessert, sit indoors or in the pleasant courtyard, & beers are served along with soft drinks.

✗ **Restaurant Tranquillété** [116 F2] This super little local eatery consists of a cheerful courtyard, with assorted shapes & sizes of tables, a handful of energetic waitresses serving customers really briskly,

& a blackboard with the dishes of the day chalked on it. The food is simple (meat, fish or chicken with chips/salad, fresh fruit for dessert) but good, & cheap, for which reason it does get busy at lunchtime.

while other more floury varieties are used especially for boiling (like potatoes), roasting, or distillation into banana beer or wine.

The banana's uses are not restricted to feeding bellies. The juice from the stem is traditionally regarded to have several medicinal applications, for instance as a cure for snakebite and for childish behaviour. Pulped or scraped sections from the stem also form very effective cloths for cleaning. The outer stem can be plaited to make a strong rope, while the cleaned central rib of the leaf is used to weave fish traps and other items of basketry. The leaf itself forms a useful makeshift umbrella, and was traditionally worn by young girls as an apron. The dried leaf is a popular bedding and roofing material, and is also used to manufacture the head pads on which Rwandan women generally carry their loads.

The banana as we know it is a cultigen – modified by humans to their own ends and totally dependent on them for its propagation. The domestic fruit is the result of a freak mutation that gives the cells an extra copy of each chromosome, preventing the normal development of seeds, thereby rendering the plant edible but also sterile. Every cultivated banana tree on the planet is effectively a clone, propagated by the planting of suckers or corms cut from 'parent' plants. This means that, unlike sexually reproductive crops, which experience new genetic configurations in every generation, the banana is unable to evolve mechanisms to fight off new diseases.

In early 2003, a report in the *New Scientist* warned that cultivated bananas are threatened with extinction within the next decade, due to their lack of defence against a pair of fungal diseases rampant in most of the world's banana-producing countries. These are *black sigatoka*, an airborne disease first identified in Fiji in 1963, and the soil-borne Panama Disease, also known as *Fusarium Wilt*. Black sigatoka can be kept at bay by regular spraying – every ten days or so – but it is swiftly developing resistance to all known fungicides, which in any case are not affordable to the average subsistence farmers. There is no known cure for Panama Disease.

So far as can be ascertained, Panama Disease does not affect any banana variety indigenous to Rwanda or neighbouring countries, but it has already resulted in the disappearance of several introduced varieties. Black sigatoka, by contrast, poses a threat to every banana variety in the world. It has been present throughout Uganda for some years, where a progressive reduction exceeding 50% has been experienced in the annual yield of the most seriously affected areas, and recent reports suggest it is rapidly spreading into parts of Rwanda and the DRC. In addition to reducing the yield of a single plant by up to 75%, black sigatoka can also cut its fruit-bearing life from more than 30 years to less than five.

International attempts to clone a banana tree resistant to both diseases have met with one limited success – agricultural researchers in Honduras have managed to produce one such variety, but it reputedly doesn't taste much like a banana. Another area of solution is genetic engineering – introducing a gene from a wild species to create a disease-resistant edible banana. Although ecologists are generally opposed to the genetic modification of crops, the domestic banana should perhaps be considered an exception, given its inability to spread its genes to related species – not to mention its pivotal importance to the subsistence economies of some of the world's poorest countries, Rwanda among them.

WHAT TO SEE

Kabgayi Cathedral & Museum [116 A4] The Kabgayi Mission, which lies a couple of hundred metres from the Butare road just 3km from Gitarama (see *Centre St André* under *Where to Stay*), was founded by Catholic missionaries in 1906, and it became the seat of the first Catholic bishop of Ruanda-Urundi, for which reason nearby Gitarama was once seriously considered as the colonial capital. Built in 1925, the massive Cathedral Basilica of Our Lady at Kabgayi, with its redbrick exterior, stained glass windows, and huge and tranquil interior, is the oldest and most historically important in the country, and worth a visit, though major repair work is currently under way following the collapse of the roof due to earthquake activity in April 2008. During the colonial era, a hospital and various training schools were set up in Kabgayi – for midwives, artisans, printers, carpenters and blacksmiths, among others.

In the early stages of the genocide, Kabgayi, situated within walking distance of the Provisional Government headquarters at Gitarama, provided refuge to tens of thousands of civilians, many of whom died of disease or starvation. The full extent of the genocide killings at Kabgayi emerged in February 2009, when a report compiled by 18 Gacaca judges revealed that at least 64,000 people who sought refuge in the church grounds were killed there, with the probable complicity of local church leaders and Red Cross workers, who allegedly buried many victims alive. A genocide memorial stands alongside the hospital, where at least 6,000 victims are currently buried in a mass grave consisting of three concrete pits.

The Kabgayi Museum, tucked away in the Evêché (Archdeacon's residence) alongside the cathedral, is theoretically open from 08.00 to 17.00 Monday to Friday, though in practice you may need to ask around to locate the caretaker. Saturday and Sunday visits are also possible if booked in advance. A nominal entrance fee is charged. Within the very small interior are many historically and culturally interesting items such as:

- Ancient hand tools and weapons: knives, hoes, spears, arrows, etc
- Tools and implements connected with the iron industry
- Ancient examples of clothing: bark cloth etc
- Musical instruments
- Methods of transportation used for chiefs, high-born women and the sick
- Clay pots and pipes
- Baskets – ornamental and for domestic use
- The prestigious Milk Bar and jugs from the palace of the last queen mother (1961)
- Old indoor games such as *igisoro*, which are still popular in Rwanda and neighbouring countries
- Ancient military officers' costumes and pips
- A national drum captured from Ijwi Island (Kivu) in 1875, thereby effectively annexing it to Rwanda
- Information about traditional medicines, and tokens (*kwe*) formerly used as currency
- Modern clothing and historical photographs

RUHANGO

Straddling the Butare road about 25km south of Gitarama, and connected to it by regular public transport, the eponymous capital of Ruhango District is another nondescript but well-equipped and surprisingly substantial town. It had a population of 43,750 according to the 2002 census, making it the twelfth largest in the country. It is of limited interest to tourists except on Friday mornings, when it hosts one of the largest markets in the country. Vendors trek in for the occasion from far afield, carrying their wares, and an astonishing range of merchandise is on sale, from livestock and vegetables to hi-fi equipment, household goods and swathes of brightly coloured cotton fabric. You could consider spending a Thursday night here and then watching activities unfold the next morning. Otherwise, the area is notable primarily for Uratare rwa Kamageri (Kamageri's Rock – see box on page 123), which is signposted by the roadside ten minutes' walk south of the town centre, and for the Poterie Locale de Gatagara described under *Excursions* below. Minibuses to/from Kigali cost Rfr1,000.

WHERE TO STAY AND EAT

Hotel Umuco Plaza (12 rooms) 0252 560017; m 078 3503542/8458700. Centrally located, & arranged around a pleasant courtyard, this sensibly priced hotel provides travellers with basic but clean accommodation close to the taxi park, as well as inexpensive meals such as goat brochettes & chips or beef stew & rice. *Sgl using common shower Rfr3,000; en-suite dbl Rfr5,000; meals Rfr800–1,000.*

Restaurant-Bar Ituzi (6 rooms) Situated right alongside the Umuco & probably only worth considering if its smarter neighbour is full, this new lodge has basic sgls using a common shower only, but the outdoor bar looks to be a pleasant spot for a drink or meal. *Rfr2,000 sgl.*

WHAT TO SEE

Poterie Locale de Gatagara (m 078 8520872/5; e bjbosco03@yahoo.fr; ⊕ 07.00–12.00 Mon–Sat, 14.00–17.00 Mon–Fri) Marked by an inconspicuous blue signpost to the right of the Butare Road about 10km south of Ruhanga, this ceramic workshop lies alongside a locally well-known church centre for the handicapped, though the two organisations are apparently unaffiliated. Using foot-driven wooden treadle wheels, Gatagara produces much of the pottery you see for sale in craft shops in Kigali, but items can be bought more cheaply here at source, from a shop piled high with bowls, mugs, teacups, vases and other ceramic wares. Note that the wares produced at Gatagara are not overtly ethnic in style, but the quality is high. You can watch the Batwa potters throwing, baking and glazing the pottery, and see the clay in all its stages.

NYANZA

Sometimes known as Nyabisindu, the unassuming town of Nyanza lies about 20km south of Ruhango, along a surfaced feeder road that branches westward from the main Butare–Kigali road at Kubijega (literally, 'Place of Storage', in reference to a trio of nearby metal warehouses). With its wide dusty streets, waist-deep gullies caused by water erosion, and rather unfocussed layout, Nyanza has something of a Wild West feel, and until recently it boasted few tourist facilities. All the same, it's a reasonably substantial town (in fact, a population of 56,000 makes it the eighth largest in the country), and it seems destined to expand further following its surprise selection ahead of Butare as the capital of South Province in the administrative shake-up of 2006. Partly as a result of this, several new hotels have sprung up in Nyanza since the third edition was published, and the town is scheduled for further development in coming years.

The recent elevation of Nyanza to provincial capital is not without historical precedent. In 1899, Mwami Musinga Yuhi V, his sense of absolute authority undermined by the growing colonial presence in Rwanda, decided to break with the royal tradition of mobility that had led to his predecessor having had an estimated

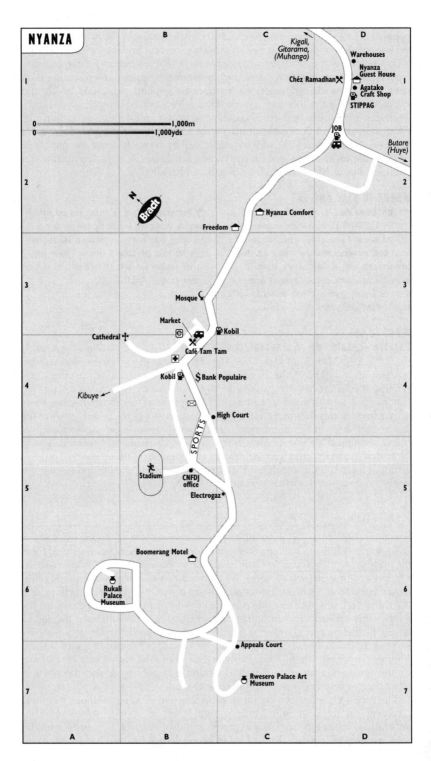

NYANZA

Kigali, Gitarama, (Muhanga)

Warehouses
Nyanza Guest House
Chéz Ramadhan
Agatako Craft Shop
STIPPAG
JOB

Butare (Huye)

0 ————— 1,000m
0 ————— 1,000yds

N **Bradt**

Nyanza Comfort
Freedom

Mosque
Market
Cathedral
Café Tam Tam
Kobil
Kobil
Bank Populaire

Kibuye

SPORTS

High Court

Stadium
CNFDJ office
Electrogaz

Boomerang Motel

Rukali Palace Museum

Appeals Court

Rwesero Palace Art Museum

A NEW VERSION OF AN ANCIENT TALE It happened during the reign of Mwami Mibambwe II Sekarongoro II Gisanura, who ruled Rwanda almost four centuries ago. He was a fair and just ruler. Among other innovations, he required his chiefs to bring jars of milk from their own cows to the court – and these were then distributed to the poor and needy, three times a day: morning, noon and evening. Some chiefs grumbled at this, although they were careful to do so out of earshot of the Mwami; others admired his generosity, and sometimes brought small gifts of vegetables or meat in addition to the milk. Wise and observant as he was, he knew well which chiefs resented his laws, which had true kindness in their hearts and which tended to misuse or misdirect their powers.

One day, so the story goes, a man was convicted of stealing from the Mwami, which was considered a most serious crime. The Mwami called two of his chiefs to the royal court, selecting them carefully, and asked each of them to devise a suitable punishment.

The chief named Mikoranya thought for many days and then scratched a careful diagram on the ground; it represented a shaft of wood extending from a hut, on which the thief would be slowly tortured in full view of the populace. His cries would echo far and wide. The chief named Kamageri, on the other hand, remembered a large flat rock that lay close to his home place in Ruhango, near Gitarama; he proposed to the Mwami that this rock should be heated until it was red hot, and the criminal should then be spread-eagled across it with his wrists and ankles securely tied, so that he roasted to a lingering death. The Mwami then asked the chiefs to demonstrate their ideas, so that he could decide which should be used, and eagerly they set to work.

After much hammering and hauling, the torture rack was in position. Mikoranya refused to pay his labourers, and two of them were whipped when they complained, but grudgingly they finished the task. For a whole week Kamageri's rock was piled with brushwood fires which were kept burning day and night (some women came under cover of darkness to use the embers for cooking), although those tending the flames were burned and choked by smoke. At last the rock glowed crimson and the heat was unbearable from many yards away. Paths leading to the area were crammed with people – men come straight from tending their cattle, old women leaning heavily on canes, young women with babies on their backs, scampering children getting under everyone's feet – all excited to see the spectacle. The chiefs sent word to the Mwami, and he arrived with his retinue.

'Is everything ready?' he asked Kamageri and Mikoranya, and they nodded proudly, expecting praise and possibly some reward. The Mwami called forward his guards, to whom he had already explained what would happen. 'Take them,' he ordered. 'And subject them to the punishments they have devised! Let Kamageri roast on his rock and Mikoranya suffer his own torture. These were cruel men. They took pleasure from brutality. There is no place for such in my kingdom.' The guards seized the two chiefs and cast them to their fate; and from the watching crowd a great cheer rose into the sky, as the people acknowledged the wisdom and goodness of their ruler.

The rock can still be seen today, at Ruhango on the Gitarama–Huye road. Tourists stop to photograph it and guides recount various versions of the story. And on the blackest nights, when the moon is hidden by cloud and stars cannot pierce the thick velvet of the sky, you may still – if you lift your head to the wind and breathe as lightly as thistledown – smell the faint ashiness of smoke drifting from Kamageri's ancient fire.

50–60 residences scattered through the kingdom. The recently enthroned Musinga selected Nyanza Hill as the site of the first permanent royal capital, a role it would retain throughout both his reign and that of his son Rudahigwa Mutara III until the traditional monarchy was abolished in 1961. Today, the traditional palace built by Musinga and first house built by Mutara III have been restored to form the highly worthwhile Rukali Palace Museum, while the newer house built by Mutara III is now the Rwesero Art Museum – both well worth the minor diversion from the Butare road, whether you use private or public transport.

GETTING THERE AND AWAY Nyanza lies 2km west of Kubijega junction (✪ S 02°20.749, E 029°46.001; 1,811m) on the main Kigali–Butare road less than two hours' drive from Kigali and just 45 minutes' drive from Butare. A good surfaced road (culminating in a one-way loop) leads all the way to the hilltop museum [122 A6]. Direct minibus-taxis to/from Butare, Gitarama and Kigali leave from the town centre, adjacent to the market [122 B3], but it is also pretty easy to pick up passing traffic at Kubijega – minibus-taxis in either direction stop alongside the JOB filling station at the junction [122 D2].

WHERE TO STAY AND EAT
Moderate
🏠 **Nyanza Comfort Hotel** [122 C2] (8 rooms) ☎ 0252 533256; m 078 8792731. Opened in 2007, this is the smartest place to stay in Nyanza, situated on the left side of the feeder road about halfway between Kubijega junction & the town centre. The rooms all have proper dbl beds with netting, tiled en-suite bathrooms, ample cupboard space & a phone, while the balcony offers an attractive view over cultivated hills surrounding Nyanza. There is no formal restaurant but the garden bar serves brochettes, omelettes & the like. *Rfr12,000/15,000 sgl/dbl; Rfr20,000 for a twin with 2 dbl beds.*

Budget
🏠 **Boomerang Motel** [122 B6] (10 rooms) ☎ 0252 533396. This is the closest hotel to Nyanza's museums, situated about two-thirds of the way along the road running there from the town centre. The clean & brightly decorated en-suite rooms have ¾ beds, nets & hot showers, & a restaurant-bar serves typical local fare for around Rfr2,000 per main course. *Rfr8,000/10,000 sgl/dbl.*

🏠 **Nyanza Guesthouse** [122 D1] (20 rooms) ☎ 0252 533121/40; m 078 8422263. Situated alongside the Kigali Rd some 200m from the Nyanza junction, next to the metal eyesores that gave Kubijega its name (see page 121), this is the longest-serving hotel in town, though it recently doubled its number of rooms. It offers comfortable accommodation in clean, tiled en-suite rooms set around a small, rather untidy garden. No food is served but Chez Ramadan immediately opposite sells cold drinks, brochettes, chips & other typical local snacks. The attached Agatako Craft Shop sells a good selection of local handicrafts. *Rfr7,000 sgl or dbl, Rfr10,000 twin.*

🏠 **Freedom Hotel** [122 C2] (17 rooms) m 078 8510424. This is the newest hotel in town, having opened more or less opposite Nyanza Comfort in late 2008, but you wouldn't think so to look at it. There's nothing much wrong with the spacious en-suite rooms, which are quiet & come with dbl beds, nets & tiled hot showers, & there are also cheaper dbl rooms using common showers & toilets. However, the attached garden bar had a pervasive smell of urine within months of opening, which doesn't bode well for the long term. *Rfr10,000 en-suite dbl; Rfr6,000 using common shower.*

WHAT TO SEE
Rukali Palace Museum [122 A6] (☎ 0252 553131; e *museumrwanda@yahoo.fr; www.museum.gov.rw;* ⊕ *09.00–17.00 daily except 1 Jan, 7 Apr, 1 May, 4 Jul; entrance Rfr3,000 non-residents, Rfr2,000 foreign residents, Rfr1,000 children, inc entry to Rwesero Art Museum, with a further photographic fee of Rfr2,000 & video fee of Rfr5,000 pp*) This is the top touristic reason for visiting Nyanza, situated on a hilltop about 2km southwest of the centre, and signposted (✪ S 02°21.468, E 029°44.395; 1,805m).

In 1862, when Speke prepared for his first audience with King Mutesa of Buganda (part of modern-day Uganda), he put on his finest clothes, but admitted that he 'cut a poor figure in comparison with the dressy Baganda [who] wore neat bark cloaks resembling the best yellow corduroy cloth, crimp and well set, as if stiffened with starch'.

Known as *impuzu* in Rwanda, the stiff, neat bark-cloth cloak described by Speke was then the conventional form of attire in this part of Africa. Exactly how and when the craft arose is unknown. One tradition has it that King Wamala of Bacwezi Kingdom (legendary precursor to both Rwanda and Buganda) discovered bark cloth by accident on a hunting expedition, when he hammered a piece of bark to break it up and instead found that it expanded laterally to form a durable material.

Bark cloth can be made from the inner bark lining of at least 20 tree species. The best-quality cloth derives from four species of the genus Ficus, known locally as *umutaba, umuhororo, umurama* and *umugombe*, all of which were extensively cultivated in pre-colonial times. Different species of tree yielded different textures and colours, from yellow to sandy brown to dark red-brown.

The common bark-cloth tree can be propagated simply by cutting a branch from a grown one and planting it in the ground – after about five years the new tree will be large enough to be used for making cloth. The bark will be stripped from any one given tree only once a year, when it is in full leaf. After the bark has been removed, the trunk is wrapped in green banana leaves for several days, then plastered with wet cow dung and dry banana leaves to help it heal. If a tree is looked after this way, it may survive 30 years of annual use.

The bark is removed from the tree in one long strip. A circular incision is made near the ground, another one below the lowest branches, then a long line is cut from base to top, before finally a knife is worked underneath the bark to ease it carefully away from the trunk. The peeled bark is left out overnight before the hard outer layer is scraped off, then it is soaked. It is then folded into two equal halves and laid out on a log to be beaten with a wooden mallet on alternating sides to become thinner. When it has spread sufficiently, the cloth is folded in four and the beating continues. The cloth is then unfolded before being left to dry in the sun.

There are several local variations in the preparation process, but the finest cloth reputedly results when the freshly stripped bark, instead of being soaked, is steamed for about an hour above a pot of boiling water, then beaten for an hour or so daily over the course of a week. The steaming and extended process of beating are said to improve the texture of the cloth and to enrich the natural red-brown or yellow colour of the bark. Although it is used mostly for clothing, bark cloth can also serve as a blanket or a shroud, and is rare but valued as bookbinding.

Oral tradition has it that the cloth was originally worn only by the king and members of his court. Ironically, however, this historical association between bark cloth and social prestige was reversed during the early decades of colonial rule, when clothing made from cotton and other fabrics became a status symbol. By the 1950s, bark cloth had practically disappeared from everyday use.

The traditional ancient palace of the Mwami has been reconstructed, together with some other buildings, 3–4km away from its original site, beside the newer Western-style palace built for Mwami Rudahigwa Mutara III in 1932. In olden times, Nyanza was the heart of Rwanda and seat of its monarchy, background to the oral tradition of battles and conquests, power struggles and royal intrigues. It is where the German colonisers came, at the end of the 19th century, to visit the

5

Mwami – and contemporary reports tell of the great pomp and ceremony these visits occasioned, as well as the impressive size of the Mwami's court.

> The capital of the kingdom was composed of a group of huts, an ephemeral town of some 2,000 inhabitants, well organised as far as the administration of the country and the comfort of the nobility were concerned... At his court the Mwami maintained the following retinue: the *'Ntore'*, adolescent sons of chiefs and notables, who formed the corps de ballet; the *'Bakoma'*, soothsayers, magicians and historians; the *'Abashashi'*, keepers of the arsenal, the wardrobe and the furniture; the *'Abasisi'* and *'Abacurabgenge'*, mimes, musicians and cooks; the *'Abanyabyumba'*, palanquin bearers and night watchmen; the *'Nitalindwa'*, huntsmen and runners; the *'Intumwa'*, artisans working for the Mwami; and finally the hangmen, attentive servants of jurists, ever ready to respond to the brief order to fetch and kill.
>
> *Traveller's Guide to the Belgian Congo and Ruanda-Urundi,*
> Tourist Bureau for the Belgian Congo and Ruanda-Urundi, Brussels, 1951

The traditional palace has been carefully reconstructed and maintained, and contains the king's massive bed as well as various utensils. English- and French-speaking guides are available to relate the history and traditions of the royal court – there is even significance attached to some of the poles supporting the roof; for example, the one at the entrance to the king's bed is named 'do not speak of what happens here' and another conferred sanctuary on anyone touching it.

The newer palace is a typical colonial-era building with its spacious rooms and wide balcony. The *Travellers' Guide* above also states: 'In certain circumstances, and with the permission of the local authorities, he [the Mwami] may be visited at his palace which is built on modern lines, furnished in good taste and richly decorated with trophies in an oriental manner.' In more recent times, the rundown palace served for several years as the part-time home of Rwanda's National Ballet (the Intore dancers, see pages 29–31). Now fully restored, it reopened in May 2008 as a museum whose exhibits relate to the two rulers who lived here during the early to mid 20th century, as well as the more ancient history of the Rwanda Empire. Several original items of royal furniture decorate the interior, and the walls are adorned with monochrome photographs. Other displays depict the palace when it was in use, and chart the history of Rwanda from the 5th century onwards.

The museum can also arrange Intore dance performances by prior notice. The performances can start at anytime from 08.00 to 20.00 and last for about two hours. Between 08.00 and 16.00 on normal weekdays, the cost is Rfr50,000 for up to five people, then another Rfr10,000 for each additional one to five people. The price rises by Rfr20,000 from 16.00 to 18.00 and by another 25% after 18.00. An additional levy of 50% is charged on weekends and public holidays. The same photographic charges as the museum are applied. If that's too steep, a DVD of the same drum/dance troupe performing at the Festival Pan-African de la Dance (FESPAD) in 2008 can be viewed in the museum at no additional charge.

Rwesero Palace Art Museum [122 C7] (✆ 0252 553131; e *museumrwanda@ yahoo.fr; www.museum.gov.rw;* ◷ *09.00–17.00 daily except 1 Jan, 7 Apr, 1 May, 4 Jul; entrance inc in ticket for Rukali Palace Museum*) Prominently perched atop Rwesero Hill (✦ S 02°22.050, E 029°44.452; 1,834m) about 1km south of Rukali, this striking building was constructed for Mutara III Rudahigwa over 1957–59, but he died in July 1959 before he could take up residence. Later used as a Supreme Court and Appeals Court, the palace fell into disuse for several years before being renovated and reopening as an arts museum in 2006. It now hosts a combination of permanent and temporary displays, featuring a fascinating combination of

HOLLYWOOD COMES TO NYANZA
Rosamond Halsey Carr

My introduction to the Mwami and his royal court was in 1956, when the Hollywood film *King Solomon's Mines* was shown to the king and queen and the royal courtiers. The movie, which was partially filmed on location in Ruanda and starred Stewart Granger and Deborah Kerr, contains some of the most authentic African dance sequences on film, including a dazzling depiction of the dance of the Intore.

The showing had been arranged by the American consulate in Léopoldville and took place in the royal city of Nyanza. Many of the European residents of Ruanda were invited, myself included. The Mwami and his queen, their courtiers, and the Tutsi nobles who took part in the film were all present. It was a mild, clear night, charged with an air of excitement and wonder. A large screen was erected in the middle of a wide dirt road. On one side of the screen, chairs had been set up for the invited guests. On the other side (the back side), a huge crowd of Banyaruanda sat with expectant faces waiting for the movie to begin.

The king and his entourage made a ceremonial entrance. One would be hard-pressed to find a more majestic figure than this giant of a monarch who could trace his family dynasty back more than four hundred years. Rudahigwa and his courtiers were dressed in traditional white robes with flowing togas knotted at their shoulders, and his queen, Rosalie Gicanda, was wrapped in billowing layers of pale pink...

The soundtrack for the film was in English and, as a result, the Africans were unable to understand the dialogue. Restlessness and murmurs of disappointment rippled through the crowd until the action sequences progressed to the familiar landscape of Ruanda. From that point on, the spectators provided their own soundtrack with cheers and improvised dialogue, as they followed the safari adventure across the desert to the royal city of Nyanza, shouting with glee each time they recognised friends – and in some instances themselves – on the big movie screen.

The city of Nyanza was almost entirely devoid of Western influence, as the Belgian administration had refrained from intruding upon the royal seat of the Tutsi monarchy. There were no hotels, and outside visitors were discouraged. When the movie ended, the Mwami and his entourage and most of the invited guests assembled at the one small restaurant in town for sandwiches and drinks.

From Land of a Thousand Hills: My Life in Rwanda *by Rosamond Halsey Carr with Ann Howard Halsey, Viking, 1999. See* Appendix 2, *page 272.*

traditional and contemporary Rwandan paintings and sculptures dating from the 1950s onwards, though most postdate the genocide. In my estimation, this is one of the finest exhibitions of its type anywhere in Africa, and in many respects it is more interesting and rewarding than the nearby palace museum.

Nyabisindu National Dairy *En route* to the palaces you'll pass this state-owned dairy, which was founded by the Belgian colonists in 1937 and is still going strong today. It's the largest dairy in Rwanda, with a production capacity of 15,000 litres. In theory you can just turn up and ask for a free tour, but in practice it would be courteous to ask about this on your way out to the palaces and then have your tour (if convenient) on the way back.

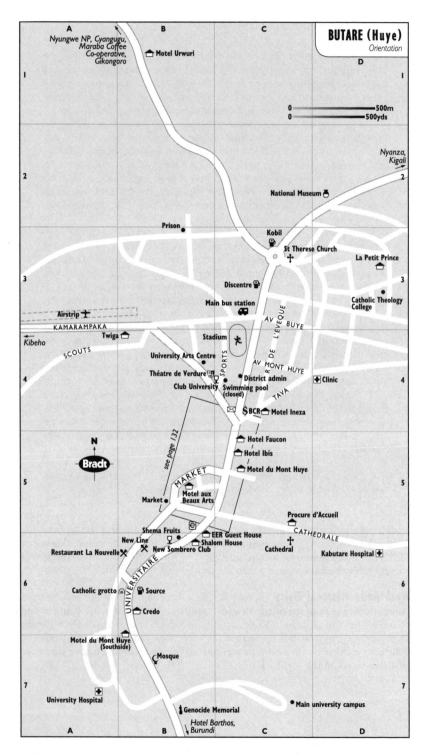

BUTARE (Huye)
Orientation

Nyungwe NP, Cyangugu,
Maraba Coffee
Co-operative,
Gikongoro

Motel Urwuri

0 ———— 500m
0 ———— 500yds

Nyanza,
Kigali

National Museum

Prison

Kobil

St Therese Church

La Petit Prince

Discentre

Main bus station

Catholic Theology
College

Airstrip

KAMARAMPAKA

Kibeho

Twiga

SCOUTS

AV DE L'EVEQUE

Stadium

R DE MONT HUYE

University Arts Centre

AV MONT HUYE

Théatre de Verdure

District admin

Club University

Swimming pool
(closed)

TAVA

Clinic

N

Bradt

BCR Motel Ineza

see page 132

Hotel Faucon

Hotel Ibis

Motel du Mont Huye

MARKET

Market

Motel aux
Beaux Arts

Procure d'Accueil

CATHEDRALE

Shema Fruits

New Line

EER Guest House

Shalom House

Restaurant La Nouvelle

New Sombrero Club

Cathedral

Kabutare Hospital

UNIVERSITAIRE

Catholic grotto

Source

Credo

Motel du Mont Huye
(Southside)

Mosque

University Hospital

Genocide Memorial

Hotel Barthos,
Burundi

Main university campus

6

Butare (Huye)

Set at an altitude of 1,755m some 30km north of the border with Burundi, the pleasant, businesslike town of Butare is often called the country's 'intellectual centre': the first secondary school in what is now Rwanda opened here in 1928, and it has been the site of the national university since 1963. During the colonial era, Butare served as the administrative centre of the northern half of Ruanda-Urundi and it was the largest town in the joint territory after the capital Bujumbura (in modern-day Burundi). Popular with colonial settlers, Butare was renamed Astrida in 1935, in tribute to Queen Astrid, the 29-year-old Swedish wife of Belgium's King Leopold III, who died in a car accident, but it reverted to its original name in 1962.

At the time of independence, it seemed almost inevitable that Butare would become the capital city of Rwanda. In the end, however, Kigali was favoured for its more central location. So while Kigali has mushroomed, Butare remains peaceful and compact – though it is still the third-largest town in Rwanda, with a population estimated at around 100,000 in 2009, and its neatly laid out centre still displays strong architectural evidence of its favoured status during the colonial era. Butare served as the administrative capital of the eponymous province prior to the administrative reorganisation of 2006, when it became capital of the new district of Huye, named after Mount Huye, which rises to 2,278m about 10km west of town. During term-time Butare has probably the country's greatest concentration of students, in relation to its size – not only at the university but also at other technical and training schools and colleges. It's something of a religious centre, too, with its massive cathedral and other churches.

GETTING THERE AND AWAY

Butare lies 136km south of Kigali (⊕ of Hotel Ibis S 02°35.993; E 29°44.508), a two-hour drive along good tarred roads. Most public minibus-taxis from Kigali to Butare leave from Nyabugogo taxi park, and will drop you either at the minibus station on the northern edge of town [128 C3] or opposite the market in the centre [132 A6/7]. The fare is Rfr1,500. Some companies offer regular express departures between the city centres – Atraco Express, for instance, operates an hourly service leaving from its office on Rue Mont Kabuye in central Kigali on the hour from 06.00 to 17.00 (m *078 8531978*). There are also direct minibuses to Butare from Cyangugu and Gitarama.

When you are ready to leave Butare, most minibus-taxis depart from the main taxi park opposite the stadium about 500m north of the town centre [128 C3]. There are also several private operators running services out of the town centre – Atraco Express [132 C4] (m *078 8841512*) on the main road offers regular departures to Kigali (every hour on the hour from 06.00 to 18.00), and a twice-daily service to Cyangugu, leaving at 08.00 and 14.00, and charging Rfr2,500. Sotra Tours next to the Faucon Hotel [132 B1] runs a Kigali service leaving every 30 minutes from 06.00 to 18.30.

The intellectual and cultural spirit of Butare – as it was then – was so strong that initially it seemed that it could resist the madness of slaughter that erupted elsewhere in the country on 6 April 1994. For decades Hutus and Tutsis had lived and studied peacefully together there. When the killing started, people flocked to Butare from outlying areas believing that they would find safety – as indeed they did, for a while. The prefect of Butare, Jean-Baptiste Habyarimana (no relation to the late president), was the only Tutsi prefect in Rwanda at the time of the genocide. He took charge, welcoming the refugees, reassuring parishioners, and demonstrating such authority that, for two weeks while the killing raged elsewhere, relative calm prevailed in Butare, punctuated by isolated instances of violence.

It couldn't last. Because of his defiance, Habyarimana was sacked from his post and murdered, to be replaced by a hardline military officer, Colonel Tharcisse Muvunyi, and an equally hardline civilian administrator. Under their orchestration, paramilitary units from Kigali were airlifted to Butare, and the killing started immediately. Ultimately, the massacres in and around Butare proved to be some of the worst of the genocide, and the death tally of 220,000 was the highest of any prefecture. Tharcisse Muvunyi later fled to Britain, where he was tracked down and arrested in Lewisham (London) in February 2000. In September 2006, the International Criminal Tribunal for Rwanda (ICTR) sentenced Muvunyi to 25 years imprisonment. This ruling was annulled on appeal in August 2008 and retrial with regards to one count of the indictment is to commence in 2009.

GETTING AROUND

The National Museum and the University are no more than about 5km apart, so theoretically everything is manageable on foot. If you should get weary or want to go further afield, however, a few beat-up taxis wait by the turning from the main street leading to the market [132 A6/7]. The prices asked seem to be standard, but, if you feel you're being overcharged, either bargain or ask to see the official tariff. In any case, agree on a price in advance. Rates may well have increased by the time you read this, but at the time of writing it costs about Rfr1,500–2,500 from the town centre to the museum, and around Rfr15,000 to Nyanza or Kibeho. Waiting time costs extra.

SECURITY

For all its laid-back atmosphere, Butare is a busy town with a mixed population, so take normal precautions such as not carrying conspicuously expensive items. The larger street kids can be a bit pushy, but treat them understandingly and they're manageable. In the evenings some may gather to sniff solvents around the petrol stations. If you go out to eat at night it's wise to take a torch/flashlight. Yes, the streets are well lit, but if there's a power cut (rare, but it happens) they become very black indeed, and finding your way back to your hotel might not be easy.

WHERE TO STAY

MODERATE

⌂ **Le Petit Prince Hotel** [128 D3] (25 rooms)
☏ 0252 531307; m 078 8358681;
e petitprincehotel@yahoo.fr. Set in large manicured gardens in the northern suburbs of Butare, opposite the Catholic University & a few mins' walk from the national museum, this new hotel is probably the pick of the smarter options in Butare, which isn't saying a great deal. The best & most expensive rooms are

mini-suites with dbl bed, lockable built-in cupboards, fridge, tiled bathroom with tub, satellite TV, phone & balcony. The cheapest rooms are smaller & some have rather awkward shapes, but still come with TV & en-suite showers. Rooms are very variable in price, size & layout, so it is worth asking to see one before you take it. Facilities include internet access, & a restaurant bar that stays open from 10.00 to 22.00. *Rfr18,000–23,400 dbl; Rfr31,800 mini-suite.*

🏠 **Credo Hotel** [128 B6] (58 rooms, soon to expand to 90) 📞 0252 530505/530855; m 078 8302216/8504176; e credohotel@yahoo.fr. Until recently, the Credo, situated 500m from the town centre along the road to the university, was generally regarded as the smartest option in Butare. It remains quite pleasant, though rather characterless, & its dazzling labyrinthine corridors suffer somewhat from the excessive use of white tiles. All rooms are en-suite, with impeccably clean WC & showers, & most also have a TV, phone & balcony. There's a peaceful view across fields at the back, while facilities include a swimming pool, restaurant & outdoor poolside restaurant-bar. With a bit of notice, car-hire can be arranged here for trips to Nyungwe Forest. It's sometimes used by tour groups or for conferences, so you'd do well to book in advance. *Rfr15,000/25,000 sgl/dbl B&B; Rfr40,000/50,000 suite.*

🏠 **Hotel Ibis** [132 C3] (11 rooms) 📞 0252 530335; m 078 8323000; e campionibis@hotmail.com. Established in 1942, this centrally located, family-run hotel is something of a local institution, & it certainly wins out over the upstart competition when it comes to character. The quaintly old-fashioned & cosy en-suite rooms all come with a private terrace, satellite TV, internet connection & phone, most have 1 dbl & 1 sgl bed, & the bedside lights are a welcome touch. The main restaurant is good though quite pricey & there's a pleasant &

BUDGET

🏠 **Motel du Mont Huye** [132 D3] (19 rooms) 📞 0252 530765. Arguably the best value of all the budget places is this centrally located but peaceful spot, which lies along a small side road away from the main street & its traffic. The clean, tiled, comfortable en-suite rooms with 1 or 2 ¾ beds all have hot water & a small balcony opening on to a central garden, & a more than adequate restaurant serves meals & snacks in the Rfr2,000–5,000 range. It's popular with Catholic Relief Services, NGOs, etc, so it's best to book in advance, though extra rooms are now available at an annexe on the university road about 100m past the Hotel Credo.

relatively inexpensive terrace snack-bar. *Rfr15,000–25,000 depending on room size.*

🏠 **Hotel Barthos** [128 B7] m 078 8460877/8626513/8666802; e barthoshotel@yahoo.fr; www.barthos.com. This comfortable & friendly new hotel has an attractive façade with art deco influences, & lies out of town near the University campus. The large rooms are simply furnished with handcrafted wood, & have an en-suite hot shower & TV. Ask for a room at the back because the front side is near the busy road. *Good value at Rfr15,000–25,000 dbl B&B.*

🏠 **Hotel Faucon** [132 B2] (10 rooms) 📞 0252 531126; m 078 8895533/3589201; e faucon@yahoo.fr. Presumably of similar vintage to the nearby Ibis, this attractive & recently renovated hotel is set in a building with thick walls, high ceilings & faint colonial-era echoes! The en-suite rooms & suites are very spacious & come with dbl bed & netting, a sitting area with armchairs & TV, & en-suite bathroom with tub. Rooms are set round a large courtyard, away from the street, & the back windows have a peaceful view of greenery. There's a good main restaurant, also a bar/snack-bar, & the substantial b/fast is possibly the best value in town. *Rfr15,000/dbl, or Rfr30,000 for a 2-bedroom apt, excluding b/fast.*

🏠 **Shalom House** [128 B6] (8 rooms) m 078 5125041; e rusodilo@yahoo.fr. Situated in the Anglican (EER) Diocese of Butare, on the south side of the town centre, this smart new dbl-storey hostel has very large tiled rooms with lockable built-in cupboards, king-size or twin beds, nets, en-suite showers & access to a ground-floor lounge with TV/DVD. The rooms are arguably the best value in this range, but there is no restaurant or bar (though it's not far to walk to the town centre). *Rfr20,000 dbl excluding b/fast.*

Rfr6,000/10,000 sgl/twin; Rfr10,000–15,000 for a 2-bedroom apt at the annexe.

🏠 **Motel Ineza** [128 C4] (12 rooms) 📞 0252 530387; m 078 0229590; e motelineza@gmail.com. Situated along a side road opposite the post office on the north side of town, this popular & pleasant hotel is most notable for its secluded garden, where you can sit out & eat, write or just enjoy the peace & quiet. Unfortunately the en-suite rooms, though very clean & equipped with mosquito netting (a rarity in Butare), are rather cramped, & the so-called dbls have a ¾ bed only. It serves a variety of snacks & light meals, & it's very close to

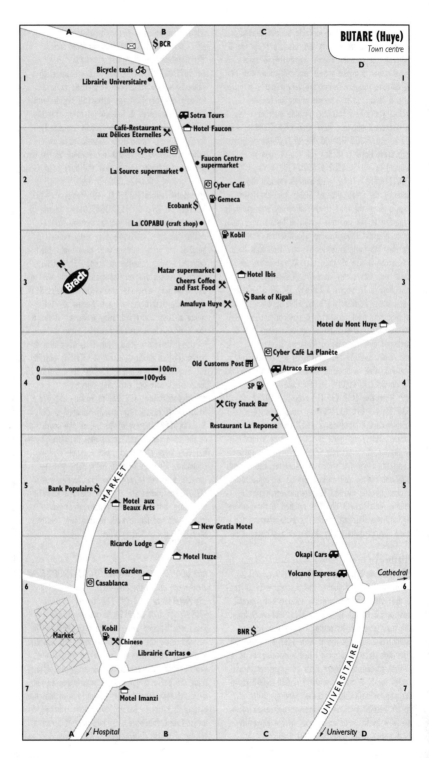

the town centre if you prefer to eat elsewhere. *Rfr4,000/7,000 sgl/dbl occupancy.*

🏠 **Motel aux Beaux Arts** [132 A5] (10 rooms) ✆ 0252 530037; m 078 8460877. The pick of a cluster of inexpensive hotels dotted around the market area, this comfortable & very reasonably priced 2-storey hotel offers clean twin & dbl rooms with washbasin, shower & WC. The restaurant no longer offers any meals other than b/fast, but there are plenty of other options for eating out within a couple of hundred metres. The presence of a large outdoor bar right next door might put off those hoping for an early night, but the bar isn't as noisy as it looks & the sound doesn't really carry to the bedrooms. *Rfr5,000–6,000 sgl, Rfr7,000–8,000 twin or dbl.*

🏠 **New Gratia Motel** [132 B5] (11 rooms) ✆ 0252 531044. Also situated close to the market, this is a reasonably comfortable set-up, with the basic but clean en-suite twins (adorned by a solitary net dangling pointlessly above the space between the 2 beds) set round a small, well-watered courtyard garden. *Rfr7,000 twin.*

🏠 **Twiga Hotel** [128 B4] (24 rooms) m 078 8855032. This friendly new hotel, which opened in 2008 in the northern suburbs about 5mins' walk from the bus station, is decorated with garish sculptures of giraffes (*twiga* in Swahili), gorillas & other wildlife. There is a pleasant-looking garden bar & restaurant, & for accommodation you have the choice of a small en-suite dbl with ¾ bed & hot shower or a larger mini-suite with dbl bed & TV. It feels like poor value at *Rfr10,000/15,000 dbl/mini-suite.*

SHOESTRING

🏠 **Ricardo Lodge** [132 B6] (10 rooms) m 078 8458144. Situated in the market area, the en-suite dbl rooms here enclose a grassy courtyard & seem among the better choices in this range. *Rfr6,000 dbl.*

🏠 **Motel Ituze** [132 B6] (7 rooms) m 078 8466229. Situated next to the Motel Gratia, this basic & rather overpriced lodge offers accommodation in dingy twin rooms using a common shower, set around a patch of grass & with deckchairs outside. *Rfr5,000–6,000 twin.*

🏠 **Eden Garden Hotel** [132 B6] (13 rooms) ✆ 0252 530446; m 078 8409083. Also in the market area, this hotel, set around a central courtyard, offers adequate accommodation in plain, clean & rather gloomy rooms using shared facilities. *Rfr4,000 twin.*

🏠 **Motel Imanzi** [132 B7] (11 rooms) m 078 8171671. Under new management, the former Hotel Dusabane opposite the market has small but adequately clean rooms with net & en-suite shower & toilet. *Fair value at Rfr4,000/6,000 sgl/dbl.*

✖ WHERE TO EAT AND DRINK

Plenty of small restaurants round the market offer snacks and good-value *mélanges* of rice, vegetables and meat for around Rfr1,000–2,000, while most hotels also serve meals in the Rfr4,000–5,000 range. Several more formal restaurants are scattered around town, notably the following:

✖ **Chinese Restaurant** [132 A7] m 078 8504115; ⏰ daily from 08.00 until the last customer leaves. Situated behind a filling station opposite the central market, this is arguably the best eatery in Butare, despite the rather scruffy exterior, serving a huge selection of Chinese fish, meat & vegetarian dishes in the Rfr4,000–6,000 range, as well as more typical grills (beef, chicken, rabbit & fish) for around Rfr4,000. You can eat indoors or on the balcony.

✖ **Cheers Coffee & Fast Food** [132 C3] ✆ 0252 531276; m 078 3172828; ⏰ 08.30–22.00 daily. This winning contemporary eatery is part of the Matar Supermarket, which stands directly opposite the Hotel Ibis. It is a good spot for b/fast, serving fresh coffee & a decent selection of freshly baked filled rolls, croissants, mini-pizzas & the like. It's also popular at lunch & to a lesser extent dinner, when a varied menu includes salads (Rfr700–1,300), sandwiches (Rfr1,000–1,500) & a selection of grills & pasta dishes (Rfr2,000–4,000).

✖ **Hotel Ibis** [132 C3] ✆ 0252 530335; m 078 8323000; ⏰ b/fast, lunch & dinner daily. There's no more characterful or popular spot for an evening rendezvous than the terrace of the venerable Hotel Ibis, with its mix 'n' match of contemporary & period décor, & attached indoor bar. It serves the usual range of grills, mostly for around Rfr4,000–5,000, though brochettes & burgers are cheaper. New additions are draft beer on tap & a pizza menu.

✕ Hotel Faucon [132 B2] ☎ 0252 531126; 📱 078 8895533/358920l; ⊕ b/fast, lunch & dinner daily. Similar in character to the Ibis a few doors up, but a touch more downmarket, the terrace bar at the Faucon is another good spot for an evening drink, & the varied menu is cheaper, with most dishes in the Rfr3,000–4,000 range.

✕ Inzozi Nziza www.bluemarbledreams.org. Translating as 'Sweet Dreams', this ice-cream & coffee shop, still under development, will be the first in Butare to serve locally developed soft-serve ice cream made freshly with local ingredients daily, as well as coffee roasted on the premises. Proceeds will support a cooperative comprised of more than 100 women from the drumming group Ingoma Nshya. The location is yet to be decided, but check their website for details.

NIGHTLIFE

There's not a huge amount: the **Sombrero Nightclub** [128 B6] near the Credo Hotel is more of a bar than a genuine nightclub, while the once popular **Piscine** behind the post office closed in 2006 and looks unlikely to reopen in any great hurry, if ever. There are plenty of small bars dotted around the market area, and the terrace bars and the hotels Faucon [132 B2] and Ibis [132 C3] remain popular places to while away the evening in the open air as Butare goes by.

SHOPPING

There are two **bookshops**: the Librairie Universitaire [132 B1] at the northern end of the main street has a fair range of books and student stationery, as well as some dusty but original handicrafts. Librairie Caritas [132 B7] at the other end of the main street has a few more touristy books and items of stationery, as well as some international magazines and games.

For **self-caterers**, the central market [132 A6/7] is a good place to buy local produce such as fruit and vegetables, and there's a good bakery nearby, alongside the Chinese Restaurant [132 A7]. For imported foods as well as freshly baked bread and other goodies, there's the excellent Matar Supermarket [132 C3], which recently relocated to a building directly opposite the Hotel Ibis. Also on the main road, other good supermarkets include the Faucon Centre [132 B2] and La Source [132 B2]. Locally made fruit juice and jams can be bought at Shema Fruits [128 B6] on the university road next to the Sombrero Nightclub.

For **handicrafts**, there's an excellent shop on the opposite side of the road to the Ibis Hotel, selling products made by the Co-opérative des Producteurs Artisanaux de Butare [132 B2] (*COPABU;* ☎ *0252 530762;* e *copabu@yahoo.fr; www.copabu.co.rw*). The items are priced, but a little gentle bargaining will do no harm, particularly if you're buying more than one. The co-op was set up in 1997 with 47 members, working in banana-leaf products, wood-carving and reed baskets. Three years later it had 954 members (99 individuals and 35 associations) of which 66% were women. Handicrafts in the Butare area have been well organised, with the help of German aid.

OTHER PRACTICALITIES

COMMUNICATIONS The **post office** [132 B1] is at the northern end of the main street. An **internet café** is attached, and there are also several private internet cafés dotted around town, most offering reasonably fast services (but slower than Kigali) at around Rfr100 per 10 minutes – try Cyber Café la Planète a few doors down from the Hotel Ibis [132 B2], or Links Cyber Café opposite the Faucon [132 B2].

MONEY The **Banque Commerciale du Rwanda** [132 B1] opposite the post office and the **Banque de Kigali** [132 C4] midway down the main street offer normal services, but there are no private forex bureaux, so you are generally better off changing money in Kigali or (if you're heading that way) Cyangugu. The BCR has Western Union.

WHAT TO SEE AND DO

NATIONAL UNIVERSITY OF RWANDA [128 C7] (*BP 56 Butare;* ☎ *0252 530122;* e *info@nur.ac.rw; www.nur.ac.rw*) Although not really a tourist 'sight', the National University is by far Butare's most important institution. Created in 1963, with only 51 students and 16 lecturers when it opened, the university had 8,221 students and 425 lecturers by 2005. It lost many of its students and personnel during the genocide and suffered considerable damage, but managed to reopen in 1995. It is now a vibrant and forward-looking institution, comprising faculties of agronomy, law, arts and human sciences, medicine, science and technology, economics, social sciences and management, and education, as well as schools of journalism and communication and modern languages. You may run across visiting professors in any of Butare's hotels and guesthouses.

Out by the university is the **Ruhande Arboretum**, started in 1934. Its objective at the outset was to study the behaviour of imported and indigenous species, to determine what silvicultural methods were most suitable, to evaluate the trees' productivity and timber quality, and to develop the best of them. Now, it is of interest for the range and variety of its species – and it's a peaceful, shady place. Get permission from the university if you'd like to visit.

If you have an interest in the arts, you might want to check out whether any student productions are running at the **Théâtre de Verdure** [128 B4] (☎ *0252 530215;* e *cua_centre@yahoo.com*), part of the Centre Universitaire des Arts, which lies along a back road behind the post office.

THE NATIONAL MUSEUM OF RWANDA [128 D2] (☎ *0252 553131;* e *museumrwanda@ yahoo.fr; www.museum.gov.rw;* ⊕ *09.00–17.00 daily except 1 Jan, 7 Apr, 1 May, 4 Jul; entrance Rfr3,000 non-residents, Rfr2,000 foreign residents, Rfr1,000 children, with a further photographic fee of Rfr2,000 & video fee of Rfr5,000 pp*) If you're in Butare – indeed even if you're in some other part of Rwanda – you should allow time to visit this beautifully presented collection of exhibits on Rwandan history and culture. The museum is exceptional. Opened in 1988, and presented to Rwanda as a gift from Belgium's King Baudouin I, it is situated on more than 20 hectares of land containing indigenous vegetation and a traditional craft training centre as well as the main 2,500m^2 museum building, whose seven spacious rooms illustrate the country and its people from earliest times until the present day. At the reception desk, various pamphlets and books are on sale. Until recently, no descriptions or background material were available in English, but most displays are now labelled in English as well as Kinyarwanda.

Room 1 (the entrance hall) has space for temporary displays as well as numerous shelves of traditional handicrafts for sale. **Room 2** presents a comprehensive view of Rwanda's geological and geographical background and the development of its terrain and population. In **Room 3** the occupations of its early inhabitants (hunter-gathering, farming and stock-raising) are illustrated, together with the later development of tools and methods of transport. The social importance of cattle is explained and there are even detailed instructions for the brewing of traditional banana beer (see box on page 136). **Room 4** displays a variety of handicrafts and the making of traditional household items: pottery, mats, baskets, leatherwork and the wooden shields of the Intore dancers. **Room 5** illustrates traditional styles and methods of architecture – and a full-scale royal hut

(Free translation)
- When the bunches of fruit are ready, cut them.
- Cover the bunches with banana leaves and leave them in the courtyard to ripen for two to three days.
- Clean out the pit in which the fruit ripened.
- Lay banana branches across the top of the pit.
- Place the bananas on top of the branches.
- Wrap the bananas in fresh banana leaves and then scatter a layer of earth on top.
- Put leaves in the ditch under the bananas and set the leaves alight. Leave for three days.
- Peel the fruit, then crush it, then mix a little water into the pulp.
- Press the pulp and filter the juice.
- Grind up a small amount of sorghum.
- Pour the juice into a large jar and add the sorghum to it.
- Leave to ferment for three days.
- The beer is ready to drink.

has been reconstructed. In **Room 6** traditional games and sports are displayed and more space is given to the costumes and equipment of the Intore dancers. Finally, **Room 7** contains exhibits relating to traditional customs and beliefs, history, culture, poetry, oral tradition and the supernatural.

If you don't fancy the walk from Butare (about 1.5km from the centre), then a taxi to the museum will cost about Rfr1,500, more if you ask it to wait. If you're coming by minibus-taxi from Kigali you can ask to be dropped off there; and, if you want to go straight back to Kigali afterwards, you could try flagging down a minibus that has come from Butare – if it has spare seats inside, it will probably stop. Or to be sure of getting one you can walk to the minibus-taxi stand, which is less than 1km away.

OTHER POINTS OF INTEREST The huge, red-brick, Roman Catholic **cathedral** [128 C6], built in memory of Belgium's Princess Astrid in the late 1930s, is the largest in the country and worth a visit. Its interior is fairly plain, but the atmosphere is tranquil and the size impressive. A service there can be a moving experience. It's possible to take a turning to the right a short distance east of the Motel Ineza and then to cross twisty tracks through the green and cultivated valley until you reach the cathedral, but ask for directions and advice.

There is some attractive architecture in the city centre, and the tranquil, tree-lined residential streets away from the centre are good territory for strolling. Major colonial landmarks along the main road through Butare include the **Old Customs House** [132 C4] (now a financial training centre) opposite the SP filling station, whose architecture would suggest it was built in the 1930s, and the handsome little **Librairie Universitaire** [132 B1], which was erected as a doctor's surgery in the 1950s and later served as a bank. A clear heritage of Belgian colonisation (in Belgium even the motorways are lit) is the generous amount of street lighting in Butare.

Spectacular displays of **traditional dance** (*Intore*) take place in Butare and can be arranged on request (and for a fee); ask at the museum (see above) about this.

EXCURSIONS FROM BUTARE

HUYE TINNERY (**m** *078 8640923;* **e** *abmabuye@yahoo.fr*) Shortly before we went to print with the 4th edition, a reader wrote in to recommend this Tinnery as an excellent place for tourists to visit. It is run by the affable Antoine Bizimana, and you can watch artisans working from start to finish – from melting the tin over an open fire to completing a beautiful tray or elephant figurine. Products are sold at the tinnery and through boutiques at various hotels in Kigali. It is located about 5km northwest of Butare on the Gikongoro road, and signposted 'Les Etains de l'Etainerie y'i Huye au Rwanda'.

KIBEHO Before the genocide, Kibeho hit the headlines because of the visions of the Virgin Mary allegedly seen there by young girls from 1981 onwards, starting with that of teenager Alphonsine Mumureke in November 1981. The phenomena were reported both nationally and internationally, and the small, remote community became a centre of pilgrimage and faith, as believers travelled from all over Rwanda and further afield to witness the miracles. During the genocide Kibeho suffered appallingly: hospital, primary school, college and church were all attacked. The church was badly burned while still sheltering survivors; a genocide memorial site stands beside it.

You pick up the Kibeho road by driving through the minibus park just north of Butare. Minibuses also make the trip, but not very frequently. It's a beautiful drive through a mixture of wooded valleys and farmland, on an unmade road. There's not a great deal to see at Kibeho, but developments are planned in order to attract tourists. If you want to spend the night, clean, comfortable, safe and inexpensive accommodation and decent meals are available by prior arrangement at the **Regina Pacis Hospitality House** (\ *0252 530242;* e *benebikira@yahoo.fr; www.paraclete.org/benebikira/hospitality*), run by the Benebikira Sisters of Rwanda, a charitable order dedicated to creating sustainable revenue-generating projects for local communities.

MARABA COFFEE CO-OPERATIVE The fertile slopes around Mount Huye, west of Butare, lie at the heart of Maraba coffee-growing country (see box on page 138), and also form one of the most scenic parts of Rwanda, all rolling green hills swathed in coffee shrubs and other lush vegetation. There's no formal tourist industry in the area, but it's easy enough to explore in a private vehicle or by bicycle – possibly even on foot – either as a day excursion from Butare, or *en route* from there to Nyungwe or Cyangugu.

The best place to start is the **Cyarumbo Coffee Washing Station**, which can be reached by following the main road west towards Cyangugu for 12km to Maraba trading centre, then continuing for another few hundred metres across a bridge, where the washing station is clearly signposted to the left. A 1.5km dirt track leads to the station, which was founded in July 2001 with the assistance of USAID and other charities. Here, you can watch co-operative members dry the coffee beans, then wash them, before removing the pod and any bad beans.

Back on the Cyangugu road, 1km past the turn-off to Cyarumbo, you might want to stop at the **National Speciality Coffee Quality Laboratory & Training Centre** (known locally as 'the Laboratory'), which stands on the right. Another 500m past this, a good dirt road to the right reaches the tiny trading centre of Simbi after 2km, then it continues deeper into the hills, to the shambas where the coffee is grown – a wonderfully scenic area with great potential for hiking and cycling.

GIKONGORO (NYAMAGABE) This modestly sized town, administrative capital of Nyamagabe District, sprawls uneventfully along a green ridge on the Cyangugu Road about 40km west of Butare. There's not a lot to see around here except for a few shops and some beautiful, dramatically hilly landscapes. But if the area appeals to you and you feel like some steepish strolling, there's decent accommodation

Rwanda's Maraba Bourbon coffee is one of the country's success stories. Beans being grown at Maraba, near Butare, have excelled in international taste tests – in a US study they were classed as second best worldwide – and are being marketed actively in the UK and US. Maraba is a very special type of Arabica coffee from Bourbon coffee trees, characterised by a smooth, full-bodied, almost fruity flavour with no astringency or after-taste.

The coffee plantation is run by the Abahuzamugambi Co-operative, many of whose members are women widowed in the genocide who were struggling to support their families. The sale of the Maraba coffee has enabled them to pay school fees, rebuild damaged homes and acquire livestock. International support from USAID, ACDI/VOCA, PEARL, the UK's Comic Relief, Union Coffee Roasters of London (www.unionroasted.com) and others provided for new washing stations and improved equipment. In 2005 the Co-operative won the prestigious City of Göteborg International Environmental Prize. Membership grew from an initial 200 in 2001 to around 2,000 in 2006 and is still increasing. In the UK, Sainsbury's has promoted Maraba coffee in several of its stores during annual Comic Relief campaigns and also sells a speciality beer containing Maraba coffee. In the US, the coffee is available from Starbucks as well as from speciality stores whose customers care more for quality than price. Sales in 2005 via the Inter-American Coffee Company (US) and Union Coffee Roasters raised over US$266,000.

Traditionally, Arabica coffee has always been Rwanda's principal export, but quality and quantity declined seriously after the genocide. According to OCIR-Café, the state coffee board, the 19,600 tonnes produced in 2001 were about half the pre-1994 output. With Maraba Bourbon, this is changing fast: almost 70,000kg were produced in 2004, and other plantations around Rwanda are achieving similar success.

In the country as a whole, there are around 8 million coffee trees on some 33,000 hectares of land, and other good coffee growing areas are Akagera, Virunga, and around lakes Kivu and Muhazi. A brand that has successfully joined Maraba on the international market is Rwanda Blue Bourbon, also used by Starbucks.

Maraba Bourbon is promoted in Rwanda's restaurants and hotels and is on sale in supermarkets, along with other Rwandan coffees. Its growth is self-perpetuating. Watch out for it – whether in the UK, the US or Rwanda – and enjoy!

available at the new three-storey **Golden Monkey Hotel** (*23 rooms;* m *078 845 3186;* e *goldenmonkeyhotel@yahoo.com*), which lies alongside the main road and charges Rfr20,000 for a smart twin or double room with netting, tiled floors, lockable built-in cupboards and en-suite hot shower and toilet.

The genocide memorial at **Murambi**, about 2km north of Gikongoro, is one of Rwanda's starkest: over 1,800 bodies, of the 27,000-odd exhumed from mass graves here, have been placed on display to the public in the old technical school. They people the bare rooms, mingling horror with poignancy, as a mute but chillingly eloquent reminder that such events must never, ever, be allowed to recur. During the genocide, under orders from the prefect and with the support of the church authorities, between 40,000 and 60,000 inhabitants were assembled together in and around the school on Murambi hill, supposedly for protection; there were 64 rooms crammed full with people. Then the *interahamwe* attacked, throwing grenades through the windows. Within four days, most of those on the premises had been slaughtered. Later, French soldiers were installed on the site as part of Opération Turquoise, and a volleyball pitch was built over one of the mass graves.

7

Nyungwe Forest National Park

If the mountain gorillas of Volcanoes National Park form the single best reason to visit Rwanda, then the less-publicised Nyungwe Forest is probably the best reason to prolong your stay. Extending for 1,015km² over the mountainous southwest of Rwanda, Nyungwe protects the largest remaining tract of medium-altitude forest anywhere in Africa, forming a contiguous forest block with the 370km² Kibira National Park in neighbouring Burundi. Nyungwe is the most important catchment area in Rwanda, providing water to some 70% of the country, and its central ridges form the watershed between Africa's two largest drainage systems, the Nile and the Congo – indeed, a spring on the slopes of the 2,950m Mount Bigugu was recently established as the most remote source of the world's longest river (see *Ascend the Nile* box on page 154).

As with other Albertine Rift forests, Nyungwe is a remarkably rich centre of biodiversity. More than 1,050 plant species are known to occur in the national park, including about 200 orchids and 250 Albertine Rift Endemics. The vertebrate fauna includes 85 mammal, 278 bird, 32 amphibian and 38 reptile species (of which a full 62 are endemic to the Albertine Rift) while a total of 120 butterfly species have been recorded. Primates are particularly well represented, with 13 species resident, including a population of about 400 chimpanzees, some of which are semi-habituated to tourist visits.

Statistics aside, Nyungwe is, in a word, magnificent. The forest takes on a liberatingly primal presence even before you enter it. One moment the road is winding through a characteristic rural Rwandan landscape of rolling tea plantations and artificially terraced hills, the next a dense tangle of trees rises imperiously from the fringing cultivation. For a full 50km the road clings improbably to steep forested slopes, offering grandstand views over densely swathed hills that tumble like monstrous green waves towards the distant Burundi border. One normally thinks of rainforest as the most intimate and confining of environments. Nyungwe is that, but, as viewed from the main road, it is also gloriously expansive.

Vast though it may be, Nyungwe today is but a fragment of what was once an uninterrupted forest belt covering the length of the Albertine Rift (the stretch of the western Rift Valley running from the Ruwenzori Mountains south to Burundi). The fragmentation of this forest started some 2,000 years ago, at the dawn of the Iron Age, when the first patches were cut down to make way for agriculture – it is thought, for instance, that the isolation of Uganda's Bwindi Forest from similar habitats on the Virunga Mountains occurred as recently as 500 years ago.

It is over the past 100 years that the forests of the Albertine Rift have suffered most heavily. Take northwestern Rwanda's Gishwati Forest, which extended over a comparable area to Nyungwe as recently as the 1930s, but had been reduced to two separate blocks covering a combined 280km² by 1989, and now covers little more than 6km². Nyungwe has fared well by comparison, bearing in mind that it is now the only substantial tract of forest left in Rwanda. First protected as the 1,140km²

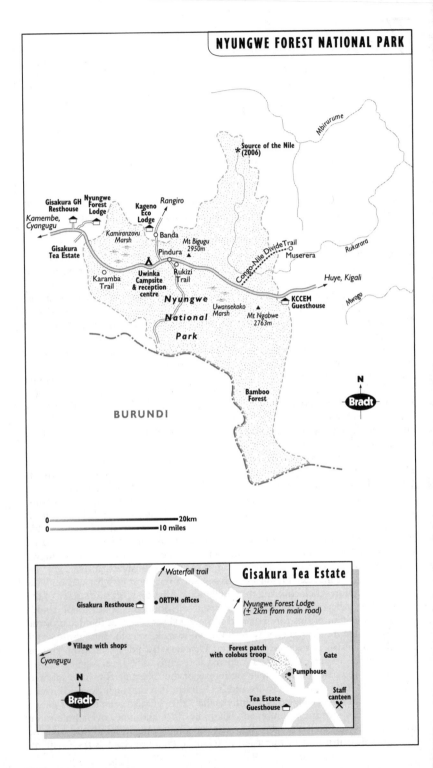

NYUNGWE FOREST NATIONAL PARK

Mbirurume

*Source of the Nile
(2006)

Gisakura GH   Nyungwe   Rangiro
Resthouse   Forest   Kageno
               Lodge   Eco
Kamembe,   Lodge
Cyangugu   Kamiranzovu   ○ Banda
               Marsh   Rukarara
Gisakura   Pindura   Mt Bigugu
Tea Estate   2950m   Congo-Nile Divide Trail
                                         ▲   Muserera
               ○   Λ   ○
               Karamba   Uwinka   Rukizi   Huye, Kigali
               Trail   Campsite   Trail
                              & reception
                              centre   Nyungwe   KCCEM
                                                                 Guesthouse   Mwogo
                                         National   Uwansekoko
                                                    Marsh   Mt Ngabwe
                                         Park   2763m

                                                              Bamboo   N
                                                              Forest   ↑

BURUNDI   Bradt

0 ▬▬▬▬▬▬▬▬▬▬ 20km
0 ▬▬▬▬▬▬▬▬▬▬ 10 miles

                    ↗ Waterfall trail   Gisakura Tea Estate

Gisakura Resthouse ⌂ ● ORTPN offices   ↗ Nyungwe Forest Lodge
                                                (± 2km from main road)

● Village with shops   Forest patch
Cyangugu   with colobus troop   Gate

   N   ● Pumphouse
   ↑   Staff
Bradt   Tea Estate   canteen
                                 Guesthouse ⌂   ✗

140

Forêt Naturelle de Nyungwe in 1933, the reserve was reduced by about 15% between 1958 and 1979 thanks to encroachment by local subsistence farmers, who also harvested it as a source of honey, bush meat, firewood and alluvial gold (an estimated 3,000 gold panners worked the Nyungwe watershed in the mid-1950s).

Fortunately, Nyungwe's extent has remained reasonably stable since 1984, when a co-ordinated forest protection plan was implemented under the Wildlife Conservation Society. This in turn led to the establishment of research projects by the likes of Amy Vedder (Angola colobus) and Beth Kaplin (L'Hoest's and blue monkeys), the creation of a vast network of tourist trails in the late 1980s, and the first reasonably comprehensive biodiversity survey as undertaken by Dowsett in 1990. The tragic events of 1994 had little long-term effect on Nyungwe, which was formally accorded national park status in 2004.

For most visitors, the main attraction of Nyungwe Forest is its primates. Chimp tracking can be arranged at short notice, and several other monkeys are readily seen, including the acrobatic Ruwenzori colobus in troops of up to 400 strong (the largest arboreal primate troops in Africa) and the beautiful and highly localised L'Hoest's monkey. Nyungwe is also highly alluring to birders, botanists and keen walkers. One of the joys of Nyungwe is its accessibility. Not only is the forest bisected by the surfaced trunk road between Butare and Cyangugu, but it is serviced by a well-organised and moderately priced guesthouse and campsite, and easily explored along a well-maintained 130km network of walking trails.

For all that, Nyungwe features on surprisingly few tourist itineraries through Rwanda. Partly, this is because the forest trails generally require more stamina than their counterparts in Volcanoes National Park, without the enticement of mountain gorillas to justify the effort. Another factor is simply that the park has long lacked any genuine tourist-class accommodation, as have the two closest towns, Butare and Cyangugu.

All this is set to change, however, as Nyungwe enters into a phase of unprecedented tourist development in 2009. Among the offerings in the pipeline are a pair of upmarket private tourist lodges scheduled to open in early 2010, a total overhaul of the Uwinka Visitors' Centre and construction of a suspended canopy walk there, the addition of several new walking trails and renaming of existing ones, a new guidebook to trails and activities reflecting these changes, and the implementation of a revised fee structure.

All these developments are likely to take effect at about the time this edition is published or shortly afterwards, which makes updating this chapter a frustratingly speculative exercise. Although we have attempted to include all probable new developments, most were still on the drawing board at the time of research and we cannot guarantee everything will go ahead as expected. Readers visiting Nyungwe are strongly urged to check on http://updates.bradtguides.com/rwanda for the latest updates.

NATURAL HISTORY

Nyungwe is a true rainforest, typically receiving in excess of 2,000mm of precipitation annually. It is also one of the oldest forests in Africa, which is one reason why it boasts such a high level of biodiversity. Scientific opinion is that Nyungwe, along with the other forests of the Albertine Rift, was largely unaffected by the drying up of lowland areas during the last ice age, and thus became a refuge for forest plants and animals which have subsequently recolonised areas such as the Congo Basin. Nyungwe's faunal and floral diversity is a function not only of its antiquity, but also of the wide variation in elevation (between 1,600m and 2,950m above sea level), since many forest plants and animals live within very specific altitudinal bands.

FLORA The forest comprises at least 200 tree species. The upper canopy in some areas reaches 50–60m in height, dominated by slow-growing hardwoods such as *Entandrophragma excelsum* (African mahogany), *Syzygium parvifolium* (waterberry), *Podocarpus milanjianus* (Mulanje cedar), *Newtonia buchananii* (forest newtonia) and *Albizia gummifera* (smooth-barked albizia). A much larger variety of trees makes up the mid-storey canopy, of which one of the most conspicuous

ALBERTINE RIFT ENDEMICS

Most of Rwanda's forest inhabitants have a wide distribution in the DRC and/or West Africa, while a smaller proportion consists of eastern species that might as easily be observed in forested habitats in Kenya, Tanzania and in some instances Ethiopia. A significant number, however, are Albertine Rift Endemics (AREs): in other words their range is more or less confined to montane habitats associated with the Rift Valley escarpment running between Lake Albert and the north of Lake Tanganyika. The most celebrated of these regional endemics is of course the mountain gorilla, confined to the Virunga and Bwindi Mountains near the eastern Rift Valley escarpment. Other primates endemic to the Albertine Rift include several taxa of smaller primates, for instance the golden monkey and Ruwenzori colobus, while eight endemic butterflies are regarded as flagship species for the many hundreds of invertebrate taxa that occur nowhere else.

Of the remarkable tally of 37 range-restricted bird species listed as AREs, roughly half are considered to be of global conservation concern. All 37 of these species have been recorded in the DRC, and nine are endemic to that country, since their range is confined to the western escarpment forests. More than 20 AREs are resident in each of Uganda, Rwanda and Burundi, while two extend their range southward into western Tanzania.

All but three of the 29 endemics that occur on the eastern escarpment have been recorded in Rwanda's Nyungwe Forest. Inaccessible to tourists at the time of writing, the Itombwe Mountains, which rise from the Congolese shore of northern Lake Tanganyika, support the largest contiguous block of montane forest in East Africa. This range is also regarded as the most important site for montane forest birds in the region, with a checklist of 565 species including 31 AREs, three of which are known from nowhere else in the world. The most elusive of these birds is the enigmatic Congo bay owl, first collected in 1952, and yet to be seen again, though its presence is suspected in Nyungwe.

Several forest-dwelling AREs share stronger affinities with extant or extinct Asian genera than they do with any other living African species, affirming the great age of these forests, which are thought to have flourished during prehistoric climatic changes that caused temporary deforestation in lower-lying areas such as the Congo Basin. The Congo bay owl, African green broadbill and Grauer's cuckoo-shrike, for instance, might all be classed as living fossils – isolated relics of a migrant Asian stock that has been superseded elsewhere on the continent by indigenous genera evolved from a common ancestor.

Among the mammalian AREs, the dwarf otter-shrew of the Ruwenzoris is one of three highly localised African mainland species belonging to a family of aquatic insectivores that flourished some 50 million years ago and is elsewhere survived only by the related tenrecs of Madagascar. A relict horseshoe bat species restricted to the Ruwenzoris and Lake Kivu is anatomically closer to extant Asian forms of horseshoe bat and to ancient migrant stock than it is to any of the 20-odd more modern and widespread African horseshoe bat species, while a shrew specimen collected only once in the Itombwe Mountains is probably the most primitive and ancient of all 150 described African species.

is *Dichaetanthera corymbosa*, whose bright purple blooms break up the rich green textures of the forest.

Of the smaller trees, one of the most striking is the giant tree-fern *Cyathea mannania*, which grows to 5m tall, and is seen in large numbers along the ravines of the Isumo (Waterfall) Trail. Also very distinctive are the 2–3m-tall giant lobelias, more normally associated with montane moorland than forest, but common in Nyungwe, particularly along the roadside. Bamboo plants, a large type of grass, are dominant at higher altitudes in the rather inaccessible southeast of the forest, where their shoots are favoured by the rare and elusive owl-faced monkey. Nyungwe also harbours a huge variety of small flowering plants, including around 200 varieties of orchid and the wild begonia.

Within Nyungwe lie several swampy areas whose biology is quite distinct from that of the surrounding forest. The largest of these is the 13km² Kamiranzovu Marsh, sweeping views of which are offered along the main road between the campsite and the guesthouse – and which can also now be explored on the guided Kamiranzovu Marsh Trail. Formerly a favoured haunt of elephants, this open area is also rich in epiphytic orchids and harbours localised animals such as the Congo clawless otter and Grauer's rush warbler. The higher-altitude Uwasenkoko Marsh, bisected by the main road towards Butare, is dominated by the Ethiopian hagenia and protects a community of heather-like plants sharing unexpected affinities with the Nyika Plateau in distant Malawi.

MAMMALS The most prominent mammals in Nyungwe are primates, of which 13 species are present, including the common chimpanzee (see box on page 144) and eight types of monkey (see below). In total, however, an estimated 86 different mammal species have been recorded in Nyungwe, including several rare forest inhabitants.

Of the so-called 'Big Five', elephant, buffalo and leopard were all common in pre-colonial times. Buffalo and elephant are now extinct. The last buffalo was shot in 1976. By contrast, between six and 20 elephants still lived in the forest as recently as 1990, but no spoor have been seen since November 1999, when the corpse of what was presumably Nyungwe's last elephant was found by rangers, cause of death unknown. Leopard, by contrast, are still present in small numbers, and regularly seen by local villagers, but as a tourist you'd be very lucky to encounter one.

A number of smaller predators occur in Nyungwe, including golden cat, wild cat, serval cat, side-striped jackal, three types of mongoose, Congo clawless otter, common and servaline genet, and common and palm civet. Most of these are highly secretive nocturnal creatures which are infrequently observed.

The largest antelope found in Nyungwe is the bushbuck. Three types of duiker also occur in the forest: black-fronted, yellow-backed and an endemic race of Wein's duiker. Formerly common, all the forest's antelope have suffered from intensive poaching as bush meat. Other large mammals include giant forest hog, bushpig, several types of squirrel (including the monkey-sized giant forest squirrel), Derby's anomalure (a large squirrel-like forest animal which has large underarm flaps enabling it to glide between trees) and the tree hyrax (a rarely seen guinea-pig-like animal whose blood-curdling nocturnal screeching is one of the characteristic sounds of the African forest).

Monkeys The 13 primate species which occur in Nyungwe represent something like 20–25% of the total number in Africa, a phenomenal figure which in East Africa is comparable only to Uganda's Kibale Forest. Furthermore, several of these primates are listed as vulnerable or endangered on the IUCN red list, and Nyungwe is almost certainly the main stronghold for at least two of them.

Disregarding the chimpanzee (see box below), the most celebrated of Nyungwe's primates is the **Ruwenzori colobus** *Colobus angolensis ruwenzori*, a race of the more widespread Angola colobus which is restricted to the Albertine Rift.

CHIMPANZEES

You'll hear them before you see them: from somewhere deep in the forest, an excited hooting, just one voice at first, then several, rising in volume and tempo and pitch to a frenzied unified crescendo, before stopping abruptly or fading away. Jane Goodall called it the 'pant-hoot' call, a kind of bonding ritual that allows any chimpanzees within earshot of each other to identify exactly who is around at any given moment, through the individual's unique vocal stylisation. To the human listener, this eruptive crescendo is one of the most spine-chilling and exciting sounds of the rainforest, and a strong indicator that visual contact with man's closest genetic relative is imminent.

It is, in large part, our close evolutionary kinship with chimpanzees that makes these sociable black-coated apes of the forest so enduringly fascinating. Humans, chimpanzees and bonobos (also known as pygmy chimpanzees) share more than 95% of their genetic code, and the three species are far more closely related to each other than they are to any other living creature, even gorillas. Superficial differences notwithstanding, the similarities between humans and chimps are consistently striking, not only in the skeletal structure and skull, but also in the nervous system, the immune system, and in many behavioural aspects – bonobos, for instance, are the only animals other than humans to copulate in the missionary position.

Unlike most other primates, chimpanzees don't live in troops, but instead form extended communities of up to 100 individuals, which roam the forest in small socially mobile subgroups that often revolve around a few close family members such as brothers or a mother and daughter. Male chimps normally spend their entire life within the community into which they were born, whereas females are likely to migrate into a neighbouring community at some point after reaching adolescence. A high-ranking male will occasionally attempt to monopolise a female in oestrus, but the more normal state of sexual affairs in chimp society is non-hierarchical promiscuity. A young female in oestrus will generally mate with any male that takes her fancy, while older females tend to form close bonds with a few specific males, sometimes allowing themselves to be monopolised by a favoured suitor for a period, but never pairing off exclusively in the long term.

Within each community, one alpha male is normally recognised – though coalitions between two males, often a dominant and a submissive sibling, have often been recorded. The role of the alpha male, not fully understood, is evidently quite benevolent – chairman of the board rather than crusty tyrant. This is probably influenced by the alpha male's relatively limited reproductive advantages over his potential rivals, most of whom he will have known for his entire life. Other males in the community are generally supportive rather than competitive towards the alpha male, except for when a rival consciously contests the alpha position, which is far from being an everyday occurrence. One male in Tanzania's Mahale Mountains maintained an alpha status within his community for more than 15 years between 1979 and 1995!

Prior to the 1960s, it was always assumed that chimps were strict vegetarians. This notion was rocked when Jane Goodall, during her pioneering chimpanzee study in Tanzania's Gombe Stream, witnessed them hunting down a red colobus monkey, something that has since been discovered to be common behaviour, particularly during the dry season when other food sources are depleted. Over subsequent years, an average of 20 kills has been recorded in Gombe annually, with red colobus being the

The Ruwenzori colobus is a highly arboreal and acrobatic leaf-eater, easily distinguished from any other primate found in Nyungwe by its contrasting black overall colour and snow-white whiskers, shoulders and tail tip. Although all colobus monkeys are very sociable, the ones in Nyungwe are unique in so far as they typically move in troops of several hundred animals. A semi-habituated troop

prey on more than half of these occasions, though young bushbuck, young bushpig and even infant chimps have also been victimised and eaten. The normal modus operandi is for four or five adult chimps to slowly encircle a colobus troop, then for another chimp to act as a decoy, creating deliberate confusion in the hope that it will drive the monkeys into the trap, or cause a mother to drop her baby.

Although chimp communities appear by-and-large to be stable and peaceful entities, intensive warfare has been known to erupt once each within the habituated communities of Mahale and Gombe. In Mahale, one of the two communities originally habituated by researchers in 1967 had exterminated the other by 1982. A similar thing happened in Gombe Stream in the 1970s, when the Kasekela community as originally habituated by Goodall divided into two discrete communities. The Kasekela and breakaway Kahama community co-existed alongside each other for some years. Then in 1974, Goodall returned to Gombe Stream after a break to discover that the Kasekela males were methodically persecuting their former community mates, isolating the Kahama males one by one, and tearing into them until they were dead or terminally wounded. By 1977, the Kahama community had vanished entirely.

Chimpanzees are essentially inhabitants of the western rainforest, but their range does extend into the extreme west of Tanzania, Rwanda and Uganda, whose combined population of perhaps 7,000 individuals is assigned to the race *P. t. schweinfurthii*. The Rwandan chimp population of around 400 individuals is now thought to be confined to Nyungwe National Park (including a small community in the Cyamudongo Forest), but it remains faintly possible that a small population recorded in the early 1990s in the more northerly and badly degraded Gishwati Forest still persists. Although East Africa's chimps represent less than 3% of the global population, much of what is known about wild chimpanzee society and behaviour stems from the region, in particular the ongoing research projects initiated in Tanzania's Gombe Stream and Mahale Mountain National Parks back in the 1960s.

An interesting pattern that emerged from the parallel research projects in these two reserves, situated little more than 100km apart along the shore of Lake Tanganyika, is a variety of social and behavioural differences between their chimp populations. Of the plant species common to both national parks, for instance, as many as 40% of those utilised as a food source by chimps in the one reserve are not eaten by chimps in the other. In Gombe Stream, chimps appear to regard the palmnut as something of a delicacy, but while the same plants grow profusely in Mahale, the chimps there have yet to be recorded eating them. Likewise, the 'termite-fishing' behaviour first recorded by Jane Goodall at Gombe Stream in the 1960s has a parallel in Mahale, where the chimps are often seen 'fishing' for carpenter ants in the trees. But the Mahale chimps have never been recorded fishing for termites, while the Gombe chimps are not known to fish for carpenter ants. Mahale's chimps routinely groom each other with one hand while holding their other hands together above their heads – once again, behaviour that has never been noted at Gombe. More than any structural similarity, more even than any single quirk of chimpanzee behaviour, it is such striking cultural differences – the influence of nurture over nature if you like – that bring home our close genetic kinship with chimpanzees.

of 400, resident in the forest around the campsite, is thought to be the largest troop of arboreal primates anywhere in Africa – elsewhere in the world, only the Chinese golden monkey moves in groups of a comparable number.

Most of the other monkeys in Nyungwe are guenons, the collective name for the taxonomically confusing Cercopithecus genus. Most guenons are arboreal forest-dwelling omnivores, noted for their colourful coats and the male's bright red or blue genitals. The most striking of Nyungwe's guenons is **L'Hoest's monkey** *Cercopithecus l'hoesti*, a large and unusually terrestrial monkey, whose cryptic grey and red coat is offset by a bold white 'beard' which renders it unmistakable. As with the Ruwenzori colobus, L'Hoest's monkey, also known as mountain monkey, is more or less confined to the Albertine Rift, and is very scarce elsewhere in its restricted range. In Nyungwe, it is the most frequently encountered monkey, with troops of 5–15 animals often seen along the roadside, within the forest, and even in the campsite.

Likely to be encountered along the road and around the campsite, the **silver monkey** *C. doggetti*, formerly considered to be a race of blue monkey *C. mitis*, is similar in build and general appearance to L'Hoest's monkey, but lacks the diagnostic white beard. The silver monkey typically lives in small family parties, though solitary males are also often encountered in Nyungwe. Some sources list the closely related golden monkey *C. kandti* for Nyungwe, but this appears to be an error – though it is not impossible that a small population of this ARE inhabits the remote bamboo forests close to the Burundi border.

These southerly bamboo forests definitely provide refuge to the rare and secretive **owl-faced monkey** *C. hamlyni*, another ARE whose modern range is restricted to a handful of montane forests. This thickset, plain grey, pug-faced monkey was first recorded in Nyungwe as recently as 1992, and it remains the least-known of the monkeys in the reserve – the 1999 WCS survey was unable to locate a single individual, but researchers monitoring the population close to the Burundi border reckon they encounter the monkeys at most twice a week.

Another guenon whose status within Nyungwe is uncertain is the **red-tailed monkey** *C. ascanius*, a small and highly active arboreal monkey most easily distinguished by its bright white nose. Generally associated with low-elevation forest, the red-faced monkey now faces extinction within Nyungwe owing to much of its habitat having been cleared for cultivation over recent decades. The solitary individual that hangs out with a colobus troop on the tea estate is presumably unlikely ever to find a breeding partner, though we have been told that a small but viable population of red-tailed monkeys survives on the fringes of the forest reserve near Banda.

Dent's monkey *C. denti*, formerly considered to be a race of mona monkey *C. Mona*, is widespread within Nyungwe, and occurs at all elevations, but it is infrequently seen by tourists. Another typical forest guenon, **Dent's mona** is distinguished from other monkeys in the forest by its contrasting black back and white belly, blue-white forehead, and yellowish ear tufts. It often moves with other guenons, and is mostly likely to be seen in the forest patch in the Gisakura Tea Estate or at Karamba, along the road to Uwinka not far from the Gisakura Guesthouse. Some sources incorrectly list the **crowned monkey** *C. pogonias* for Nyungwe, but this is a West African lowland species, considered by some to be a race of mona monkey.

Unlikely to be seen within the forest proper, the **vervet monkey** *C. aethiops* is a grizzled grey guenon of savanna and open woodland, with a distinctive black face mask. Probably the most numerous monkey in the world, the vervet is occasionally encountered on the forest verge and around the Gisakura Guesthouse, where it is often quite tame and regularly raids crops.

Another savanna monkey occasionally seen along the road through Nyungwe is the **olive baboon** *Papio anubis*, a predominantly terrestrial primate which lives in large troops. After the chimpanzee, this is by far the largest and stockiest of the forest's primates, with a uniform dark olive coat and the canine snout and large teeth characteristic of all baboons. The olive baboon is very aggressive and, like the vervet monkey, it frequently raids crops.

Intermediate in size between the olive baboon and the various guenons, the **grey-cheeked mangabey** *Cercocebus albigena* is an arboreal monkey of the forest interior. Rather more spindly than any guenon, the grey-cheeked mangabey has a uniform dark-brown coat and grey-brown cape, and is renowned for its loud gobbling call. It lives in small troops, typically around ten animals, and is localised in Nyungwe because of its preference for lower altitudes.

Other primates In addition to chimpanzees and monkeys, Nyungwe harbours four types of prosimian, small nocturnal primates more closely related to the lemurs of Madagascar than to any other primates of the African mainland. These are three species of **bushbaby** or galago (a group of tiny, hyperactive wide-eyed insectivores) and the sloth-like **potto**. All are very unlikely to be encountered by tourists.

BIRDS Nyungwe is probably the single most important birdwatching destination in Rwanda, with 278 bird species recorded, of which the majority are forest specialists and 26 are regional endemics whose range is restricted to a few forests along the Albertine Rift. Birdwatching in Nyungwe can be rather frustrating, since the vegetation is thick and many birds tend to stick to the canopy, but almost everything you do see ranks as a good sighting.

You don't have to be an ardent birdwatcher to appreciate some of Nyungwe's birds. Most people, for instance, will do a double-take when they first spot a great blue turaco, a chicken-sized bird with garish blue, green and yellow feathers, often seen gliding between the trees along the main road. Another real gem is the paradise flycatcher, a long-tailed blue, orange and (sometimes) white bird often seen around the guesthouse. Other birds impress with their bizarre appearance – the gigantic forest hornbills, for instance, whose wailing vocalisations are almost as comical as their ungainly bills and heavy-winged flight. And, when tracking through the forest undergrowth, watch out for the red-throated alethe, a very

PROPOSED TOURISM PRICING FOR NYUNGWE NATIONAL PARK

Package		Foreign Visitor	Foreign Resident	Nationals/EA members	Comment
Trails	1 day	US$40	US$30	Rfr3,000	Includes entrance fees
	2–3 days	US$60	US$45	Rfr4,000	and a trek on any
	4–7 days	US$80	US$60	Rfr5,000	nature trail.
Chimpanzee visits	1 day	US$90	US$60	Rfr5,000	Include entrance fees,
	2–3 days	US$110	US$95	Rfr7,000	nature walk, and US$50
	4–7 days	US$130	US$110	Rfr10,000	chimp visit fee
Other primates	1 day	US$70	US$45	Rfr3,000	Includes entrance fees,
	2–3 days	US$90	US$60	Rfr4,000	nature walk and US$30
	4–7 days	US$110	US$75	Rfr5,000	primate visit fee
Annual pass	Single		US$100	Rfr15,000	Includes entrance fees
	Couple		US$150	Rfr25,000	plus nature walk, but not
	Family		US$200	Rfr30,000	chimp or primate visits

localised bird with a distinctive blue-white eyebrow. The alethe habitually follows colobus troops to eat the insects they disturb, and based on our experience it sees humans as merely another large mammal, often perching within a few inches!

The priorities of more serious birdwatchers will depend to some extent on their experience elsewhere in Africa. It is difficult to imagine, for instance, that a first-time visitor to the continent will get as excited about a drab Chubb's cisticola as they will when they first see a paradise flycatcher or green pigeon. For somebody coming from southern Africa, at least half of what they see will be new to them, with a total of about 60 relatively widespread East African forest specials headed by the likes of great blue turaco, Ross's turaco, red-breasted sparrowhawk and white-headed wood-hoopoe.

From an East African perspective, however, it is the Albertine Rift Endemics that are the most alluring. Depending on your level of expertise, you could reasonably hope to tick off half of these over a few days in the forest. Of the 26 avian AREs found in Nyungwe National Park, the following are reasonably common: handsome francolin, Rwenzori turaco, red-faced woodland warbler, collared apalis, mountain masked apalis, yellow-eyed black flycatcher, Rwenzori batis, stripe-breasted tit, regal sunbird, blue-headed sunbird, purple-breasted sunbird, dusky crimsonwing and strange weaver. Also common but rather more localized, Grauer's rush warbler and red-collared mountain babbler are respectively confined to Kamiranzovu Swamp and Mount Bigugu. The nocturnal Rwenzori nightjar and secretive creeper-loving Grauer's warbler are both common but difficult to observe. Short-tailed warbler, Shelley's crimsonwing, red-throated alethe, Kungwe apalis, Archer's robin-chat, Kivu ground thrush, dwarf honeyguide and Albertine owlet are uncommon, and Rockefeller's sunbird is very rare.

CHAMELEONS

Common and widespread in Rwanda, but not easily seen unless they are actively searched for, chameleons are arguably the most intriguing of African reptiles. True chameleons of the family Chamaeleontidae are confined to the Old World, with the most important centre of speciation being the island of Madagascar, to which about half of the world's 130 described species are endemic. Another two species of chameleon occur in each of Asia and Europe, while the remainder are distributed across mainland Africa, with at least eight species recorded from Rwanda, most of which are forest species associated with Nyungwe National Park.

Chameleons are best known for their capacity to change colour, a trait that is often exaggerated in popular literature, and which is generally influenced by mood more than the colour of the background. Some chameleons are more adept at changing colour than others, the most variable being the common chameleon *Chamaeleo chamaeleon* of the Mediterranean region, with more than 100 colour and pattern variations recorded. Many African chameleons are typically green in colour but will gradually take on a browner hue when they descend from the foliage in more exposed terrain, for instance while crossing a road. Several change colour and pattern far more dramatically when they feel threatened or are confronted by a rival of the same species. Different chameleon species also vary greatly in size, with the largest being Oustalet's chameleon of Madagascar, known to reach a length of almost 80cm.

A remarkable physiological feature common to all true chameleons is their protuberant round eyes, which offer a potential 180° degree vision on both sides and are able to swivel around independently of each other. Only when one of them isolates a suitably juicy-looking insect will the two eyes focus in the same direction as the chameleon stalks slowly forward until it is close enough to use the other unique weapon in its armoury. This is its sticky-tipped tongue, which is typically about the same length as

The guides at Nyungwe are improving and some are excellent, but others have only limited knowledge. For this reason, you will be highly dependent on a field guide, and without a great amount of advance research you are bound to struggle to identify every bird that you glimpse. Given the above, relict forest patches and the road verge are often more productive than the forest interior, since you'll get clearer views of what you do see.

OTHER CREATURES While monkeys and to a lesser extent birds tend to attract the most attention, Nyungwe's fauna also includes a large number of smaller animals. With only 12 species recorded, snakes are relatively poorly represented, due to the chilly climate – probably good news for most visitors – but colourful lizards are often seen on the rocks, and at least five species of chameleon occur in the forest. Nyungwe also harbours more than 100 different types of colourful butterfly, including 40 regional endemics. Look out, too, for the outsized beetles and bugs that are characteristic of all tropical forests. Equally remarkable, but only to be admired at a distance of a metre or so, are the vast columns of army ants that move across the forest trails – step on one of these columns, and you'll know all about it, as these guys can bite!

FURTHER INFORMATION A basic fact-sheet about the forest is available from the ORTPN tourist office in Kigali. An excellent booklet entitled *Nyungwe National Park* is sold for Rfr7,000 at ORTPN offices countrywide (including Uwinka). More practical is the new 104-page *Guide to Trails and Excursions in Nyungwe National Park*, a colour booklet that should be available by 2010.

its body and remains coiled up within its mouth most of the time, to be unleashed in a sudden, blink-and-you'll-miss-it lunge to zap a selected item of prey. In addition to their unique eyes and tongues, many chameleons are adorned with an array of facial casques, flaps, horns and crests that enhance their already somewhat fearsome prehistoric appearance.

In Rwanda, you're most likely to come across a chameleon by chance when it is crossing a road, in which case it should be easy to take a closer look at it, since most chameleons move painfully slowly and deliberately. Chameleons are also often seen on night game drives, when their ghostly nocturnal colouring shows up clearly under a spotlight – as well as making it pretty clear why these strange creatures are regarded with both fear and awe in many local African cultures. More actively, you could ask your guide if they know where to find a chameleon – a few individuals will be resident in most lodge grounds.

The flap-necked chameleon *Chamaeleo delepis* is probably the most regularly observed species of savanna and woodland habitats in East Africa. Often seen crossing roads, the flap-necked chameleon is generally around 15cm long and bright green in colour with few distinctive markings, but individuals might be up to 30cm in length and will turn tan or brown under the right conditions.

Characteristic of East African montane forests, the horned chameleons form a closely allied species cluster of some taxonomic uncertainty. They are typically darker than the savanna chameleons and, significantly, the males of all taxa within this cluster are distinguished by up to three nasal horns that project forward from their face. In Rwanda, the cluster is represented by the Rwenzori three-horned chameleon *C. Johnstoni*, a range-restricted ARE that can grow up to 30cm long and is reasonably common in Nyungwe National Park, where it supplements a diet of insects with more substantial fare such as small lizards.

Keen birdwatchers should try to lay their hands on the out-of-print checklist of the forest's birds, which gives Latin, English and French names as well as a good indication of each species' habitat and relative abundance within the reserve.

A more esoteric publication, of interest primarily to researchers and to a lesser extent birdwatchers, is the WCS Working Paper ed 19 *Biodiversity Surveys of the Nyungwe Forest Reserve in Southwest Rwanda* (Plumptre, Andrew, 2002), which includes detailed results of a mammal and bird inventory that took place in 1999. It can be downloaded from the website www.wcs.org/science.

GETTING THERE AND AWAY

Nyungwe Forest Reserve is bisected by the main surfaced road between Butare and Cyangugu. The Uwinka Reception Centre and Campsite lies alongside the main road, and is well signposted 90km from Butare and 54km from Cyangugu. The Gisakura Guesthouse is also on the main road, 18km closer to Cyangugu, on the right side of the road and about 2km after you exit the western boundary of the forest reserve coming from Butare. Nyungwe Forest Lodge lies between the two. Note that there is some talk that the section of the main Butare–Cyangugu road that passes through Nyungwe will close to non-touristic traffic as and when the main road between Kibuye and Cyangugu is surfaced.

PARK FEES

Costs can mount up at Nyungwe, with all the possibilities, so plan carefully and check beforehand in case of increases. An entrance fee of US$20 per person per day is charged to non-residents and foreign residents. Chimpanzee tracking costs US$50 for non-residents or US$30 for resident foreigners, while other guided walks cost US$30 per person for non-residents or US$15 for resident foreigners (with substantial discounts available to children under the age of 15). Citizens of Rwanda pay an entrance fee of Rfr1,000 and Rfr2,000–4,000 per person for the various guided walks. Note that these fees are likely to be replaced by those in the box on page 147. It's normal to tip the guides if you feel they've done a good job.

WHERE TO STAY AND EAT

UPMARKET

Nyungwe Forest Lodge (24 rooms) ✆ 0252 504330; m 078 8351000; www.nyungweforestlodge.com. Scheduled to open in Jan 2010, this new lodge has a lovely setting within the Gisakura Tea Estate, right on the forested park boundary. Situated between the junction to Gisakura Tea Estate & the Gisakura Guesthouse, it lies about 2km from the main Cyangugu road, along a dirt road signposted to the right coming from the direction of Butare. Accommodation is in timber chalets that look out over the forest gallery, & facilities will include a spa, restaurant & boardroom. As with Akagera Safari Lodge & Gorillas' Nest in Kinigi, it is owned by Dubai World & managed as part of the Mantis Collection. *US$300 dbl B&B.*

Kageno Eco-lodge (2 rooms) ✆ (US) 1 212 227 0509; e info@kageno.org; www.kageno.org. Set on the hillside above Banda village, about an hour's drive north of the main Butare–Cyangugu road, this new lodge forms part of a community project that has already constructed a health centre, pharmacy & fresh source of clean water for 5,000 people in the village (see website for more details). Designed by an award-winning New York architectural firm & scheduled to open in Apr 2010, it will comprise 2 luxurious solar-powered stone-&-tile bungalows, each with 2 queen-size beds, a couch that opens into a 3rd bed, western bathrooms, a dining area, & general amenities on par with a 3-star hotel. The site offers lovely views over the forest to Lake Kivu, & is ideally located for tracking a chimp community that sticks close to the village during the fruiting season of Apr–Sep. There will be a restaurant & gift shop selling traditional handicrafts. *US$250/420/520 sgl/dbl/trpl FB.*

MODERATE

🏠 **Gisakura Guesthouse** (6 rooms) m 078 8675051; e ghnyungwe@yahoo.com; ⊕ S 02°26.281; E 029°05.548; 1,931m. Also known as the ORTPN Guesthouse, though it is now privately managed, this cosy little place stands 2km outside the forest close to the Gisakura Tea Estate. It offers comfortable no-frills accommodation using clean communal showers & toilets, & serves good meals for Rfr4,000–5,000 along with a small selection of beers & sodas. For travellers dependent on public transport, the location 18km from Uwinka is a little inconvenient, but it is well placed for the excellent Isumo Trail & visits to the colobus troop on the Gisakura Tea Estate. Vervet monkeys occasionally pass through the guesthouse grounds, a fair variety of birds are present in the small patch of forest in front of the guesthouse, while several sunbird species are likely to be seen when the garden is in bloom. A number of nearby relict forest patches offer good birdwatching, as well as a chance of encountering forest monkeys. *Rfr15,000/20,000/25,000 sgl/twin/dbl B&B.*

BUDGET

🏠 **KCCEM Guesthouse** (20 rooms) m 078 8501583/8447739; e kctckitabi@yahoo.com. The recently founded Kitabi College of Conservation & Environmental Management, which stands alongside the new Kitabi Gate on the eastern boundary of the park, operates a very reasonably priced guesthouse & canteen. There are 4 bungalows, each with 5 small but clean bedrooms & 2 shared bathrooms with toilet & hot shower, & pretty views over a valley covered in tea plantations & forest. The canteen charges Rfr2,500 for lunch or dinner & Rfr1,500 for b/fast. *Rooms Rfr6,000/10,000 sgl/dbl.*

🏠 **Gisakura Tea Estate Guesthouse** (3 rooms) m 078 8489251; ⊕ S 02°27.102; E 029°05.194; 1,953m. Situated on the Gisakura Tea Estate, about 1km back towards the forest boundary from Gisakura Guesthouse, this is a more basic & affordable option, but it's advisable to call ahead before you arrive. In addition to simple accommodation, there is a communal lounge, beers & sodas are available at the nearby estate canteen, & meals can be arranged with a few hours' notice. The guesthouse lies less than 500m from the forest patch where colobus are resident, & the area offers good birding. Other trails can be arranged at the ORTPN office next to the Gisakura Guesthouse, a 20-min walk away. To reach the tea estate's guesthouse, follow the dirt road into the tea estate (signposted 'Usine à thé Gisakura') for about 500m until you reach a large traffic circle, then follow the central road branching from this circle (at roughly 2 o'clock) for about 200m. *Rfr10,000 dbl.*

CAMPING

⛺ **Uwinka Reception Centre & Campsite** m 078 8436763; ⊕ S 02°28.696; E 029°12.007; 2,442m. Set in the heart of the forest, yet only a couple of hundred metres from the main road, the campsite here has a perfect (albeit rather chilly) location on a high ridge, with individual sites scattered over a wide area of forest. It's also the most convenient for hikes, particularly if you have no vehicle, as the trailhead for the coloured Uwinka Trails start from here, for tracking the 400-strong troop of colobus, & for the soon-to-open canopy walk. There's a small orchid nursery nearby. A semi-habituated troop of L'Hoest's monkey passes through every morning & most afternoons, as does the occasional troop of silver monkey & a variety of forest birds. The main road adjacent to the campsite is also worth exploring, for the great views & variety of birds. Drinks are available at reasonable prices, & a restaurant is planned for the new upgraded visitors' centre, but for the time being campers must bring all food. Also bring sufficient warm clothing to offset the chilly night temperatures at high altitude. *Camping costs US$20 pp per night for non-residents, US$10 for residents, & Rfr2,000 for citizens. When the new price schedule is implemented, this will change to US$20 for all foreigners or Rfr5,000 for all East African nationals who have used other tourism products, & US$40 for non-residents, US$30 for residents, & Rfr5,000 for East African nationals who haven't used other tourism products.*

TRAILS AND ACTIVITIES

A large selection of walking possibilities and other excursions is available within Nyungwe. Visitors with a vehicle and sufficient interest could easily keep themselves busy for a week without significantly retracing their steps. The options for travellers without private transport are limited, however, and depend greatly on which accommodation option they choose.

The main centre of activities, the hilltop Uwinka Reception Centre is the trailhead for the main trail network, and is also a good site for chimpanzee tracking and colobus viewing. There are also good walking options out of the Gisakura Reception Centre (alongside Gisakura Guesthouse) and Kitabi Reception Centre (at the eponymous entrance), as well as several trails that lead from other points along the main road. All reception centres are open 07.00–17.00 daily. The village of Banda is the best base for chimpanzee tracking but this activity can also be undertaken from Uwinka or the isolated Cyamudongo Forest bloc between Nyungwe and Cyangugu.

All forest trails are steep and often very slippery, so dress accordingly. Jeans, a thick shirt and good walking shoes are the ideal outfit, and a waterproof jacket will be useful during the rainy season.

UWINKA AND SURROUNDS The main centre of activities is the hilltop Uwinka Reception Centre (m *078 8436763/8866625;* e *reservation@rwandatourism.com*), which forms the trailhead for the main network of trails, and is also a good site for chimpanzee tracking and colobus viewing. By the time you read this, Uwinka will probably have been transformed by renovations and additions funded by USAID. These include a new Interpretation Centre with a deck overlooking the forest, a restaurant and canteen, two trailhead shelters, and a Visitor Centre. There are also plans to expand the parking lot and redo the stairs uphill from there. More exciting still is the construction of a new canopy walk along the Igishigishigi Trail, as detailed below.

A relict of the earliest attempt to develop tourism at Nyungwe in the late 1980s, a network of six walking trails leads downhill from Uwinka into the surrounding forested hills. At the time of writing, each trail is designated by a particular colour, but a new set of names has been adopted and should come into use by 2010, and we have used both in the table below. The footpaths are all well maintained and clearly marked, but don't underestimate the steepness of the slopes or – after rain – the muddy conditions, which can be fairly tough going at this high altitude.

The Uwinka Trails pass through the territory of a habituated troop of 400 colobus monkeys. During the rainy season, a troop of chimpanzees often moves into this area as well, and it is up to you to decide whether to pay extra to track

UWINKA TRAILS			*With Tracey Clarke*
New name	**Old name**	**Length & grading**	**Meaning**
Imbaraga trail	Red trail	9.8km, 6hrs, difficult	Imbaraga means strength, reflecting how difficult the trail is
Umuyove trail	Pink trail	5.5km, 3.5hrs, moderate	Umuyove is a mahogany, many large specimens of which are seen on this trail
Umugote trail	Blue trail	3.6km, 3hrs, moderate	Umugote is a Syzygium tree, which is common on this trail
Igishigishigi trail	Green trail	2.4km, 1.5hrs, easy	Igishigishigi means a tree fern, which is more common here than elsewhere in Nyungwe
Buhoro Trail	Grey trail	2km, 1.5hrs, easy	Buhoro means slow, and this short trail is an easy slow walk
Irebero trail	Yellow trail	3.6km, 3hrs, moderate	Irebero means a viewpoint, and there are some magnificent ones on this trail

them. You can reasonably expect to see some primates along any of the Trails, as well as a good variety of forest birds, though the latter require patience and regular stops where there are open views into the canopy. Unless you opt for a specific primate visit, chance will be the decisive factor in what you see, though the Umugote Trail is regarded as especially good for primates and birds, while the Imbaraga Trail is good for chimpanzees and passes four waterfalls. Birdwatchers should explore the main road close to Uwinka, as they will probably see a greater variety of birds here than from within the forest. About 500m east of the campsite, the road offers some stunning views over the forested valleys, and passes a stand of giant lobelias.

Canopy walkway Scheduled to open before the end of 2009, a canopy walkway similar to the famous one in Ghana's Kakum National Park is currently being constructed on the Igishigishigi Trail. Suspended between giant trees about 1km from Uwinka, the walkway will be at least 200m long, and it will offer views into the forest canopy (superb birding opportunity) east of a stream bed lined with tall trees and ferns. The canopy walkway experience can be undertaken as a round trip using the Igishigishigi Trail, or integrated into the Umuyove or more challenging Imbaraga Trail.

Mangabey tracking Sightings of the grey-cheeked mangabey are infrequent unless you make a special excursion, a trip which requires a private vehicle. A mangabey troop, resident in a patch of forest along the Banda road, has been habituated by researchers, who normally spend every Monday and Friday with it (consequently, these are the best days to visit the monkeys, as they will already have been tracked down when you arrive). The turn-off to Banda, 800m from the Uwinka Campsite towards Butare, is signposted 'Eclise Episcopa de Rwanda'. The monkeys are usually found between 5km and 10km along the turn-off. Tracking the mangabeys is regarded as a formal primate visit, and must be done in the company of a guide. L'Hoest's, silver and colobus monkeys are also often seen in this area.

Chimpanzee tracking at Uwinka/Banda A habituated chimpanzee community has its territory on the forested slopes that divide Uwinka from the village of Banda, and it can be tracked from either base. The most reliable season for tracking is April to September, when fruiting trees lure the chimps close to Banda, and they can often be seen within a kilometre of the village. At other times of year the chimps range more widely, but they are still very habituated once you do locate them. It is advisable to start early, around 05.30, in order to pick them up close to their overnight nests. The best starting point is usually Banda, which lies about 15km from the main road and about one hour's drive from Gisakura or Kitabi and 45 minutes from Uwinka. For those without a vehicle (or when the Banda Road is impassable, as may be the case after heavy rain), it is also possible to track the chimps from Uwinka, but be prepared for a tough hike on steep slippery slopes!

OTHER TRAILS AND ACTIVITIES The many trails and activities below are covered from east to west, starting with the Ngabwe Trail near Kitabi entrance gate on the Butare road and ending at the Cyamudongo Forest, a western annex to the main national park.

Ngabwe Trail (4.7km, 3 hours, moderate) Set on the slopes of Ngabwe near the park's eastern boundary, this new circular trail passes through a wide variety of vegetation zones over a relatively short distance, and there is a spectacular camping/picnic site with a toilet and benches at the summit. It starts about 200m

On 19 September 2005, three men set out to make a complete ascent of the Nile from the sea to the source.

Known as the Ascend the Nile Expedition, Neil McGrigor, Cam McLeay and Garth McIntyre took to the water in Rashid in Egypt and travelled in tiny inflatable boats ('Zap Cats'), just 4m long and with outboard engines, for the entire length of the river, over 6,700km. Their journey took them through five challenging countries: Egypt, Sudan, Uganda, Tanzania and finally Rwanda.

The expedition was self-sufficient but did receive some support from Fortnum & Mason, the famous store based in London's Piccadilly, which had previously supplied Stanley's 1875 expedition with goodies such as thick-cut marmalade, humbugs and sardines. Hampers were delivered to the team throughout their journey.

En route they faced enormous difficulties, not least ascending the many river rapids, facing crocodiles head on and avoiding numerous pods of hippos. The weather ranged from searing heat to continuous rain, while the river changed from a wide blue delta in Egypt to a muddy puddle at its source in Rwanda.

Apprehension and frustration turned to real fear and sorrow when, in November 2005, the men came under attack from rebels in Uganda. A close friend of the team was killed and the remaining members were injured. The expedition's future was in doubt. But the team decided to continue to their goal.

On 3 March 2006 they resumed, crossing Lake Victoria and reaching the border of Tanzania and Rwanda. It was this part of the journey that offered unexpected challenges: larger-than-predicted rapids, cold nights and achingly slow progress on foot through the Nyungwe Forest as the team edged ever closer to the Nile's new source that they were so determined to find.

Finally, on 31 March 2006, they reached their goal at the headwater of the Rukarara River, a tributary of the Akagera which in turn drains into Lake Victoria. With their patient guides, the team planted a flag to mark the spot on the slopes of Mount Bigugu and the celebrations began. News of the expedition and its findings made its way across the world, reaching as far as China and Russia.

Using research and modern navigation equipment, they have been able to demonstrate that they discovered another, longer source than that pinpointed by Dr Kandt in 1898. Kandt had not had the benefit of either the maps drawn by the Belgians in 1937 or the Global Positioning System from which the team had re-measured the entire length of the Nile – which turns out to be some 107km longer than previously recorded! It's possible to walk to the source; see under *Other trails and activities*, opposite.

The co-ordinates of the new longest source, deep in Rwanda's Nyungwe Forest, are: Latitude S 02°16'055.962"; Longitude E 29°19'052.470"; Elevation 2,428m/7,966ft. For more details of the expedition, see www.ascendthenile.com.

down a side road on the left some 3km past Kitabi entrance gate, and passes through areas of mature forest rich in strangler figs, as well as shrubbier and heath communities. L'Hoest's, silver and colobus monkeys are common here, while mangabey, chimpanzee and black-fronted duiker are seen occasionally. The trail can be extended to an 8-hour walk through Kitabi Tea Plantation. The trail ends 1.2km closer to the gate than where it started.

Congo-Nile Divide Trail (42.2km, 3–4 days, difficult) Cut in 2007, the only multi-day trek in Nyungwe's Congo-Nile Divide Trail follows the spectacular ridge that forms the continental divide between the Congo and Nile watersheds. It's a challenging but rewarding wilderness hike, and includes a visit to a sedge marsh identified as the source of the White Nile by Richard Kandt a century before *Ascend the Nile* identified a more remote source in 2006. There are stunning views most of the way, switchback ascents to several tall peaks, and the trail passes through a cross-section of the park's main habitats, including bracken fields, primary and secondary forest, bamboo forest, ericaceous shrub, marsh and open fields swathed in wildflowers. The park authorities recommend traversing from north to south, starting at a trailhead near Musarara about 3 hours north of Gisakura on a rough dirt road, and three overnight stops is ideal, though fit hikers could cut back to two. The trail ends on the main Butare–Cyangugu road 7km west of Uwinka.

Source of the Nile It is possible to visit the newly identified Source of the Nile (see box *Ascend the Nile* opposite) near Gisovu Tea Factory by advance arrangement with ORTPN. It is an easy walk, taking 45–60 minutes in either direction from the trailhead, but the drive there from Gisakura or Kitabi takes 3–4 hours in either direction on rough dirt roads. The trailhead is more quickly reached from Kibuye, a 60-minute drive following the Cyangugu Road southward then taking the signposted turn-off for Gisovu Tea Factory, but you will need to ring through to Uwinka to arrange for a guide to meet you there.

Muzimu Trail (5.2km, 3.5 hours, moderate) This remote trail lies in the northeast of the park, and the trailhead lies two hours' drive in either direction from Gisakura. It passes through an area dominated by open heath-like vegetation and tangled scrub, and is particularly rewarding for wildflowers and non-forest birds. It is notable for offering several 360° panoramic views over the park, with Lake Kivu shimmering below, and – on a clear day – the volcanic peaks of the Virungas on the distant horizon.

Bigugu Trail (6.7km in either direction, 6 hours, difficult) Aimed squarely at the 'because it's there' fraternity, the steep and slippery 7km trail leads to the 2,950m Bigugu Peak, which is the highest point in Nyungwe National Park. Suitable only for reasonably fit walkers, the trail starts about 4km from Uwinka along the Butare Road (the trailhead is clearly marked). Birders come here to see the localised red-collared mountain babbler, but the area also boasts some wonderful wildflowers, ranging from red-hot pokers and orchids to giant lobelias.

Rangiro Road The dirt road to Rangiro, which leaves the main tar road about 1.5km east of Uwinka, is regarded as the best excursion for dedicated birdwatchers. This is because the road passes through both high- and low-elevation forest within a relatively short distance, and affords good views into the canopy in several places. A 4x4 vehicle is essential, and a guide recommended. In addition to birdwatching, the Rangiro road offers some stunning views over the mountains, and is a good place to see mangabeys, silver monkeys, and a variety of butterflies. You can continue all the way to Banda, where the local community tours are offered.

Kamiranzovu Marsh Trail (6km, 3 hours, moderate) This botanically exciting trail leads from the forested main road downhill to the relatively low-lying Kamiranzovu Marsh, which is the park's largest wetland habitat, set within a caldera-like depression. It was the favoured haunt of Nyungwe's elephants before they became extinct, and it remains fabulously rich in orchids, particularly during the rainy season, and localised swamp-associated birds such as Grauer's rush warbler and Albertine owlet (the latter is most likely to be seen on a nocturnal visit, with a guide who has a recording of its call).

Karamba Trail (4km, 3 hours, easy) One of the easiest walks in Nyungwe, and the best for birdwatching, this circular trail ascends through a relatively flat and open area to a 360° viewpoint. The absence of big trees is largely because of human disturbance, first as a gold mine and market, then as a quarry for road-building material, and most recently as an army camp. The footpath is on quartzite rock, so it's less muddy than other trails at Nyungwe, but it forms a stream after rain. About 500m into the walk, there is a large hole offering a perfect cutaway view of all rainforest strata. Plants here include white *Satyrium* orchids and giant tree ferns normally seen in moist, rainforest valleys. At the viewpoint is a bench where you can look out for birds and monkeys. The Karamba area is the best part of Nyungwe for Dent's mona monkey, and the large troop that lives here sometimes keeps company with red-tailed monkeys.

Isumo (Waterfall) Trail (10.6km, 4 hours, moderate) This superb trail starts at the Gisakura Guesthouse and can be shortened by driving the first 3km to the car

THE NILE RIVER

The Nile is the world's longest river, flowing for more than 6,650km (4,130 miles) from its most remote headwaters in Burundi and Rwanda to the delta formed as it enters the Mediterranean in Egypt. Its vast drainage basin occupies more than 10% of the African mainland and includes portions of nine countries: Tanzania, Burundi, Rwanda, the DRC, Kenya, Uganda, Ethiopia, Sudan and Egypt. While passing through southern Sudan, the Nile also feeds the 5.5 million hectare Sudd or Bar-el-Jebel, the world's most expansive wetland system.

A feature of the Nile Basin is a marked decrease in precipitation as it runs further northward. In the East African lakes region and Ethiopian Highlands, mean annual rainfall figures are typically in excess of 1,000mm. Rainfall in south and central Sudan varies from 250–500mm annually, except in the Sudd (900mm), while in the deserts north of Khartoum the annual rainfall is little more than 100mm, dropping to 25mm in the south of Egypt, then increasing to around 200mm closer to the Mediterranean.

The Nile has served as the lifeblood of Egyptian agriculture for millennia, carrying not only water, but also silt, from the fertile tropics into the sandy expanses of the Sahara. Indeed, it is widely believed that the very first agricultural societies arose on the floodplain of the Egyptian Nile, and so, certainly, did the earliest and most enduring of all human civilisations. The antiquity of the name Nile, which simply means river valley, is reflected in the ancient Greek (Nelios), Semetic (Nahal) and Latin (Nilus).

Over the past 50 years, several hydroelectric dams have been built along the Nile, notably the Aswan Dam in Egypt and the Owen Falls Dam in Uganda. The Aswan Dam doesn't merely provide hydroelectric power, it also supplies water for various irrigation schemes, and protects crops downriver from destruction by heavy flooding. Built in 1963, the dam wall rises 110m above the River and is almost 4km long, producing up to 2,100 megawatts and forming the 450km-long Lake Nasser. The construction of the Aswan Dam enforced the resettlement of 90,000 Nubians, whilst the Temple of Abu Simbel, built 3,200 ago for the Pharaoh Rameses II, had to be relocated 65m higher.

The waterway plays a major role in transportation, especially in parts of the Sudan between May and November, when transportation of goods and people is not possible by road due to the floods. Like other rivers and lakes, the Nile provides a variety of fish as food. And its importance for conservation is difficult to overstate. The Sudd alone supports more than half the global populations of Nile lechwe and shoebill (more than 6,000), together with astonishing numbers of other water-associated birds – aerial surveys undertaken between 1979 and 1982 counted an estimated 1.7 million glossy park at the forest edge. The first part of the trail – in essence following the road to the car park – passes through rolling tea plantations dotted with relict forest patches which are worth scanning closely for silver and other monkeys. These small stands of forest can also be rich in birdlife; keen ornithologists might well want to take them slowly, and could perhaps view this section of the trail as a worthy birdwatching excursion in its own right.

The trail then descends into the forest proper, following flat contour paths through a succession of tree-fern-covered ravines, and crossing several streams, before a sharp descent to the base of a pretty but small waterfall. Monkeys are often seen along the way (the Angola colobus seems to be particularly common) and the steep slopes allow good views into the canopy. This trail can be very rewarding for true forest interior birds, with a good chance of spotting AREs such as Ruwenzori turaco and yellow-eyed black flycatcher.

ibis, 370,000 marabou stork, 350,000 open-billed stork, 175,000 cattle egret and 150,000 spur-winged goose.

The Nile has two major sources, often referred to as the White and Blue Nile, which flow respectively from Lake Victoria near Jinja and from Lake Tana in Ethiopia. The stretch of the White Nile that flows through southern Uganda is today known as the Victoria Nile (it was formerly called Kiira locally). From Jinja, it runs northward through the swampy Lake Kyoga, before veering west to descend into the Rift Valley over Murchison Falls and empty into Lake Albert. The Albert Nile flows from the northern tip of Lake Albert to enter the Sudan at Nimule, passing through the Sudd before it merges with the Blue Nile at the Sudanese capital of Khartoum, more than 3,000km from Lake Victoria.

The discovery of the source of the Blue Nile on Lake Tana is often accredited to the 18th-century Scots explorer James Bruce. In fact, its approximate (if not exact) location was almost certainly known to the ancients. The Old Testament mentions that the Ghion (Nile) 'compasseth the whole land of Ethiopia', evidently in reference to the arcing course followed by the river along the approximate southern boundary of Ethiopia's ancient Axumite Empire. There are, too, strong similarities in the design of the papyrus 'tankwa' used on Lake Tana to this day and the papyrus boats depicted in Ancient Egyptian paintings. Furthermore, the main river feeding Lake Tana rises at a spring known locally as Abay Minch (literally 'Nile Fountain'), a site held sacred by Ethiopian Christians, whose links with the Egyptian Coptic Church date to the 4th century AD. Bruce's claim is further undermined by the Portuguese stone bridge, built circa 1620, which crosses the Nile a few hundred metres downstream of the Blue Nile Falls and only 30km from the Lake Tana outlet.

By contrast, the source of the White Nile was for centuries one of the world's great unsolved mysteries. The Roman Emperor Nero once sent an expedition south from Khartoum to search for it, but it was forced to turn back at the edge of the Sudd. In 1862, Speke correctly identified Ripon Falls as the source of the Nile, a theory that would be confirmed by Stanley in 1875. Only as recently as 1937, however, did the German explorer Burkhart Waldecker locate the most remote of the Nile's headwaters in Burundi: a hillside spring known as Kasumo which forms the source of the Ruvyironza River, a tributary of the 690km long Kagera, the most important river to flow into Lake Victoria. Remarkably, however, the absolute location of the most remote source of the Nile still remains up for grabs in the early 21st century – as you can see in the box *Ascend the Nile* on page 154.

Based partially on text kindly supplied by Laura Sserunjogi, of the Source of the Nile Gardens in Jinja, Uganda.

Gisakura Tea Estate A relict forest patch in this tea estate, only 20 minutes' walk from the Gisakura Guesthouse, supports a resident troop of around 40 Ruwenzori colobus monkeys. This troop is very habituated, far more so than the larger troop at Uwinka, and the relatively small territory the monkeys occupy makes them very easy to locate and to see clearly. Oddly, a solitary red-tailed monkey moves with the colobus, and has done so for at least a decade (it was observed during the research trip of all four editions of this book!) – some of the guides say that it is the troop leader.

Other guides may tell you the odd monkey out at Gisakura is not a red-tailed but a mona (also known as Dent's monkey, and unlikely to be observed elsewhere in East Africa) or a hybrid red-tailed/mona. The apparent cause of this confusion is that a solitary mona monkey does spend some of its time in the same forest patch, and the guides are unable to distinguish it from its red-tailed cousin. In January 2006, this writer saw a red-tailed and a mona monkey concurrently from the rim, but several hundred metres apart, the former with the main colobus troop, the latter on its own. The two are easy to tell apart – the mona, though it has some white on its face, lacks the almost artificial-looking white beacon of a nose that distinguishes the red-tailed monkey!

Particularly in the early morning, the relict forest patch is also an excellent birdwatching site, since it lies in a ravine and is encircled by a road, making it easy to see deep into the canopy. Most of what you see are forest fringe or woodland species (as opposed to forest interior birds), but numerically this proved to be the most rewarding spot in Nyungwe, with some 40 species identified in an hour, notably black-throated apalis, paradise and white-tailed crested flycatcher, Chubb's cisticola, African golden oriole, green pigeon, olive-green cameroptera, three types of sunbird, two greenbuls and two crimson-wings.

Note that a visit to this forest patch is treated as a primate walk by the ORTPN office and a corresponding fee is charged.

Cyamudongo Forest Covering an area of about 6km², this patch of montane forest, situated about 45 minutes' drive south of the Shagasha Tea Estate on the main road between Gisakura and Cyangugu, is now protected as an isolated annexe to Nyungwe National Park. Despite its small size, Cyamudongo still harbours a community of perhaps 25 chimpanzees, currently being habituated, and often easier to locate than the chimps in the main forest block in the dry season (July, August, December), when the chimps tend to range more widely in search of food. Once located, the chimps here are fairly approachable. Other mammals present include L'Hoest's monkey, and – as one of the few true high-altitude forests left in Rwanda – Cyamudongo may well still harbour a few rare forest species that are no longer found in the main forest block at Nyungwe. Indeed, a new and presumably endemic purple orchid *Polystachya bruechertiae* was discovered here as recently as 2008.

Chimp tracking (and other guided walks) can be arranged at Uwinka or the Nyungwe park headquarters. You will need your own transport and a national park guide, and the drive from Gisakura takes about one hour, branching south from the main road to Cyangugu at the Shagasha Tea Estate. This enforces a seriously early start on chimp trackers, though we have heard vague talk of a community-based camp being installed here, something that might well happen during the lifespan of this edition. Either way, there are several forks along the road between the tea estate and the forest, so you may need to ask directions (bearing in mind that the forest is known locally as Nyirandakunze after a deceased queen).

Cyamudongo can also be approached from the south, as an extension of a drive to the hot springs at Bugarama. The closest town is Nyakabuye, a sprawl of traditional homesteads and a few tall concrete buildings centred around a bustling marketplace. Nyakabuye lies about 20km from Bugarama town, and 5km past the hot springs, in an area of plantation and bamboo forest. From the town, a steep road leads uphill for 8km, past traditional homesteads (evidently totally unused to tourists), before it winds through the indigenous forest for 2km. The forest ends at a T-junction in front of a large pine plantation, where a left turn along a 15km road, through rolling hills planted with tea, emerges on the surfaced Butare–Cyangugu road at the Shagasha Tea Estate.

It isn't easy to reach Cyamudongo Forest without private transport. With patience, it should be possible to catch a lift as far as Nyakabuye on the back of a truck from Bugarama. According to locals, Nyakabuye is also serviced by some sort of public transport direct from Kamembe (Cyangugu) on Wednesdays and Fridays. You'll almost certainly have to walk the 8km from town to the forest boundary, a steep but attractive trail, along which you are bound to attract a lot of friendly attention from curious children (and adults, for that matter). No formal accommodation exists in the area, but it is difficult to imagine that anybody would refuse permission to pitch a tent at one of the homesteads which line the road up to the forest, or that any significant risk would be attached to doing so. But the reality, as with any truly off-the-beaten-track travel, is that this trip should only be attempted by adventurous, flexible travellers who are prepared to deal with a total absence of tourist facilities.

8

Lake Kivu

Running for almost 100km along the Congolese border, Kivu is one of the string of 'inland seas' that submerge much of the Albertine Rift floor north of Zambia and south of the Sudan. With a surface area of 2,200km², Kivu is not comparable in extent to the most expansive of the Albertine Rift lakes, Tanganyika and Albert, but a maximum depth of 480m and total water content of 333km³ place it among the 20 deepest and 20 most voluminous freshwater bodies in the world. It is also very beautiful, with its deep blue water hemmed in by steeply terraced escarpments containing several peaks of 2,800m or higher, and the northern shore overlooked by the smoking outline of volcanic Nyiragongo.

A shallower incarnation of Kivu probably formed about two million years ago as a result of the same tectonic activity that created the Albertine Rift and other associated lakes. Back then, Kivu was probably contiguous with the much lower-lying Lake Edward on the Uganda-DRC border, and it would have been part of the Nile watershed (as Lake Edward still is today). About 20,000 years ago, however, lava from the Virungas created a natural dam at what is now the northern end of Kivu, isolating it from Lake Edward and causing its surface to rise dramatically to a present-day altitude of 1,470m. As a result, the Rusizi River, which formerly drained out of Lake Tanganyika and into Kivu, reversed its flow. Today, the Rusizi flows out of the lake's southern tip at Cyangugu, then follows the Burundi-DRC border southward before emptying into Lake Tanganyika and the Congo Basin.

Kivu supports a somewhat impoverished fauna by comparison with other Rift Valley lakes of similar size. This is thought to be due to the unusually high level of local volcanic activity. The geological record suggests that the release of methane trapped below the lake's surface has resulted in regular mass extinctions every few thousand years. As a result, fewer than 30 fish species are known from the lake, and while this does include 16 endemics, it pales by comparison with the many hundreds of species recorded from Lakes Victoria and Tanganyika. Volcanic activity and/or high methane levels probably also explain the complete absence of hippo and croc from the lake. The rumoured absence of bilharzia from Kivu is strongly contradicted by anecdotal reports from expatriates, so anybody who swims in the lake should assume they have been exposed to the disease.

With its attractively irregular shoreline lined by verdant slopes and sandy beaches, Kivu has long served as a popular weekend getaway for residents of this otherwise landlocked country. There are three main resort towns on the Rwandan lakeshore, of which Gisenyi, the most northerly, has far and away the best and most varied tourist facilities, thanks partly to its proximity to the popular Volcanoes National Park. Further south, Kibuye has the advantage of being far closer to Kigali, and it is also now served by a good quality lakeshore hotel, while Cyangugu can easily be visited in conjunction with Nyungwe National Park and Butare, but it currently lacks accommodation approaching international standards. The

285km² Idjwi Island, which falls within Congolese territory, is the second largest inland island in Africa and tenth largest in the world.

CYANGUGU (RUSIZI)

The most southerly of Rwanda's Lake Kivu ports, Cyangugu (pronounced 'Shangugu') is also the most amorphous, sprawling along a 5km road through the green hills that run down to the lake shore. The capital of Rusizi District, it consists of discrete upper and lower towns whose combined population of 75,000 make it the seventh-largest settlement in the country. Known as Kamembe, the upper town, which stands high above the lakeshore at a breezy altitude of about 1,620m, is a lively business centre, and the site of the main taxi stand, market, banks and supermarkets, as well as a clutch of local guesthouses and restaurants. Aside from the views of the lake, and a couple of flaking colonial-era buildings, Kamembe is all energy and no character – bustling it may be, but in truth you could be in pretty much any small undistinguished African town anywhere on the continent.

Far more intriguing is the lower town – Cyangugu proper – which has an almost cinematic quality, coming across rather like an abandoned film set used years ago to make a movie about some colonial West African trading backwater. Cyangugu is

LIMNIC ERUPTIONS

Shortly before midnight on 15 August 1984, villagers living around Cameroon's Lake Monoun recall being awoken by an explosive noise emanating from within the lake. Come dawn the next morning, 37 residents of a nearby low-lying valley lay mysteriously dead, their skin damaged and discoloured, the surrounding air overhung with the remnants of a pungent smoky cloud; bizarre circumstances that gave rise to any number of macabre and implausible theories: a vicious terrorist attack, a chemical weapon test gone horribly wrong, the malicious work of an angry lake spirit…

The truth was somewhat more prosaic, yet no less frightening. And even before scientific investigators were able to release their tentative findings, it happened again, only 100km further northwest, when an acrid cloud of gas erupted from beneath the surface of a 200m-deep crater lake called Nyos on 22 August 1986. Within the space of hours, 1,750 local villagers living in the surrounding valleys had suffocated to death, together with thousands of animals, with the furthest casualty occurring a full 27km from the lakeshore.

In March 1987, a UNESCO Conference was held at Yaounde to discuss the previously unknown phenomenon, unique to very deep lakes, which investigators called a *limnic eruption*. What seemed to have happened, in simplistic terms, is that carbon dioxide of volcanic origin seeps continuously into the lower strata of a deep lake, where its high solubility allows it to accumulate in volumes up to five times heavier than normal water, becoming increasingly volatile as it approaches saturation point – the carbonated pressure at the bottom of the lake might be three times greater than that of a sparkling wine or soda! By now, the time bomb is ticking. All it takes is a seemingly innocuous external trigger – a light landslide, a heavy storm, an otherwise inconsequential subterranean volcanic activity – to upset the lake's stratification. Then, suddenly, a cloud of noxious carbon dioxide will belch out from the lake surface, diffusing into lower-lying areas and effectively suffocating all oxygen-dependent creatures in its path until finally it dissipates.

Over the next few years, a French research team travelled around Africa trying to establish whether any other very deep lakes might be at similar risk to Monoun and Nyos. And as it turned out, the only contender for this unwanted distinction is Kivu, situated on the lake shore, alongside a bridge across the Rusizi River where it flows out of the lake, which is also the main border crossing between southern Rwanda and the DRC. The town consists of little more than one pot-hole-scored main road, yet within its abrupt confines it does have a decidedly built-up feel, and must once have been rather grand and prosperous. Today, however, many of the old multi-storey buildings have been reduced to shells – victims of one or other war, perhaps, or just decades of neglect – generating an aura of dilapidation underscored by the anomalous Hotel du Lac Kivu, with its freshly painted modern exterior, and the neatly cropped lawn of the Home St François. The outmoded façades of Cyangugu speak of better times past, and while the town's aura of tropical ennui is less than invigorating, it is also somehow rather affecting.

Between and eastward of the two of them (off the map) is Cyangugu's current residential area. Former Bishop of Cyangugu Kenneth Barham, who owns and runs the Peace Guesthouse (see page 165), describes it:

> From the top of the High Street you look across at Mont Cyangugu with the
> 'mudugudu' of 50 'shelter-housing' properties and the high court at the top of the hill.
> This hill is designated the Prefecture of the future. The Medical HQ for the Province
> is there, the Education Centre is now built there, three law courts are there and the

whose lower strata, below around 300 metres (1,000ft), are infused with 55 billion cubic metres of dissolved methane gas and 256 cubic metres of carbon dioxide, a mix made doubly unstable by the high level of volcanic activity around the northern lakeshore. Indeed, it seems more than likely that the periodic faunal extinctions punctuating Kivu's fossil record can be attributed to prehistoric limnic eruptions, and experts regard another such incident as inevitable. Of course, it may not happen for hundreds or thousands of years – but were it to happen tomorrow, the consequences for the two million human inhabitants of the Kivu Basin would be devastating!

At the time of writing, the Cameroonian lakes are in the process of being 'degassed' – a procedure that involves laying a pipe to the lowest strata of the lake and pumping the pressurised water so that it shoots out from the lake surface in a spectacular 50m-high fountain to release the carbon-dioxide safely into the atmosphere. Some fear that the degassing process might itself trigger another disaster, others reckon that it is simply not happening fast enough, but so far things have gone smoothly enough, and optimists believe the two lakes will be degassed to the point of benignity by 2010.

As for Kivu, the risk of future disaster would most likely be reduced were the lake's practically inexhaustible reserves of methane to be extracted as a source of fuel and energy for local and possibly international consumption. Prior to 2004, this only took place on a very small scale to fuel the Bralirwa brewery near Gisenyi. However, following several trial extractions elsewhere on the lake, the Rwandan government has now committed to the large-scale extraction of methane for conversion to electricity at a new plant to be built outside Kibuye as part of the US$325 million KivuWatt Project, which was formally awarded to the international company ContourGlobal in March 2009. It is planned that the project will be constructed in two phases, with the first 25 MW of electrical power coming online in 2010, and another 75 in 2012. This will represent a twenty-fold increase in Rwanda's energy production, and the surplus will be sold to neighbouring countries.

For further information about the phenomenon of limnic eruptions and methane extraction at Lake Kivu, check out the websites http://perso.wanadoo.fr/mhalb/nyos and www.contourglobal.com/rwanda.html.

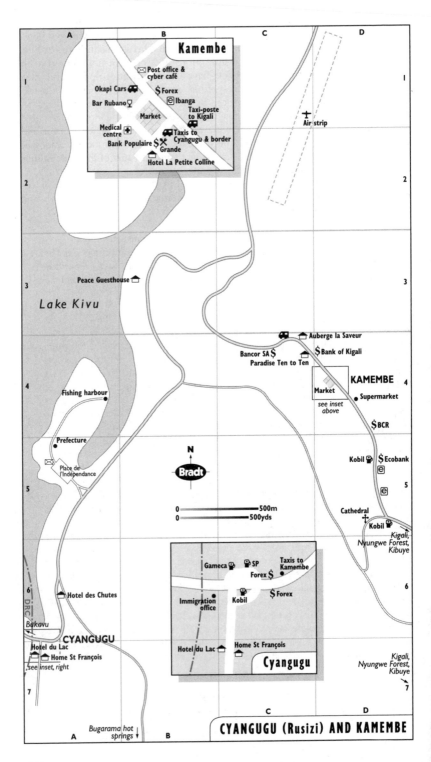

Kamembe

⊠ Post office &
cyber café

Okapi Cars 🚐 $ Forex
Bar Rubano 🍷   ⓔ Ibanga
                              Taxi-poste
          Market   to Kigali 🚐
Medical ✚
centre   🚐 Taxis to
Bank Populaire $ ✕ Cyangugu & border
                  Grande
        Hotel La Petite Colline

✈ Air strip

Peace Guesthouse 🏠

Lake Kivu

🚐 🏠 Auberge la Saveur
Bancor SA $
Paradise Ten to Ten $ Bank of Kigali

Fishing harbour ⚓   Market ▦   **KAMEMBE**
                                                                        • Supermarket
                                        *see inset
                                         above*
• Prefecture
                                                                              $ BCR
⊠ Place de
l'Indépendance   Kobil 🚘 $ Ecobank
                                                            ⓔ
N
Bradt   ⓔ
                                        Cathedral ✝
0 ————————— 500m   Kobil 🚘
0 ————————— 500yds   *Kigali,*
                                                            Nyungwe Forest,
                                                            Kibuye
                        Gameca 🚘 🚘 SP Taxis to
                                          Kamembe
                                  Forex $
🏠 Hotel des Chutes
                        Immigration • $ Forex
🚐   office   Kobil 🚘
DRC   Forex $
Bakavu
CYANGUGU
🏠 Hotel du Lac   Hotel du Lac   🏠 Home St François
🏠 🏠 Home St François
see inset, right   **Cyangugu**

Kigali,
Nyungwe Forest,
Kibuye

Bugarama hot
springs ▼

CYANGUGU (Rusizi) AND KAMEMBE

space for the Prefecture is there. I have built a Dispensary, which I am expanding into a specialist unit for dentistry and eye work. Our St Matthew's Primary School is there. It is the residential heart of Cyangugu, as opposed to the commercial centre on the other hill. You get to it by turning left on the tarmac as you enter the town, passing our cathedral and turning up a gravel road just after the river.

While the former prefecture of Kibuye had the sad distinction of being the site of the most extensive extermination of Tutsis during the genocide, the prefecture of Cyangugu came second. Before the French set up their 'safe zone', it was estimated that 85–90% of Tutsis here had died. Many communities were completely wiped out. More recently, the town was particularly hard hit by an earthquake that was felt throughout the great lakes region on 4 February 2008, and measured 6.1 on the Richter Scale. Several houses collapsed, and 30 people were killed when a church roof collapsed at Shangi, about 5km north of Kamembe.

Unless you are thinking of crossing into the DRC, Cyangugu has to be classed as something of a dead end in travel terms. It is, however, the closest town to Nyungwe, and might therefore make an attractive alternative base for self-drive visitors to this national park. The lakeshore setting is lovely, too, and the atmospheric old town forms a good base from which to explore more off-the-beaten-track destinations such as the Bugarama Hot Springs and islands of Gihaya and Nkombo.

GETTING THERE AND AWAY
By air Rwandair Express (see advertisement on page 274) runs thrice-weekly flights between Kigali and Cyangugu.

By road The road from Butare to Cyangugu is surfaced in its entirety but in relatively poor condition west of Gikongoro. Regular minibus-taxis connect Kigali and Butare to Cyangugu – or more accurately to Kamembe, which is where the main minibus stand [164 B1] for Cyangugu is situated. The fare from Kigali is around Rfr4,000 and from Butare around Rfr2,500.

A steady stream of minibus-taxis run back and forth between Kamembe and the border post at Cyangugu, at a cost equivalent to US$0.25 for the 5km trip. The Peace Guesthouse [164 B3] and Hotel des Chutes [164 A6] both lie within 50m of the taxi route, as does the main harbour and port.

Direct transport between Kamembe and Kibuye is restricted to one bus daily. This costs Rfr2,800, takes 5–6 hours, and leaves the bus park between 07.00 and 07.30 (sit on the left for the best views of the lake). Be warned that there are no minibus-taxis from the border post to Kamembe at this time in the morning.

GPS reading for Cyangugu (Hotel du Lac) is ⊕ S 02°29.390, E 028°53.596 (1,473m) and for Kamembe (Ten to Ten Hotel) ⊕ S 02°28.410, E 028°54.513 (1,613m).

By boat Public lake transport may restart one day; check the current position with ORTPN. Meanwhile the Hotel Centre Béthanie (in Kibuye) has boats for hire linking Cyangugu to Kibuye and thence to Gisenyi (see page 174). In Cyangugu, the Hotel des Chutes [164 A6] can sometimes arrange lake transport.

WHERE TO STAY
Moderate
🏠 **Peace Guesthouse** [164 B3] (20 rooms) BP 52 Cyangugu; ✆ 0252 537799; m 078 8522727; e info@peaceguesthouse.org; www.peaceguesthouse.org. Overlooking the lake about 1km from Kamembe along the scenic road towards Cyangugu proper, this popular guesthouse was

constructed by the Anglican Church in 1998 & offers a wide selection of accommodation, ranging from en-suite bungalows to simple rooms using common hot showers. Several Rwandan VIPs — including the president — have stayed here, & overall it's probably the most attractive option in Cyangugu, though the accommodation is starting to look rather rundown & the costlier rooms feel a bit overpriced. Adequate meals are available in the restaurant, but no alcohol is served, & there are no longer internet facilities. The Peace Guesthouse also has 4 houses to rent for longer-stay visitors. *Sgl using common shower Rfr7,080; en-suite dbl Rfr14,160; bungalows & villas with 2 dbl bedrooms & en-suite hot bath Rfr47,200–94,400.*

⌂ **Paradise Ten to Ten Hotel** [164 C4] (30 rooms) ☎ 0252 537796; m 078 8645390. Situated in the heart of Kamembe, a location that has little going for it aside from its proximity to the bus station, this modern 3-storey block, ostensibly the smartest option available in & around Cyangugu, does suffer from something of a character deficit. The large tiled en-suite rooms, though a little frayed at the edges, come with nets, TV, fan, private balcony & hot water. Other facilities include a good restaurant, a rooftop bar, room service & a massage & sauna, & a swimming pool is planned. The echoing passages might make you vulnerable to noise from other guests, & things can get very noisy on Fri/Sat when the nightclub continues until the early hours. *Rfr20,000 ordinary dbl, Rfr25,000 dbl with a lake view, Rfr35,000 suite.*

⌂ **Hotel des Chutes** [164 A6] (17 rooms) ☎ 0252 537405/537015; m 078 8829807. Set on a rise about 500m back from the border post, this pleasant & good-value hotel has an attractive

location overlooking the lake, & the shady balcony is fun for a drink or snack. Following recent renovations, the rooms are also now among the best on offer in Cyangugu, with clean tiled floors, comfortable beds & crisp, fresh linen, TV, netting, hot bath, & in some instances a lake-facing private balcony. The restaurant serves good meals & snacks. You may be able to fix lake transport to Kibuye at reception. *Rfr11,000/15,000 en-suite twin/dbl.*

⌂ **Hotel du Lac** [164 C7] (20 rooms) ☎ 0252 537172; m 078 8300518/8844146. Formerly the smartest option in Cyangugu, this wonderfully located hotel remains a beacon of relative prosperity amidst the row of semi-dilapidated buildings that runs along the river immediately south of the border post with the DRC. Unfortunately, the rooms are a bit shabby & seem poor value by comparison with other hotels in this range. The hotel's best feature is the open-air riverfront bar & restaurant, which serves excellent brochettes & grilled chicken, as well as more substantial meals. There's also a large — but on last inspection empty — swimming pool! *Rfr12,000 en-suite dbl with hot water & fan, Rfr15,000 for a larger room with TV, Rfr20,000 for a suite with a barren volleyball court of a spare room, whose role is difficult to discern.*

⌂ **Hotel La Petite Colline** [164 B2] (10 rooms) ☎ 0252 537824; m 078 3346234; e musoni74@ yahoo.fr. Situated in Kamembe more or less opposite the market, this locally styled hotel has lots of character & the semi-outdoor bar with banana-leaf roof is full of inventive decorations alongside more traditional African art. There's a nice feel about the place, & it is very close to the bus station, but the en-suite rooms are a little basic at the asking price. *Rfr10,000–20,000 en-suite dbl.*

Budget

⌂ **Home St François** [164 C7] (24 rooms) ☎ 0252 537915. Situated directly opposite the Hotel du Lac, this church-run lodge is easily the best budget option in Cyangugu — in fact as good a deal as you'll find anywhere in Rwanda. The rooms are spacious, clean & secure, some with en-suite hot shower, others with access to a common hot bath.

Meals are very cheap but nothing to shout about, so you are probably better off eating at the nearby Hotel du Lac or Hotel des Chutes. The atmosphere is very homely, if not exactly full of cheer, & reception no longer refuses accommodation to unmarried couples. *Rfr8,000 dbl.*

✕ **WHERE TO EAT AND DRINK** The nicest place to eat is the **Hotel du Lac** [164 C7], which has a pleasant riverside terrace and charges Rfr2,500–3,000 for a tasty lunchtime buffet or Rfr3,000–5,000 for à la carte dishes, including superb barbecued peri-peri chicken and brochettes. Also recommended is the terrace restaurant at **Hotel des Chutes** [164 A6], which has a reasonable menu in a similar price range. Up in Kamembe the restaurant at the **Paradise Ten to Ten Hotel** [164 C4] is correct but a bit boring, while the more atmospheric **La Petite**

Colline [164 B2] serves a varied selection of steaks, fish, chicken, pasta dishes and pizzas in the Rfr3,000–5,000 range. All these places are attached to hotels and open for breakfast, lunch and dinner daily. There are also plenty of small places around the market area serving adequate food.

OTHER PRACTICALITIES
Internet There are several internet cafés in Kamembe. If you are heading on to Kibuye and need to check email, it's best to do so in Kamembe as no internet facilities are available in Kibuye.

Money The banks provide the normal **foreign exchange** services at the usual snail's pace. There are now quite a number of forex bureaux dotted around the border post and market area, offering an instant service for cash, generally at better rates than the banks – but do keep your wits about you. The Bank of Kigali [164 D4] has Western Union.

WHAT TO SEE AND DO Cyangugu forms the obvious base from which to explore the far southwest of Rwanda, a region which sees very few tourists. The southwest boasts a couple of points of interest in the form of the Bugarama Hot Springs and islands of Gihaya and Nkombo, though you could argue that these landmarks provide a good pretext to explore a remote corner of Rwanda as much as they rank as worthwhile goals in their own right. With access to a private vehicle, this area could be explored as a day trip out of Cyangugu. Using what limited public transport exists, you're definitely in for an adventure: you should probably plan on spending at least one night out of Cyangugu, and should be prepared for long waits at the roadside, or a lot of walking.

Note that some old travel guides refer to the **Rusizi Falls** (Les Chutes de Rusizi) on the Rusizi River along the border with the DRC. In reality, whatever waterfall may once have existed here is now submerged beneath the waters of the Mururu Dam, which was built in 1958 about 10km south of Cyangugu as a source of hydroelectric power and also serves as an obscure border crossing into the DRC.

Another possible excursion from Cyangugu, at least when things are quiet in the DR Congo, is to the town of **Bukavu** across the border. If you do go into DR Congo, and you're of a nationality that needs a visa for Rwanda, then unless you have a multiple-entry (rather than a single-entry) Rwandan visa you'll have to pay again to re-enter Rwanda.

Bugarama hot springs Situated slightly less than 60km from Cyangugu by road, the Bugarama hot springs lie at the base of a limestone quarry, 5km from the Cimerwa Cement Factory, in a lightly wooded area dotted by large sinkholes. The springs bubble up into a large green pool which, as viewed from the roadward side, is initially somewhat disappointing. You can, however, follow a path around the edge of the pool, past a large sinkhole to your left, then leap over the outlet stream to the base of the cliff. Here you are right next to the main springs, which bubble into the pool like a freshly shaken and opened fizzy-drink bottle, and are sizzling hot to the touch.

In a private vehicle the springs can be reached in about 90 minutes from Cyangugu, but they are rather more inaccessible using public transport. The first part of the trip involves following the partially surfaced road that connects Cyangugu to Ruha (a border post with Burundi) for approximately 40km to the junction town of Bugarama. You need to turn left at this junction, along a dirt road that passes through Bugarama and a series of small villages, until after 11km you reach the strip of tar outside the Cimerwa Cement Factory. Here you must turn right, passing the factory gate. After another 5km, immediately past a signpost reading Secteur Nyamaranko, you'll see a hillside quarry and three-way fork to your left. Follow the leftmost fork for about 100m, then turn right on to a small dirt track, and after 100m or so you'll see the pool in front of you. If in doubt, ask for directions to the 'Amashyuza' (aka 'Amahyuza'). From here, it would be possible to continue on the Cyamudongo Forest (see page 158).

Using public transport, one (very slow) bus and several minibus-taxis cover the Ruha road daily, leaving from Kamembe rather than Cyangugu proper, and taking up to two hours to reach Bugarama town. Bugarama itself isn't much to shout about – a hot, dusty small town ringed by plantations of plantains and pines – and there is no regular public transport along the 16km road between the town and the springs. However, finding a lift on a pick-up truck – at least as far as the cement factory – shouldn't present a major problem. From there, the 5km walk is along flat terrain, and shouldn't take longer than an hour in either direction.

Gihaya and Nkombo Islands A short boat ride away from Cyangugu, this pair of islands in Lake Kivu makes for a diverting half-day outing, and forms a good excuse to get out on to the lake, without really qualifying as essential excursion. Gihaya is the smaller island, best known as the site of a derelict mansion set in large shady lawns that locals variously claim was built as a holiday home for King Baudouin II of Belgium or for President Juvenal Habyarimana. The 20km-long Nkombo Island, which was badly hit by the 2008 earthquake, offers plenty of opportunity for exploration, but the main attraction seems to be a rather impressive fruit-bat colony near a jetty at the south end of the island. En route, the lake is very pretty, with sweeping views to the heavily settled Congolese shore around Bukavu, and there is plenty of birdlife to be seen, notably cormorants and pelicans, as well as the unusual local boats – comprising three dugouts bound together – called amato.

Motorboats taking 8–10 passengers can be arranged at Cyangugu Port, or you could make advance contact with Agence Nyungwe (m *078 3324220/3427222*), and local dugouts with paddlers can also be arranged. Either way, you're looking at around Rfr20,000 for the boat hire, but the trip is far quicker with a motor, around 20 minutes each way as opposed to one hour.

KIBUYE (KARONGI)

The most conventionally pretty of the lake ports and capital of Karongi District, this modestly sized town (population 78,000) sprawls across a series of hills interwoven with the lagoon-like arms of the lake. Now that the new road from

---

THE CREATION OF LAKE KIVU

A NEW VERSION OF AN ANCIENT TALE Long, long ago, before the beginning of what we now remember, there was nothing but a dry, grassy plain covering the area where Lake Kivu lies today. It was a hard, hot place, whose people had to work ceaselessly to scrape a living from the land. One of these people was a man whose heart was kind; he helped his older neighbours to till their ground and to gather in their crops. His wife scolded him for this, saying: 'Why do you spend so much time filling their grain-stores when our own lies empty?' But Imana had seen his good deeds and was pleased, and wanted to reward the man, so he gave him a cow whose udders yielded milk, millet, beans and peas. Imana warned the man that he must not speak of his special cow to others, lest they envy him and try to steal it, so the man milked his cow in secret and carried home the produce to his wife who began to scold him a little less.

A day came when the man was called away to work at the Mwami's court. Anxiously, he asked Imana what he should do about his cow. Imana said that his wife might be told, and might milk it in the meantime, but that she must not pass on the secret of the cow to others.

With her husband away from home, the woman invited a young man to her house. He dined off the milk and the millet and the beans and the peas, and he wondered how her poor land could produce so much. He searched all round her homestead for an extra storeroom or piece of land but he found nothing, and the cow looked just like an ordinary cow. Insistently the young man questioned the woman, using all kinds of persuasion to discover her secret, and eventually she weakened. She milked the cow in front of him and he was so amazed that he ran to the neighbours, crying: 'Here is an animal that will feed us all – we need work on the land no more!'

Imana heard this, and he frowned deeply, and that night he prepared a punishment. Before going to bed, the woman went out into her field to empty her bladder as usual, thinking to take only a few moments. But the flow was unstoppable. On and on it went, flooding her house and her fields and the land around about. Deeper and deeper it became, until the woman herself was drowned in it and even the trees were covered. Her household utensils – her wooden bowl and her woven mat and the gourd which held her grain – floated away into the distance, broke into bits and became islands. And as the morning sun rose into the sky it lit the new and shining surface of Lake Kivu as it is today.

When the man returned from working at the Mwami's court he found a lake of sweet water lapping at the edge of his fields. The land had become soft and fertile. Fish swam in the lake, and waterbirds bobbed on the wavelets. Of the cow there was no sign, but she had left behind a big heap of millet and peas and beans which he then planted, and his crop and all those after it grew richly on the irrigated land.

And Imana smiled.

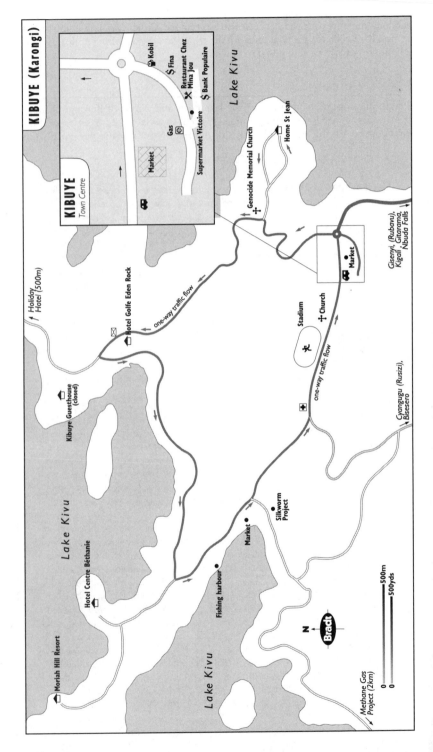

KIBUYE (Karongi)

KIBUYE
Town Centre

Market

Gas

Kobil
Fina
Restaurant Chez
Mina Jou
Bank Populaire
Supermarket Victoire

Lake Kivu

Genocide Memorial Church

Home St Jean

Holiday
Hotel (500m)

Hotel Golfe Eden Rock

one-way traffic flow

Kibuye Guesthouse
(closed)

Stadium

Church

one-way traffic flow

Gisenyi, (Rubavu),
Kigali, Gitarama,
Nbuda Falls

Lake Kivu

Cyangugu (Rusizi),
Bisesero

Market

Lake Kivu

Hotel Centre Béthanie

Moriah Hill Resort

Silkworm
Project

Market

Fishing harbour

Lake Kivu

N

Bradt

500m
500yds

0
0

Methane Gas
Project (2km)

Kigali has been completed, Kibuye is the lakeside town most quickly accessible from the capital, though it has not caught on with foreign tourists and Rwandan holidaymakers the way Gisenyi has. That said, at weekends you'll often find families from elsewhere in Rwanda enjoying the small beaches and the swimming, some of them former exiles who returned after the genocide and are rediscovering their country. Hills planted with pines and eucalyptus give the locale a pristine, almost Alpine appearance, in contrast to the atmosphere of fading tropical languor which to some extent afflicts the other ports. It's a green, peaceful and appealing place, whose sudden views of the lake sparkling amid overhanging trees are true picture-postcard material.

It's hard to believe, amid today's sunlight and tranquillity, that during the genocide the prefecture of Kibuye experienced the most comprehensive slaughter of Tutsis anywhere in Rwanda. Previously there had been around 60,000 in the prefecture, an unusually high proportion of about 20%. When the French troops arrived afterwards they estimated that up to nine out of every ten had been killed. Whole communities were annihilated, leaving no witnesses to the crime. Near the sports stadium you will see just one of the mass graves, with a sign announcing: 'More than 10,000 people were inhumated here. Official ceremony was presided over by H E Pasteur Bizimungu, President of the Republic of Rwanda. April 26th 1995.' Now birds chirp on the surrounding wall and the laughter of children in the nearby primary school echoes across the enclosure. Here and throughout Rwanda, memories of the genocide remain acute but daily life carries on determinedly around them. As does tourism.

Looking ahead, Kibuye is set to benefit from two significant new government initiatives during the lifespan of this edition. The first is the already contracted construction of a plant to convert methane extracted from the lake to electrical power about 3km south of town (see box page 163), a move that will give the local economy a genuine shot in the arm when the first phase comes online in 2010. The second, less certain, development is the probable construction of new surfaced roads south to Cyangugu and north to Gisenyi, the former part of a long-term plan to divert most incidental traffic away from the main road connecting Butare to Cyangugu via Nyungwe National Park.

GETTING THERE AND AWAY

By road The main access is by an excellent road from Kigali via Gitarama, started by the Chinese in 1990. On some stretches it's a considerable feat of engineering, cutting through hillsides and teetering around steep valleys. The drive takes at least two hours in a private vehicle. Minibus-taxis are available from Nyabugogo bus station as well as from certain private operators in central Kigali (Atraco departs for Kibuye at 06.15, 08.15, 10.15, 12.15 and 13.15) and cost Rfr1,700 (or Rfr1,200 coming from Gitarama). GPS (Hotel Golfe Eden Rock) is ⊕ S 02°03.559, E 029°20.893.

Travelling from elsewhere on the lakeshore, the drives are mostly on dirt roads, though this may change if the planned surfaced roads to Cyangugu and Gisenyi ever go ahead. For now, the trip from Cyangugu or Nyungwe National Park takes about four hours in a private vehicle (the junction of the Cyangugu–Nyungwe Road and dirt road to Kibuye is at ⊕ S 02°25.355, E 029°04.196) and the trip to Gisenyi about three. Note that the trip to Gisenyi involves following the Kigali road east for 17km as far as Rubengera (⊕ S 02°02.916, E 029°24.849), then turning left on to a clearly marked dirt road. There are two buses daily from Gisenyi, charging Rfr2,500. No minibus-taxis run regularly between Cyangugu and Kibuye, but there's one bus daily in either direction, leaving at 08.00 and taking about an hour longer than a private vehicle would.

When you arrive in Kibuye by minibus-taxi, alight at the crossroads at the entrance to the town if you want the Hotel Golfe Eden Rock or the Home St Jean; continue to the final stop by the sports stadium for the Béthanie. There are sometimes some bicycle-taxis around if your bags are heavy. If you are driving in Kibuye, note that the main surfaced loop road around the sprawling town is one-way in an anti-clockwise direction.

By boat Public lake transport should eventually restart now that the situation with the DRC is calmer. In the meantime, the Hotel Centre Béthanie has two boats for hire linking Kibuye to Cyangugu and Gisenyi. The smaller boat holds up to four passengers and takes about one hour to get between Kibuye and either Gisenyi or Cyangugu, while the larger boat, which holds up to 20 passengers, takes about 2–3 hours for each leg. Whichever boat you charter, the cost for the Kibuye–Gisenyi leg is Rfr150,000 and for the Kibuye–Cyangugu leg Rfr220,000. Bookings can be made through the hotel reception.

WHERE TO STAY
Upmarket

🏠 **Moriah Hill Resort** (20 rooms) m 078 8512222/8307660; e moriah.hill@yahoo.fr; www.moriah-hill.com. Opened in 2007, this is far & away the smartest hotel in Kibuye, boasting an isolated location further along the same peninsula as the established Hotel Centre Béthanie. Spanning 4 storeys, the bright white main hotel building is somewhat intrusive, but it has been designed so that all rooms have large balconies with views across the lake to a nearby forested peninsula, & are perfectly positioned to catch the sunset. The rooms are large & comfortable, with dbl beds, satellite TV, fridge, seats & table, & a spacious modern bathroom with tub & shower. The restaurant, in a separate building, has plenty of indoor & outdoor seating & an unusually imaginative menu with most main courses falling in the Rfr5,000–7,000 range. A motorboat can be hired at Rfr55,000 per hr, & kayaks will be available soon. *Rfr56,000/59,000 sgl/dbl B&B; Rfr71,000 suite.*

🏠 **Birambye Lodge** www.birambye.org. This planned lodge (whose name is the Kinyarwanda word for sustainability) will be built opposite the L'Esperance Orphanage, which lies on the Lake Kivu shore about 50km from Kibuye close to the junction for the Source of the Nile in northern Nyungwe National Park. It will be designed by Birambye International, which has a long-term partnership with a Rwandan NGO called Genocide Survivor Student Association, to meet all the criteria of sustainable development, & profits will be invested in the education, health & training of the orphans at L'Esperance. Check the website for news.

Moderate

🏠 **Hotel Centre Béthanie** (42 rooms) ☎ 0252 568235; f 0252 568509. This lively, friendly Presbyterian lodge is definitely the best value in this range, boasting a beautiful lakeshore position on a wooded peninsula, though it seems a shame that most of that wood consists of eucalyptus, pine & other exotic trees. The brick chalet-style rooms are a bit cramped together, but very clean, & they come with hot showers, netting & a view of the lake. A decent restaurant overlooking the lake serves no alcohol but a good selection of main dishes in the Rfr3,000–4,000 range, & a selection of lighter meals & snacks for around Rfr2,000. Normally there is plenty of space but it can fill up if there's a religious gathering or seminar, so it's safer to book in advance. Internet access costs Rfr1,000 per hr & a boat is available for hire at around Rfr30,000–35,000 per hr. *Rfr10,000/15,000 twin/dbl; Rfr30,000 suite excluding b/fast.*

🏠 **Hotel Golfe Eden Rock** (60 rooms) ☎ 0252 568524; e golfedenrock@yahoo.fr. Situated near to the (currently closed) Kibuye Guesthouse & roughly opposite the post office, this large hotel has a great location, with excellent views over the lake, & it has pleasant en-suite rooms with a dbl bed, netting & polished floor. Ask for a room that leads on to the lower balcony. Facilities include an internet café & a decent restaurant with indoor & outdoor seating. *Rfr12,000/16,000 sgl/dbl B&B; Rfr20,000 suite.*

🏠 **Holiday Hotel** (28 rooms) m 078 8350535/8555594; e holidayhotel@yahoo.fr. The newest addition to the Kibuye accommodation scene opened in Jan 2009 on the lakeshore about 1km north of the Golfe Eden Rock. It consists of a circular 3-storey building & a row of chalets set in uninspired gardens running down to the lakeshore. The rooms in the main building are poorly designed to accommodate a king-size bed, but they do have TV, large tiled en-suite bathroom with tub, & a small balcony. The semi-detached rooms in the chalets are also small & overall quite similar, but they seem less awkwardly laid out. Either way, it feels like poor value at Rfr35,000 for a dbl with lake view or Rfr30,000 without.

Budget
🏠 **Home St Jean** (26 rooms) ☏ 0252 568526; e homesaintjean@yahoo.fr. The cheapest accommodation option in Kibuye, this Catholic guesthouse is tucked away down a lane to the right-hand side of the large church that you'll see on a hill as you enter Kibuye from the east. It is signposted from near the church, but rather indistinctly. The lodge took a battering during the genocide but it reopened in 1996 &, following recent renovations, it is now very comfortable &

🏠 **Kibuye Guesthouse** Formerly the pick of the accommodation in Kibuye, this state-owned guesthouse has an idyllic location beside a small beach on the grassy lake shore, with great views & Technicolor sunsets. It is closed at the time of writing but signs of construction work in 2009 suggest that it is likely to reopen under private management in the not too distant future.

good value. An attractive feature of the lodge is the tremendous hilltop views of the lake & access via a steep footpath through neat gardens to a small swimming beach. A small restaurant serves brochettes, pizzas & more substantial meals in the Rfr2,000–5,000 range, & it has a well stocked bar. The nicest rooms are the en-suites (with ¾ bed) in the new block facing the lake. Rfr6,000/8,000 sgl/dbl using common shower; Rfr10,000–15,000 en suite.

✗ **WHERE TO EAT AND DRINK** The pick is undoubtedly the **Moriah Hills Hotel**, but it isn't so convenient for people staying elsewhere (unless you have a car) and it is relatively pricey at Rfr5,000–7,000 for a main course. Elsewhere, the **Golfe Eden Rock** serves a good selection of snacks and meals in the Rfr3,000–5,000 range, but service is on the slow side, and nobody seems overly concerned about serving the meal you actually order. The restaurant at the **Béthanie** is also good, with a standard menu, and a lot more efficient. All these hotel restaurants serve breakfast, lunch and dinner daily. In town, the **Restaurant Chez Mina Jou** serves a filling and tasty lunchtime 'plat' for Rfr800. There are plenty of places for a quick beer or fruit juice when you're strolling.

OTHER PRACTICALITIES The **post office** down near the Kibuye Guesthouse has international telephone and fax facilities. **Internet** facilities are limited, but access is available at the Moriah Hills and Golfe Eden Rock, as well as the more central Gas Internet. There is no forex bureau.

WHAT TO SEE AND DO
Around town Kibuye is such a relaxed, pleasant town that it's enjoyable just strolling and watching life unfold. There's a big **market** on Fridays, in an open area just beyond the hospital, when people come in from outlying villages and across the lake from Idjwi Island. The week-long market in the centre of town hasn't a huge range but is still worth a browse. A new development likely to be completed during the lifespan of this edition is the **Environmental Museum of Kibuye** (*www.museum.gov.rw*), which will be built on the lakeshore close to the Hotel Golfe Eden Rock, and will house a variety of natural and prehistoric artefacts from the region.

As the sketch map shows, you can do a **circular walk** along the main one-way road around Kibuye. This offers some beautiful views across the lake and can be stretched to fill a couple of hours or so, depending on how often you stop to photograph, watch birds, or just enjoy the surroundings. Views are slightly better going clockwise rather than anticlockwise – with the added advantage that you'll be facing any oncoming traffic, so can take evasive action more quickly! Once you've passed the hospital on your way up to the Béthanie there's nowhere to get a drink until you're back down by the Golfe Eden Rock, so you may want to carry some water.

Genocide memorial church As you enter Kibuye from the east, you'll see a large church perched on a hill above the town. During the genocide, over 11,400 died there. Lindsey Hilsum caught the stark horror of it in an article in *Granta* issue 51:

> The church stands among trees on a promontory above the calm blue of Lake Kivu. The Tutsis were sheltering inside when a mob, drunk on banana beer, threw grenades through the doors and windows and then ran in to club and stab to death the people who remained alive. It took about three hours.

For some time the church remained empty and scarred. Then gradually work started – new mosaics were sketched out and then completed, and new stained glass filled the broken windows. New hangings adorned the altar. A memorial has been built outside by the relatives of those who died there and nearby. During the week it is generally empty, for anyone who wants to go to reflect peacefully on the past, but on Sundays now it is filled with worshippers and their singing wafts out across Lake Kivu. Sometimes commemorative services are held. A memorial of this kind is arguably more evocative and moving than the skulls of Nyamata or the corpses of Murambi. Here there is an echoing beauty, which is no bad accompaniment to thoughts of death. Try to find time for a few reflective minutes in this deeply memorable place.

Boat trips Apart from longer trips to Cyangugu and Gisenyi (see below) there are possibilities for trips on Lake Kivu and to nearby islands. The steep-sided Napoleon's Island, said to be shaped like its namesake's hat, supports quite a number of birds as well as a colony of thousands of fruit bats, which rise from the slopes like a massive chattering cloud when disturbed. By contrast, tiny Amahoro (Peace) Island is a popular chill-out spot with a restaurant, volleyball, swimming, camping (bring your own tent as the ones offered are rather tatty), and a short walking trail around its rocky northern extension. The Hotel Centre Béthanie and Moriah Hills Resort (see under hotel listings above) both have motorboats for hire, and you can ask around locally for cheaper boat transport. Because the charge for motorised boats is per hour, you'll pay a lot more if the boat waits for you at one of the islands than if you are dropped and arrange to be collected later.

Ndaba Falls On your way back by minibus-taxi along the road to Gitarama, look out for this waterfall some distance away on your right about 20km out from Kibuye. Passengers will point it out to you if you warn them beforehand – in French it's the Chutes de Ndaba. In the rainy season it's an impressive 100m cascade, in the dry season a fairly unimpressive straggle. You can ask for the minibus to drop you at the viewpoint. Going in the other direction it's harder to spot.

GISENYI (RUBAVU)

The most important tourist centre and largest port on the Rwandan shore of Lake Kivu is Gisenyi, an attractively faded resort town situated about 110km north of Kibuye by road, and 60km west of the gorilla-tracking base of Ruhengeri. Gisenyi is the fifth-largest town in Rwanda, with a population estimated at more than

In the hills high above Kibuye, often shrouded in mountain mist, Bisesero is a place of great sadness and great heroism. Of the estimated 800,000 or so people who lost their lives throughout the whole country during the genocide, more than 6% were slaughtered here in this one area; but the resistance they mounted against the killers – and maintained for almost three months – was the strongest and most courageous in all of Rwanda.

When the genocide began on 7 April 1994, Tutsis from the whole surrounding region converged on Bisesero for refuge, numbering around 50,000 at their height. Then the killers came, an assortment of military, trained *interahamwe* and villagers, heavily armed and equipped with vehicles. The people of Bisesero had machetes and other rudimentary weapons and managed to survive relatively well until mid-May, killing a number of their attackers and repulsing others. But it was bitterly cold in the hills and raining heavily, and they were short of food.

On 13 May the attackers returned in full force, including many militia and soldiers, and with weapons that the refugees in Bisesero could not match, although they did their best to group themselves effectively and fought fiercely hand-to-hand. The battle raged for eight hours and resumed the next day. By the end, around half of the refugees had died. The exhausted survivors had little choice but to hide in the forest and put up what sporadic resistance they could. The attacks continued relentlessly. By the time the French arrived at the end of June, only around 1,300 of the 50,000 were still alive. But – they had survived.

Set on a hillside about 30km from Kibuye, Bisesero Genocide Memorial, maintained by the National Museum of Rwanda (www.museum.gov.rw), comprises nine small buildings, each of which represents one of the nine communes that formerly made up the province of Kibuye. Within these buildings are a chilling collection of human bones and skulls, along with other documents of the terrible events at Bisesero. The site of the memorial is now called the 'Hill of Resistance' because of the heroic events that took place there. It's a sad, moving and evocative place, where the sense of history is very strong.

80,000, and the capital of Rubavu District. It is also better equipped for upmarket tourism than any urban centre outside of the capital, and it thus forms a good alternative base from which self-drive tourists can visit the gorillas, whilst also possessing a seductive tropical ambience that makes it a great place to settle into for a few days.

Good roads connect Ruhengeri and Gisenyi to Kigali and southern Uganda, and the region as a whole has an agreeably moderate year-round climate and consistently attractive mountain scenery. Its location close to the Uganda and DRC borders made it an unsettled area both before and for some time after the genocide, because of army and guerrilla activity. From a tourist's perspective, security is no longer a serious concern, but it would still be a good idea to seek local advice before heading off the beaten track.

Gisenyi is split into an upper and lower town, of which the former consists of an undistinguished grid of busy roads centred around a small market, with a northern skyline dominated by the distinctive volcanic outline of Nyiragongo, whose active crater belches out smoke by day and glows ominously at night. The lower town is a more spacious and atmospheric conglomeration of banks, government buildings, old colonial homesteads and hotels, beside a shore lapped by the waters of Lake Kivu. The waterfront, with its red sandy beaches, pleasing mismatch of architectural styles, and shady palm-lined avenues, has the captivating

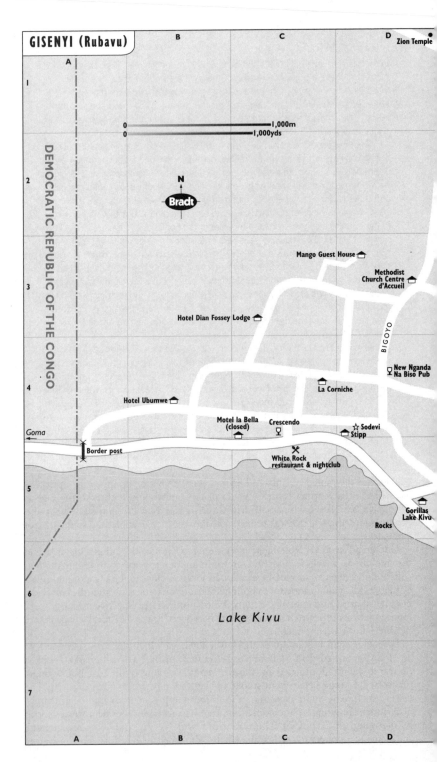

GISENYI (Rubavu)

Zion Temple

DEMOCRATIC REPUBLIC OF THE CONGO

0 — 1,000m
0 — 1,000yds

N
Bradt

Mango Guest House

Methodist
Church Centre
d'Accueil

Hotel Dian Fossey Lodge

BIGOYO

New Nganda
Na Biso Pub

La Corniche

Hotel Ubumwe

Goma

Border post

Motel la Bella
(closed)

Crescendo

Sodevi
Stipp

White Rock
restaurant & nightclub

Gorillas
Lake Kivu

Rocks

Lake Kivu

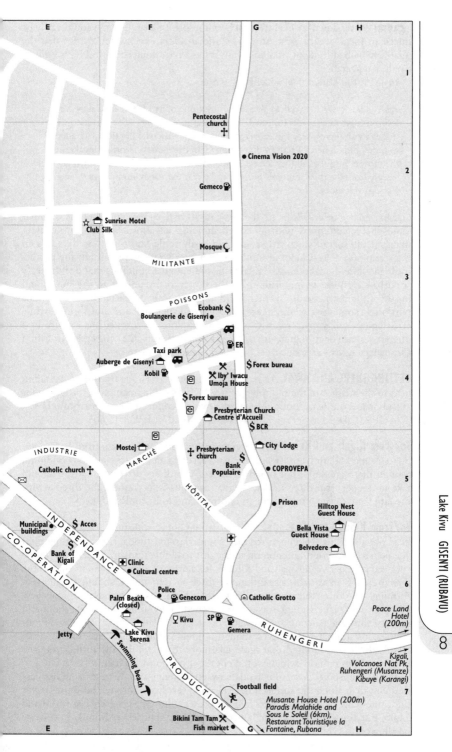

Pentecostal church †

● Cinema Vision 2020

Gemeco ⌨

☆ ⌂ Sunrise Motel
Club Silk

Mosque ☾

MILITANTE

POISSONS

Ecobank $
Boulangerie de Gisenyi ●

Taxi park 🚌

Auberge de Gisenyi ⌂ 🚌

Kobil ⌨

⌨ ER

$ Forex bureau

✕ Iby' Iwacu
Umoja House

$ Forex bureau

ⓔ

ⓔ

⌂ Presbyterian Church
Centre d'Accueil

$ BCR

ⓔ

Mostej ⌂

MARCHÉ

† Presbyterian church

⌂ City Lodge

$

Bank Populaire

● COPROVEPA

INDUSTRIE

Catholic church †

⊠

HÔPITAL

● Prison

Hilltop Nest Guest House ⌂

Bella Vista Guest House ⌂

Belvedere ⌂

Municipal buildings ●

$ Acces

$

Bank of Kigali

INDEPENDANCE

CO-OPERATION

✚ Clinic
● Cultural centre

Police ●

🅿 Genecom

⌂ Catholic Grotto

Palm Beach (closed) ⌂

Jetty

⌂ Lake Kivu Serena

⚲ Kivu

SP 🅿 🅿

Gemera

RUHENGERI

Peace Land Hotel (200m)

Kigali, Volcanoes Nat Pk, Ruhengeri (Musanze) Kibuye (Karangi)

Swimming beach ⚓

PRODUCTION

Football field 🏃

Bikini Tam Tam ✕
Fish market ●

Musante House Hotel (200m) Paradis Malahide and Sous le Soleil (6km), Restaurant Touristique la Fontaine, Rubona air of a slightly down-at-heel tropical beach resort. Indeed, Gisenyi could easily be mistaken for a sweaty West African or Indian Ocean backwater, except that the relatively high altitude of 1,500m means it has a refreshing climate at odds with its tropical appearance.

In 1907, the Duke of Mecklenburg wrote:

> Kissenji possesses an excellent climate, for by virtue of its 1,500 metres above sea level all enervating heat is banished. The natural coolness prevalent in consequence makes a visit there a very agreeable experience. The man who has this place allotted to him for his sphere of activity draws a prize. In front are the swirling breakers of the most beautiful of all the Central African lakes, framed in by banks which fall back steeply from the rugged masses of rock; at the rear the stately summits of the eight Virunga volcanoes.

Gisenyi today offers little in the way of formal sightseeing, but its singular atmosphere, combined with an excellent range of affordable accommodation, makes it the sort of town that you could easily settle into for a few days. It's an interesting place to wander around, too, whether your interest lies in the prolific birds that line the lakeshore, the fantastic old colonial buildings that dot the leafy suburban avenues, lazing around on the beach, or mixing in to the hustle and bustle of the market area. Further afield, the 6km walk or *matatu* drive to Rubona port offers some lovely lake views and, a little further on, some hot springs; while at Rubona itself you can easily arrange to explore the immediate vicinity in a dugout canoe or pirogue. It's also possible to visit the engaging Imbabazi Orphanage nearby (see details and box on pages 183 and 184).

GETTING THERE AND AWAY All buses and minibus-taxis leave from the bus station next to the market in the old town centre [177 F4]. The main port for Gisenyi is at Rubona, about 6km south of town; the two are connected by regular minibuses. The GPS (Lake Kivu Serena Hotel) is ✛ S 01°42.077, E 029°15.605.

To/from Kigali and Ruhengeri Gisenyi lies approximately 60km from Ruhengeri by road, and 160km from Kigali. The road is sealed and mostly in good condition, though there are some pot-holed stretches. The direct drive from Kigali should take no longer than three hours. Regular minibus-taxis connect the three towns; the fare from Gisenyi to Ruhengeri is Rfr800 and to Kigali Rfr1,800.

To/from Kibuye and Cyangugu To drive from Gisenyi to Kibuye, you first need to head out along the Ruhengeri road for about 5km to Pfunda, before turning right at a poorly signposted junction on to the dirt road that leads to Rubengera on the surfaced road between Kigali and Kibuye. It's a drive of about 110km in all, and the dirt stretch is in variable condition, so three to four hours should be allowed. Although the dirt road runs parallel to Lake Kivu, it offers disappointingly few glimpses of the lake, though this is compensated for by some spectacular mountain scenery and relic patches of Gishwati Forest (see *Gishwati Forest* page 186). From Kibuye, it's another 100km to Cyangugu, a three-to-four-hour drive, mostly along dirt roads. It is rumoured that these lakeshore roads will be surfaced during the lifespan of this edition, which would cut the driving time in half.

Public transport along the road between Gisenyi and Kibuye is rather less frequent than along the surfaced road heading east from Gisenyi, but buses cover the route daily at a fare of Rfr2,500. At present they leave Gisenyi at 06.00 and 14.00, but this could vary. You'll need to change vehicles at Kibuye if you are heading on to Cyangugu.

Boat transport on Lake Kivu lapsed while relations with the DRC were volatile but is now picking up. At the time of writing there is no scheduled public transport between the lake ports, but the Hotel Centre Béthanie in Kibuye has boats for hire (see page 172). By the time you read this there may be more operators, so ask around – be aware that safety standards may not always be 100% and check what equipment is available.

WHERE TO STAY

Gisenyi has a range of accommodation to suit most tastes and budgets, and prices are generally quite reasonable, though they have risen considerably in recent years. Most of the accommodation is on the lakefront, about 15 minutes on foot from the bus and minibus-taxi stand; travellers who don't want to walk down will find a few taxis lined up at the petrol station next to the bus stand. There are a couple of cheap guesthouses close to the bus station, but on the whole it is more pleasant to stay by the lake.

Upmarket

Lake Kivu Serena Hotel [177 F6]47 (66 rooms) \ 0252 541111; e kivu@serena.co.rw; www.serenahotels.com. The former Kivu Sun, which opened in 2004 on the site of the old Meridien Izubu & was acquired by the prestigious Kenyan-based Serena Group in 2007, is the only urban hotel outside of the capital that truly conforms to international standards, & it forms a justifiably popular w/end retreat for Kigali-based expatriates & NGO workers. The green & well-wooded lakeshore grounds lead down to a sandy swimming beach, the spacious & comfortable en-suite rooms all have AC, mini-bar, safe, DSTV & en-suite bathroom with tub/shower. Other facilities include a sparkling swimming pool, a fitness centre with sauna & massage, a gift shop, well trained English-speaking staff, free WiFi access throughout the building, & a highly rated restaurant with indoor & outdoor tables & a varied menu serving grills, curries & salads in the Rfr4,000–6,000 bracket. Visa & MasterCard accepted. US$154/204/315 sgl/dbl/suite B&B.

Gorillas Lake Kivu Hotel [176 D5] (35 rooms) \ 0252 540600/1; e gorillashotel@rwanda1.com; www.hotelgorillas.com. Opened in late 2008 on the site of the sorely missed Hotel Regina, this modernistic upmarket addition to the Gisenyi waterfront doesn't match the class of the Serena, but

it feels like a reliable & efficient choice at half the price. The bland but neat rooms come with a twin or king-size bed, WiFi, writing desk, built-in wardrobes, flat-screen DSTV, & a small bathroom with combined tub/shower. Other facilities include a massive swimming pool & an excellent restaurant with a varied selection of main courses in the Rfr4,000–6,000 range. A health spa, fitness centre, business centre & gift shop are planned. Decent value. US$90/110 sgl/dbl B&B.

Stipp Hotel [176 D4] (26 rooms) \ 0252 540450/540060; e stipphotels@rwanda1.com; www.stippag.co.rw. Boasting a suburban location about 1km northwest of the Serena, this renovated colonial building, which opened as a hotel in early 2005, lies in attractive landscaped grounds overlooking the lake, but is separated from the shore by a road & a tall wall. It is of similar standard to the Gorillas Hotel, but a lot smaller, with smart modern décor, a more personalised feel, & reasonable rates. There is a large, clean swimming pool, the restaurant serves a varied selection of meals for around Rfr5,000–7,000 per main course, & the large carpeted en-suite rooms all come with DSTV, internet access & (in most cases) a lake view. Rfr50,000 dbl; Rfr79,500 suite.

Moderate

Paradis Malahide [176 G7] (10 rooms) m 078 8648650/8756204; e parmalahide@yahoo.fr; www.paradismalahide.com. Situated in Rubona, 6km south of the town centre, this is the top midrange choice around Gisenyi, combining a rustically beautiful lakeshore setting with very comfortable accommodation in rondawels (circular cottages) with stone floors, reed ceilings, dbl beds with nets & en-

suite hot shower. A good terrace restaurant is attached, serving meals in the Rfr4,000–5,000 range as well as cheaper snacks such as omelettes & brochettes, & there's a well stocked bar. The lodge is ideally sited to enjoy sunsets over the lake while kamikaze pied kingfishers dive into the water & local fishermen cruise past in their distinctive boats (consisting of 3 dugouts held together by long poles). There is also a motorboat for hire at Rfr15,000 per 30mins, if you want to explore the surrounding lakeshore or to visit Akeza Island to catch the sunset or enjoy candlelit dinners or a family picnic. To get to Paradis Malahide, follow the road towards Rubona for about 5km; when you can see the brewery ahead of you, turn sharp right, continue along the lake shore & you'll come to it on your left. *Rfr30,000 dbl B&B.*

🏠 **Musante House Hotel** [177 G7] (18 rooms) m 078 8309269/8503054. Tucked away on a quiet alley along the Rubona Rd about 200m past the Restaurant Bikini Tam-Tam, this is a quiet, homely & reasonably priced hotel with good lakeshore access & 3 classes of room, all of which are en-suite dbls. A restaurant & bar are attached, & the compact green garden is inhabited by a pair of crowned cranes. *Rfr12,000–15,000 for a small room without TV & with cold water only; Rfr18,000 for a larger room with TV, balcony, hot shower; all rates inc b/fast for 1.*

🏠 **Peace Land Hotel** [177 H6] (32 rooms) ✆ 0252 540007/8; m 078 8511760; e peacelandhotel07@ yahoo.com; www.peacelandhotel.com. This new multi-storey hotel stands about 500m along the Ruhengeri Rd in the hills above Gisenyi. It offers great views over the town & lake, especially from the rooftop restaurant/bar, but feels a bit remote from both. 5 types of tiled en-suite room are available, ranging from ordinary sgls with ¾ bed & combined tub/shower to spacious VIP rooms with king-size bed, netting, TV, sitting area & balcony. The rooms are pretty acceptable value, but most are accessed via a labyrinthine network of tiled staircases & corridors that could be a nightmare to manoeuvre in rainy weather. *Rfr15,000/23,000 sgl/twin without TV; Rfr28,000/33,000 sgl/dbl with TV; Rfr38,000 VIP room; all B&B.*

🏠 **Hotel Dian Fossey Lodge** [176 C3] (20 rooms) m 078 8517591; e hoteldianfossey@yahoo.fr. Despite considerable upgrades since the last edition was researched, this suburban lodge set in a cluttered compound decorated with large Disney-on-acid animal sculptures has to be classified as something of an architectural hodgepodge. You'd be unlikely to select it on aesthetic grounds, but the staff seems friendly enough, & the tiled en-suite rooms represent above-average value for money in this range. *Rfr17,000 sgl with ¾ bed & net; Rfr25,000 dbl with queen-size bed, TV, tub & ample cupboard space; Rfr30,000 suite with king-size bed, sofa, TV & fridge.*

🏠 **Belvedere Hotel** [177 H6] (26 rooms) m 078 8506555; e belvederehotel@yahoo.fr. This is a solidly built but unremarkable modern hotel situated alongside the Ruhengeri Rd a few hundred metres from the town centre. It has pleasant landscaped gardens with a terrace restaurant & view over the town & lake, but it's not as alluring as staying on the lakeshore. The rooms all have a queen-size bed, netting, flat-screen TV, writing desk & en-suite bathroom with combined tub/shower. *Rfr25,000/30,000 for an ordinary sgl/dbl, Rfr40,000/45,000 for a larger room, all B&B.*

🏠 **Hotel Ubumwe** [176 B4] (12 rooms) ✆ 0252 540267; m 078 8506647; e ubumwehotel2006@ yahoo.fr. Set in leafy suburbia close to the Congolese border, this friendly & comfortable but unremarkable hotel has bright en-suite rooms with king-size beds, hot showers & small balconies in the new wing & rather more run-down rooms in the old wing. The 1st-floor restaurant has a balcony with lake views, & serves a varied selection of main courses for Rfr4,000–6,000 & lighter meals for around Rfr2,500. It's 20mins' walk from the town centre, & set back a block from the lake. *Rfr20,000/25,000 sgl/dbl in old wing; Rfr30,000 dbl in new wing.*

🏠 **Mostej Hotel** [177 F5] (20 rooms) ✆ 0252 540485; m 078 8836693; e mostej.hotel@ yahoo.fr. Boasting an indifferent location alongside the main dirt road connecting the market area to the lakeshore, this solidly built & modern-looking hotel, which opened in late 2008, has a somewhat bland & functional feel, & optimistically high rates. All rooms are en-suite with hot shower & DSTV, but the cheaper rooms are quite cramped & have a ¾ bed, whereas costlier rooms have a king-size bed, small balcony & large bathroom. *Rfr15,000/25,000 small sgl/dbl; Rfr35,000/45,000 large sgl/dbl; all rates B&B.*

🏠 **Palm Beach Hotel** [177 F6] (15 rooms) The pick of the moderate options for the 3rd edition, this lakeshore hotel alongside the Serena has a striking art-deco façade & light airy ambience to the interiors. It also used to host the best continental restaurant in town & an equally likeable beachfront bar. It closed in 2008 for renovations, & seems likely to reopen during the lifespan of this edition.

🏠 **Motel La Bella** [176 C4] (3 rooms) This characterful & affordable gem, which lies about 300m further out of town than the Stipp Hotel, consisted of a well-maintained old colonial house, with wooden floors, slatted windows & whitewashed exterior, set on a large, attractive lawn sloping down to the lakeshore. It also closed in 2008 & its future is uncertain.

Budget

⌂ **Hilltop Nest Guesthouse** [177 H5] (4 rooms) m 078 8503209. This low-key self-catering guesthouse lies, as its name suggests, on a hill overlooking the lake & town centre. It has comfortable rooms with king-size bed, net, plenty of cupboard space & in some cases a TV. There's an equipped kitchen & pleasant balcony with a view, or you could eat at the Belvedere next door. *Rfr15,000 dbl.*

⌂ **La Corniche** [176 C4] (4 rooms) m 078 8322234. Set alongside a pleasant garden bar & restaurant a short walk north of the lakeshore, this is an adequate & homely lodge. Most rooms have 1 sgl & 1 dbl bed, & an en-suite hot bath or shower. Some rooms are nicer than others so look before you commit. *Rfr15,000 dbl.*

⌂ **Sunrise Motel** [177 E2] (12 rooms) ☏ 0252 540779; m 078 8461676. Tucked away in the backstreets north of the market & bus station, this pleasant new hotel has small but clean rooms with carpet, writing desk & en-suite hot shower & tub. It's about the best deal in this range, but best avoided on Fri & Sat nights, when the adjoining Club Silk nightclub parties until the wee hours (the club is soundproofed but there's bound to be a lot of noise in the parking area). *Rfr10,000/13,500 sgl/dbl.*

Shoestring

⌂ **Presbyterian Church Centre d'Accueil** [177 G4] (13 rooms) ☏ 0252 540397. This agreeable church-run lodge near the market & main taxi park has long been the best deal in this range, despite its distance (about 10mins' walk) from the lake, with bright & fresh rooms set in spaciously laid out grounds that also contain a basic but good-value restaurant. *Rfr6,000 en-suite dbl or twin with nets & hot water; Rfr9,000 trpl; Rfr1,500 for a bed in a 6- or 8-berth dorm.*

⌂ **Methodist Church Centre d'Accueil** [176 D3] (8 rooms) m 078 8560317. Set in pleasant grounds to the north of the town centre, this good-value & friendly but rather isolated lodge offers accommodation in clean private rooms with ¾ bed, washbasin & shared shower/toilet, as well as in 3-bed dorms. Meals are prepared by request & there's a (very distant) view of the lake. The downhill walk to the beach takes 10–15mins. *Rfr5,000 dbl; Rfr8,000 twin; Rfr2,000 dorm bed.*

⌂ **Auberge de Gisenyi** [177 F4] m 078 8703456. Situated close to the taxi park & market, this is a standard local guesthouse & bar/restaurant with small en-suite rooms (cold water, hot buckets by request). *Rfr6,000/7,000 sgl/dbl.*

⌂ **City Lodge** [177 G5] (10 rooms) m 078 8881281. Situated on a dirt road near the market, this adequate local hotel has large rooms with dbl beds & shared ablution facilities. *Rfr8,000 dbl.*

⌂ **Sous le Soleil** [177 G7] (4 rooms) m 078 8490254. Situated in Rubona, between the brewery & Paradis Malahide, this a nice lakeshore location & the basic rooms with ¾ beds are about as cheap as it gets in Gisenyi. *Rfr4,000.*

✕ **WHERE TO EAT AND DRINK** Most of the smarter hotels have adequate to good restaurants. For top-notch continental cuisine, the new **Gorillas Lake Kivu Hotel** [176 D5] should be your first port of call, but it lacks the outdoor ambience of the almost-as-good **Lake Kivu Serena** [177 F6]. Elsewhere, you can also eat well in the pretty gardens of the **Stipp Hotel** [176 D4], while the **Paradis Malahide** [177 G7] in Rubona serves wonderful fresh fish accompanied by a great view across the bay. There are plenty of budget eateries around the market area, of which the **Auberge de Gisenyi** [177 F4] and **Café-Resto Iby'Iwacu** [177 G4] are recommended. The **Boulangerie de Gisenyi** [177 G3] opposite the market is a very well stocked supermarket with a good bakery. For dedicated clubbers, the **Sodevi Nightclub** [176 D4], set in a pretty garden bar, and **Club Silk** [177 E2] next to the Sunrise Motel are both active on Friday and Saturday nights.

✕ **White Rock Restaurant, Bar & Nightclub** [176 C5] m 078 5102122; ⊕ 12.00–22.00 Wed–Sun, the nightclub operates on Wed & Sat nights only. This is the most attractive place to eat in Gisenyi, centred on a large covered deck right above the lakeshore, but with indoor seating too, & a pool table & nightclub downstairs. The varied menu includes salads, sandwiches, soups & burgers for around Rfr2,500, pasta dishes in the Rfr3,500–4,000 range, full fish & meat meals at around Rfr4,500–6,000, & a tempting choice of desserts for Rfr2,000–3,500. The bar is well stocked but disproportionately pricey, so you may want to start or finish with a cheaper drink at the nearby Crescendo bar.

♀ **Crescendo Bar** [176 C4] 📱 078 8501388; ⊕ 12.00–23.00 daily. Situated opposite the White Rock, this agreeable palm-shaded garden bar serves inexpensive drinks & a limited selection of snacks, including brochettes & grilled chicken. The daytime vocal accompaniment of the garden's plentiful birdlife is replaced by the gentle sound of lapping water by night.

✕ **La Corniche** [176 C4] 📱 078 8322234. Set in a pretty suburban garden, this place is notable for its expansive lunchtime buffets, which are great value for the hungry at Rfr2,500–3,500. It functions mainly as a garden bar in the evenings, but a limited selection of affordable snacks is available.

✕ **Bar-Restaurant Bikini Tam-Tam** [177 G7] Situated alongside the Rubona Rd. This is a great spot for sundowners — indeed for a drink at any time of day — & the perfect lakefront position is only slightly undermined by the aromatic fish market next door. A limited selection of snacks & grills is available in the Rfr1,500–3,500 range.

✕ **Restaurant Touristique la Fontaine** [177 G7] ☎ 0252 540525; 📱 078 8689733; ⊕ lunch & dinner daily. Set in attractive landscaped lakeshore gardens in Rubona, a few gates up from the Paradis Malahide, this pleasant al fresco restaurant, also known as Chez Maman Chakula, serves continental-style meat, rabbit & fish dishes in the Rfr4,000–7,000 range. It also offers a range of cheaper snacks & local dishes, & a bar.

OTHER PRACTICALITIES For **foreign exchange**, most of the banks marked on the map will change US dollars cash, but you'll get better rates and more efficient service at any of several forex bureaux dotted around the market area [177 F/G4]. The Banque de Kigali [177 E6] also has Western Union. **Internet** facilities are widespread: several good cyber cafés can be found in the market area [177 F4] and the Serena [177 F6] and Gorillas hotels [176 D5] both have WiFi access. For **handicrafts**, the shop run by the COPROVERA cooperative [177 G5] on the main road running south from the market is worth a look.

WHAT TO SEE AND DO

Rubona Set on an attractive peninsula 6km from the town centre, Rubona is the main harbour for Gisenyi and the site of Rwanda's largest brewery, Bralirwa. It is connected to the town centre by a surfaced road and regular minibus-taxis, a scenic route which would make for a pleasant stroll in one or other direction. Rubona is a bustling little satellite town, and fun to stroll around, but it is mainly of interest to travellers looking for lake transport, or photographers attracted by the hundreds of small fishing pirogues or dugout canoes that dot the harbour (look out for the distinctive catamaran-style boats consisting of three dugouts held together by poles). The fish in this bay have an unusual diet, as dregs from the brewing process at Bralirwa Brewery are thrown into the water regularly!

Another compelling reason to visit Rubona is the presence of the Paradis Malahide (see page 179), which offers some of the best-value accommodation in the area, and – even if you don't want to spend the night – makes an excellent spot for a sundowner drink or al fresco lunch.

Hot springs A little beyond Bralirwa are some hot springs, claimed by the local people living nearby to have a curative effect. Allegedly, bathing in the waters relieves fatigue, cures skin rashes and even helps to mend simple fractures. More prosaically, in some places the springs are hot enough – and are used by the villagers – to boil potatoes and cassava. John and Rosemary Cox add: 'We left our vehicle on the road and walked down to where the springs steam and bubble out to the lake. It would be hard to bathe in their shallow pools but lots of friendly children were playing and splashing in them and were quite happy to be photographed. Adults were likewise happily on hand to help us disengage the 4×4 when it got stuck reversing to return to the hotel.'

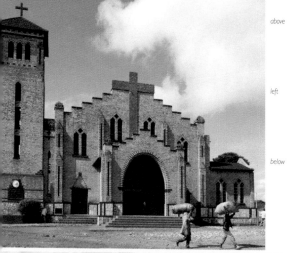

above   In 2008 Kigali became the first African urban centre to be presented with the Habitat Scroll of Honour award (AVZ) page 77

left   The huge Roman Catholic cathedral in Butare was built in the late 1930s and is the largest in the country (AVZ) page 136

below   The town of Gisenyi, on the shores of Lake Kivu, possesses a seductive tropical ambience that makes it a great place to spend a few days (AVZ) page 174

left   Rwanda's burgeoning tea industry now creates employment for around 60,000 people and more than 10 million kilograms of tea are exported from Rwanda yearly (CR/MP/FLPA) page 55

below   The fishing boats on Lake Kivu comprise three dugout canoes bound together, called *amato* (AVZ) page 161

bottom   Woman working in the fields on the lower slopes of the Virunga Mountains, Volcanoes National Park (NF) page 228

above left	Intore traditional drummer — drumming is of great artistic importance in Rwanda and a full drum ensemble typically consists of either seven or nine drums (AVZ) page 29
above right	At the Rukali Palace Museum in Nyanza the traditional palace of the *mwami* has been carefully reconstructed and maintained, and contains the king's massive bed (AVZ) page 124
below left	Woman preparing food in Kigali — Rwandan favourites include goat kebabs (brochettes), grilled or fried tilapia (a type of lake fish) and bean or meat stews (AVZ) page 54
below right	Coffee washing station — the best areas for growing coffee are Akagera, Virunga, and around lakes Kivu and Muhazi (AVZ) page 138

top   **Buffalo** *Syncerus caffer*
(AVZ) page 253

left   **Burchell's zebra** *Equus
burchelli* (AVZ) page 254

below   **Ankole bull** (AVZ) page 244

above **Bushbuck** *Tragelaphus scriptus*
(AVZ) page 253

above right **Hippopotamus**
Hippopotamus *amphibious*
(AVZ) page 253

right **African elephant** *Loxodonta africana*
(AVZ) page 254

below **Impala** *Aepyceros melampus*
(AVZ) page 252

above left Shoebill *Balaeniceps rex* (AVZ) page 256
above right Grey-crowned crane *Balearica regulorum* (AVZ) page 255
below left Red-throated alethe *Alethe poliophrys* (AVZ) page 147
below right Montane double-collared sunbird *Nectarinia ludovicensis* (CR/MP/FLPA) page 6

top left   **Golden monkey *Cercopithecus kandti***
(AVZ) page 227

above left   **Red-tailed monkey *Cercopithecus ascinius***
(AVZ) page 146

top right   **Chimpanzee *Pan troglodytes***
(FL/FLPA) page 144

above right   **Olive baboon with young *Papio cynocephalus
anubis*** (AVZ) page 147

below   **Extending for 1,015km² over the mountainous southwest of Rwanda, Nyungwe Forest National Park protects 13
resident primate species** (TM/MP/FLPA) page 139

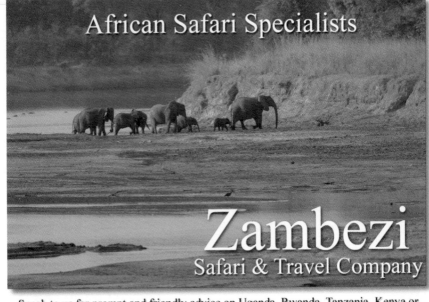

Dancing Pots Operated by New Dawn Associates (m *078 8513652;* e *www.newdawnassociates.com*) in collaboration with the Abatigayubuke community outside Gisenyi, the Dancing Pots experience is designed to give visitors the opportunity to interact with the inhabitants of a forward-looking Batwa settlement. Hunter-gatherers by tradition, these historically marginalised people comprise less than a half percent of the population, and suffer from high levels of illiteracy, unemployment and landlessness. At Abatigayubuke, however, the Batwa have harnessed traditional skills such as pottery and performing arts to make a living and become integrated into the greater community. A visit incorporates traditional dance performances, pottery and the opportunity to talk about the Batwa traditions and lifestyle. A day visit from Gisenyi costs between US$50 and US$80 per person, depending on group size (minimum size is four), with 70% of income going to the community.

Ingoboka Coffee Cooperative (m *078 8513652; www.newdawnassociates.com*) Comprising 350 members, this lakeside cooperative is one of the largest producers of coffee in the Gisenyi area, and it forms the centrepiece of the new 'From Crop to Cup' experience offered by New Dawn Associates. This offers visitors the opportunity to experience and observe the entire coffee production chain, starting with a visit to one of the cooperative member's *shambas* on Nyamirundi Island (whose volcanic soils are attributed with the fine non-acidic flavour of the coffee produced) and continuing to the Gashishi Washing Station on the mainland, before finally enjoying a cup of hand-ground coffee with their hosts. A day visit from Gisenyi costs between US$55 and US$70 per person, depending on group size (minimum five), with 70% of income going to the community. The best time to go is during the main coffee harvesting season of March to June.

Imbabazi Orphanage Not far from Gisenyi is the Imbabazi orphanage (*www.rwandaproject.org*), a positive and heart-warming project started in December 1994 by Rosamond Halsey Carr at her plantation in nearby Mugongo to shelter some of the many genocide orphans and displaced children. After moving to Gisenyi in the 1990s and spending some years there, it returned to new and purpose-built premises in Mugongo at the end of 2005. See box on page 184.

Visitors are welcome, and are likely to find themselves being sung and danced to by the smiling, lively bunch of children. One of the buildings in the orphanage is currently being converted to a visitor centre documenting the life of its founder, scheduled to open in late 2009. To get there from Gisenyi, follow the Ruhengeri road out of town for about 20km to Kabari junction, where the 8km dirt road to Mugongo is signposted to the left. Public transport runs to within about 2km of Imbabazi, but you could also walk – it's a beautiful road with spectacular views of two of the volcanoes and Lake Kivu.

Kiaka Cooperative (\ *0252 540853;* m *078 8426429;* e *kiakacoop@yahoo.fr; www.kiaka.com;* ⊕ *10.00–16.00 daily*) Situated at Kanama, about 15km from Gisenyi along the road to Ruhengeri, this Atelier de Menuiserie (Carpentry Shop) showcases the highly regarded work of the Cooperative des Artisans de Kanama. The hefty furniture here is probably of greater interest to expatriates than tourists, but it also stocks a decent selection of basketwork, pottery, carvings and other handicrafts, and you can visit the workshop to watch the craftsmen in action.

Goma The capital of the strife-torn Congolese province of Nord-Kivu, Goma lies on the lakeshore a mere 1km from the Rwandan border post and 3.5km from the centre of Gisenyi. With a population of around 250,000, it is much larger than Gisenyi (or, for that matter, than any Rwandan town other than Kigali). In times past, Goma was renowned for its live music scene and bustling nightlife. However, since July 1994, when Nord-Kivu received an influx of around one million Hutu refugees from Rwanda, leading to an acute food and water shortage, and a cholera outbreak that claimed thousands of lives, the town has been blighted by a succession of natural and artificial disasters.

Natural disaster struck in January 2002, when the eruption of nearby Nyiragongo sent a lava flow up to 1km wide through the city centre. Most of the human population was evacuated to Gisenyi, and lava destroyed more than 4,500 buildings. Although much of the town has been cleared and rebuilt, the seas of craggy lava still lie beside the road with truncated buildings arising from them.

Goma has frequently been a focal point of the lengthy Congolese civil war initiated by a coup in 1997. The most recent fighting broke out on 25 October 2008, when the town and environs witnessed heavy battles between the UN-backed Congolese army and the Congrès National pour la Défense du Peuple (CNDP) rebel movement led by the Tutsi general Laurent Nkunda. Unknown thousands died in the conflict, and some 250,000 civilians were forced to flee their homes, leading to what the United Nations called 'a humanitarian crisis of

ROSAMOND HALSEY CARR AND THE IMBABAZI ORPHANAGE

As a young fashion illustrator in New York City, Rosamond Halsey married an adventurous hunter-explorer, Kenneth Carr, and journeyed with him to the Congo in 1949. After their eventual divorce, Kenneth left; Rosamond stayed on. In 1955 she moved to northwest Rwanda to manage a flower plantation, Mugongo, and later bought it. For the next 50 years she witnessed the end of colonialism, celebrated Rwanda's independence and became one of Dian Fossey's closest friends. (In the film Gorillas in the Mist, her role is played by Julie Harris.)

During periods of violence and upheaval, Mrs Carr always stayed fast at her home in Mugongo while others fled. But when the genocide began in April 1994 the American Embassy finally insisted that she leave. After several months in the US, she received word that Sembagare, her friend and plantation manager of 50 years, had survived what turned out to be three attempts on his life. In August 1994, aged 82, she returned in a cargo plane, to find her home in ruins and 50 years' worth of possessions either stolen or destroyed. At Mugongo, she and Sembagare did the only thing that made sense to them: they converted an old pyrethrum drying-house and set up the Imbabazi Orphanage, to care for the genocide orphans.

In 1997 the orphanage was forced to move from Mugongo for security reasons, and, having changed locations four times, settled in Gisenyi for several years. At the end of 2005 it moved 'back home' to Mugongo. From time to time some children are traced and reclaimed by family members – while others arrive and are taken in. Mrs Carr died on 29 September 2006 at the age of 94 (she was officially Rwanda's oldest resident) and was buried at Mugongo. She lived in a house on Gisenyi's lake shore right up until her death, and would still visit the orphanage several times a week to manage its affairs. The Mugongo farm continues to provide the orphanage with fresh vegetables and many Rwandan businesses (and weddings!) with fresh flowers, and is the sole source of income for the families who work there.

Imbabazi receives funds from various friends and organisations, many of them in the US. (Search 'Imbabazi Orphanage' on the internet and you'll find links to some.) Visitors to Mugongo can meet the children and decide on the spot – as often happens – to catastrophic dimensions'. Despite several calls for ceasefires, the fighting continued intermittently until 22 January 2009, when Nkunda was arrested after crossing into Rwanda. On 23 March 2009, the CNDP signed a peace treaty with the Congolese government, but Goma remains potentially volatile, and it will take years to recover from the fighting.

Provided the situation holds stable, Goma makes for an interesting half-day excursion from Gisenyi. You don't need a visa as such but an entrance fee of US$30 is levied at the border. If you're one of the nationalities that needs a visa to enter Rwanda, then make sure that it's multiple-entry rather than single-entry, otherwise you'll have to pay for a fresh visa to return to Rwanda from DRC. The frontier post normally opens at 08.00 and closes at 18.00 sharp, although there's talk of extending this. Goma has taken a beating but was a gracious and attractive town and is well worth a stroll. At the time of writing, if you're heading into the countryside around the town, it's advisable to do so in the company of a local person – for reasons not of safety but of hassle.

If you feel like an adventure, see the box, *Climbing Nyiragongo*, on page 186 – but for this climb you must have proper equipment and be accompanied by a competent guide. And even if the political situation is stable, step cautiously in the vicinity of the crater: in July 2007 a tourist from Hong Kong died after falling 100 metres whilst taking photographs.

sponsor one or more of them, whether for small general needs or for secondary school education. A novel fundraising scheme, 'Through the Eyes of Children', began in 2000, originally as a photographic workshop conceived by photographer David Jiranek. Using disposable cameras, the children at the orphanage took photos of themselves and their surroundings, exploring their community and finding beauty as Rwanda struggled to rebuild after the genocide.

At first the photos were developed locally, displayed on the orphanage walls and put into albums by the children. A year later, the children were invited by the US Embassy to exhibit their work in Kigali, with all proceeds going towards their education. In the 2001 *Camera Arts Magazine* Photo Contest, eight-year-old Jacqueline won first prize for portraiture, and the project has won an Honourable Mention in an international competition featuring professional and non-professional photographers from around the world.

UNICEF invited the Imbabazi children to participate in its 2003 *State of the World's Children* report. As a result the report's cover photograph was of Murakete, taken by her friend Umuhoza at the orphanage. Also published inside are other photos of the children using their disposable cameras. In addition, New York University invited the project to exhibit at the Gulf & Western Gallery at the NYU Tisch School for the Arts in New York City in December 2002 and January 2003. The photos were also shown at the premiere of the Human Rights Watch International Film Festival in New York in June 2003. For more information, check the comprehensive website www.rwandaproject.org.

Since Rosamond Halsey Carr founded the Imbabazi Orphanage in 1994, she and her staff have cared for more than 400 orphans. The orphanage, still based at Mugongo, is currently home to about 100 children, aged from seven to 21 years.

Rosamond Halsey Carr is the author of *Land of a Thousand Hills: My Life in Rwanda* (she wrote the book with her niece, Ann Howard Halsey), chronicling her love affair with Rwanda and describing the country in all its variety and beauty; see *Further Information*, page 272. She is also the subject of a short documentary film *A Mother's Love: Rosamond Carr & A Lifetime In Rwanda*.

We were eight people in total, ranging in age from a 12-year-old boy to about 45 years. On Saturday morning we were at the Rwanda–DRC border in Gisenyi at 08.00. After all the custom procedures to enter DRC, we met up with one of the volcanologists and our guide. They accompanied us to the foot of the volcano where we negotiated a price of US$30 per person and US$20 for the guide. Some of the people hired a porter for US$10.

We left the base office at exactly 10.00. The first bit of the trail goes through beautiful rainforest. It is amazing to see all the indigenous trees and hear the different bird songs. After a while we left the forest to walk on old lava from the 2002 eruption. We followed the lava to our lunch spot, which was about halfway up the volcano. When the volcano erupted in 2002 the lava came out of the side of the mountain and not the top. We saw the place where it emerged and there was still some smoke coming out. The lava flowed down the path we had come up, then stopped before it reached the town. But it then found another way under the volcano and came out of the side of the mountain at another place, near the airport, from where it went through the town and ended up in Lake Kivu.

After lunch we went through rainforest again. The path was now much steeper and we also had some rain. We reached the 'huts' at about 16:30. There used to be three metal huts – one is now down completely, half of the second one is still standing and the third one is still OK. We pitched one tent inside hut number 2 and the other two tents outside.

The guide, guard and porter slept in hut number 3. They also carried up a bag of charcoal and we could warm ourselves up and get our clothes dry. We also used this hut for doing all our cooking. Outside it was quite chilly but the amazing view over the other volcanoes, lake and town made up for it.

After a rest and dinner we climbed for a final 30 minutes to the summit. It was dark so we used torches and head lamps. We could only see a red glowing mist in the big volcano pot. We could hear the lava bubble down under. It sounded like the waves of the sea. We could see the lights of the two towns and all the fishing boats down on the lake.

We were back on the summit the next morning just after sunrise. We traversed for about half an hour around the volcano rim. All the mist lifted out of the huge pot and we could see the lava down at the bottom. What an amazing sight. We were standing on top of a live volcano!

On the way down we investigated the crater at our lunch spot more closely and then followed the lava back to the base. It was an amazing weekend!

Note: This box has not been updated for this edition due to political volatility in the DR Congo, but we include it in the hope that it will be safe to visit the area again soon.

Gishwati Forest In the early 20th century, Gishwati was the second-largest tract of indigenous forest in Rwanda, extending over roughly 1,000km² along the Albertine Rift escarpment from the base of the Virungas halfway down Lake Kivu. By 1989, when Rwanda's last forest-dwelling Batwa hunter-gatherers were evicted from Gishwati, it consisted of two main forest blocks which together covered less than a quarter of its former extent. More forest was cleared in the early 1990s to make way for a forestry plantation and dairy project, and most of what remained was cut down in 1998–99, to accommodate the land needs of returned refugees.

This short-sighted decision not only resulted in immense biodiversity loss, but also has led to several landslides that have killed many people, as well as the drying up of streams that once provided water to communities outside the forest. In 2008, floods blamed on deforestation destroyed hundreds of homes. Today, a mere 6km² of true forest remains at Gishwati. Chimpanzees, still known to occur in the reserve in the late 1980s, are almost certainly now locally extinct. Outside of the Virungas, Gishwati was also the only confirmed haunt of the golden monkey, but it seems unlikely that a viable population of this endangered species remains. There has been no recent bird inventory, but it is possible that Albertine Rift endemics such as regal sunbird and strange weaver are still present.

The most substantial remnant of Gishwati can be visited from the road between Gisenyi and Kibuye, and there is serious talk of developing it for tourism in the near future. However, there are tricky issues to overcome. In 2009, the Forestry Management Support Project (PAFOR) had planted around 70,000 seedlings on some 40 acres of land, but these were then uprooted by settlers angry at having been told they must move out of the forest to what they claim is a less fertile area. At the time of writing, they are being promised incentives such as schools, markets and a health centre in the new area, and the Rwandan government allocated one billion Rwandan francs to a three-year restoration project scheduled to start in October 2009. However, it remains to be seen whether and exactly how the problem will be resolved on the ground. For now, Katot Meyer writes:

The road passes a small patch of indigenous forest to the east exactly 40km from Gisenyi. I went for a walk there. Very few people were on the road and luckily I could slip into the forest without any kids following me. There are a lot of trails, most of them with cattle tracks on, but I saw not a soul. Peace and quiet in Rwanda? I thought it to be impossible. There were birds singing in the trees, frogs at the river crossing, an absolute feast. At some places the undergrowth is very thick but as long as you stay on the paths this is an incredible hiking area. I could see the forest stretching over quite a few hills but in some places on the horizon cultivators had already invaded it. I would have thought that the areas closest to the main road would be in the greatest danger, yet I found many trees that had fallen from natural causes and were just left to rot. As in all Rwandan Forest areas, wear long trousers for walking.

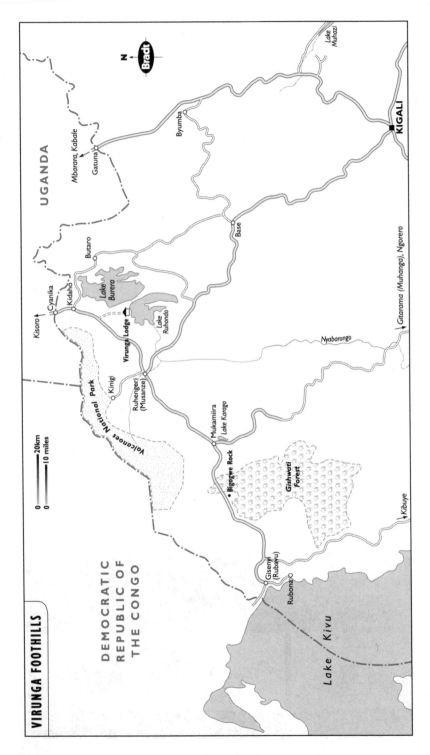

VIRUNGA FOOTHILLS

9

Ruhengeri (Musanze) and Surrounds

Location, they say, is everything, and on this score Ruhengeri, the fourth-largest town in Rwanda, with a population estimated at around 90,000, is privileged indeed. As the closest town to the Volcanoes National Park (see *Chapter 10*), it is the most convenient urban base from which to track mountain gorillas, as well as boasting a memorably stirring backdrop in the form of the distinctive volcanic outlines of the three most easterly mountains in the Virunga chain.

Despite its strategic importance as a tourist hub and its status as capital of Musanze District, Ruhengeri is an unremarkable town, sprawling amorphously from the tight grid of pot-holed roads that surround the central market. But as travel bases go, it's difficult to fault: the mood is friendly and free of hassle, and – at an altitude of 1,850m – the temperate climate is most agreeable. The market is lively and worth a visit, and there are some pleasant strolls around town, as well as the possibility of excursions further afield to Lakes Burera, Ruhondo and Karago.

GETTING THERE AND AWAY

The main taxi park [195 F7] is on a patch of open ground at the edge of the compact town centre, a short distance south of the central market past the Urumuli Hotel. However, the superior express services to Gisenyi and Kigali operated by the likes of Virunga Express, Sotra Express and Atraco leave from in front of the respective company's office, all of which are clustered together on Avenue du 5 Juillet west of the central market [195 G2]. The GPS for the Hotel Muhabura is ✪ S 01°29.883, E 029°37.954.

TO/FROM KIGALI Kigali and Ruhengeri are linked by a 96km surfaced road. It's in fair condition, though the combination of outrageous bends, the occasional pothole, and some seriously manic local drivers requires caution. Even so, you should cover the distance in 90 minutes.

Regular minibus-taxis connect Kigali (Nyabugogo bus station) and Ruhengeri, leaving in either direction when they have a full complement of passengers. Tickets cost Rfr1,500 and the trip takes around 90 minutes. The most reliable minibus service is Virunga Express (aka Virunga Ponctuel), which has departures in either direction every 15 minutes or so between 06.00 and 17.00. The Kigali office is just outside Nyabugogo bus station and the Ruhengeri office is on Avenue du 5 Juillet next to the Home d'Accueil Virunga [195 G2]. Atraco and Sotra respectively run hourly and half-hourly services between Kigali and Ruhengeri from 06.00 to 19.00.

About 35km out of Kigali, on your left, you'll see a small but ornate cemetery, very different in style from those elsewhere in Rwanda. The graves there are those of Chinese workers who died during the building of this road and others in Rwanda – the excellent Kigali–Kibuye road is also one of theirs.

TO/FROM GISENYI The 62km drive between Ruhengeri and Gisenyi follows a fairly good (and by Rwandan standards unusually straight) surfaced road, and should take no longer than an hour and a quarter. Minibus-taxis between the two towns leave regularly and cost around Rfr1,000. As with the Kigali trip, the most reliable service is Virunga Express/Ponctuel, which departs hourly from 06.00 to 19.00.

Driving from Ruhengeri to Gisenyi, you pass (on the left) a surfaced road that goes first to Lake Karago (see page 202) and then continues southwards to join the Gitarama–Kibuye road, as shown on the map on pages ii–iii of the colour section. It winds high up into the hills and the views are breathtaking. It passes through hamlets and beside tea plantations, so there is human interest too, but the main attraction has to be the wonderfully panoramic landscape. You could consider it as an alternative way of returning to Kigali from either Ruhengeri or Gisenyi. Hikers can probably get lifts as transport goes to and from the tea plantations – and there is even the odd bus.

TO/FROM UGANDA The border crossings between Uganda and Rwanda are covered more fully on page 39. Coming to Ruhengeri straight from Kampala, the most efficient option is to catch a bus or minibus heading directly to Kigali, where you can pick up a minibus-taxi to Ruhengeri.

Coming from the west of Uganda, you will have to pass through Kabale, from where you can either cross directly into Rwanda at the Katuna border post, or else continue within Uganda to Kisoro and cross at the Cyanika border post. If you have private transport, or are visiting Kisoro anyway, then the Cyanika route is the

CLIMBING MOUNT KABUYE
Doug Teschner, updated by Philip Briggs

This 2,643m peak is a pleasant hike, all the more attractive because it can be done easily in a day from Kigali without having to leave before dawn – and you're still back in town before dark. Also, as it's so close to the main road, you can get there by public transport. The hike involves 1,000m of ascent and takes two to four hours to the top (a four-to-seven-hour round trip of about 12km) for most people.

The 'mountain' is visible to the east side of the Kigali–Ruhengeri road, about an hour out of Kigali or 45 minutes out of Ruhengeri. It stands out as a hill that is bigger than the rest. You may wish to obtain a topographic map (Gakenke, map number 9) from the Ministry of Public Works in the Gikondo section of Kigali, but it is not necessary as long as visibility is good enough to see the mountain (which it almost always is).

The junction village for Mount Kabuye is Gakenke, which straddles the main surfaced road 31km from Ruhengeri and 63km from Kigali. Just north of this village, turn eastward into what appears to be a paved road signposted 'Hospital Nemba 1km'. The road becomes dirt within 100 metres and soon after you need to take the first switchback to the left through 'town', which leads to a soccer field on the right after about 1km. After another 300 metres, you pass the hospital to the right, then 400m further a downhill fork to the right leads you to another football pitch with a small kiosk-like shop and a wooden footbridge across the river on the far side. The guy who owns the shop will probably offer to guard your car, but if in doubt you could always park in the hospital grounds.

Hikers should cross the wooden bridge and follow the road, climbing steadily to its end (about 2km). After 30 minutes, look for a little shack on the right which (if open) will sell you warm Fanta and you may even be able to arrange for a child to carry some to the top. This is a good way to keep hydrated and support the local economy.

Where the road ends at a pipe, there is an obvious steep section of trail. Above this, there are multiple trails and it is not always easy to pick the best one, but you can better option. Kisoro and Ruhengeri lie approximately 40km from each other along a mostly tarred road. On public transport, you'll have to change vehicles at the border, and can expect to pay around Rfr600–800 for each leg.

Otherwise, given the poor state of the road between Kabale and Kisoro (as well as the limited amount of public transport), the most circuitous route between Kabale and Ruhengeri on paper is almost certainly the most efficient in practice: that is to catch a minibus-taxi from Kabale to Kigali (you might need to change vehicles at the border), from where you can pick up another to Ruhengeri. A variation on this would be to stop at Byumba on the Kabale–Kigali road, then travel along the back road to Base on the Ruhengeri–Kigali road, but this will almost certainly entail spending a night in Byumba (see page 235).

TOURIST INFORMATION

ORTPN The ORTPN office in Ruhengeri town is on the first floor of the municipal buildings on Avenue du 5 Juillet [194 C4]; look out for the signpost opposite the Bank of Kigali, about 300m south of the Muhabura Hotel. A second ORTPN office is situated 12km out of town at the Volcanoes National Park headquarters in Kinigi. At the time of writing, depending on availability, last-minute gorilla-tracking permits can be booked through either of these offices. To make such a booking, pop in at around 17.00 on the day before you want to track, since this is when the next day's bookings are radioed through from the main booking office in Kigali. This situation might change during the lifespan of this edition.

easily readjust on smaller trails if you lose the main one. The best route goes right at the top of the steep section and stays just to the right of the ridge, passing by the local water supply and eventually passing a school (prominently visible from below) in a big clearing. Above the school, the trail follows the right side of the ridge to a T-Junction. Turn left and enjoy the short flat stretch before turning right and heading steeply back up the very scenic ridge through farmlands and by houses with the mountain prominently visible above. If the sky is very clear, views of the volcanoes will appear off to the left.

After a while, the trail switches over to the left side of the ridge and soon reaches a flattish place on the ridge proper. Turn right after 50m for a scenic rest on rocks in a eucalyptus grove. You're about two-thirds of the way to the top. After your rest, continue up the steepening ridge toward the summit cone. A short steep section up a grassy patch leads to a rocky trail, which slabs off to the left and eventually swings around the peak to reach the pass on the left (north) side of the summit.

At the pass, leave the main trail by turning right on a smaller one. You're now 15 minutes from the top. Follow this vague path up the ridge, through new eucalyptus trees, to nearly the top. The precise but somewhat indistinct summit (visible *en route* from a prior false top) is reached by leaving the path for the final 20m. If it is very clear, you can see all the Virunga volcanoes and Lake Ruhondo to the north. Just down on the other side of the summit, there is a pine forest which offers shade on a sunny day.

As in all places in Rwanda, expect to be followed by a pack of children, although I have found that each time we go (I have done it five times), there are fewer, as they seem to be getting used to visitors.

Descend the same way, or pick another. The valley off to the right (looking down) is very beautiful, but it adds at least an hour to the descent.

TOUR OPERATORS

Ruhengeri has two:

Highland Gorilla Tour & Travel [195 E6] ☏ 0252 546765; m 078 8414488; e ngyiroger@yahoo.fr; www.shyiradiocese.org.rw. Situated in the same building as the Centre d'Accueil de l'Eglise Episcopale. Can also arrange car hire.
Amahoro Tours Market St; ☏ 0252 546877; m 078 8687448; e info@amahoro-tours.com; www.amahoro-tours.com. The main agent for

homestays in the area (see box on page 198), as well as involving visitors in local activities of their choice (canoeing, fishing, dancing, drumming, traditional medicine, beekeeping, local cuisine, etc). They can also arrange gorilla visits & all the normal tourist programmes. This is a developing enterprise, so check the helpful website or email for the latest information.

WHERE TO STAY

Until recently, almost all accommodation options within Ruhengeri itself fell into the budget or shoestring category, but this has changed following the recent opening of several midrange hotels in the town, along with the spanking new upmarket-ish Hotel Gorillas. Nevertheless, gorilla trackers seeking high-quality accommodation are pointed towards the quartet of smarter lodges situated close to the Volcanoes National Park headquarters at Kinigi, or to the sumptuous Virunga Lodge near Lake Burera (all covered later in the chapter). A new, luxury tented camp called Ikoro, originally scheduled to open on the outskirts of town in mid-2007, was still under construction in mid-2009.

UPMARKET

Ikoro Tented Camp [195 H1] (10 tents) m 078 8671572; www.elegantafrica.com. This uncompleted camp has a lovely woodland setting with a view of the volcanoes on the outskirts of Ruhengeri. It will consist of 10 luxury en-suite safari tents, each with a private veranda, as well as 5 dedicated camping sites, each with its own washing (hot showers) & cooking facilities. Materials & furnishings are being sourced locally. Facilities will include a restaurant, bar, lounge & internet access. It's located on the Ruhengeri/Cyanika road about 1km past the turn-off to Kinigi. It is likely to open in 2010, an event that will be posted on the Bradt update website. *US$150 per dbl tent per night; US$40 per campsite.*

Hotel Gorillas [194 C3] (24 rooms) ☏ 0252 501717/8; m 078 8487777; e info@relaysgorillashotel.com; www.relaysgorillashotel.com. Situated directly opposite the venerable Hotel Muhabura, this new branch of the Gorillas Hotel chain (also represented in Kigali & Gisenyi) is easily the smartest option in Ruhengeri town, though it lacks the individual character of its more rustic counterparts in the Virunga foothills around Kinigi. Facilities include a restaurant & bar, & free WiFi for hotel residents; a massage/sauna room, business centre & gift shop are likely to follow. *US$110/130 sgl/dbl B&B.*

MODERATE

La Palme Hôtel [194 B3] (12 rooms, more under construction) ☏ 0252 546428/9; e palmehotel02@yahoo.fr. Rated highly by several local tour operators, this small hotel — extension under construction — lies in small but green grounds at the northwest end of Av 5 Juillet, more or less opposite the landmark Hotel Muhabura. The carpeted rooms, which come with dbl beds, mini-bar, en-suite hot shower & DSTV, are nothing special at the price, but the service & food are both very good, & facilities include a cyber café. *US$60/90 sgl/dbl B&B; US$110 suite.*

Hotel Muhabura [194 C3] (15 rooms) ☏ 0252 546296; m 078 8364774; e muhabura12@yahoo.fr or info@hotelmuhabura.com; www.hotelmuhabura.com. The oldest tourist lodging in Ruhengeri, dating to Dian Fossey's time, this likeable old favourite lies in green grounds on the outskirts of town along Av 5 Juillet in the direction of Gisenyi. It is a very characterful & reasonably priced set-up, offering accommodation in 2 types of room: spacious en-suite dbls with hot bath & shower & larger apartments with similar facilities. A smarter new wing is under construction. A good bar &

restaurant serves a wide selection of continental dishes inside or outdoors for Rfr4,000 upwards. *Rfr20,000/25,000 sgl/dbl occupancy B&B.*

⌂ **Centre d'Accueil de l'Eglise Episcopale** [195 E6] (42 rooms) ☎ 0252 546857; m 078 8558501; e ishema_hotel@hotmail.com or info@ishemahotel.com; www.ishemahotel.com. Also known as the Ishema Hotel (but not signposted as such), the recently expanded & renovated EER Guesthouse lies in large grounds on Av du 5 Juillet near the junction with Rue de Pyrèthre, about 1km from the taxi park. Accommodation ranges from smart dbl rooms & suites with king-size or 2 ¾ beds, net, flat screen DSTV & en-suite bathroom with combined tub/shower in the new 2-storey main building, to more basic en-suite dbls & rather dour sgls using common showers in the ground floor outbuildings. It has the only swimming pool in Ruhengeri, a good restaurant & coffee shop, & the welcome is very friendly, but the accommodation feels overpriced. *Rfr30,000/45,000/60,000 en-suite sgl/dbl/suite in the new building. Rfr18,000/25,000/30,000 en-suite or Rf7,000/9,000 using common facilities in the old buildings.*

⌂ **Sainte Anne Hotel** [195 H2] (16 rooms) ☎ 0252 546461; m 078 8448958; e info@sainteannehotel.com; www.sainteannehotel.com. This new 3-storey hotel, opened in Oct 2008, is set on a quiet side road a block northeast of the market.

BUDGET

⌂ **Centre Pastoral Notre Dame de Fatima** [195 E4] (35 rooms) ☎ 0252 546780/4; e cpndefatima@yahoo.fr. The best deal in this range, by virtue of not having raised prices significantly since it opened in 2004, is this modern-looking hostel situated on the edge of the town centre opposite the stadium & alongside an affiliated Catholic church. Although a bit institutional for some tastes, it has a useful location, very clean rooms, a decent bar & restaurant, an on-site internet café, & very reasonable rates. *Rfr10,000/12,000 sgl/dbl using common showers; Rfr15,000/17,000 en-suite sgl/dbl; Rfr30,000 apt with TV; Rfr3,000 dorm bed.*

⌂ **Amahoro Guesthouse** [195 G5] (7 rooms) m 078 8687448. Operated by Amahoro Tours, this

SHOESTRING

⌂ **Home d'Accueil Virunga** [195 G2] (8 rooms) ☎ 0252 546904. Not to be confused with the Virunga Hotel directly behind it, the former Home d'Accueil Virunga was for years the pick of the cheaper places scattered around the town centre.

Accommodation is in neat & clean en-suite rooms with tiled floor, a queen-size or 2 ¾ beds, flat screen DSTV, lockable cupboards, & a compact bathroom with tub or shower as you prefer. There's an internet café, WiFi in all rooms, & a pleasant terrace & indoor restaurant serving African & Western dishes from Rfr3,500 upwards. *Rooms seem fair value at Rfr30,000/35,000 sgl/dbl occupancy.*

⌂ **Virunga Hotel** [195 G1] (25 rooms) m 078 8448958; e info@virungahotel.com; www.virungahotel.com. Another new addition to the Ruhengeri accommodation scene, this efficient multi-storey hotel lies on the same road as the Sainte Anne, & is overall very similar in price & standard. The en-suite rooms have a queen-size or 2 ¾ beds, flat screen DSTV & a compact bathroom with hot shower. There's a decent restaurant on the ground floor, & internet access just a door down. *Rfr25,000/30,000/40,000 sgl/dbl/twin.*

⌂ **Relay's Gorilla Hotel** [195 G2] (29 rooms) m 078 3565507. The location above the Silverback Top Link Nightclub might be of some concern on Fri & Sat nights, but on weekdays this is a pleasant enough lower midrange hotel, with a conveniently central location near the bus station, & large clean rooms with TV, phone & en-suite hot tub or shower. *Rfr20,000 for smaller rooms with dbl beds; Rfr40,000 for larger rooms with king-size bed & balcony.*

small self-catering guesthouse in the back-roads north of the town centre bills itself as a 'home stay' rather than a guesthouse, & guests can be introduced to various aspects of Rwandan culture or shown how to prepare Rwandan food. Accommodation is in neat tiled twin or dbl rooms that share a bathroom, kitchen & lounge with TV & a small library. *US$20 per room.*

⌂ **La Brise Musanze** [194 A2] (14 rooms) ☎ 0252 546408; m 078 8865561. Situated at Musanze about 3km out of town on the Gisenyi Rd, this is a good-value rustic hotel offering accommodation in large, comfortable en-suite rooms with TV set in pretty green gardens. *Rfr16,000 dbl or twin; Rfr20,000 mini-suite.*

Standards have slid slightly of late, but this welcoming small lodge, situated on Av 5 Juillet diagonally opposite the market, remains a good choice in this range. The en-suite rooms all have nets & hot water, a good courtyard restaurant is

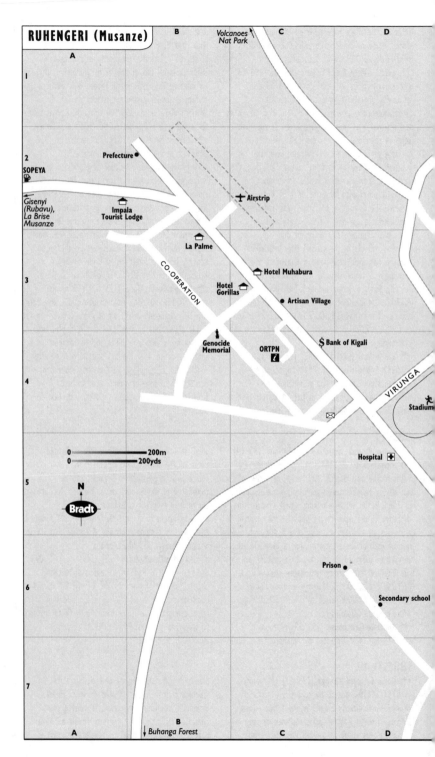

RUHENGERI (Musanze)

A

B   Volcanoes
     Nat Park

C

D

1

2   Prefecture ●

SOPEYA

← Gisenyi
(Rubavu),
La Brise
Musanze

Impala
Tourist Lodge

✈ Airstrip

La Palme

CO-OPERATION

Hotel Muhabura

3   Hotel
    Gorillas

● Artisan Village

Genocide
Memorial

ORTPN

$ Bank of Kigali

4

VIRUNGA

Stadium

Hospital ✚

0 ━━━ 200m
0 ━━━ 200yds

5

N

Bradt

Prison ●

6   Secondary school ●

7

A

B
↓ Buhanga Forest

C

D

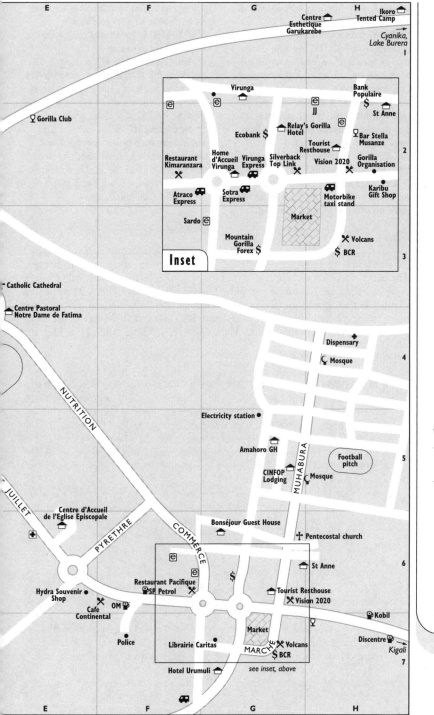

E   F   G   H

Ikoro
Tented Camp

Centre
Esthetique
Garukarebe

Cyanika,
Lake Burera

I

Virunga

Bank
Populaire

St Anne

Relay's Gorilla
Hotel

Ecobank

Bar Stella
Musanze

Gorilla Club

Tourist
Resthouse

Home
d'Accueil
Virunga

Virunga
Express

Restaurant
Kimaranzara

Silverback
Top Link

Vision 2020

Gorilla
Organisation

2

Atraco
Express

Sotra
Express

Motorbike
taxi stand

Karibu
Gift Shop

Sardo

Market

Mountain
Gorilla
Forex

Volcans

BCR

Inset

3

Catholic Cathedral

Centre Pastoral
Notre Dame de Fatima

Dispensary

Mosque

4

Electricity station

Amahoro GH

MUHABURA

Football
pitch

5

CINFOP
Lodging

Mosque

Centre d'Accueil
de l'Eglise Episcopale

PYRETHRE

COMMERCE

Bonséjour Guest House

Pentecostal church

St Anne

6

Hydra Souvenir
Shop

Restaurant Pacifique
SP Petrol

Tourist Resthouse
Vision 2020

Cafe
Continental

OM

Kobil

Police

Market

Volcans

Discentre

Kigali

Librairie Caritas

MARCHE

BCR

Hotel Urumuli

see inset, above

7

JUILLET

NUTRITION

E   F   G   H

attached, & safe parking is available. *Rfr5,000 sgl; Rfr6,000–9,000 dbl or twin.*

🏠 **Centre Esthetique Garukurebe** [195 H1] (9 rooms) ☎ 078 8833255. Two name changes since the last edition was published suggest that the former Motel Ituzi has been through some unstable times management-wise, but it remains a decent enough choice provided that you don't mind the isolated location on the Cyanika road, some 3km from the town centre past the turning to Kinigi. Inexpensive local meals are available. *Rfr6,000–10,000 en-suite twin or dbl.*

🏠 **CINFOP Lodging** [195 G5] (56 rooms) ☎ 078 8790603. Based out of an office & restaurant in the grid of back-roads immediately north of the town centre, this unique establishment consists of 8 different houses whose individual rooms are rented out by the night. *It's pretty good value at Rfr4,000–5,000 for a room using common showers, & Rfr10,000 for an en-suite.*

🏠 **Tourist Resthouse** [195 H2] (6 rooms) ☎ 0252 546635; ☎ 078 8520758. Centrally located on Rue de Muhabura, this friendly little lodge has clean but cramped en-suite rooms with ¾ bed, net & sporadic hot water. *Rfr8,000 sgl or dbl occupancy.*

🏠 **Hotel Urumuli** [195 G7] (6 rooms) ☎ 0252 546820. Conveniently located along a back road close to the market & literally around the corner from the new taxi park, this small hotel has rather poky en-suite rooms with nets, flaking paint & no hot water. *Rfr6,000/8,000 sgl/dbl.*

✖ WHERE TO EAT AND DRINK

As with hotels, there is plenty of choice when it comes to eating out in Ruhengeri. The most extensive and expensive menus are in the smarter hotels, all of which serve breakfast, lunch and dinner daily. The **Gorillas Hotel** [194 C3] is the pick if you want to splash out, serving high-quality French-influenced cuisine, with most main courses coming in at around Rfr5,000–6,000. Most of the other midrange hotels, including the La Palme [194 B3], Sainte Anne [195 H2] and

---

BAGENGE'S ROCK

A NEW VERSION OF AN ANCIENT TALE Ruganzu II Ndori was one of the greatest of Rwanda's warrior kings. One source puts his reign at 1510–43, another at 1600–24, so... who knows! His father, Ndahiro II, had catastrophically lost the Royal Drum, Rwoga, in battle, causing a time of great hardship for Rwanda: for 11 years the land was tortured by drought, sorghum withered in the ground, cows were barren and women conceived only sickly children. Considering the family cursed, the powerful *abiiru* (dynastic ritualists) banished Ruganzu from the kingdom – but after Ndahiro's death chiefs traced him and returned him to power.

Immediately rain began to fall on the parched land, sorghum grew fresh and sweet, cows produced rich milk and many calves, and woman became pregnant with fine, healthy sons. Ruganzu introduced the last of the Royal Drums, Karinga, to replace the lost Rwoga. He chose an adoptive Queen Mother from another clan; she was a poet and created a new form of dynastic poem. Ruganzu's conquests were many and much praised.

One day – so the ancient stories relate in various ways – the king and his entourage were visiting a part of Rwanda that today is just off to the right of the Kigali-Ruhengeri road where it crosses the River Base. A sign to Nemba Hospital is nearby – as is a large rock known as 'Bagenge's Rock'.

Bagenge was the local chief in whose home the King was lodging for the night – and he had spent all that day in a state of great anxiety. The cause for his concern was the great rock, which was well known for moving about at night and relentlessly crushing anything that came within its path, whether mice, children, men, cattle or possibly even kings. Bagenge knew that death or injury to the King risked returning Rwanda to its previous state of drought and disaster.

Virunga [195 G1], have more than serviceable restaurants, with food in the Rfr4,000–5,000 range, but none really stands out.

Far more alluring is the **Muhabura Hotel** [194 C3], where a selection of grills, stews and mild curries start at around Rfr4,000 for a heaped plate, and the semi-shaded balcony ranks as high on the ambience front as anywhere in Ruhengeri. Beers and other drinks are only slightly more expensive than at the local bars and restaurants in town.

The **Home d'Accueil Virunga** [195 G2] has a popular courtyard restaurant serving a fair selection of grilled and fried meals in the Rfr1,000–2,000 range (great fish and chips). The courtyard restaurant in the **Hotel Urumuli** [195 G7] is similar in standard and price: the whole tilapia (a freshwater fish), chicken and goat kebabs are all recommended and excellent value. The **Tourist Resthouse** [195 H2] also has an inviting menu, dominated by stews rather than grills.

Most of the above restaurants serve alcoholic drinks, but more dedicated drinking holes include the **Bar Stella Musanze** [195 H2] opposite the Tourist Resthouse, and the **Silverback Top Link** [195 G2] below Relay's Gorilla Hotel, which serves decent snacks and operates as a nightclub on Friday and Saturday nights.

SHOPPING

Good places to buy local handicrafts include the **Karibu Gift Shop** [195 H2] on the far east of Avenue du 5 Juillet, the **Hydra Souvenir Shop** [195 E6] on the same road but west of the main town centre and the craft shop in the Hotel Muhabura [194 C3]. On the right of the Cyanika road just beyond the Centre Esthetique Garukurebe is **Fecar Inganzo**'s handicrafts workshop.

He prepared a great feast, the greatest that the region had seen for some years, and the smell of the spit-roasted meats and pungent spices caused many a nearby villager's mouth to water. There was wine too, in great abundance, and banana beer; and after the feast dancers leaped and drummed and chanted in the firelight. Bagenge's aim was to entertain the King and his entourage until they fell deeply asleep, so that none would wander off and fall victim to the rock.

But kings sleep less than ordinary men. In the quiet of the night Ruganzu awoke. He wanted to feel air fresh upon his face and to plan new conquests in a silence unbroken by the snores of his attendants. He strolled off along the soft mud path and stood in the open, above the valley, looking upwards at the stars.

The ground shook, a shadow blotted out the starlight and the great rock lurched ominously towards the King. Ruganzu raised his staff threateningly and stood his ground. Disconcerted by such courage, the rock hesitated. Gently the King spoke (for he was wise, and knew that soft words hold the greatest power).

'Greetings, my subject. I hail you and I accept the offering you bring: the offering of your size and strength, to use for the good of my kingdom. Guard this village well. Protect the children who play in your shadow. Comfort the weary traveller who leans against you. Shelter the plants growing around your base. Remain in this spot for ever, the friend of all who live nearby. Perform this task well, my subject, and many centuries from now men will still remember you and tell this tale.'

As you will see, if you visit Bagenge's Rock today, it has indeed performed its task well and stayed peacefully in the same spot. All the same, if you wander the paths by night, keep your ears alert for the rumble of a sudden stealthy movement, because Rwanda is a Republic now and the power of kings is very much reduced …

Visiting Rwanda, it's impossible not to be curious about the country's complex culture. How do people make their living? What's it like being a kid in Rwanda? How has the genocide affected people's lives? Many typical Rwanda package tours don't do much to answer these questions, but, through community-based tourism, tourism that invites you to meet and interact with locals and ask as many questions as you want, you'll gain much insight.

After a day of gorilla trekking, stop in the village of Nyakinama near Ruhengeri and meet Berita Ntawangakoje, the head of a woman's weaving association who together with six other widows makes and sells handicrafts woven from banana bark. She'll show you designs for baskets, mats, and handbags and explain how she boils flowers to produce natural dyes. Following a demonstration, you can try your hand at weaving a small basket. The women can also teach you how to make *urwagwa*, banana beer, Rwanda's traditional libation. Afterwards, sip – don't gulp – the potent nectar of the brewing process.

Visit a Kagano community living near the national park and listen to them sing songs about their old way of life, living in the forest with the gorillas. Cecil, the community matriarch, will tell you about her people's struggles with poverty, but also of her initiatives to improve their situation. Go to the garden of a traditional healer and learn about the herbal remedies Rwandans use to treat illness. Spend the afternoon at an orphanage, where young children eagerly await the chance to practise their English and show you how to play the Rwandan version of duck-duck-goose. In the evening, attend a dinner where you'll be served local food and hear stories about the genocide and its causes and after-affects – questions are always welcome. Or, watch a performance of Intore drumming and dancing.

You can participate in these and other cultural activities through Amahoro Tours (*www.amahoro-tours.com*), a local tour operator that has specialised in this type of tourism since its inception. Amahoro Tours is managed by Greg Bakunzi, a Rwandan who spent the first part of his life in a refugee camp in Uganda and then came to Rwanda after the genocide in 1994 to build a new life. Witnessing the tourists coming through Ruhengeri on their way to the gorillas, Greg came to the belief that tourism had the power to lift Rwandans out of poverty and instil a sense of purpose and pride in the community. So, with help of the German NGO Sustainable Development through Tourism (*www.sd-tourism.org*), Greg established Amahoro Tours in 2003. Through partnerships with local associations and other groups, Amahoro offers packages that expose visitors to traditional Rwandan culture and provide the locals with extra income through goods and services sold to the tourists.

After seeing the positive benefits of tourism on the groups involved in Amahoro's community tourism programmes, Greg and his association partners decided to start the charity Amahoro Integrated Development Program (AIDP; *www.aidpafrica.org*) in 2007, to help those not yet benefiting from tourism, namely orphaned and abandoned children. AIDP now sponsors an interim housing centre for orphaned and abandoned children, a housing scheme that places widows and foster children together in newly constructed houses, and a volunteer teacher programme at local schools. All AIDP projects can be visited by tourists and accept short- and long-term volunteers.

If you're coming to Ruhengeri to go gorilla trekking, take an extra day or two to visit with the locals and experience authentic Rwandan culture up close. Not only will you enrich your travels, you'll help make a real difference in your hosts' lives. How often can you do that on vacation?

In and around the central market [195 G7] are a variety of small stalls and businesses – tailors, cobblers, people ironing clothes with old coal-filled irons, etc. In fact a new market is due to open not far from the centre sometime soon, in a triangular plot with shops and stalls around the edge and open space in the middle, which may or may not replace the old one. Anyone will direct you there.

Formerly the only **bookshop**, the Librairie Caritas [195 G7] 100m west of the market had closed at the time of research.

OTHER PRACTICALITIES

FOREIGN EXCHANGE The branch of the **Bank of Kigali** [194 C4] close to the Muhabura Hotel, **Banque Commerciale du Rwanda** [195 H3] behind the market and **Ecobank** [195 G2] north of the market offer limited (ie: cash only) foreign exchange facilities. The Bank of Kigali has Western Union too.

For travellers who arrive from Uganda, there are no private forex bureaus in Ruhengeri, so try to obtain some Rwandan francs when you cross the border. Otherwise, assuming that you have US dollars or euro cash, most of the hotels will sort you out at a rate fractionally lower than the street rate in Kigali, which is probably a safer bet than trying to change money on the street or in the market.

INTERNET There are a few **internet** cafés dotted around town, charging the usual rates of around Rfr400 per hour – try JJ Internet [195 H1] next to the Virunga Hotel for a really quick connection.

SWIMMING There is a clean **swimming pool** at the Centre d'Accueil de l'Eglise Episcopale [195 E6]; a nominal fee is charged to travellers staying at other hotels.

EXCURSIONS FROM RUHENGERI

Most people who visit Ruhengeri treat it purely as a base from which to track gorillas (see *Chapter 10*). But several local points of interest make for worthwhile

---

UBUSHOBOZI PROJECT   *Elizabeth Todd*

If you are looking for a fantastic off the beaten path excursion in Ruhengeri, the Ubushobozi Project (**m** 078 8827028; **e** *dusifidele@yahoo.fr; www.ubushobozi.org*) is a small, grassroots non-profit organisation devoted to educating and training at-risk and orphaned teenage girls. In a stable, social and caring environment, the girls are taught sewing (and have become highly skilled), basic computer and business skills, life skills, and attend daily English class. They make beautiful bags (among other items), which are excellent souvenirs/gifts. Each is handmade and all proceeds go directly back into the project so not only are you getting a cool item, you're making a donation. The programme's director and house manager, Dusingizimana Fidele, is a charismatic guy, speaks great English, and has a million stories about Rwanda (he grew up in Imbabazi Orphanage and was a photographer in the famous Rwanda Project). If you want to see a programme up close and firsthand that's empowering and changing the course of young girls' lives while supporting the women and men of the local community, you won't be disappointed. We visited after gorilla trekking. It's a really nice and interesting way to spend an afternoon. It's most definitely a feel-good excursion. Contact Dusingizimana Fidele at the number above to arrange a visit.

day or overnight excursions from Ruhengeri, notably the little-visited Lakes Karago, Burera and Ruhondo. For visitors seeking upmarket accommodation, the Virunga Lodge at Lake Burera and a pair of lodges at Kinigi are far more alluring than anything on offer in Ruhengeri itself.

BUHANGA ECO-PARK This undeveloped park lies 8km outside of Ruhengeri (✪ S 01°34.061, E 029°38.169; 1,628m); just head out of town past the post office until you reach the Nyakinama College, turn right on to a rough dirt track after another 500m, and you'll reach it after another 500m or so. Consisting of a small patch of forest dominated by spectacular dragon trees, this culturally significant site (see box *Ryangombe and the Buhanga Forest*, page 202) is under development as a nature trail, with a bar and possibly a hotel promised some time in the future. It's of some interest to birdwatchers too: the exquisite and very seldom seen Angola pitta was recorded here in 2006 and 2008 (both times in May), a recent Nubian woodpecker sighting is the second for Rwanda, and rather more improbably we've heard unconfirmed reports of the green broadbill (an ARE known only from the Congo and one locality in Uganda).

MUSANZE CAVE AND NATURAL BRIDGE The impressive Musanze Cave lies in the grounds of a school about 2km from the town centre off the Gisenyi road. The main cave, reportedly 2km long, has an entrance the size of a cathedral, and is home to an impressive bat colony. The large ditch out of which the cave opens is littered with pockmarked black volcanic rubble, and at the opposite end there is a natural bridge which was formed by a lava flow from one of the Virunga volcanoes.

Legend has it that Musanze Cave was created by a local king, and that it has been used as a refuge on several occasions in history. There are plans to develop it as a tourist attraction – but meanwhile it's advisable not to enter. It was the site of a massacre during the genocide; local people consider it a tomb and don't take kindly

crowned tchagra, and **yellow-bellied** and **fawn-breasted waxbills**, and there is even the chance of finding **narina trogon** (seen 1.5km from the centre of Ruhengeri). **Klaas's diederik** and **red-chested cuckoos** are heard all the time during October to May.

Mpenge River and its associated wetland area is about 1km from the fuel station (Kobil) at the southern end of Ruhengeri (also the location of a local market twice a week). Early mornings here can produce **black crake**, **cape** and **pied wagtails**, **white-browed** and **red-capped robin-chats**, and a variety of weavers. These include **baglafecht**, **slender-billed**, **northern brown-throated**, **yellow-backed (black-headed)** and **Holub's golden weavers**, which are all easily viewed and identified. The surrounding reed-beds and papyrus are easily accessible for viewing Palearctic warblers during the period from September/October to April/May.

The Rugezi Swamps are another location where the endangered **Grauer's swamp warbler** breeds and a host of reed-bed and papyrus specials can be found. This could also make up part of a journey around lakes Bulera and/or Ruhondo, where flooded areas (such as the northern shore of Lake Bulera) are the scene for jaw-dropping antics of **pied kingfishers. Yellow-billed storks**, **African spoonbills**, **little grebes**, **African jacanas**, **grey herons**, **intermediate-**, **cattle-** and **little egrets** frequent these areas as well. The **black saw-wings** are particularly obliging here and provide good viewing and photo opportunities.

The road to the southern part of Lake Ruhondo (turning off from the road to Kigali at the stone crushers) follows the Mukungwa River for part of the way, where **malachite kingfishers** can be observed from close proximity. The area is dominated by cultivated land but the irrigation 'ditches' often hide **hamerkop**, **African spoonbill**, **yellow-billed storks** and **sacred ibis. Fan-tailed widowbirds** are also seen close to the road. It is ideal for good sightings of swallows such as the **Angola, wire-tailed**, **mosque, barn** (October–May), and **lesser-striped** varieties.

A few days birding in Ruhengeri can thus be very productive and result in a very respectable bird list which would include quite a few 'specials'.

Marcell Claassen (m 078 8671572; e marcell@elegantafrica.com) is a birding guide based in Ruhengeri with ten years guiding experience in southern and East Africa. Birding excursions of varying length anywhere in Rwanda can be conducted independently of or combined with and built into existing itineraries. His regular updates on birding in Rwanda can be viewed at http://rwandabirdingguide.blogspot.com/.

A NEW VERSION OF AN ANCIENT TALE None could shoot an arrow so far and straight as Ryangombe, the greatest warrior and hunter of his time. None could run so fast or stalk so silently. The sun dimmed its rays in respect when he was taking aim and the rain paused as he pursued his quarry. He defended the forest against farmers who would fell trees to make space for their crops, and the branches murmured their thanks as he rested in their shade. Women competed for his favours, opponents feared him, storytellers throughout the realm extolled his exploits and his name was lauded far and wide. So powerful was Ryangombe that he challenged even the mighty King Ruganzu, who ruled Rwanda almost seven centuries ago.

Ryangombe's favourite hunting-ground was the Buhanga Forest, in the volcano foothills not far from Ruhengeri: a place of ancient trees, dark ravines and thrusting rocks, where sunlight throws patterns on the leafy floor and butterflies bask on mossy logs. Birds swoop and perch among the branches and small creatures scuttle in the undergrowth. In this forest is the sacred pool called Gihanga, empty in the rainy season but full to overflowing in the dry season, where Rwanda's early monarchs would come to bathe and drink the water.

It was on a dark, dark day here in the Buhanga Forest that Ryangombe faced his final opponent – no king or fellow warrior but a wild and angry buffalo, which burst upon him from the shelter of the trees. Its horns tore into his flesh and the forest floor was reddened by his blood. His companions, seeing their hero slain and wishing to be at his side in the higher world, taunted the buffalo until it gored them also and trampled their limbs with its hooves. The bodies of the young men lay beneath the great tree Umuvumu, still in the forest today, until Imana raised them to their final home on the slopes of Karisimbi. If you climb the mountain nowadays, you may – if your spirit is fair and you know how to listen with your heart – still hear their voices carried on the breeze as they talk and laugh together.

After Ryangombe's death, traditional healers from throughout the Great Lakes region would journey to the spot in Buhanga Forest where he fell. From the trees in that place they would take a branch back to their homelands, and use it as the base to build a shrine – Ingoro – from which to worship him and send prayers to their gods.

Sit quietly in Buhanga Forest today and you can sense its ancient history. Kings and healers and legendary heroes have walked its paths and felt its power. And – who knows – that sudden rustle that you hear behind you may even be the soft and stealthy footfall of Ryangombe as he stalks some ghostly prey.

to tourists scrambling about inside. Please respect this: either view from a distance or go with a local guide.

To get to Musanze Cave from the town, follow Avenue du 5 Juillet past the Hotel Muhabura towards Gisenyi. Just short of 2km from the town centre, you'll see the large steel Entrepots Opravia Musanze to your left. Turn right directly opposite this building, following a curved dirt track which after about 100m leads to a football field and school. The cave lies in a ditch on the opposite side of the football field.

LAKE KARAGO This small lake set off the Gisenyi Road is less impressive than the larger Burera and Ruhondo lakes to the east of Ruhengeri, but it is also a lot more accessible on public transport, and sufficiently attractive that it served for years as the site of the president of Rwanda's holiday home. Lake Karago makes for a pleasant rustic excursion from Ruhengeri, the main attraction being the characteristically mountainous Rwandan landscape around the lake and a set of rapids along the river that runs into the lake. There were also quite a few birds around when we visited, notably pelicans and herons.

Lake Karago can easily be visited as a day trip out of Ruhengeri, or *en route* between Ruhengeri and Gisenyi. It lies 1.5km from Mukamiira, a small junction town on the main Ruhengeri–Gisenyi road. Regular minibus-taxis cover the 20km between Ruhengeri and Mukamiira, where you need to turn left at the main junction towards Ngororero. The walk from Mukamiira to the first viewpoint over the lake takes about 15 minutes. From here, several footpaths lead to the shore, a 10–20-minute descent, depending on how muddy it is and which path you use. For the continuation of the road after Lake Karago, see page 190.

LAKE BURERA The largest and most beautiful of the lakes in the vicinity of Ruhengeri, and overlooked by what is arguably the best tourist lodge anywhere in Rwanda, Burera (aka Bulera) has been almost entirely neglected by travellers until recently. With a private vehicle, however, the dirt road that loops around Burera's eastern shore makes for a superb day outing, while adventurous backpackers could happily spend several days exploring the lake using a combination of motorcycle-taxis, boats, and foot power. No budget accommodation exists anywhere on the lake shore, but the area is dotted with small villages where it shouldn't be a problem to get permission to pitch a tent, and there is talk of the Episcopal Church property on the Musangabo Peninsula being made into a guesthouse – check with the church's guesthouse in Ruhengeri for further details.

Lake Burera is visually reminiscent of Uganda's popular Lake Bunyonyi – not too surprising when you realise that these two bodies of water lie no more than 20km apart as the crow flies. Burera's eccentric shape is defined by the incredibly steep hills that enclose it. The slopes which fall towards the lake are densely terraced and intensively cultivated: very little natural vegetation remains among the fields of plantains, potatoes, beans and other crops, while the most common tree is the Australian eucalyptus. The stunning and distinctive scenery around the lake is enhanced by the outlines of the Virunga Mountains, the closest of which towers 10km away on the western horizon.

Getting around
By road For travellers with their own transport, the circuit around the lake is straightforward enough. The road is mostly in good shape, and likely to present no problems provided that your vehicle has reasonable clearance (a 4x4 would be advisable during the rainy season). The full round trip from Ruhengeri covers about 150km, 90km of which are on dirt, and realistically takes a minimum of five hours to complete. Better, arguably, to leave after breakfast, carry a picnic lunch, and make a day of it, stopping along the way to enjoy the views and rustic villages.

To follow the circuit, head out of Ruhengeri along the surfaced road towards Cyanika, passing the turn-off for Virunga Lodge to your right after 16km, then continuing for another 6km to Kidaho, where you need to turn right into a dirt road signposted 'Lake Burera'. After about six relatively flat kilometres along this track, the lake becomes visible to the right: on the shore you'll see a small fishing village (so far as can be ascertained, also called Kidaho) and dozens of small boats used to ferry locals around the lake.

A few hundred metres past this village, a side road leads around the small Musangabo peninsula, where a platform (and potentially soon a guesthouse) run by the Episcopal Church offers stunning views in all directions. The church also operates a motorboat that can be hired for the one-hour return trip to the Rusumo Falls (around Rfr6,000) per party or the two-hour round trip to the bridge between lakes Burera and Ruhondo (around Rfr10,000 per party).

'We have always lived in the forest. Like my father and grandfathers, I lived from hunting and collecting in this mountain. Then the Bahutu came. They cut the forest to cultivate the land. They carried on cutting and planting until they had encircled our forest with their fields. Today, they come right up to our huts. Instead of forest, now we are surrounded by Irish potatoes!' – Gahut Gahuliro, a Mutwa born 100 years earlier on the slopes of the Virungas, talking in 1999.

The Batwa (singular Mutwa) pygmies are the most ancient inhabitants of interlacustrine Africa, and easily distinguished from other inhabitants of the region by their unusually short stature and paler, more bronzed complexion. Semi-nomadic by inclination, small egalitarian communities of Batwa kin traditionally live in impermanent encampments of flimsy leaf huts, set in a forest clearing, which they will up and leave when food becomes scarce locally, upon the death of a community member, or when the whim takes them. In times past, the Batwa wore only a drape of animal hide or bark cloth, and had little desire to accumulate possessions – a few cooking pots, some hunting gear, and that's about it.

The traditional Batwa lifestyle is based around hunting, undertaken as a team effort by the male members of a community. In some areas, the favoured modus operandi involves part of the hunting party stringing a long net between a few trees, while the remainder advances noisily to herd small game into the net to be speared. In other areas, poisoned arrows are favoured: the hunting party will move silently along the forest floor looking for potential prey, which is shot from a distance, then they wait until it drops and if necessary deliver the final blow with a spear. Batwa men also gather wild honey, while the women gather edible plants to supplement the meat.

Today, the combined Batwa population of Rwanda, Burundi, Uganda and the eastern DRC is estimated at around 100,000 people. As recently as 2,000 years ago, however, East and Southern Africa was populated almost solely by Batwa and related hunter-gatherers, whose lifestyle differed little from that of our earliest common human ancestors. Since then, agriculturist and pastoralist settlers, through persecution or assimilation, have marginalised the region's hunter-gatherers to a few small and today mostly degraded communities living in habitats unsuitable to agriculture or pasture, such as rainforest interiors and deserts.

The initial incursions into Batwa territory were made when the first Bantu-speaking farmers settled on the forested montane escarpment of the Albertine Rift, some time before the 16th century, and set about clearing small tracts of forest for subsistence agriculture and posture. This process of deforestation was greatly accelerated in the early 20th century. By the 1930s, the few substantial tracts of highland forest remaining in the region had all been gazetted as forest reserves by the colonial authorities. In one sense, this move to protect the forests was of direct benefit to the Batwa, since it ensured that what little remained of them would not be lost to agriculture. But the legal status of the Batwa was altered to their detriment – true, they were still permitted to hunt and forage within the reserves, but, where formerly these forests had been recognised as Batwa communal land, they were now government property.

Another 50 years would pass before the Batwa were faced with the full ramifications of having lost all legal entitlement to their ancestral lands in the colonial era. In the 1970s and 1980s, the Batwa communities resident in most of the region's conservation areas were evicted, a move backed by international donors who also insisted that hunting and other forest harvesting – the traditional subsistence activities of the Batwa – should be criminalised. Adding insult to injury, while compensation was awarded to non-Batwa farmers who had settled within protected areas after they were gazetted and illegally cleared forest to make way for cultivation, the evicted Batwa received compensation only if they had destroyed part of the forest reserve in a similar manner.

In the early 1990s, Rwanda's last forest-dwelling Batwa were evicted from the Gishwati Forest Reserve to make way for a World Bank project intended to protect the natural forest. The World Bank later concluded that the project had failed, with more than half of the original forest having been cleared for pasture prior to 1994, and it admitted that the treatment of indigenous peoples had been 'highly unsatisfactory'. Since 1998, returned refugees have been settled in the remaining forest, resulting in further destruction, but the former Batwa residents of Gishwati are mostly still landless.

Today, more than 40% of Batwa households in Rwanda are landless, and none has legal access to the forest on which their traditional livelihood depends. Indeed, most Batwa now eke out a marginal living from casual wage labour on other peoples' farms, porterage, simple craftwork (particularly pottery), and singing and dancing at festivals – many are in essence forced to live as beggars. Furthermore, with Batwa men no longer able to fulfil their traditional roles as hunters and providers, many have turned to alcohol and drug (or spousal) abuse, leading to the imminent collapse of Batwa cultural values.

Locally, the Batwa are viewed not with sympathy, but rather as objects of ridicule. The extent of local prejudice against them can be garnered from a set of interviews posted on the Ugandan website www.edrisa.org. The Batwa, report some of their Bakiga neighbours: 'smoke marijuana … like alcohol … drink too much … make noise all night long … eat too much food … cannot grow their own food and crops … depend on hunting and begging … don't care about their children … the man makes love to his wife while the children sleep on their side' – a collection of circumstantially induced half-truths and outright fallacies that make the Batwa come across as the debauched survivors of a dysfunctional hippie commune!

Prejudice against the Batwa is not confined to their immediate neighbours. The 1997 edition of Richard Nzita's otherwise commendable *People and Cultures of Uganda* contrives, in the space of two pages, to characterise the pygmoid peoples of Uganda as beggars, crop raiders and pottery thieves – even cannibals! Conservationists and the Western media, meanwhile, persistently stigmatise the Batwa as gorilla hunters and poachers – this despite the strong taboo against killing or eating gorillas that informs every known Batwa community. Almost certainly, any gorilla hunting that might be undertaken by the Batwa today will have been instigated by outsiders.

This much is incontestable: the Batwa and their hunter-gatherer ancestors have inhabited the forests of the Albertine Rift for countless millennia. Their traditional lifestyle places no rigorous demands on the forest and could be cited as a model of that professed holy grail of modern conservationists: the sustainable use of natural resources. The Batwa were not major participants in the deforestation of the region, but they have certainly been the main human victims of this loss. And Batwa and gorillas cohabited the same forests for many millennia prior to their futures both being imperilled by identical external causes in the 20th century. As Jerome Lewis writes: 'They and their way of life are entitled to as much consideration and respect as other ways of life. There was and is nothing to be condemned in forest nomadism … The Batwa … used the environment without destroying or seriously damaging it. It is only through their long-term custody of the area that later comers have good land to use.'

Quotes from Lewis and Gahuliro are sourced from Jerome Lewis's exemplary report Batwa Pygmies of the Great Lakes Region, *downloadable for a nominal fee at http://www.minorityrights.org/1056/reports/batwa-pygmies-of-the-great-lakes-region.html.*

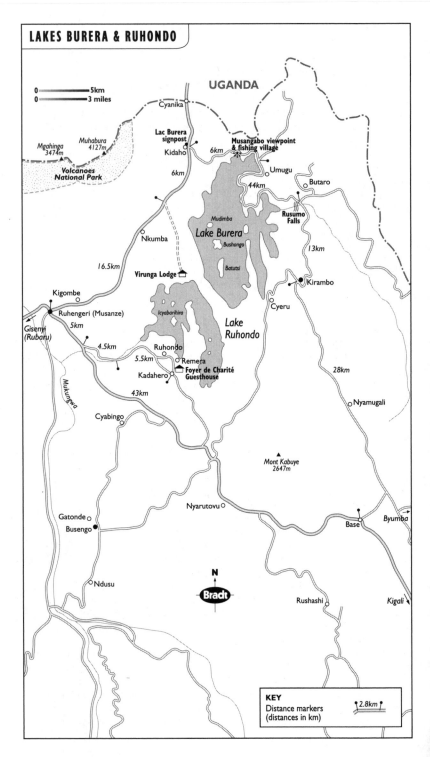

LAKES BURERA & RUHONDO

UGANDA

0 ————— 5km
0 ————— 3 miles

Cyanika

Mgahinga
3474m

Muhabura
4127m

Volcanoes National Park

Lac Burera signpost

Kidaho

6km

6km

Musangabo viewpoint & fishing village

Umugu

Butaro

44km

Rusumo Falls

Mudimba

Lake Burera

Bushonga

13km

Nkumba

Batutsi

16.5km

Virunga Lodge

Kirambo

Icyabarihira

Cyeru

Lake Ruhondo

Kigombe

Ruhengeri (Musanze)

Gisenyi
(Rubaru)

5km

4.5km

Ruhondo

5.5km

Foyer de Charité Guesthouse

Remera

28km

Mukungwa

Kadahero

43km

Nyamugali

Cyabingo

▲ *Mont Kabuye*
2647m

Gatonde

Busengo

Nyarutovu

Base

Byumba

Ndusu

N

Bradt

Rushashi

Kigali

KEY
Distance markers
(distances in km)

2.8km

The largest centre on the eastern shore of the lake is Butaro, which maps would suggest is only about 10km from Musangabo. In reality, the two are divided by a spectacular 44km stretch of road which hugs the cultivated contours about 100–200m above the lake shore. *En route*, the road passes through the small market village of Umugu. Butaro itself lies a couple of kilometres off the main road; about 50m from the junction, the attractive Rusumo Falls (not to be confused with their namesake on the Tanzania border) tumble over a cliff to the fields next to the lake. If you take a closer look, just above the waterfall, you'll find the confluence of two rivers, one laterite in colour, like most rivers in the region, the other black.

After Butaro, the road veers away from the lake, and the views are few and far between, which leaves you with the option of returning the way you came (65km of which 50 are on dirt) or pushing on to complete the circuit (85km of which 41 are on dirt). Assuming that you decide to sally forth, the next main settlement you will reach, after 13km, is Kirambo. Here, you can either turn left along a side road which leads to the village of Ruyange in a cultivated river valley at the southern tip of Lake Burera (a 20km round trip), or else continue straight ahead towards Base on the main Kigali–Ruhengeri road. Base lies 28km past Kirambo, and is almost equidistant between Kigali and Ruhengeri.

By public transport For travellers without a vehicle, the absence of public transport along parts of this circuit makes it inaccessible or challenging, depending on how you see these things. For a day trip to Burera, it is easy enough to get as far as Kidaho – any Cyanika-bound minibus-taxi can drop you there, though you will probably be expected to pay the full fare of around Rfr800 – from where a motorcycle-taxi to the Musangabo Peninsula will cost around Rfr500. With an early start, you should also have time to catch a boat-taxi from the fishing village next to the peninsula to the lake shore below Butaro and the Rusumo Falls, and to return the same way. The boat-taxi takes 30–60 minutes in either direction, and costs around Rfr1,000 per person. It should also be straightforward and affordable to hire a boat privately, either to go to the falls or else just to explore the lake.

Beryl Hutchison writes: 'I made the journey to Lake Burera by minibus and got to the peninsula by bicycle-taxi. It was such a beautiful and tranquil place. There were no motorised boats so I hired a pirogue. I was told that the journey to Rusumo Falls takes about four hours and although the boatman was willing I decided against it. Instead we had a row round the lake and then got out of the pirogue and walked through the shambas to the Ugandan border.'

Lake Burera could also be explored more extensively by boat, but it is an option suitable only for those with a pioneering spirit. The obvious place to start a trip of this sort would be Musangabo, though boats are the main form of transport throughout the area, so it should be easy enough to hire a boat and paddler anywhere. In addition to Rusumo Falls, there are at least four large islands in the southern half of the lake: Mudimba, Munanira, Bushongo and Batutsi. In theory, it should be possible to boat to the south of Lake Burera, hike across the narrow strip of hilly terrain that separates it from Lake Ruhondo, and then pick up another boat to the Foyer de Charité on the southern shore of that lake (see *Lake Ruhondo*, page 209). We've never heard of a traveller who attempted this, so drop us a line to let us know how it goes!

On foot Keen walkers might also think about exploring the area over a few days. We've not heard of anybody doing this, so it would be uncharted territory, and would probably be practical only if you have a tent and are prepared to ask permission to camp at the many villages and homesteads you encounter. It would probably be advisable to carry some food (though fish and potatoes should be easy to buy along the way). It is difficult to imagine that any serious security concerns are attached to hiking in this Uganda border area; you'll come across loads of local pedestrians for company, and travellers are still something of a novelty in this rural region.

The road to the east of the lake can effectively be viewed as an unusually wide hiking trail: it offers great views the whole way, is used by very few vehicles, and follows the contours for most of its length. The most beautiful stretch for hiking is the 44km between Musangabo and Butaro (which can also be covered by boat), and you would be forced to walk the 13km between Butaro and Kirambo. From Kirambo, there is a limited amount of public transport to Base, where it is easy to find a lift on to Ruhengeri or Kigali.

Where to stay

Virunga Lodge (8 rooms) \ 0252 502452/576530 or (UK) +44 0870 8708480; m 078 8302069; e salesrw@volcanoessafaris.com or salesuk@volcanoessafaris.com; www.volcanoessafaris.com; ✪ S 01°26.694, E 029°44.517. Boasting one of the most stunning locations in Africa, this exclusive lodge lies on a 2,175m hilltop above lakes Burera & Ruhondo. In addition to stunning views over the lakes to its southeast, the panorama stretches northwest to embrace 4 of the Virunga Volcanoes, providing a magnificent overview of this wild volcanic landscape.

THE NYABINGI CULT

Traditionally the most popular spirit among the Bakiga of southwest Uganda and neighbouring parts of Rwanda is that of a respected rainmaker called Nyabingi, who – possibly in the mid to late 18th century – was murdered by a rival medium at her home in Mukante in the Bufundi Hills of the Rwanda-Uganda border area. After the death of Nyabingi, legend has it, her attendants were visited by numerous ill or barren Bakiga villagers, who would make sacrifices to the late rainmaker's spirit, which would cure their ailment if it approved of the items offered. Over subsequent decades, the spirit possessed a succession of Bakiga mediums, mostly but not always women, who would be blessed with Nyabinga's powers of healing, rainmaking and curing infertility.

Several Nyabingi mediums incited local uprisings against colonialism. The first such rebel was Queen Muhumusa, of mysterious origin, but possibly a former wife of the late Rwandan King Rwabuguri Kigeri. In 1909, Muhumusa was imprisoned by the German authorities in Rwanda after threatening that her son Ndungutse would capture the throne and boot the colonists out of his kingdom. Upon her release in 1911, the Queen crossed the border into Uganda and settled at Ihanga Hill near Bubale, 12km from present-day Kabale on the Kisoro Road. She then announced that she had come in search of a cave wherein was secured a sacred drum which, she claimed, would call up a limitless stream of calves when beaten by her and her son. As the news of the magic drum spread though Kigezi, hundreds of young Bakiga men joined in the quest for its location, hoping for a share of the spoils, and Muhumusa received wide support from local chiefs.

The Christian Muganda chiefs installed by the British in southwest Uganda regarded the growing cult surrounding Muhumusa to be evil and insurrectionist, and refused to have anything to do with it. This angered Muhumusa, who attacked the home of one such chief, burning it to the ground, killing several people, and threatening to impale her victim on a sharpened pole, along with any other disrespectful chiefs she could capture. The colonial authorities responded to this affront by attacking Muhumusa's residence with 50 troops and a cannon. At least 40 of the medium's followers were killed on the spot and buried in a mass grave, and several more died of wounds after fleeing the battle site. Muhumusa was captured and imprisoned in Mbarara, where she remained until her death in 1945. The British authorities then proceeded to criminalise the Nyabingi cult through the Witchcraft Ordinance of 1912.

If you're after organic bush chic rather than transatlantic luxury, this is arguably the finest lodge anywhere in Rwanda, offering accommodation in spacious stone-&-wood chalets with king-size beds, superb views from the private verandas, & an eco-friendly ethos underscored by the extensive use of solar power. Originally fitted with biodegradable toilets & manually filled hot bucket showers, the bathrooms are currently being upgraded with hot & cold running water, & conventional flush toilets, a process that should be complete by the end of 2009. This is an excellent base for gorilla tracking, with the one caveat being that the distance from Kinigi enforces an earlier start than other lodges (ideally at 06.00 – but the staff are used to this &

organise early wake-up calls, showers & b/fast as a matter of course). It lies about 30mins' drive from Ruhengeri, turning right off the Cyanika Rd after 16km at Nyaragondo junction (⊕ S 01°25.073, E 029°43.509). Major renovations are planned for late 2009. *US$500 pp inc all meals, alcoholic & non-alcoholic drinks, laundry, massage, activities around the lodge & all government taxes.*

⌂ **Paradise Motel** m 078 8478512;
e harelimanaviateur@yahoo.fr. Situated in Kirambo, about 13km south of Butaro, this small new establishment is very friendly & helpful, & it also serves meals, including outstanding rabbit & fried potatoes! *Rfr10,000 for an en-suite trpl with cold water only.*

LAKE RUHONDO Separated from Lake Burera by a 1km-wide strip of land (thought to be an ancient lava flow from Mount Sabinyo), Lake Ruhondo is, like the more

In order to help win over local converts, the earliest Christian missionaries to Rwanda and southwest Uganda used words associated with the Nyabingi cult in their sermons and descriptions of Christian rituals. The Virgin Mary was portrayed as a spiritual icon similar to but more powerful than Nyabingi, and many locals adopted the Mother of Jesus as a substitute for the traditional spirit associated with healing and fertility. By the 1930s, the Nyabingi cult, if not completely dead, had gone so far underground as to be undetectable – while it became increasingly common for locals to claim having seen the Virgin Mary at sites of worship formerly associated with Nyabingi.

At least one former Nyabingi shrine has more recently been adopted by a nominally Christian cult. The Nyabugoto Caves near the small town of Kunungu in southwest Uganda were in times past occupied by a renowned medium who regularly cured barren Bakiga women. In the late 1970s, it was reported that a local woman called Blandina Buzigye witnessed a large rock formation in this cave transform into the Virgin Mary before her eyes. It was in the same Ugandan cave, ten years later, that a former prostitute called Credonia Mwerinde founded a fertility cult that mutated into the doomsday movement whose entire membership was locked inside a blazing church by the leaders in a shocking massacre that attracted world headlines in March 2000.

Oddly enough, the term Nyabingi found its way across the Atlantic to Jamaica, where admirers of the rebellious Queen Muhumusa incorporated what are known as nyabinghi chants into their celebrations. Sometimes abbreviated to *bhingi*, the chants and dances were originally performed to invoke 'death to the black or white oppressors' but today they are purely ceremonial. Three differently pitched drums are used to create the nyabinghi beat, which – popularised in the late 1950s by the recording artist Count Ossie – has been a huge rhythmic influence on better-known secular Jamaican genres such as ska and reggae. Nyabinghi is also the name of a fundamentalist but strictly pacifist Rastafarian cult which regards the late Ethiopian emperor Haile Selassie as having been an earthly incarnation of God. Indeed, according to some Rastafarian cultists in Jamaica, the neglected Nyabingi spirit abandoned its home in the Rwanda-Uganda border area in 1937 and relocated to Ethiopia, where it took possession of Haile Selassie during the Italian Occupation. The present whereabouts of the spirit is unknown.

northerly lake, an erratically shaped body of water whose shore follows the contours of the tall, steep hills that characterise this part of Rwanda. In common with Lake Burera, Ruhondo's shores are densely cultivated, and little natural vegetation remains, but it is nevertheless a very beautiful spot, offering dramatic views across the water to the volcanically formed cones of the Virunga Mountains looming on the horizon. Ruhondo is also an easy target for an overnight excursion, since good accommodation is available – though availability should be confirmed in advance.

The lake is most accessible from the southwest, where the Foyer de Charité guesthouse has a superb location on a hilltop overlooking the lake, with sweeping views across to the volcanoes in the northwest, and potentially stupendous sunsets. Several footpaths lead down the steep slopes below the mission to the lake shore, a knee-crunching descent and lung-wrenching ascent. At the lake, it is easy to negotiate a fee to take a pirogue to one of the islands, or to the hydro-electric plant on the opposite shore, where a small waterfall connects Lake Ruhondo with Lake Burera.

Getting around The best route to the Foyer de Charité starts on the main Kigali road about 5km south of Ruhengeri. Coming from Ruhengeri, you need to turn left along a dirt road signposted for Remera which initially leads through a marshy area dotted with traditional brickmaking urns, before following a cultivated river valley. After 2.8km, take a left fork, then almost 2km after that turn right to cross a bridge over the river. The road is flat until this point, but now it starts to ascend gently, with the lake becoming visible to the left about 2.5km past the bridge. Several footpaths lead from this viewpoint to the lake shore, an easier ascent than the one from the Foyer de Charité. Beyond the viewpoint, the road continues to climb for 3km to the village of Kadahero, where a left turn leads after about 200m to the mission.

This is all straightforward enough provided that you have a vehicle, ideally a 4x4, and that – if driving along the tar from Kigali – you don't inadvertently take an earlier road signposted for Remera (this road does lead to the mission, but it's longer and rougher). There is no public transport, however, and hitching might prove to be frustrating. One option would be to catch public transport towards Ruhengeri as far as the turn-off to Remera, then to walk the final 10km to the mission (the last 6km would be steep going with a rucksack). The alternative is to hire a motorcycle-taxi from Ruhengeri – the going rate is around Rfr1,500–2,000 one-way – and arrange to be collected at a specified time.

Where to stay

Foyer de Charité (45 rooms) ☎ 0252 547024; m 078 8510659; e vdprw@yahoo.fr. Established as a religious retreat in 1968, this mission was renovated in 1995 after it had been damaged during the genocide. It remains first & foremost a religious retreat, but respectful lay visitors are usually permitted to stay provided that they make advance arrangements. Comfortable guest rooms with wash basins are available, as are communal solar-heated showers, inexpensive & filling meals, & cold beers & sodas. There is little in the way of formal entertainment (the beautiful singing at evening mass in the chapel might qualify I suppose), but it's a lovely place to relax for a couple of days, & there's plenty of room for exploration on the surrounding roads. It is essential to make contact in advance, as the mission closes to lay visitors for special religious events — which probably add up to around 100 days annually. *Room rates are negotiable, but expect to pay around Rfr8,000/12,000 sgl/dbl.*

10

Volcanoes National Park

The 160km² Volcanoes National Park protects the Rwandan sector of the Virunga Mountains, a range of six extinct and three active volcanoes that straddle the Ugandan and Congolese borders and protect more than half the world's population of the charismatic mountain gorilla. Also sometimes referred to by its French name, Parc des Volcans, it forms part of a contiguous 433km² trans-frontier conservation unit that also includes Virungas National Park and Mgahinga National Park, which respectively protect the Congolese and Ugandan sectors of the Virunga Mountains. The three national parks function separately today, but prior to 1960 the Rwandan and Congolese sectors were jointly managed as the Albert National Park.

Renowned for the habituated mountain gorillas that inhabit its forested slopes, Volcanoes National Park is also an immensely scenic and ecologically diverse destination, spanning altitudes of 2,400m to 4,507m, and dominated by the string of volcanoes after which it is named. This chain of steep, tall, free-standing mountains, linked by fertile saddles formed by solidified lava flows, is one of the most stirring and memorable sights in East Africa. The tallest mountain in the chain, and the most westerly part of the national park, is Karisimbi (4,507m) on the border with the DRC. Moving eastwards, the other main peaks within the national park are Visoke (aka Bisoke) on the DRC border; Sabyinyo at the junction of Rwanda, Uganda and the DRC; and Gahinga (aka Mgahinga) and Muhabura (aka Muhavura) on the Uganda border.

It is no surprise that visiting the mountain gorillas remains the most popular tourist activity in Volcanoes National Park. And since 2006, a total of 56 gorilla-tracking permits have been available daily, eight for each of the seven habituated troops. However, it would be reductive to bill Volcanoes National Park solely as a gorilla-tracking destination. A wide variety of other hikes and activities are offered, making it possible to spend several days in the area without running out of things to do. The most popular activity after gorilla tracking is a visit to a habituated troop of the rare golden monkey, an Albertine Rift endemic whose modern range is more-or-less restricted to the Virungas. A relatively negligible 1,280 tourists undertook this excursion in 2008, less than one percent of the 17,089 gorilla-tracking permits issued in the same year. Fewer still embarked on the more demanding day treks to the crater lake on Bisoke peak and Dian Fossey's grave at Karisoke, while the overnight hike to the summit of Karisimbi attracted a mere 100 takers.

Gorillas and golden monkeys aside, primates are poorly represented by comparison with most other large forests in Rwanda and Uganda. Little information is available regarding the current status of other large mammals in the mountains, but 70-plus species have been recorded in neighbouring Mgahinga National Park, and most probably also occur in the larger Rwanda sector. Elephant and buffalo are still quite common, judging by the amount of spoor encountered on forest trails, but are very timid and infrequently observed. Also present are giant forest hog, bushpig, bushbuck, black-fronted duiker, spotted hyena, and several

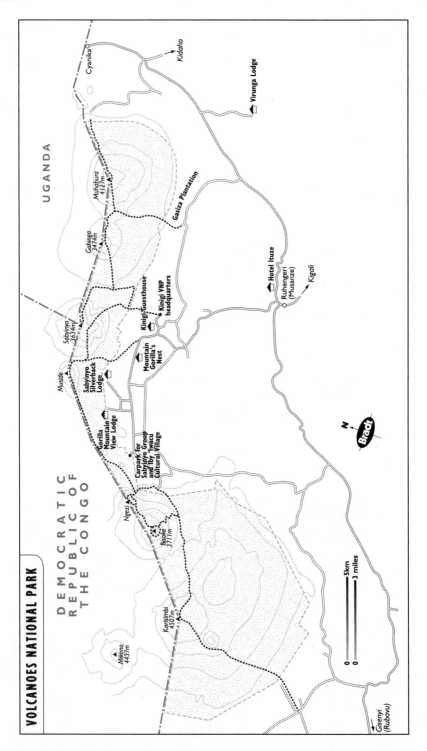

VOLCANOES NATIONAL PARK

UGANDA

DEMOCRATIC
REPUBLIC OF
THE CONGO

Cyanika

Kidaho

Virunga Lodge

Muhabura
4127m

Gahinga
3474m

Gasiza Plantation

Sabyinyo
3634m

Kinigi Guesthouse

Kinigi VNP
headquarters

Hotel Ituze

Mushe

Mountain
Gorilla's
Nest

Ruhengeri
(Musanze)

Kigali

Sabyinyo
Silverback
Lodge

Gorilla
Mountain
View Lodge

Carpark for
Sabyinyo Group
and Iby' Iwacu
Cultural Village

N

Bradt

Nezi

Bisoke
3711m

Karisimbi
4507m

Mikeno
4437m

0   5km
0   3 miles

Gisenyi
(Rubavu)

varieties of small predator. Recent extinctions, probably as a result of deforestation, include the massive yellow-backed duiker and leopard.

A bird checklist for Volcanoes National Park compiled in 1980 totalled 180 species. About 15 previously unrecorded species were noted during a 2004 biodiversity survey, but it is possible that several other forest specialists have vanished since 1980. A local speciality is the vulnerable swamp-dwelling Grauer's rush warbler, while at least 16 Albertine Rift endemics are present, including handsome francolin, Ruwenzori turaco, Ruwenzori double-collared sunbird, Ruwenzori batis, strange weaver, dusky crimson-wing, collared apalis, red-faced woodland warbler and Archer's ground robin.

HISTORY, CONSERVATION AND ECOTOURISM

The ecology of the Virungas remained practically unknown to western science until 1902, when the German explorer Oscar von Beringe ascended Mount Sabyinyo and became the first European to encounter – and to kill – a mountain gorilla (see box, page 10) Over the following two decades, at least 50 individual mountain gorillas were captured or killed in the Virungas, prompting the Belgian government to establish the Albert National Park by decree on 21 April 1925, protecting a triangle formed by the Karisimbi, Mikeno and Visoke volcanoes.

At the time of its creation, this was the first national park in Africa to be known as such. The Institut du Parc National Albert was created by decree on 9 July 1929. A further decree on 12 November 1935 determined the final boundaries of the Albert National Park, then covering 809,000ha. About 8% of the park lay in what is now Rwanda and today constitutes the Volcanoes National Park, while the rest was in the Congo. At the time of independence, Rwanda's new leaders confirmed that they would maintain the park (the gorillas were already well known internationally), the pressing problem of overpopulation notwithstanding.

SCHALLER AND FOSSEY The gorilla population of the Virungas is thought to have been reasonably stable in 1960, when a census undertaken by George Schaller indicated that some 450 individuals lived in the range. By 1971–73, however, the population had plummeted to an estimated 250. This decline was caused by several factors, including the post-colonial division of the Albert National Park into its Rwandan and Congolese components, the ongoing fighting between the Hutu and Tutsi of Rwanda, and a grisly tourist trade in poached gorilla heads and hands – the latter used by some sad individuals as ashtrays! Most devastating of all perhaps was the irreversible loss of almost half of the gorillas' habitat between 1957 and 1968 to local farmers and a European-funded agricultural scheme.

George Schaller initiated the first study of mountain gorilla behaviour in the 1950s, and his pioneering work formed the starting point for the more recent and well-known behavioural study undertaken by the American primatologist Dian Fossey a decade later. Fossey arrived in Rwanda to study its mountain gorillas in 1967, supported by the eminent Kenyan palaeontologist Louis Leakey, who had earlier been responsible for placing Jane Goodall at Gombe Stream in Tanzania. She founded the Karisoke Research Centre high on the forested slopes of Mount Karisimbi, and for the next 18 years used it as the base for her ongoing studies of Volcanoes National Park's mountain gorillas.

It is largely thanks to Fossey's single-minded and somewhat paramilitary campaign to discourage poaching in Volcanoes National Park that this activity was curtailed while there were still some gorillas to save. For this, she would pay the ultimate price. The brutal murder of Dian Fossey at the Karisoke Research Centre in December 1985, though officially unsolved, is widely thought to have been the work of one of the many poachers whom she antagonised in her efforts to save her gorillas. Three years after her death, Fossey's life work was exposed to a mass audience with the release of *Gorillas in the Mist*, a cinematic account of her life that was filmed on location in Volcanoes National Park. The film grossed more than US$60 million worldwide, was nominated for five Academy Awards, and generated unprecedented global interest in mountain gorillas and ecotourism in the Virungas.

GORILLA TOURISM 1979-94 In 1979, Amy Vedder and Bill Weber initiated the first gorilla tourism project in Rwanda's Volcanoes Park, integrating tourism, local education and anti-poaching measures with remarkable success. Initially, the project was aimed mainly at tourists in overland trucks, who paid a paltry – by today's standards – US$20 per person to track gorillas. Even so, gorilla tourism was raising up to ten million US dollars annually by the mid 1980s, making it Rwanda's third-highest earner of foreign revenue, and the industry was given a further boost with the release of the film *Gorillas in the Mist* in 1988.

By that time, Volcanoes National Park was the best organised and most popular gorilla sanctuary in Africa, and gorilla tourism was probably Rwanda's leading earner of tourist revenue. What's more, the mountain gorilla had practically

INTERNATIONAL CONSERVATION ORGANISATIONS

Mountain gorillas are the focus of several conservation organisations. The most important international organisations currently working in Rwanda are listed alphabetically with a summary of their activities:

DIAN FOSSEY GORILLA FUND INTERNATIONAL Founded in 1978, the Atlanta-based DFGFI funds and operates the Karisoke Research Centre (*www.gorillafund.org; select 'Karisoke Research Centre'*), originally established by Dr Dian Fossey in 1967. Although the original research centre was destroyed during the 1990s, it has been replaced by a new centre employing 80 staff in Ruhengeri town. It continues to monitor three gorilla groups and to carry out daily anti-poaching patrols from a base outside the park. DFGFI aims to strengthen research and protection efforts through education, local capacity building, and support to a Geographic Information Systems unit based within the national university.

THE GORILLA ORGANIZATION (*www.gorillas.org*) This London-based organisation manages several projects designed to integrate traditional conservation and research with economic development and education in Rwanda, Uganda, DR Congo, Cameroon and Gabon. These include:

- Beekeepers, who are supported to develop modern sustainable honey farms at the edge of, rather than inside, the park boundary.
- Fresh water in village schools using local engineering technology to provide water cisterns. Water collection is one of the main causes of encroachment in the gorilla habitat, and children living close to the forest often miss school to collect water for their families.
- Training in sustainable agriculture for farmers in areas adjacent to gorilla habitat.
- Tree planting to alleviate environmental degradation, since most fuel used in households comes from wood.
- Virunga Wildlife Clubs in schools, which organise field trips, tree planting and environment-week activities, and a Conservation Network that links local organisations in the Virunga region.

become the national emblem of Rwanda, and it was officially recognised to be the country's most important renewable natural resource. To ordinary Rwandans, gorillas became a source of great national pride: living gorillas ultimately created far more work and money than poaching them had ever done. As a result, a census undertaken in 1989 indicated that the local mountain gorilla population had increased by almost 30% to 320 animals.

Gorilla tourism came to an abrupt halt in 1991, when the country erupted into the civil war that culminated in the 1994 genocide. In February 1992, the park headquarters were attacked, two park employees were killed, and the Karisoke Research Centre established by Fossey had to be evacuated. The park was closed to tourists and, although it reopened in June 1993, it had to be evacuated in April 1994 because of the genocide.

WAR AND THE GORILLAS The Rwandan civil war raised considerable concern about the survival of the gorillas, as land mines were planted there by various military factions, and the mountains provided an escape route to thousands of fleeing refugees. Remarkably, however, when researchers were finally able to return to the park, it was discovered that only four gorillas could not be accounted

INTERNATIONAL GORILLA CONSERVATION PROGRAMME (*www.mountaingorillas.org*) IGCP is a joint initiative of three organisations, the African Wildlife Foundation, Fauna and Flora International and the World Wide Fund for Nature. IGCP's overall goal is the sustainable conservation of the world's remaining mountain gorillas and their habitat. IGCP aims to enhance communication and cooperation between protected-area authorities through regional meetings, training programmes, cross-border patrols and communications networks; and advises governments on environmental policy and legislation enforcement. IGCP provides training and support for park staff, and has established a Ranger-based Monitoring programme throughout the Virunga region.

MOUNTAIN GORILLA VETERINARY PROJECT (*www.mgvp.org*) MGVP provides veterinary care to the mountain gorillas. The project's vets monitor the health of individual gorillas in both the research and tourist groups, and are able to intervene in emergency situations, such as a gorilla becoming trapped by a life-threatening snare. Since disease transmission from humans is a serious threat to the gorillas' survival, MGVP also monitors the health of government and project staff working in the park, and organises seminars addressing health and hygiene issues. The MGVP receives funding from the Morris Animal Foundation and is affiliated to the Maryland Zoo in Baltimore, USA.

WILDLIFE CONSERVATION SOCIETY (*www.wcs.org/international/Africa/rwanda*) With strong historic links to the mountain gorillas, WCS's major programme in Rwanda is now the Nyungwe Forest Conservation Project, although it is still involved with the Volcanoes and Akagera National Parks. WCS is also implementing training programmes in monitoring and research with its partners, including the ORTPN (Office Rwandais du Tourisme et des Parcs Nationaux). It provides direct support to the management of parks and wildlife, and supports ORTPN in tackling immediate threats. In addition, the volcanoes fall within the focus of WCS's **Albertine Rift Project** (*www.albertinerift.org*). The objective of this programme is to improve conservation by providing information for park managers, building capacity to better manage these areas, and encouraging collaboration across national boundaries. Biological and socio-economic surveys are used to identify priority conservation areas and to plan measures to alleviate poverty in the communities that border them.

for. Two of those missing were old females who most probably died of natural causes; the other two might have been shot, but might just as easily have succumbed to disease. It is also encouraging to note that the war had no evident effect on breeding activity, a strong indication that it was less disruptive to the gorillas than had been feared.

But in this most volatile part of Africa little can be taken for granted. Just as Rwanda started to stabilise politically, the DRC descended into anarchy. For years, eastern Congolese officials, who lived far from the capital, received no formal salary and were forced to devise their own ways of securing a living, leading to a level of corruption second to none in the region. At least 16 gorillas were killed in three separate incidents in the DRC between 1995 and 1998, since when the Congolese part of the Virungas was effectively closed to tourists and researchers alike prior to re-opening in 2005.

Under the circumstances, it is remarkable to learn that the latest gorilla count – undertaken in 2003 – shows a continued increase to at least 380 individuals in the Virungas. No further killings were reported between 2003 and 2007, but then at least ten Congolese mountain gorillas were shot in four separate incidents in the space of months, culminating in the arrest of the alleged perpetrators in September of that year. More recent reports placed the Rwandan gorilla population at 260 in 2008 and the Congolese population at 210 in early 2009, and even if one allows for some overlap between the countries, it suggests the current mountain gorilla population of the Virungas population is probably in excess of 400.

PROS AND CONS OF GORILLA TOURISM Any concern about the fate of a few gorillas might seem misplaced in the context of a genocide that claimed a million human lives. But it is these self-same gorillas which have allowed Rwanda to rebuild the lucrative tourist industry that was shattered by the war. Gorilla tracking resumed on a permanent basis in July 1999, and Volcanoes National Park has remained open ever since, a period during which the volume of permits sold annually increased almost tenfold (from 1,934 in 1999 to 17,089 in 2008). Mostly, it's the gorillas that bring tourists to Rwanda, but once there they will usually spend money in other parts of the country, providing foreign revenue and creating employment beyond the immediate vicinity of Volcanoes National Park.

There are those who query the wisdom of habituating gorillas for tourist visits. One area of concern is health, with humans and gorillas being sufficiently close genetically for there to be a real risk of passing a viral or bacterial infection to a habituated gorilla, which might in turn infect other members of its group, potentially resulting in all their deaths should they have no resistance to the infection. Another concern is that habituating gorillas to humans increases their vulnerability to poachers, a theory backed up by the fact that most mountain gorillas poached since the mid-1990s belonged to habituated troops.

Given the above, a reasonable response might be to query the wisdom of habituating gorillas in the first place. The problem facing conservationists is that gorillas cannot be conserved in a vacuum. At current prices, the Rwandan authorities can potentially earn US$28,000 daily in tracking permits alone, much of which is pumped back into the protection and management of the Volcanoes Park, and distributed into local communities bordering the park. There are also the broader benefits of job creation through tourism in and around the Virungas. And even in terms of pure conservation, habituation has many positive effects, allowing researchers and rangers to monitor the gorillas on a daily basis, and to intervene when one of them is ill, injured or in a snare.

Put crudely, while tourism is probably integral to the survival of the mountain gorilla, the survival of the mountain gorilla is certainly integral to the growth of

The birth of a child in Rwanda is a big event for the family and neighbourhood, and the naming of the child at the Kwita Izina ceremony is traditionally the chance to welcome him or her into the wider world. The baby is carried outside and shown to the public, and young children suggest names for this infant who has recently joined them. The parents then select one of the names. It's a lively gathering, accompanied by plenty of food, drink and, of course, dancing.

In the past few decades, the Kwita Izina naming tradition has also been applied to young mountain gorillas, with the park guides taking on the role of proposing the names – which are based on the behaviour, circumstances and background of the infants or their mother. This gorilla-naming ceremony was a low-key private affair up until 2004, but in June 2005 it was held publicly at the Mountain Gorilla's Nest Hotel in Kinigi, and the official naming of 23 gorillas was followed by a celebration party with traditional music and dancing. On the same day, a Gorilla Fundraising Gala was held at the Kivu Sun Hotel (now Lake Kivu Serena) in Gisenyi.

So successful was the inaugural public ceremony that it has now become an annual event, held in mid to late June, when all gorillas born over the past 12 months are given a formal name to the accompaniment of traditional music and dance. Visitors are most welcome to attend these events, which raise valuable funds for the protection of the mountain gorillas; tour operators will fit it into your itinerary by request. As well as the naming, there is the opportunity to 'adopt' (sponsor) a gorilla and/or to make general donations to the animals' welfare.

For more information, tickets and details of sponsorship contact ORTPN (details on page 84) or check www.kwitizina.org.

Rwanda's tourist industry. Ultimately, it's a symbiotic situation that motivates a far greater number of people to take an active interest in the fate of the gorillas than would be the case if gorilla tourism were to be curtailed.

GETTING THERE AND AWAY

The park headquarters at Kinigi (✪ S 01°25.783, E 029°35.717) form the springboard for gorilla tracking and other activities in Volcanoes National Park, all of which require the participant to check in at 07.00. More rustic sprawl than village, Kinigi is situated at an altitude of around 2,200m on the eucalyptus-strewn southern footslopes of the Virungas some 12km north of Ruhengeri town. There's plenty of public transport from Kigali and Gisenyi (see pages 189 and 190) to Ruhengeri, from where the recently surfaced road to Kinigi is signposted to the left of the main Cyanika Road about 300m past the Centre Pastoral Notre Dame de Fatima.

Kinigi is a pretty enough spot, offering great views of the volcanoes as well as some pleasant low-key walking opportunities, though somewhat compromised by the conspicuous absence of indigenous vegetation on the densely cultivated volcanic soils. Visitors on organised trips generally overnight at one of midrange-to-upmarket lodges in and around Kinigi before they go gorilla tracking, which eases the pressure to get to the headquarters in time on the morning of departure.

At the other extreme, with a private vehicle it is possible to drive up from Gisenyi or Kigali on the day you track, though you would need a very early start to reach the assembly point at Kinigi by 07.00 – allow at least two hours from Kigali or one hour from Gisenyi. Another popular upmarket base for gorilla tracking is Virunga Lodge, which overlooks Lake Burera about 30–45 minutes' drive from Kinigi.

Due to the paucity of cheap accommodation near Kinigi, budget-conscious travellers generally prefer to stay in Ruhengeri, 15–20 minutes drive away. Unfortunately, the limited public transport from Ruhengeri isn't sufficiently reliable to guarantee arrival at Kinigi in time, so you will need to rent a vehicle/driver to tie in with gorilla tracking times; for more details see under *Gorilla tracking* on page 220.

WHERE TO STAY AND EAT

There is no accommodation within the national park and overnight camping is forbidden. However, there is now a choice of four midrange-to-upmarket lodges situated within a few kilometres of the park headquarters at Kinigi, all listed below. Another option is the superb but more distant (30–45 minutes' drive) Virunga Lodge overlooking Lake Burera (see page 208), and people with limited time and a high tolerance for very early mornings sometimes base themselves at a hotel in Gisenyi or even Kigali, an option that became less attractive after the assembly time at Kinigi was shifted from 08.00 to 07.00 a few years back. Meanwhile, travellers on a restricted budget almost invariably overnight in Ruhengeri (see pages 192–6) and make their way to Kinigi early in the morning.

EXCLUSIVE

🏠 **Sabyinyo Silverback Lodge** (8 rooms) ☏ +254 20 2734000; m 078 5101759; e reception.rwanda@governorscamp.com; www.governorscamp.com. Opened in 2007, this is currently the swishiest lodge in the vicinity of the Virungas, if not Rwanda, set on community land at an altitude of 2,515m on the footslopes of Mount Sabyinyo, only 10mins' drive from the park headquarters. The land is owned by the Sacola Community Trust & leased to Governors' Camp, a long-serving & award-winning Kenyan luxury safari camp operator which built the lodge & also manages it. A community fee of US$58 pp per night is levied, & the community also receives a 17% cut of the lodge's profits. Accommodation consists of 5 stone cottages, 2 suites & 1 4-bed family suite, all spread out across the grassy slopes. The stylish & well-equipped rooms combine ethnically influenced decor with something of a country house feel, &

come complete with log fire, minibar, tea/coffee-making facilities, mini-safe, direct radio contact with the main building (in lieu of a phone line), 24hr electricity, & a fabulously earthy bathroom with tub & shower. The restaurant & lounge area is in the main building & serves a different 3-course set menu daily. In addition to gorilla tracking, it offers birding expeditions, & trips to Ruhengeri & lakes Kivu & Burera. The steep climb from the car park to the accommodation makes this lodge highly unsuited to disabled travellers, though it should be perfectly manageable by anybody fit & supple enough to track gorillas. Rates include full-board accommodation but exclude drinks, gorilla-tracking permits, transfers to/from Kigali & community fee. Visa is accepted. *US$1,010/1,508 sgl/dbl high season (16 Jul–31 Oct; 15–31 Dec); US$878/1,312 mid season (1 Jan–31 Mar; 1 Jun–15 Jul; 1 Nov–14 Dec); US$426/852 low season (Apr & May).*

UPMARKET

🏠 **Mountain Gorilla's Nest** (40 rooms) ☏ 0252 546331; m 078 8351000; www.gorillanestlodge.com; ✪ S 01°26.365, E 029°34.729. Situated at an altitude of 2,295m between Kinigi & the Volcanoes National Park boundary, this well-established lodge lies in neat grounds enclosed by an intrusive circle of tall Antipodean eucalyptuses that block what would otherwise be a great view of the ragged-edged rim of Sabyinyo. As things stand, it is functional rather than characterful, but extensive renovations are planned following a recent buyout

by Dubai World & inclusion in the Mantis Collection, a South African group of exclusive lodges. These should be complete by mid-2010, when the lodge will be up to 4- or 5-star standards, with fewer but larger rooms. Facilities will include a spa & the 9-hole golf course is likely to be rehabilitated. Rates are likely to be around *US$300 dbl B&B.*
🏠 **Gorilla Mountain View Lodge** (15 rooms with 10 more planned) m 078 8305708/9; e info@3bhotels.com; www.3bhotels.com. The newest lodge in the Virunga area, built by the original owners of

Gorilla's Nest, opened in Jan 2009 & is likely to eventually form part of a hotel chain called 3B, linking several major tourist attractions in Rwanda. Standing on the grassy, breezy saddle that connects Sabyinyo & Bisoke, it offers superb views to all 6 of the volcanoes in the Rwandan part of the Virungas, & is a good place to pick up typical highland seedeaters, sunbirds, cisticolas & other birds. Accommodation is in large & attractively designed free-standing cottages with queen-size or twin beds, tea/coffee-making facilities, private balconies, fridge, mini-safe, log fire, a spacious bathroom with a hot shower, & generator power 04.30–07.00, 12.00–13.00 & 18.00–23.00. The restaurant & bar area, a massive thatched building with stone floors, is still under construction at the time of writing. It's pretty good value at *US$200/250 sgl/dbl FB or US$500 VIP dbl.*

MODERATE

⌂ **Kinigi Guest House** (11 rooms) ☎ 0252 547156; m 078 8433606; e kinigi2020@yahoo.fr; www.rwanda-kinigi-guesthouse.com. Situated in peaceful green gardens just 300m from the park headquarters, this likeably low-key lodge is run by the charity ASOFERWA (see box below) & its en-suite

---

ASOFERWA

If you spend the night close to the entrance to Rwanda's Volcanoes National Park prior to gorilla tracking, you may choose to stay at the friendly Kinigi Guest House (see above), which is run by the non-profit women's association ASOFERWA or Association de Solidarité des Femmes Rwandaises (*Kigali office:* ☎ *0252 586394;* e *asoferwa@rwanda1.com*). Profits from the Guest House are ploughed back into ASOFERWA's programme.

This body was set up in August 1994 to help those left vulnerable and struggling as a result of the genocide, of whom many were women and children: widows, orphans, teenage mothers, traumatised women, victims of AIDS (through rape) and other forms of physical and moral violence, the old and handicapped, women in detention centres with their babies, and minors in re-education centres accused of genocide. All of these feature in ASOFERWA's work.

Among the multiple and urgent needs in 1994, ASOFERWA's first task was to provide shelter and other basic requirements for widows and for children being cared for by an older sibling. This was carried out within the framework of the 'Peace Villages' constructed throughout Rwanda under the national resettlement and rehousing programme. A village consists of 100 to 150 houses and a population of 600 to 1,200. Widows rehoused under this scheme were asked, in return, to take in orphans and care for them, while ASOFERWA helped them to set up income-generating schemes (agriculture, handicrafts, livestock, small kiosks or boutiques). These also benefit the surrounding community, as do the villages' educational and medical facilities.

The work quickly expanded and international funding agencies gave support and sponsorship. Orphans have been found homes, women's groups set up, schools and training centres opened, young people given practical skills, a tannery, a modern dairy farm and a literacy training centre established. ASOFERWA also still works with mothers in prison and with minors accused of genocide, whether in prison, during their re-education or after their return to their community. In one area a mobile medical team cares for the psycho-social needs of rape victims.

The needs are still great; but speak to any of ASOFERWA's active and dedicated team and you'll be in no doubt that they're equal to the task. Someone at the Guest House will gladly give you more information. And, if you have any clothing or other practical items that you don't want to take back home with you after your stay, you could ask at Reception whether they may be useful for the people involved in any of the projects.

have an almost Swiss appearance.)rtable public areas, a good r, & the view of the volcanoes is

superb. *Rfr20,000/25,000 sgl/dbl; Rfr30,000 VIP dbl; Rfr5,000 per bed in a 4-berth dorm. All rates B&B.*

GORILLA TRACKING

Tracking mountain gorillas in the Virungas is a peerless wildlife experience, and one of Africa's indisputable travel highlights. It is difficult to describe the simple exhilaration attached to first setting eyes on a wild mountain gorilla. These are enormous animals: the silverbacks weigh about three times as much as the average man, and their bulk is exaggerated by a shaggily luxuriant coat. And yet despite their fearsome size and appearance, gorillas are remarkably peaceable creatures, certainly by comparison with most primates – gorilla tracking would be a considerably more dangerous pursuit if these gentle giants had the temperament of vervet monkeys, say, or baboons (or, for that matter, humans).

More impressive even than the gorillas' size and bearing is their unfathomable attitude to their daily human visitors, which differs greatly from that of any other wild animal. Anthropomorphic as it might sound, almost everybody who visits the gorillas experiences an almost mystical sense of recognition: we regularly had one of the gorillas break off from chomping on bamboo to study us, its soft brown eyes staring deeply into ours, as if seeking out some sort of connection.

Equally fascinating is the extent to which the gorillas try to interact with their visitors, often approaching them, and occasionally touching one of the guides in apparent recognition and greeting as they walk past. A photographic tripod raised considerable curiosity in several of the youngsters and a couple of the adults – one large female walked up to the tripod, stared ponderously into the lens, then wandered back off evidently satisfied. It is almost as if the gorillas recognise their daily visitors as a troop of fellow apes, but one too passive to pose any threat – often a youngster will put on a chest-beating display as it walks past tourists, safe in the knowledge that they'll accept its dominance: something it would never do to an adult gorilla. (It should be noted here that close contact with humans can expose gorillas to fatal diseases, for which reason the guides try to keep their tourists at least 5m away – but the reality is that there is little anybody can do to stop the gorillas from flouting rules of which they are unaware.)

The magical hour with the gorillas is relatively expensive and getting there can sometimes be hard work. The hike up to the mountain gorillas' preferred habitat of bamboo forest involves a combination of steep slopes, dense vegetation, slippery underfoot conditions after rain, and high altitude. For all that, the more accessible gorilla groups can be visited by reasonably fit adults of any age, and in 20 years of African travel we have yet to meet anybody who has gone gorilla tracking and regretted the financial or physical expense.

PERMITS Eight permits per day are issued for each of the seven habituated groups in the Volcanoes Park, making a daily total of 56 permits. At the time of writing, all these habituated groups stay within tracking range on a more-or-less permanent basis, but gorillas are not governed by international boundaries and it is always possible that groups which originated in Uganda or the DR Congo might cross there again. Trackers are not allocated a specific group in advance but the guides do generally make an effort to match people to a group based on their apparent fitness – Sabyinyo and usually Group Thirteen being the least demanding hikes and Susa the most challenging. The strictly enforced minimum age for tracking gorillas is 15.

A gorilla-tracking permit costs US$500 including park entrance, a price that has been fixed since July 2007 and is likely to rise at some point during the lifespan of this edition (see http://updates.bradtguides.com/rwanda for updates). The permit is best bought in advance through the ORTPN office in Kigali or through a tour operator in Kigali or abroad. Depending on availability, permits can also be bought on the spot at Ruhengeri or Kinigi. There is no guarantee a permit will be available on any given day: the likelihood is highest during the main rainy season of April and May, when trekking operates at around 50% of full capacity, but you may need to wait for days or even weeks in the peak season of June to September, when booking 6–12 months ahead is strongly advised. In any event, the procedure regarding last minute bookings could always change, so you are strongly advised to check this beforehand with ORTPN in Kigali – see box *Booking a gorilla permit* on page 49. Either way, it is advisable for independent travellers to visit or ring the ORTPN office in Kinigi (m *078 8771633*) the afternoon before they intend to go tracking in order to confirm arrangements. Through June to September, when demand is high, permits for specific days can sell out well in advance, so be sure to book as far ahead as possible.

Trackers are required to check in at the park headquarters at Kinigi at 07.00, where they can enjoy a complimentary cup of tea or coffee (and if necessary make use of the last clean flush toilets they'll see for a few hours) before being allocated to one of the seven habituated groups. If you want to visit or to avoid any specific group, it helps to be there a little early so you have time to chat to the rangers. A briefing is held at around 07.30 after which you must drive to the appropriate trailhead, so the actual tracking generally starts at 08.15–08.30.

HABITUATED GROUPS The most difficult to reach of the permanent groups is the **Susa Group**, which lives on the slopes of Mount Karisimbi. Consisting of more than 40 individuals, including four silverbacks and several youngsters, this is the second-largest group of mountain gorillas in the world (there is a larger research group) and it was the one originally studied by Dian Fossey. A visit to the Susa Group is delightfully chaotic and totally unforgettable, with gorillas seemingly tumbling out of every bush and bamboo stand. The Susa Group is the first choice of most fit visitors, but it takes about an hour to drive from Kinigi to the starting point, and you should be prepared for a severe hike. The ascent from the car park to the forest boundary, though not as steep as it used to be from the new starting point, will also take the best part of an hour. On a good day, it will take no more than 20 minutes to reach the gorillas from the boundary; on a bad day you might be looking at two hours or more in either direction and it has been known to take as long as seven hours to locate the group in the dry season (the record from the previous day will give an indication of how deep in the gorillas are, as they generally don't move too far in one day).

At the other end of the severity scale is the trek to the **Sabyinyo Group**, whose permanent territory lies within the Volcanoes Park, on a lightly forested saddle between Mount Sabyinyo and Mount Gahinga. Depending on exactly where the gorillas are, the walk from the car park to the forest boundary is flat to gently sloping, and will typically take 20–30 minutes. Once you're in the forest, the gorillas might take anything from ten minutes to an hour to reach, but generally the slopes aren't too daunting, though they can be slippery after rain. The Sabyinyo Group consists of 11 individuals, with two silverbacks. Although it is less numerically impressive than the Susa Group, the Sabyinyo Group does seem more cohesive and one gets a clearer impression of the group structure and interaction. What's more, the dominant male Guhondo is the heaviest gorilla (of any race) ever measured, at 220kg.

Group Thirteen spends most of its time on the same saddle as the Sabyinyo Group. When it is in that area, it is normally as easy to reach as the Sabyinyo

Group, but it does sometimes move deeper into the mountains and the hike can then be significantly longer. Group Thirteen's name dates to when it was first habituated, and numbered 13 gorillas, but today it numbers an impressive 26 individuals, including 13 adult females serviced by an ultra-promiscuous silverback, who acquired all the females from the Nyakagezi Group after it fled into Rwanda from Uganda following the arrival there of the Kwitonda Group from the DR Congo in 2006. Group Thirteen seems to be a favourite of many of the guides, probably because its silverback is more relaxed and approachable than those in other groups.

MOUNTAIN GORILLAS: ECOLOGY AND TAXONOMY

The largest living primates, gorillas are widespread residents of the equatorial African rainforest, with a global population of perhaps 150,000–200,000 concentrated mainly in the Congo Basin. Until 2001, all gorillas were assigned to the species *Gorilla gorilla*, split into three races: the western lowland gorilla *G. g. gorilla* of the western Congo Basin, the eastern lowland gorilla *G. g. graueri* in the eastern Congo, and the mountain gorilla *G. g. beringei* living in highland forest on the eastern side of the Albertine Rift. The western race was formally described in 1847, but the eastern races were only described in the early 20th century – the mountain gorilla in 1903, a year after two individuals were shot on Mount Sabyinyo by Oscar von Beringe, and the eastern lowland gorilla in 1914.

The conventional taxonomic classification of gorillas has been challenged by recent advances in DNA testing and fresh morphological studies suggesting that the western and eastern gorilla populations, whose ranges lie more than 1,000km apart, diverged some two million years ago. For this reason, they are now treated as discrete species: *G. gorilla* (western) and *G. beringei* (eastern). One distinct western race – the Cross River gorilla *G. g. dielhi* of the Cameroon-Nigeria border region – fulfils the IUCN criteria for 'Critically Endangered', since it lives in five fragmented populations, only one of which is protected, with a combined total of fewer than 300 individuals. In 2000, the Cross River gorilla and mountain gorilla shared the unwanted distinction of being placed on a shortlist of the world's 25 most endangered primate taxa.

The status of the western gorilla is relatively secure, since it is far more numerous in the wild than its eastern counterpart, and has a more extensive range spanning half-a-dozen countries. In the 1980s, the western gorilla population was estimated at 100,000, but that figure was adjusted to 50,000 circa 2006, largely due to hunting for bushmeat and the lethal Ebola virus (which had killed 5,000 gorillas in central Africa prior to 2006, according to a study published in *Science*. Encouragingly, however, a Wildlife Conservation Society survey undertaken over 2006/7 found more than 100,000 previously unreported gorillas in the Lake Tele region of the DR Congo.

The future of the eastern gorilla – still split into a lowland and a mountain race – is far less certain. In the mid 1990s, an estimated 17,000 eastern lowland gorillas remained in the wild, but is widely thought that the population has dropped to 5,000 or fewer since the outbreak of the ongoing Congolese civil war in the DRC. Rarer still, but more stable, is the mountain gorilla, which consists of a mere 700 individuals confined to two ranges: the border-straddling Virunga Volcanoes and Bwindi National Park in Uganda.

The first study of mountain gorilla behaviour was undertaken in the 1950s by George Schaller, whose pioneering work formed the starting point for the more recent research initiated by Dian Fossey in the 1960s. Fossey's acclaimed book *Gorillas in the Mist* remains perhaps the best starting point for anybody who wants to know more about mountain gorilla behaviour.

The mountain gorilla is distinguished from its lowland counterparts by several adaptations to its high-altitude home, most visibly a longer and more luxuriant coat. It is

The **Amahoro Group**, numbering 14, and the more recently habituated **Umubano Group**, with 10 individuals, share an overlapping territory on the slopes of Mount Visoke. Both of these groups have one silverback and the hikes to reach them are typically intermediate in difficulty between those of Susa and Sabyinyo. As their names suggest, the Amahoro (literally 'Peace') and Umubano ('Live Together') groups have a quite harmonious relationship despite their territorial overlap, probably because there are strong familial links between them, with several individuals having brothers and sisters in the other group.

Two new gorilla groups have opened to tourism in recent years, both of which

on average bulkier than other races, with the heaviest individual gorilla on record (of any race) being the 220kg dominant silverback of Rwanda's Sabyinyo Group. Like other gorillas, it is a highly sociable creature, moving in defined troops of anything from five to 50 animals. A troop typically consists of a dominant silverback male (the male's back turns silver when he reaches sexual maturity at about 13 years old) and sometimes a subordinate silverback, as well as a harem of three or four mature females, and several young animals. Unusually for mammals, it is the male who forms the focal point of gorilla society; when a silverback dies, his troop normally disintegrates. A silverback will start to acquire his harem at about 15 years of age, most normally by attracting a young, sexually mature female from another troop. He may continue to lead a troop well into his 40s.

A female gorilla reaches sexual maturity at the age of eight, after which she will often move between different troops several times. Once a female has successfully given birth, however, she normally stays loyal to the same silverback until he dies, and she will even help to defend him against other males. (When a male takes over a troop, he generally kills all nursing infants to bring the mothers into oestrus more quickly, a strong motive for a female to help preserve the status quo.) A female gorilla has a gestation period similar to that of a human, and if she reaches old age she will typically have raised up to six offspring to sexual maturity. A female's status within a troop is based on the length of time she has been with a silverback: the alpha female is normally the longest-serving member of the harem.

The mountain gorilla is primarily vegetarian, with bamboo shoots being the favoured diet, though they are known to eat 58 different plant species in the Virungas. It may also eat insects, ants being a particularly popular protein supplement. A gorilla troop will spend most of its waking hours on the ground, but it will generally move into the trees at night, when each member of the troop builds itself a temporary nest. Gorillas are surprisingly sedentary creatures, typically moving less than 1km in a day, which makes tracking them on a day-to-day basis relatively easy for experienced guides. A troop will generally only move a long distance after a stressful incident, for instance an aggressive encounter with another troop. Gorillas are peaceable animals with few natural enemies and they often live for up to fifty years in the wild, but their long-term survival is critically threatened by poaching, deforestation and exposure to human-borne diseases.

It was previously thought that the Virunga and Bwindi gorilla populations were racially identical, not an unreasonable assumption given that a corridor of mid-altitude forest linked the two mountain ranges until about 500 years ago. But recent DNA tests indicate the Bwindi and Virunga gorillas show sufficient genetic differences to suggest that they have formed mutually isolated breeding populations for many millennia, in which case the 'mountain gorilla' should possibly be split into two discrete races, one – the Bwindi gorilla – endemic to Uganda, the other unique to the Virunga Mountains. Neither race numbers more than 400 in the wild, neither has ever bred successfully in captivity, and both meet several of the criteria for an IUCN classification of 'Critically Endangered'.

Volcanoes National Park   GORILLA TRACKING

10

are usually quite easy to reach. The **Hirwa Group**, comprising nine individuals, was formed in 2006 by a silverback who had broken away from the Susa group about two years earlier, and it usually inhabits the foothills of Mount Sabyinyo on the Gahinga side. At about the same time, the 16-strong **Kwitonda Group** crossed into Uganda from the DR Congo, probably due to the Congolese civil war, and stayed in Mgahinga National Park for a while, forcing the smaller Uganda-based Nyakagezi Group to cross into Rwanda. The Kwitonda Group crossed into Rwanda in late 2006, and it now inhabits the lower slopes of Mount Muhabura, a relatively easy hike (comparable to that for the Sabyinyo Group). As a result of these territorial shifts, the Nyakagezi Group clashed several times with Group Thirteen, whose silverback poached all the Nyakagezi females before the rest of the (now all-male) group beat a retreat back to Uganda.

TRANSPORT Until recently, no public transport connected Ruhengeri to the park headquarters at Kinigi, 12km from town. Following the surfacing of the road, a few

HOW TOUGH IS IT?

This is one of the most frequently asked questions about gorilla tracking in Rwanda. And it is also perhaps the most difficult to answer. So many variables are involved, and if they all conspire against you, you could be in for a genuinely exhausting outing (indeed, on rare occasions, the guides have had to carry tourists down). On the other hand, if everything falls in your favour, the excursion will be little more demanding than the proverbial stroll in the park.

The trek to see the gorillas has two distinct phases. The first is the hike from the closest car park to the forest and national park boundary, which usually takes 30–60 minutes depending on the speed of the party and the group they are visiting. The second is the trek into the forest in search of the gorillas, which will usually have been located by the advance trackers by the time tourists reach the forest edge. This might take anything from 10 minutes to two hours, but 20–30 minutes is typical, especially for those groups whose territory lies closer to the forest edge.

The first part of the trek is predictable, and it is usually quite flat and undemanding, unless you are going to the Susa Group, which involves a longer and steeper ascent. The second part is more difficult to predict, as it will depend on the exact location of the gorillas on the day, and on the steepness of the terrain en route. Other factors in determining how tough it will be include the density of vegetation (bending and crawling through the jungle can be tiring, especially if you have to dodge vicious nettles) and whether it has rained recently, in which case everything will be muddier and quite slippery underfoot.

At risk of stating the obvious, age and fitness levels are the key factors in how difficult the hike will feel. Susa Group aside, moderately fit people under the age of 40 seldom feel any significant strain, but a high proportion of trackers are in their 50s or 60s, in which case the hike might be somewhat tougher. As one reader of the last edition wrote: 'We think you underestimate how strenuous the gorilla trip is. We are both 61 but fit and well, bicycling to work each day, and still we had to take regular breaks due to problems with breathing'. That said, while many older travellers do find the track quite demanding, it is very unusual that they are so daunted as to turn back.

An important factor in determining how difficult the hike will be is which group you are allocated. As a rule, the hike to the Susa Group is the most demanding (but also the most rewarding, with more than 40 gorillas on show), while the Sabyinyo Group is the most reliably straightforward to reach. The hikes to Kwitonda, Hirwa and Group Thirteen are also usually quite undemanding, whereas the hikes to the Amahoro and Umubano Groups tend to be more difficult, but not as tough as the Susa Group.

minibus-taxis cruise the route every day, but they don't go as far as the park headquarters, and they cannot be relied upon to get you to Kinigi in time for the 07.00 assembly. In any case, there is no public transport from Kinigi to any of the car parks from where one enters the forest to start tracking, and, while individual travellers may be able to beg lifts with other tourists, it's not a reliable option.

Because of this, most independent travellers hire a vehicle and driver for the morning. ORTPN in Ruhengeri can advise on this and both Highland Gorilla Tour & Travel and Amahoro Tours (see page 192) can arrange vehicle hire. In the rainy season you may need a 4x4 to reach the trekking car parks; in the dry season an ordinary *taxi-voiture* should be adequate and will cost far less. The going rate for a 4x4 from/to Ruhengeri is around US$80 for the round trip, or US$100 for the more remote Susa Group. If you spend the night beforehand at the Mountain Gorilla's Nest, the Kinigi Guest House or the ORTPN Campsite, all quite close to the Kinigi park office, you stand a reasonable chance of hitching a lift up there from the main road; but you'll still need transport in the morning to reach the start of

Unfortunately, these things aren't set in stone, and any group might be unusually demanding (or easy) to reach on a bad day. Furthermore, nobody can guarantee which group you will be allocated in advance. However, the guides at Kinigi do make a conscious attempt to match individuals to the most suitable group, especially if they are asked to. Generally, the party for the Susa Group consists of lean-looking under-30s, while the opposite holds true for the Sabyinyo party.

Two further factors are uneven underfoot conditions and high altitude. Most visitors to Africa live in towns and cities where roads and sidewalks are paved, and parks are serviced by neatly maintained footpaths, so they are unused to walking on the more irregular and seasonally slippery surfaces typical of the ascent paths and forest floor. It will help enormously in this regard to wear strong waterproof shoes or hiking boots with a good tread and solid ankle support. Furthermore, if you think you might struggle in these conditions, there is a lot to be said for avoiding the rainy seasons, in particular March–May, when conditions can be dauntingly muddy.

Don't underestimate the tiring effect of altitude. The trekking takes place at elevations of 2,500–3,000m above sea level, not high enough for altitude sickness to be a concern but sufficient to knock the breath out of anybody – no matter how fit – who has just flown in from a low altitude. For this reason, visitors who are spending a while in Rwanda might think seriously about leaving their gorilla tracking until they've been in the country a week or so, and are better acclimatised. Most of Rwanda lies at above 1,500m, and much of the country is higher – a couple of days at Nyungwe, which lies above 2,000m, would be good preparation for the Virungas. Likewise, if you are coming from elsewhere in Africa, try to plan your itinerary so that you spend your last pre-Rwanda days at medium to high altitude: for example, were you flying in from Kenya, a few days in Nairobi (2,300m) or even the Maasai Mara (1,600m) would be far better preparation than time at the coast.

Guides will generally offer you a walking stick at the start of the hike, and, even if you normally shun such props, it is worth taking up the offer to help support you on those slippery mountain paths. If you have luggage, hire a porter too. Once on the trail, take it easy, and don't be afraid to ask to stop for a few minutes whenever you feel tired. Drink plenty of water, and carry some quick calories – biscuits and chocolate can both be bought at supermarkets in Ruhengeri. The good news is that most people who track gorillas find the hike to be far less demanding than they expect, and in 99% of cases, whatever exhaustion you might feel on the way up will vanish with the adrenalin charge that follows the first sighting of a silverback gorilla!

the trek. Whatever method you choose, make sure that it's reliable – if you don't turn up at the appointed time you risk invalidating your US$500 permit and having to miss out on the gorillas.

WHAT TO WEAR AND TAKE Put on your sturdiest walking shoes, and thick trousers and a long-sleeved top as protection against vicious stinging nettles. It's often cold when you set out, so start off with a sweatshirt or jersey (which also help protect against nettles). The gorillas are thoroughly used to people, so it makes little difference whether you wear bright or muted colours. Whatever clothes you wear to go tracking are likely to get very dirty as you slip and slither in the mud, so if you have pre-muddied clothes you might as well wear them. When you're grabbing for handholds in thorny vegetation, a pair of old gardening gloves are helpful. If you feel safer with a walking-stick, you'll be offered a wooden one at the start of the ascent.

Carry as little as possible, ideally in a waterproof bag of some sort. During the rainy season, a poncho or raincoat might be a worthy addition to your daypack, while sunscreen, sunglasses and a hat are a good idea at any time of year. You may well feel like a snack during the long hike, and should certainly carry enough drinking water – at least one litre, more to visit the Susa Group. Bottled water is sold in Ruhengeri. Especially during the rainy season, make sure your camera gear is well protected – if your bag isn't waterproof, seal your camera gear in a plastic bag (for further details about photographing gorillas see the box *Photographic tips* on pages 56–7).

Binoculars are not necessary to see the gorillas. In theory, birdwatchers might want to carry binoculars, though in practice only the most dedicated are likely to make use of them – the trek up to the gorillas is normally very directed, and walking up the steep slopes and through the thick vegetation tends to occupy one's eyes and mind.

If you are carrying much gear and food/water, it's advisable to hire one of the porters who hang about at the car park in the hope of work. This costs Rfr5,000 per porter. Locals have asked us to emphasise that it is not demeaning or exploitative to hire a porter to carry your daypack; on the contrary, tourists who refuse a porter for 'ethical reasons' are simply denying income to poor locals and making it harder for them to gain any benefit from tourism.

You may need to show your passport or some other form of identification when you check in; find out about this from ORTPN beforehand.

REGULATIONS AND PROTOCOL Tourists are permitted to spend no longer than one hour with the gorillas, and it is forbidden to eat, urinate or defecate in their presence. It is also forbidden to approach within less than 5m of the gorillas, a rule that is difficult to enforce with curious youngsters (and some adults) who often approach human visitors. Smoking is forbidden anywhere within the national park boundary ('it's unhealthy for the animals', according to one rather earnest guide, which seems to be taking concerns about passive smoking to stratospheric absurdity – more genuine justifications are litter, fire and annoying other tourists).

Gorillas are susceptible to many human diseases, and it has long been feared by researchers that one ill tourist might infect a gorilla, resulting in the possible death of the whole troop should they have no immunity to that disease. For this reason, you should not go gorilla tracking with a potentially airborne infection such as flu or a cold, and are asked to turn away from the gorillas should you need to sneeze.

To the best of our knowledge, no tourist has ever been seriously hurt by a habituated gorilla, but there is always a first time. An adult gorilla is much stronger than a person, and will act in accordance with its own social codes. Therefore it is vital that you listen to your guide at all times regarding correct protocol in the presence of gorillas.

GOLDEN MONKEY TRACKING

Although it's the gorillas that tend to hog the limelight, the little-known golden monkey *Cercopithecus kandti* (sometimes treated as a distinctive race of the more widespread blue monkey *C. mitis*) is also IUCN-listed as 'endangered', with a similarly restricted range within the Albertine Rift. As such, it's a rare treat for visitors to be able to view a newly habituated group of about 15 of these delightful creatures in the Volcanoes National Park. Visits can be arranged through any ORTPN office; they last for one hour and are for a maximum of six people; the cost is US$100 for non-residents and US$65 for foreign residents, including entry to the park. Booking is seldom necessary, but it would be advisable to do so in advance if you have to track on one specific day.

Endemic to the Albertine Rift, the golden monkey is characterised by a bright orange-gold body, cheeks and tail, contrasting with its black limbs, crown and tail-end. It was previously found in the Gishwati Forest, which since the return of the post-genocide refugees has become too degraded; and there may be a small population somewhere in the Nyungwe Forest; but it is thought that the only viable population is on the Virunga volcanoes. Within this restricted range it is the numerically dominant primate, and reasonably common – the number of individuals protected within Volcanoes National Park is a matter of conjecture, but a 2003 survey estimated a population of 3,000–4,000 in its smaller neighbour, Uganda's Mgahinga National Park.

In early 2002, ORTPN approached the Dian Fossey Gorilla Fund International (DFGFI) to discuss the possibility of habituating the golden monkeys for purposes of tourism. The DFGFI welcomed the chance to learn more about this little-studied monkey and to help promote tourism in the park. First, two possible groups were selected for habituation – they are in areas of the park that would be suitable as part of a nature trail for tourists. Field assistants were then trained in habituation and data collection techniques, and work could begin.

The first few months were terribly frustrating. Dense vegetation (bamboo) made approaching the groups very difficult and the monkeys would flee at the first sight of humans. In time, the researchers were able to refine their techniques and determine at what time of day the monkeys were most active, which made them easier to locate. Gradually the monkeys came to accept the presence of the observers for longer and longer periods. Meanwhile the researchers were gathering more and more data about their diet, habitat use, social structure and behavioural ecology, all of which must be understood if the project is to succeed in the long term.

The first group was 'opened to the public' in summer 2003 and has delighted visitors. It's a very different experience from gorilla-viewing, where the huge creatures are entirely visible as they react and interact. The golden monkeys in their bamboo thicket are smaller, nimbler and can be harder to locate and follow, though based on our most recent (2009) experience, they are a lot more relaxed now than a few years back and the quality of sightings can be superb. The benefits of this project are mutual; for tourists, the pleasure of observing a rare species of monkey; for researchers, the satisfaction of learning more about a little-known species; and for the endangered golden monkeys, far less threat of extinction, as they are studied, protected and better understood.

OTHER HIKES

Several non-primate-related hikes are now offered to visitors to Volcanoes National Park. Most of these are day hikes, attracting a uniform charge of US$100 for non-residents and US$65 for foreign residents, including park entrance, but the overnight ascent of Karisimbi is a two-day excursion costing US$175. ORTPN

10

will provide guides for all hikes, but trekkers should have suitable clothing and (if overnighting on Karisimbi) bring their own camping equipment. Hikes can be booked through the ORTPN office in Kigali, Ruhengeri or Kinigi (if you want to pay by Visa, it can only be done in Kigali). Note that all hikes depart from the park headquarters at Kinigi at around 07.30 (check-in time 07.00), the same departure time as for gorilla tracking, which means that visitors can undertake only one activity per day within the park.

One popular hike is to **Dian Fossey's tomb** and the adjacent gorilla cemetery at the former Karisoke Research Camp. This trek involves a 30-minute drive from the park headquarters to the trailhead then a 10-minute stroll to the park boundary. From here, the ascent through the forest takes anything from 90 minutes to three hours, depending on your fitness and how often you stop to enjoy the scenery,

THE VIRUNGAS

Straddling the borders of Uganda, Rwanda and the DRC, the Virungas are not a mountain range as such, but a chain of isolated freestanding volcanic cones strung along a fault line associated with the same geological process that formed the Rift Valley. Sometimes also referred to as the Birunga or Bufumbira Mountains, the chain comprises six inactive and three active volcanoes, all of which exceed 3,000m in altitude – the tallest being Karisimbi (4,507m), Mikeno (4,437m) and Muhabura (4,127m).

The names of the individual mountains in the Virunga chain reflect local perceptions. Sabyinyo translates as 'old man's teeth' in reference to the jagged rim of what is probably the most ancient and weathered of the eight volcanoes. Muhabura is 'the guide', and anecdotes collected by the first Europeans to visit the area suggest that its perfect cone, topped today by a small crater lake, still glowed at night as recently as the early 19th century. Gahinga is variously translated as meaning 'pile of stones' or 'the hoe', the former a reference to its relatively small size, the latter to the breach on its flank. Of the other volcanoes that lie partially within Rwanda, Karisimbi – which occasionally sports a small cap of snow – is named for the colour of a cowry shell, while Visoke simply means watering hole, in reference to the crater lake near its peak.

The vegetation zones of the Virungas correspond closely to those of other large East African mountains, although much of the Afro-montane forest below the 2,500m contour has been sacrificed to cultivation. Moist broad-leaved semi-deciduous forest dominates up until the 2,800m contour, whilst the slopes at altitudes of 2,800–3,200m, where an average annual rainfall of 2,000mm is typical, support bamboo forest interspersed with stands of tall hagenia woodland. At higher altitudes, the cover of Afro-alpine moorland, grassland and marsh is studded with giant lobelia, senecios and other outsized plants similar to those found on Kilimanjaro and the Ruwenzori. Above 3,600m, biodiversity levels are very low and the dominant vegetation consists of a fragile community of grasses, mosses and lichens. A total of 1,265 plant species identified across the range to date includes at least 120 that are endemic to the Albertine Rift.

The most famous denizen of the Virungas is the mountain gorilla, which inhabits all six of the extinct or dormant volcanoes, but not – for obvious reasons – the more active ones. The Virungas also form the main stronghold for the endangered golden monkey, possibly the last one now that their only other confirmed haunt, the more southerly Gishwati Forest, has been cleared to cover less than 1% of its original extent. Recent estimates based on dung surveys tentatively place the buffalo population at close to 1,000, while the total number of elephants might be anything from 20 to 100. Other typical highland forest species include yellow-backed duiker, bushbuck and giant forest hog. The mountains' avifauna is comparatively poorly known, as evidenced by sightings of 36 previously unrecorded species during a cross-border biodiversity study undertaken while the descent takes 1–2 hours. Fossey's old living quarters – which she nicknamed the mausoleum – are now in ruins, and several other landmarks in the camp are signposted. The hike offers a good opportunity to see birds and other creatures typical of the Virungas *en route*.

Far more demanding is the day hike to the 3,711m peak of **Mount Visoke**, which is topped by a beautiful crater lake. Departing from a car park at an altitude of around 2,500m, the footpath up the mountain leads after one hour to a clearing that was used as a resting point by Dian Fossey *en route* to Karisoke. From here, it takes another 2–3 hours to get to the peak, passing through lobelia and hagenia woodland, and following a path that is steep and muddy at the best of times, and outright treacherous after rain – you'll be sinking to your knees in the bog with almost every step, and do much of the descent sliding along on your butt. Indeed,

in early 2004, bringing the total checklist for the Virungas to 294, including 20 Albertine Rift endemics.

Still in their geological infancy, none of the Virunga Mountains is more than two million years old and two of the cones remain highly active – indeed, they are together responsible for nearly 40% of documented eruptions in Africa. The most dramatic volcanic explosion of historical times was the 1977 eruption of the 3,465m Mount Nyiragongo in the DRC, about 20km north of the Lake Kivu port of Goma. During this eruption, a lava lake that had formed in the volcano's main crater back in 1894 drained in less than one hour, emitting streams of molten lava that flowed at a rate of up to 60km per hour, killing an estimated 2,000 people and terminating only 500m from Goma Airport.

In 1994, a new lake of lava started to accumulate within the main crater of Nyiragongo, leading to another highly destructive eruption on 17 January 2002. Lava flowed down the southern and eastern flanks of the volcano into Goma itself, killing at least 50 people. Goma was evacuated, and an estimated 450,000 people crossed into the nearby Rwandan towns of Gisenyi and Ruhengeri for temporary refuge. Three days later, when the first evacuees returned, it transpired that about a quarter of the town – including large parts of the commercial and residential centre – had been engulfed by the lava, leaving 12,000 families homeless. The lava lake in Nyiragongo's crater remains active, with a diameter of around 50m, and, although there has been no subsequent eruption, the crater rim still glows menacingly above Gisenyi's nocturnal skyline and a new lava lake has started to form about 250 metres below the level of the 1994 one.

Only 15km northwest of Nyiragongo stands the 3,058m Mount Nyamuragira, which also erupted in January 2002. Nyamuragira vies with Ol Doinyo Lengai in Tanzania as probably the most active volcano on the African mainland, with 34 eruptions recorded since 1882. Only the 1912–13 incidence resulted in any known direct fatalities, though 17 people were killed and several pregnancies terminated as a result of ash-contaminated drinking water in the 2000 eruption. Nyamuragira most recently blew its top on 27 November 2006, spewing lava hundreds of metres into the air, along with a large plume of ash and sulphur dioxide that destroyed large tracts of cultivated land and forest.

It is perhaps worth noting that these temperamental Congolese volcanoes pose no threat to visitors to the mountain gorillas, as the relevant cones are all dormant or extinct. That might change one day: there is a tradition among the Bafumbira people that the fiery sprits inhabiting the crater of Nyamuragira will eventually relocate to Muhabura, reducing both the mountain and its surrounds to ash. Another Bafumbira custom has it that the crater lake atop Mount Muhabura is inhabited by a powerful snake spirit called Indyoka, which lives on a bed of gold and need only raise its head to bring rain to the surrounding countryside.

given that the crater lake is usually obscured by clouds during the rainy season, this is one walk definitely best suited to drier times of year. The descent takes about 2–3 hours, so allowing for at least 30 minutes on the top, you are looking at an overall hiking time of around 6–8 hours, depending greatly on your fitness level and the season. Bring food and plenty of water, and don't refuse the walking stick that will be offered to you at the parking lot.

KARISIMBI CLIMB, JANUARY 2009 *Wil Resing*

4 JANUARY This was not my first visit to the Virungas. I had visited the Susa group back in 2002, the golden monkeys in 2004 and hiked Bisoke in 2006. But now my eyes were set on Karisimbi, at 4,507m the sixth-highest mountain in Africa, after Kilimanjaro, Mount Kenya, Ruwenzori, Mount Meru (Tanzania) and Ras Dashen in Ethiopia's Simien Mountains.

Before heading for Ruhengeri, I visited ORTPN in Kigali twice for information. And twice I was told that I did not have to make an advance reservation for the Karisimbi hike, I must just pitch up at the ORTPN headquarters at Kinigi and pay. But once in Ruhengeri, Francis (my taxi driver in the volcanoes region, m *078 8448958*), told me this was not possible. I called the park warden and he confirmed that normally you must book a Karisimbi trek a couple of days ahead so that they can make preparations. (As an aside, I went to ORTPN in Kigali after I returned from Karisimbi, and the staff there apologised profusely for having given me the wrong information, and assured me that it would not happen again – I'm confident they will do their best to avoid similar mistakes in future.)

Finally, I was told they would make an exception: I could leave the next morning. I did not have to be at Kinigi at 07.00, the normal reporting time, but at 08.30. Just before darkness fell, the sky cleared after an afternoon shower, and the magnificent volcanoes appeared – Muhabura, Gahinga, Sabyinyo, Bisoke and Karisimbi – though the summit of Rwanda's highest remained hidden in the clouds, as if it wanted to tell me: *I won't reveal myself to you entirely, you have to conquer me first.*

5 JANUARY At Kinigi I was told I should have booked before and that they don't normally organize Karisimbi treks for solo tourists. But they agreed to make an exception. I paid them the US$175 for the two-day trek, US$10 to rent a tent, and I met my guide, who spoke perfect English and French. The drive from Kinigi to the trailhead was 16km and took 30 minutes. At 10.15 we arrived at the car park where the road finished. There we met the porters; one for me and one for the guide, at Rfr5,000 per day, not included in the price. I paid my porter after the trip. The guide paid for his own porter. Both guide and porters wore rubber boots: not a bad idea compared with my mountain shoes, as the trail is very muddy.

We set off at 10.20, starting at around 2,600m altitude. The guide carries a phone for communication with rangers/soldiers patrolling the park. At 10.30, we cross the stone wall that separates the park from the potato fields. Now we are in the jungle. Here, several armed soldiers join us, as protection against buffalo and elephants. We walk the same trail as for the Bisoke climb. With my binoculars I see a group of tourists approach the Amahoro group. There is a lot of fresh buffalo dung on the trail.

After an hour's gradual ascent, we reach a junction at 2,967m, with some benches. A signboard points right for Bisoke and left for Karisoke. We go left. A light rain starts falling. We walk close to Dian Fossey's tomb and gorilla graveyard, but don't visit, which would involve paying extra. I put on my rain trousers, also good protection against the stinging nettles that hem in the narrow trail. The rain trousers become essential to combat the mud, which is everywhere – not so much a mountain hike as a swamp walk! We see a

Recommended only to dedicated hikers, the overnight trek to **Karisimbi** is even more demanding, but as the highest peak in the range, it also offers the greatest vegetational diversity, rising through clumped bamboo and aromatic hagenia forest to the spectacularly otherworldly vegetation of the sub-alpine and Afro-Alpine zones, which are dominated by clumped moss and heather and stands of giant senecios and lobelias. Be warned that you will be camping in near freezing

squirrel, and hear what the guide reckons to be a gorilla research group not normally visited by tourists.

We cross different vegetation zones: bamboo and wild celery on the lower slopes, ideal food for gorillas. Then hagenia forest, with old man's beard moss on the branches. Then, above 3,000m, the marvellous giant groundsel and giant lobelia. At 15.50 we reach camp (3,700m), a similar altitude to Bisoke, which can be seen behind us. So today we climbed 1,100 metres in five and a half hours. I don't feel the effect of the altitude, but my legs are tired.

The staff pitch my tent. At 17.00 the sky clears and I finally see a glimpse of the top of Karisimbi, as well as Mikeno volcano in the Congo. I count how many we are now: one guide, two porters and seven soldiers, for just one *muzungu*! The wood is damp, so it's difficult to make a good fire and my porter uses the opening of his rubber boots to blow air into it. Around the fire we share the food we brought. At 20.00 I head to my tent for a deserved rest.

6 JANUARY Dawn at 05.30. I eat biscuits and drink water. Beautiful morning light. We leave at 06.10. The trail gets steeper, while the fog closes in. Sometimes I have to use my hands to crawl over the labyrinth of trees and branches above the muddy ground, which I would not like to fall into. On several occasions my porter has to give me a hand to pull me up. The terrain is more difficult than I had expected.

At about 4,000 metres we are above the tree line. The slope becomes more exposed and a cold wind blows. My guide already wears a hat and gloves; I put them on now too. The last couple of hundred metres we walk on volcanic scree (fortunately not loose, more like grey gravel). The wind gets harder and visibility drops to 25m. I see more and more junk and rubbish lying on the ground, and wonder where all this dirt comes from. Metal pipes, empty cans, etc. Suddenly I realise I don't climb any more. It is 08.45 and we are on the summit!

The rubbish is construction waste, left by the builders of the huge telecom mast at the summit. The Congolese border must be somewhere here, but the fog is so thick I don't have a clue where. There are two abandoned huts for the builders of the mast. One is open and we use it as a shelter. I put on all my warm clothes and take pictures outside, while my Rwandan companions, unused to this bitter cold, remain inside. The temperature is maybe 0°C, but the wind chill factor makes it feel much colder. My guide hugs and congratulates me: 'You are very strong, many people don't make it to the summit'.

At 09.15, we start the descent, arriving in camp at 11.00. The warm clothes can be taken off again. It is basically the same way down. *En route*, the sun starts shining, for the first time in two days. We spot a beautiful reedbuck and cross the stream where Dian Fossey was amazed to see gorillas looking at their own reflection in the water. At 15.10 we are at the car park, so today we hiked for about nine hours, including breaks: 800m up and 1,900m down. We pay the porters and get into Francis's car. I turn around for a last quick look at Karisimbi, but Rwanda's roof has vanished in the clouds again. Did I really conquer her heart? Although she is invisible and far away once more, I know for sure she conquered mine.

conditions, so good camping gear and plenty of warm clothing are a prerequisite, and you'll need to be self sufficient when it comes to food and water. There are also plans to open up **Gahinga** and **Muhabura** to a day and overnight hike respectively.

IBY'IWACU CULTURAL VILLAGE

Situated next to the car park at the trailhead for the Sabyinyo Group and Group Thirteen, this award-winning venture was founded in 2004 by Edwin Sabuhoro of Rwanda Eco-Tours to help improve the livelihood of communities living around Volcanoes National Park, thereby reducing human pressure on the park's resources. The cultural village is essentially the public flagship for an ambitious project that provides legitimate employment in fields such as vegetable and mushroom farming, beekeeping and tourism to about 1,000 former and potential poachers.

Best arranged a day or so in advance, Iby'Iwacu offers a busy programme that lasts about two hours and slots in ideally after a morning's gorilla tracking. The setting is a fantastic wood-and-thatch replica of a traditional Rwandan palace, second only in size to the restored palace at Nyanza Museum, and an ideal stage for traditional Intore dancers to share their drumming and dance routines. Also on offer are a short community walk, a church visit, a consultation with a traditional healer, shooting a bow and arrow with one of the local Batwa pygmies, and demonstrations of activities such as grinding millet and sorghum, making banana beer and harvesting potatoes and other crops.

Although Rwanda Eco-Tours plays a role in marketing and advising Iby'Iwacu, the cultural village is owned entirely by local communities, and the fee of US$20 person is split so that 40% goes directly to community members who perform and do other activities, while 60% goes to a village fund managed by a committee that channels it into various charitable efforts, from buying seeds for farmers to sponsoring schoolchildren and buying scholastic materials. For further details and bookings, contact Rwanda Eco-Tours in Kigali (⤷ *0252 500331/500057;* m *078 8352009; www.rwandaecotours.com*) or the local project leader at Kinigi (m *078 8451289*).

11

Eastern Rwanda

East of Kigali, the highlands of the Albertine Rift descend towards the western rim of the Lake Victoria Basin, a relatively flat and low-lying region marked by a distinctly warmer and more humid climate than the rest of Rwanda. Geographically, the most significant feature of eastern Rwanda is probably the **Akagera River**, which forms the border with Tanzania and feeds the extensive complex of lakes and marshes protected within **Akagera National Park** – the most important attraction in eastern Rwanda, covered in the next chapter.

Akagera aside, the east of Rwanda lacks any major tourist attractions. Other landmarks include the **Rusumo Falls** on the Tanzania border and **Lake Muhazi**, both of which are diverting enough if you are in the area, but not really worth making a major effort to reach, although the drive along the northern shore of Lake Muhazi is attractive. The area of rolling hills and cattle farming in the far northeast near the Uganda border offers far-reaching views – but this is an area for strolling and people-watching rather than any great excitement. The handful of towns that dot the region are uniformly on the dull side, although some have lively markets and the breezy highland town of **Byumba** in the northeast is surrounded by extensive tea plantations.

The main roads through eastern Rwanda are surfaced and covered by the usual proliferation of minibus-taxis. Accommodation options are limited by comparison with those in other parts of the country, but all the main towns have at least one reasonably comfortable – and reasonably priced – hotel. Because it lies at a lower altitude than the rest of the country, the Tanzania border area is the one part of Rwanda where malaria is a major rather than a minor risk, particularly during the rainy season.

THE BYUMBA (GICUMBI) ROAD

RWANDA NA GASABO The first substantial right turn off the main Kigali–Byumba road, about 25km out of Kigali, takes you on a winding route to Rwanda Na Gasabo or the original Rwanda hill. This is where (allegedly) the first of the ancient kings, travelling to Rwanda from the northeast, stopped at the top and set up his kingdom. It's high, with a flat top and a view in all directions. After leaving the main road, continue for a short distance to a cluster of houses where there's a sharp left turn on to a narrow road that climbs steeply. Just follow this upwards and you'll reach the top of the hill. (A 4x4 is advisable, particularly after rain.) People are generally around, so ask directions if you're unsure. The view is spectacular. There are plans to develop this site for tourism (reconstructed dwellings, interpretation boards...) but at present it's peaceful.

Legends abound! The ancient King Gihanga (see box on page 246) is said to have left two of his cows here; their names were Rugira and Ingizi. One day another king went hunting and threw a branch after an animal; the tip sank into

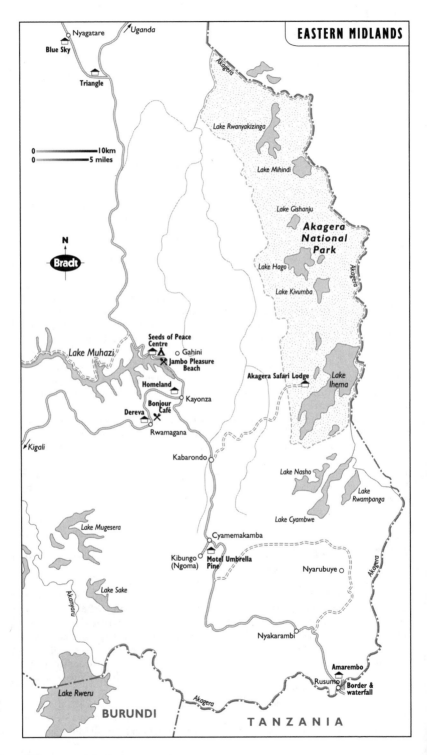

the ground and took root, becoming a species found nowhere else in Rwanda. The great trees planted as the gateway to his land are still standing, after many centuries. Then again, there was a magic earthenware pot in the court; it would fill with water of its own accord to signify that rain was on the way. Also the monarch had a very special group of royal drummers, whose drumming awakened him in the morning and sent him to sleep at night. And so on. You may well meet someone up there who will tell you other tales.

LAKE MUHAZI (NORTHWESTERN SHORE) About five minutes further up the Kigali–Byumba road after the Gasabo turning, another right turn at ✛ S 01°45.753, E 030°07.788, signposted for the village of Rwesero, is the start of a beautiful (but sometimes rough) road that follows the northern bank of the 60km long Lake Muhazi in an easterly direction to emerge near Gahini on the main surfaced road flanking Akagera National Park. The road offers a succession of tranquil, watery views (and numerous birds), with the possibility of stopping for a meal or drink at one of the resorts near Rwesero. Allow a half-day for this road, including stops – you can do it in less, but it's a shame to hurry and the surface is sometimes quite rutted. The road also crosses several small creeks on rough wooden 'bridges' so is best done in the dry season and certainly in a 4x4. It may well become impassable in a couple of places when the lake rises: ask about this. Hitching could be difficult; transport comes in from either end but doesn't necessarily go the whole way through.

This part of the lake was much studied by the Germans as they explored their new territory. Writing in 1907, a Doctor Mildbraed rather crossly commented:

> The west end of Lake Muhasi terminates in a papyrus swamp, and therefore promised rich spoils for zoological treasure-hunters. We were all the more keenly disillusioned to find the fauna far more meagre in character in this great water basin – the first we had explored in Africa – than we had been led to suppose in Germany. In spite of the luxurious vegetation at this part of the lake, the most diligent search was needed before we found a few sponges and polypi attached to some characeous plants.

Where to stay and eat Very soon after leaving the main road you cross a small iron bridge; then, after about 25 minutes (or longer if you stop to look at birds and enjoy the lakeside views), you'll come to two simple places to eat or sleep, wonderfully located at the water's edge within a few hundred metres of Rwesero. The first place on the right as you come from Kigali is the **Café-Resto Hakurya y'i Gasabo** (✛ S 01°47.545, E 030°10.160, 1,444m), which has a very slow bar/restaurant, a camping area, and three small, en-suite double rondawels for Rfr10,000 each – unfortunately, there is no telephone on the site, so it's not possible to make an advance reservation. The much smarter and better organised **Rwesero Beach Resort** (✆ 0252 502821; m 078 3737490) also has a bar/restaurant serving an varied selection of snacks and meals in the Rfr 2,500–5,000 range. You can eat indoors or on a floating wooden deck suspended above the lake. There's also a picnic place, children's playground and campsite, and it is probably the better option for day trippers seeking a lakeside snack or drink. Both places have boats, so you can fish on the lake – or cross to the opposite bank and camp there. There's plenty of birdlife around too, including pied and malachite kingfishers and fish eagle, and otters are sometimes seen in the area.

BYUMBA (GICUMBI) The sprawling town of Byumba, which lies about 75km north of Kigali, some 3km off the main road to Kibale (Uganda), is the seventh largest in Rwanda (population estimated at 75,000 in 2009) and the highest settlement of note, perched at an altitude of 2,220m above the Mulindi Valley. It is the capital of

Gicumbi District, whose rich volcanic soils lie at the heart of Rwanda's burgeoning tea industry, which has assumed a growing economic importance in recent years and now creates employment for around 60,000 people. More than 10 million kilograms of tea is exported from Rwanda yearly, much of it to the UK and Pakistan, with annual earnings of up to US$20 million accounting for more than 30% of state revenue since 2004. Byumba offers nothing in the way of tourist attractions, though the neat green tea plantations that blanket the surrounding countryside are very pretty – you could well spend a couple of days here just walking and enjoying the expansive views – and the 45km dirt road connecting it to Base (pronounced *bah-zay*, on the main road between Kigali and Ruhengeri) is one of the most scenic in the country, though it's also rather rough and requires at least two hours to cover.

There is plenty of transport to Byumba from Kigali and the Gatuna border with Uganda. The 42km road between Byumba and Base, notable for spectacular views of the tea estates around Base, is serviced by at least one bus daily, leaving Byumba in the early morning and returning from Base later in the day. There don't seem to be any minibus-taxis along this route, but hitching isn't impossible. On the Kigali–Byumba road about 10km outside Kigali is the rather surprising Highland Flowers Rose Farm, growing high-quality roses for sale locally and for export to Europe. The **Banque Commerciale du Rwanda**, 100m from the minibus station, changes US dollars cash and theoretically travellers' cheques; it also has Western Union.

Where to stay

Hotel Urumuli (27 rooms) ☎ 0252 564111; m 078 8346295; e hotelurumuli@yahoo.fr; www.hotelurumuli.com. Recently reopened after radical renovations, this is once again the pick of the accommodation in Byumba, assuming you're not on a budget. Sgl, dbl & twin rooms with DSTV, phone & en-suite hot shower are available, & there's also a 2-bedroom suite. Facilities include an internet café & a decent bar-restaurant serving the usual Rwandan fare. The hotel lies at the top of the long main street, about 2km from the public taxi park

but is served by private minibuses such as Atraco. *Rfr25,000 sgl, Rfr30,000 dbl or twin; Rfr60,000 suite.*

Centre Diocésain de Formation et de Conférence (13 rooms) ☎ 0252 564375; ⊕ S 01°35.167, E 030°03.410. If the Urumuli is too pricey for your pocket, this is the most appealing alternative, situated about 500m back towards the taxi park. It has clean en-suite rooms, & food & drinks are available, but the rooms can get busy with church guests, so try to book ahead. *Rfr15,000 sgl or dbl.*

THE NYAGATARE ROAD

RWAMAGANA One of several unremarkable small towns in eastern Rwanda, Rwamagana is of interest to travellers primarily as a base from which to explore Lake Muhazi and possibly Akagera National Park, though it does boast a couple of marginally interesting colonial buildings including a large church. The town lies about 60km from Kigali, no more than an hour's drive along a good surfaced road covered by regular minibus-taxis, some of which are 'express' while others also serve villages nearby. In Kigali they leave from the Nyabugogo bus station and call at Remera bus station *en route*. On your return you may also be dropped off at Kigali's central bus station in Avenue du Commerce.

Where to stay

Dereva Hotel (60 rooms) ☎ 0252 567244; m 078 8322228; e derevahotel@yahoo.com; ⊕ S 01°56.831, E 030°26.336, 1,534m. Set in large green grounds alongside the main road, the Dereva

offers what are probably the most commodious lodgings in this part of Rwanda, though it does feel a bit overpriced. The attached restaurant serves large meals in the Rfr3,000–5,000 range; it's a great place to try the traditional groundnut-based stew called *igisafuriga*. The management here can arrange a 4x4 for an Akagera safari for around Rfr50,000, inclusive of driver & fuel but not park entrance fees. *Rfr10,000/20,000 en-suite sgl/dbl with nets & hot showers, Rfr15,000/25,000 for a similar room with DSTV, or Rfr20,000/30,000 for a suite-like apartment.*

⌂ **Bonjour Café** (5 rooms) 📱 078 0372273. Situated a few metres from the main road, this friendly little hotel — basically a converted homestead — is far better value than the Dereva. The large en-suite rooms have a dbl bed, net & hot shower, & meals & drinks are served in the garden. *Rfr10,000 dbl.*

KAYONZA This small, rather scruffy settlement is situated 78km from Kigali, at the junction (✪ S 01°53.975, E 030°30.454) of the main north–south road connecting Kagitumba on the Rwanda border to Rusumo on the Tanzania border. Kayonza is, if anything, even less remarkable than Rwamagana, though once again it serves as a possible base for exploring Lake Muhazi and Akagera National Park and is readily accessible from Kigali on public transport (minibuses leave from Nyabugogo bus station). Volunteers working in Kayonza reckon there is some good walking to be had by heading out of town in the general direction of Akagera National Park.

⌂ **Where to stay**

⌂ **Homeland Hotel** (12 rooms) 📱 078 8673683. This new hotel, situated about 500m from the main junction along the Kigali Rd, is the smartest place to stay in Kayonza, & it could serve as a useful & relatively affordable base for a day visit to Akagera National Park. It has comfortable en-suite rooms with hot showers & writing desk, & a courtyard bar & restaurant serves chilled drinks & hot snacks & meals. *Rfr10,000/15,000/25,000 sgl/dbl/twin.*

LAKE MUHAZI (EASTERN SHORE) In common with most lakes in Rwanda, Muhazi is an erratically shaped body of water whose shores follow the contours of the surrounding hills. Roughly 60km long but nowhere more than 5km wide, Muhazi is a classic 'flooded valley' type of lake, its serpentine shape broken by numerous tendrils stretching northward or southward along former tributaries. It is a pretty spot, not as beautiful perhaps as the lakes around Ruhengeri, but – at least for travellers dependent on public transport – with the added virtue of easy accessibility. The birdlife here is highly rewarding, and the lake harbours an unusually dense population of spotted-necked otter, though no other large mammals are found in the area. The eastern tip of Lake Muhazi lies beside the surfaced Nyagatare road, about 8km north of Kayonza, opposite the turn-off to the small but attractive little town of Gahini, set high above the lake.

⌂ **Where to stay and eat**

⌂ **Seeds of Peace Centre** (25 rooms) 📞 0252 567422; 📱 078 8652792; e gahini@ rwanda1.com; ✪ S 01°50.502, E 030°28.496; 1,460m Run by the Episcopal Church, this pretty lakeshore resort, set opposite the turn-off to Gahini, is intermittently well organised for tourism, offering boating, swimming, birdwatching, a (booze-free) restaurant offering fresh lake fish, camping, a picnic place & 2 reconstructed traditional dwellings. It also has rondawels, each with 2 bedrooms, bathroom, kitchen & lounge, & a new double-storey block with more conventional en-suite hotel rooms. Profits go back into the diocese for its work in the local community. *Rfr12,000/15,000 sgl/dbl B&B, or Rfr20,000 for a 2-bedroom apartment.*

⌂ **Gahini Guest House** 📞 0252 567422; e gahini@rwanda1.com. Also run by the Episcopal Church, this cheaper guesthouse, situated in Gahini itself, lacks the lakeside setting of Seeds of Peace, but you can easily walk down to the lakeshore resort for meals & recreation. *Rfr10,000/15,000 en-suite sgl/dbl; Rfr2,000 for a bunk bed in a capacious dorm.*

✗ **Jambo Pleasure Beach** There's no accommodation at this resort a few hundred metres past Seeds of Peace along the road towards Rwamagana, but the restaurant is generally regarded to be superior, & it does serve beers & other alcoholic drinks. Camping space is available. The karaoke bar here is popular at w/ends.

11

A NEW VERSION OF AN ANCIENT TALE The monarch Ruganzu II Ndori was so great and famous a king that the mountains, rocks and forests of Rwanda were proud when he passed among them. One day, one of the rocks boasted to an eagle flying overhead that the king and his entourage had walked across it that same morning.

'Krarrk!' croaked the eagle in mocking disbelief. 'With my keen eyes I can spot the smallest mouse as it slips into its hole or the thinnest snake coiled in the shadows. Yet I see no sign that the king has passed your way.'

The rock scratched its weather-beaten head and thought deeply. Then it devised a plan. The next time King Ruganzu approached, it softened itself slightly so that his footsteps left an impression on its surface. Now the eagles and the crows and the skimming bee-eaters could see clearly that the king had walked upon the rock.

Word got around, and other rocks soon adopted the same tactic. If you visit Rwanda today, you may still see various traces of Ruganzu's footprints. Then one of the more ambitious rocks thought: 'If I create a jug, and fill it with beer, the monarch can drink his fill when he passes and I will become the chief rock within his kingdom.'

Carefully it formed itself into a jug, and filled that jug with cool, refreshing banana beer, and the king and all his courtiers drank their fill. But then some other rocks nearby saw what was happening and were jealous; they quickly made bigger and better jugs, and filled some of them with sorghum beer too so that the monarch had a choice.

Today, if you visit the old district of Murambi, you can still see half-a-dozen of these jugs, and if you're very lucky you may even catch a fleeting, aromatic scent of ancient beer. The region is called Rubona rwa Nzoga (Rubona of the beer); and the local tradition is that whatever time a guest may arrive at a house, the hosts will always have a jug of beer ready and waiting to quench his thirst.

Of course rocks in several other parts of Rwanda eventually copied the idea and made their own jugs too … but they never matched the quality or quantity of Murambi's beer, which remained the monarch's favourite throughout his reign.

Murambi was incorporated into Kayonza District in 2006. Minibus-taxis go to Kiramuruzi (between Gakenke and Kiziguro on the Akagera National Park map on page 248), from where Rubona rwa Nzoga is about 30 minutes' walk. But don't expect exact replica jugs …

NYAGATARE This scattered but rapidly growing town of around 15,000 souls is the administrative centre of the sizeable but thinly populated Nyagatare District, which extends over the most northeasterly corner of Rwanda to the borders with Uganda and Rwanda. Prior to 2006, Nyagatare was also the capital of the now-defunct Umutara Province, much of which lay within the north of Akagera National Park and the adjacent Mutara Wildlife Reserve before these areas were de-gazetted in 1997 to accommodate returned refugees. Set along the eastern bank of the forest-fringed Muvumba River, Nyagatare must originally have been just outside the boundary of the Mutara Wildlife Reserve. It lies at a relatively low altitude of 1,355m, making it hotter than other parts of Rwanda, and it retains something of a dusty frontier feel, surrounded by rolling hills whose cover of scrubby acacias and tall cactus-like euphorbia trees is far closer in appearance to Akagera than any other settled part of Rwanda.

It would be an act of febrile distortion to describe Nyagatare as any sort of travel magnet. All the same, if you are seeking a wholly un-touristy experience, you could do worse than spend a night or two here. The surrounding area is great walking country – ask for (and take note of) local permission and advice, fill up your water bottle and then just stroll off across fields, plains, hillsides… It's a wonderfully clear, open panorama (unlike in much of the rest of Rwanda with its jutting hills and intensive cultivation), fresh and gently green at moister times of year, parched and tinder dry just before the rainy season. For wildlife enthusiasts, local farmers claim that antelope and zebra often cross the border of Akagera to graze peacefully amongst their cattle, while the riparian woodland along the river as it passes the small town centre offers some potentially rewarding birdwatching. Also, in Nyagatare as in all of Rwanda, you can while time away pleasantly by people-watching and engaging in conversation – thanks to its proximity to Uganda and high population of returned refugees, this is one part of Rwanda where English is far more widely spoken than French.

With its relatively dry climate and infertile soils, this northeastern corner of Rwanda was very thinly settled prior to the gazetting of Akagera in 1935. It remains one of the few parts of the country dominated by pastoralism rather than agriculture: you won't travel far here without coming across herds of cattle – mostly the long-horned Ankole – plodding from clump to clump of bristly scrub. And as one might expect of an area so recently settled, there's a pioneering feel about the hamlets and villages here, which were built (often with foreign funds) to accommodate the returning refugees. Squatting defiantly on the empty plains, these are the houses of a child's pictures: plain and single-storied, with a small square window on either side of the front door. In fact they're dotted all over Rwanda, but the open landscapes here make them more visible.

Getting there and away Nyagatare lies about 175km from Kigali along a (mostly good) surfaced road via Rwamagana and Kayonza. The drive should take up to three hours in a private vehicle, branching left from the main road continuing to the Uganda border about 3km before you reach the town centre. Regular minibus-taxis run to Nyagatare from Kigali, costing Rfr1,500 per person. Most minibus-taxis leave from the Nyabugogo bus station, but if you prefer to leave from the city centre, there's an Atraco Express departure hourly from 07.00 to 16.00, and you can also pick up direct transport from the Remera taxi park on the east side of Kigali. Regular public transport also connects Nyagatare to the Uganda border and Kayonza. The GPS (Blue Sky Hotel) is ✤ S 01°17.340, E 030°19.655.

LAKE MUHAZI GOLF AND COUNTRY CLUB

Thanks to its proximity to Kigali, Lake Muhazi has been earmarked as a focal point of formal tourist development by the government of Eastern Province. Some 2,600ha of adjacent property has been set aside for tourist development, and a 200m conservation buffer zone has been created along the lakeshore. The most ambitious planned development is this golf and country club, construction of which commenced in late 2009. Likely to open before the end of 2010, the club is set on an 80ha stand on the eastern lakeshore about 10km south of the Rwamagana road and less than an hour's drive from Kigali. It will centre on the country's first 18 hole golf course, which will be open to day visitors for a fee, and accommodation will consist of about 50 luxurious guestrooms and suites, all with lake-facing balconies, and five presidential suites with private swimming pools. Other facilities will include a trio of restaurants, a wellness spa, three interlinked indoor and outdoor swimming pools, and a watersport centre. For further details, visit www.eagledevelopers.com or www.easternprovince.gov.rw.

11

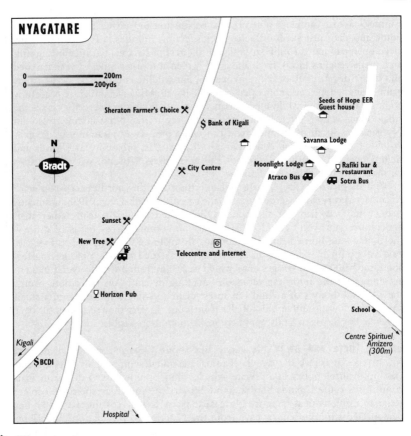

NYAGATARE

0 ━━━━━━ 200m
0 ━━━━━━ 200yds

Sheraton Farmer's Choice ✗

$ Bank of Kigali

Seeds of Hope EER
Guest house 🏠

🏠 Savanna Lodge

N
🏠 Bradt

✗ City Centre

Moonlight Lodge 🏠

Atraco Bus 🚐

♀ Rafiki bar & restaurant

🚐 Sotra Bus

Sunset ✗

New Tree ✗ 🚗

🄴 Telecentre and internet

♀ Horizon Pub

School ●

Centre Spirituel
Amizero
(300m)

Kigali

$ BCDI

Hospital ↘

🏠 Where to stay

🏠 **Blue Sky Hotel** (30 rooms) ☎ 0252 563431; 📱 078 8301914; e b_skyhotel@yahoo.com. This prominent multi-storey hotel stands a block back from the main road. The cheaply fitted rooms feel a touch overpriced for what you get, but they are definitely the smartest option in town. In the evenings the bar is busy with local people & the restaurant serves a good-value buffet or à la carte menu — although b/fast is a touch measly. A swimming pool & open-air bar are planned; other facilities include a sauna & massage room. *Rfr10,000 sgl with ¾ bed & no TV; Rfr15,000/20,000 sgl/dbl with TV.*

🏠 **Centre Spirituel Amizero** (17 rooms) ☎ 0252 565051; 📱 078 8842765. Situated in nice gardens about 1km from the main road & taxi park, this out-of-town Presbyterian resthouse is the best overall value in Nyagatare, but it's not so convenient for those without a private vehicle. The en-suite brick-faced rooms have nets, TV & (usually) hot water, & an inexpensive restaurant serves b/fast for Rfr1,200 & lunch or dinner for Rfr2,400. *Rfr6,000/10,000 sgl/dbl; Rfr2,000 per dorm bed.*

🏠 **Seeds of Hope EER Guesthouse** (20 rooms) ☎ 0252 567422; 📱 078 8468295. Situated in large grounds just around the corner from the Blue Sky, this friendly but rather basic & rundown guesthouse, run by the Episcopal Church, offers the best value in the town centre. The restaurant looks rather forlorn & under-stocked so you are probably better eating elsewhere. *Rfr3,000/6,000 en-suite sgl/twin; Rfr2,000/4,000 sgl/twin with shared bathroom; Rfr8,000 VIP room.*

🏠 **Savanna Lodge** (8 rooms) The pick (just about) of a trio of very basic lodges clustered to the southeast of the Blue Sky, this offers basic accommodation in small sgl rooms with shared facilities. *Rfr3,000.*

✗ Where to eat

The best option is probably the **Blue Sky Hotel**, which serves heaped plates of meat or chicken with the starch of your choice for around

Rfr2,500, and is open for breakfast, lunch and dinner. Otherwise, a good half-dozen eateries are scattered around town, serving the usual lunchtime *mélanges* of meat, rice and vegetables, including the **Sunset**, **New Tree** and winningly named **Sheraton Farmers' Choice Restaurant**.

Other practicalities The tiny main street offers – surprisingly – a photo laboratory, internet café, post office, filling station, dry cleaners, barber, general store and a sign-writer who also sells (rather gaudy) local paintings. There is no forex bureau, so travellers coming from Uganda should change money at the border.

THE RUSUMO ROAD

KIBUNGO (NGOMA) The largest town in the southeast of Rwanda (population 65,000), Kibungo sprawls westward from the main Rusumo Road about 25km south of Kayonza. It is the administrative centre of the recently created Ngoma District, a region suffering not only from the aftermath of the genocide, but also from several debilitating rainfall failures over recent years, so that it has often been dependent on outside food aid. It is a convenient base for the Akagera National Park if you don't fancy paying to stay at the upmarket game lodge or camping in the park itself, and it also forms a possible springboard for a half-day trip to the Rusumo Falls. Otherwise, Kibungo is no more distinguished than other towns in this part of Rwanda, with its main focal point being a small grid of scruffy roads lying 3km west of the altogether more dynamic junction suburb known as Cyasemakamba (or Cyamakamba).

Getting there and away Kibungo lies 100km from Kigali along a good surfaced road, branching southward at the main traffic circle in Kayonza after 75km. The drive should take no more than two hours. Regular minibus-taxis connect Kigali to Kibungo – Atraco has departures from the city centre hourly between 06.45 and 17.45 – and there is also plenty of minibus-taxi transport on to Rusumo. The main taxi park in Kibungo is at Cyasemakamba more or less opposite the Umbrella Pine Hotel [242 D3], but Atraco also has a terminal in the town centre proper [242 B6]. The GPS for Cyasemakamba junction is ✛ S 02°08.091, E 030°33.448 and for the town centre it's ✛ S 02°09.283, E 030°32.778.

Where to stay and eat

🛏 **Motel Umbrella Pine** [242 D3] (8 rooms)
☏ 0252 566269. Situated in Cyasemakamba 200m south of the main traffic circle, this simple but attractive, friendly & hard-working little place has been a reliable bet for some years now. There are shortcomings – dodgy plumbing, water shortages during the dry season – but the staff are so willing that it's worth a try. The rooms have hot water & nets, & the restaurant not only serves good, inventive meals, but can rustle up a picnic if you need it for visiting Akagera. The hotel can be hard to spot, tucked away behind a petrol station on the right coming from Kigali. *Rfr10,000/15,000 en-suite sgl/twin B&B.*

🛏 **Centre St Joseph** [242 C4] (35 rooms)
☏ 0252 566303. Situated 100m from the feeder road to Kibungo, this Catholic-run guesthouse has to rank as the best-value lodging in town. Rooms range from simple sgls using shared toilets &

showers, to large en-suite mini-suites with dbl bed & sitting area, to full apartments, & they are all clean & well maintained. The restaurant has indoor & outdoor seating & it serves good, inexpensive local fare, as well as soft & alcoholic drinks. *Rfr3,000 sgl; Rfr10,000 dbl mini-suite; Rfr15,000 apartment.*

🛏 **Sunset Guesthouse** [242 C4] (6 rooms) ☏ 0252 566767. Also situated alongside the feeder road about 700m from the junction, this low-key guesthouse consists of a converted homestead set in a small quiet garden bar. The en-suite rooms have large beds & are very good value, & the bar serves a limited selection of snacks. *Rfr8,000 dbl.*

🛏 **Garden of Rest Guesthouse** [242 B7] (4 rooms) ☏ 0252 566396; m 078 8467815. This appealing small resthouse is situated in Kibungo proper, 100m downhill from the main surfaced road through town,

11

241

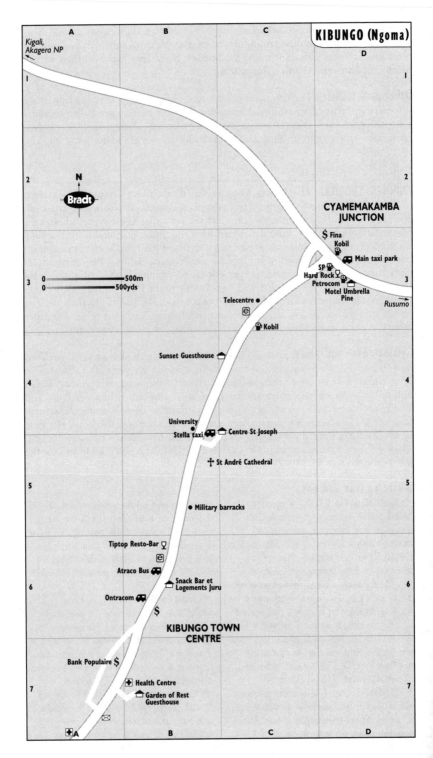

KIBUNGO (Ngoma)

A   B   C   D

Kigali,
Akagera NP

N
Bradt

0 _____ 500m
0 _____ 500yds

CYAMEMAKAMBA
JUNCTION

Fina
Kobil
Main taxi park
SP
Hard Rock
Petrocom
Motel Umbrella
Pine

Rusumo

Telecentre ●
e

Kobil

Sunset Guesthouse

University
Stella taxi   Centre St Joseph

✝ St André Cathedral

● Military barracks

Tiptop Resto-Bar ♀
e
Atraco Bus
Snack Bar et
Logements Juru
Ontracom

$

KIBUNGO TOWN
CENTRE

Bank Populaire $

✚ Health Centre
Garden of Rest
Guesthouse

✚A

& it offers comfortable en-suite accommodation in clean, tiled dbl rooms with netting & en-suite shower. The outdoor bar & restaurant looks good too. *Rfr10,000 dbl.*

Other practicalities There is a post office [242 A7] and small bank [242 B6] on the main road, but no facilities for foreign exchange. The only internet café is at the orange Telecentre [242 C3] about halfway between Cyasemakamba junction and the Sunset Guesthouse. A couple of bars and restaurants are dotted around the junction [242 D3], serving chilled beers, goat kebabs and other local fare – the food isn't comparable to that of the Umbrella Pine, but it is a lot cheaper.

NYAKARAMBI If you are heading to Rusumo, it's definitely worth stopping at this large village, which straddles the road from Kibungo about 20km before the Rusumo border crossing. This part of Rwanda is noted for its distinctive **Imigongo** (cow-dung) 'paintings' – earthy, geometric designs which are mostly used to decorate the interiors of houses. In Nyakarambi, however, a couple of the houses have cow-dung paintings on their outer walls, and about 2km south of the town there's a craft co-operative. This is where most of the geometric paintings and

TRAVELLING FROM KIGALI TO MWANZA (TANZANIA)   *Izzie Robinson*

We managed it in two days, but be warned – the second day is a long day. Also we could have just been lucky…

Getting from Kigali to the Tanzania border at Rusumo Falls involved getting up early and locating a minibus. The journey to Rusumo was not a long one, and it proved to be the last comfortable minibus ride for a long while. We passed through Rwandan immigration, walked across the bridge and up the hill to the Tanzanian post. We hadn't been sure about this border so we had got our visas in advance in Kigali. As it was Tanzanian visas were available there.

Then we looked round for some transport. Nothing! After a little wait, a car pulled up and we negotiated a price with the driver to take us to Ngara. The journey only took a couple of hours, so we were there in good time to find accommodation and buy some fruit from the market. We also tried to get a seat on the Mwanza bus, but it turned out that the bus was broken. A helpful man suggested we buy seats on the Kahama-bound bus and try to get on to Mwanza from there.

We stayed in a cheap little hostel which was clean and pleasant, and we were even offered a wake-up call at 5am. It didn't materialise but it's the thought that counts. We headed off in the dark and managed to get the front two seats next to the driver – a good move for our first experience of Tanzanian minibuses. After cramming in as many people as humanly possible and then some, our bags were then rammed into the back space. We reckon this was the moment when the coffee pot we'd carried all the way from Ethiopia broke into a million pieces!

As dawn broke, we set off at speed, passing small barefoot children shivering on the way to school. We got to Kahama by 11.00 and there we learnt there was no bus to Mwanza, but if we went to Shinyanga we could continue from there. We shrugged and bought a ticket. To get to Shinyanga we travelled on a proper bus as opposed to a minibus, giving us slightly more room.

In Shinyanga we found a bus going to Mwanza (yay!) but it was empty and we ended up sitting miserably in the sun for hours and hours waiting to go. Up to that point the roads had been OK, but the stretch to Mwanza was painfully slow as we crawled in and out of large crater pot-holes. It was after dark by the time we got to Mwanza, where we had to walk around with our bags trying to find a room. But at least we got there.

pottery you see in Kigali originate from, but it's more fun (and cheaper) to buy them at source, especially as the people who run the co-operative aren't at all pushy. The sign outside reads 'Cooperative Kakira – Art "Imigongo"' and shows geometric patterns. A small brochure, sometimes available in the workshop, explains (in more or less these words) the origin of the form in the early 19th century:

> In olden times, there was Kakira, son of Kimenyi, King of Gisaka in Kibungo province (southeastern Rwanda). Kakira invented the art of embellishing houses and making them more attractive. To decorate the inside walls, cow dung was used, in patterns with prominent ridges. Then the surfaces were painted, in red and white colours made from natural soil (white from kaolin, red from natural clay with ochre), or else in shining black made from the sap of the aloe plant – *ikakarubamba* – mixed with the ash of burned banana skins and fruits of the solanum aculeastrum plant. It was the art of mixing together the soil, fire, raw materials from the cow and medicinal art that is the source of this work.

ANKOLE CATTLE

From mountain gorillas to elephants, Rwanda is blessed with its fair share of impressive wild beasts. But it is also a major stronghold for what is unquestionably the most imposing of Africa's domestic creatures: the remarkable long-horned Ankole breed of cattle associated with the pastoralist peoples of the Uganda and Rwanda border areas.

Sometimes referred to as the Cattle of Kings thanks to their association with the royal lineages of Uganda and Rwanda, Ankole cattle come in several colours, ranging from uniform rusty-yellow to blotched black-and-white, but they always have a long head, short neck, deep dewlap and narrow chest, and the male often sports a large thoracic hump. What most distinguishes Ankole cattle from any familiar breed, however, is their preposterous, monstrous horns, which grow out from either side of the head like inverted elephant tusks, and in exceptional instances can reach a length up to 2.5m – dimensions unseen on any Rwandan or Ugandan tusker since the commercial ivory poaching outbreak of the 1980s.

The ancestry of Ankole cattle has been traced back to Eurasia as early as 15000BC, but the precursors of the modern long-horned variety originate in Ethiopia, where the humpless Egyptian longhorn (as depicted on ancient Egyptian pictographs) and humped Asian zebu were crossed about 4,000 years ago to form a long-horned, humped breed known as the Ethiopian sanga. A number of credible oral traditions indicate that the sanga was introduced to northwest Uganda in medieval times, probably as part of the same wave of southward migration from Ethiopia associated with the foundation of the legendary Bacwezi Kingdom in Uganda circa AD1350.

Hardy, and capable of subsisting on limited water and poor grazing, these introduced cattle were ideally suited to local conditions, except that they had no immunity to tsetse-borne diseases, which forced the pastoralists who tended them to keep drifting southward. The outsized horns of the modern cattle are probably a result of selective breeding subsequent to their ancestors' arrival in southern Uganda about 500 years ago, at around the time the Ankole Kingdom was founded near modern-day Mbarara. Although the long horns were bred primarily for aesthetic reasons, the artificial process of breeding might have involved an element of natural selection. When threatened by large predators such as hyena or lion, it is customary for Ankole cattle to form a tight circle with horns facing outward, and it has also been noted how the calf often walks closely in front of its mother, protected by her horns.

Both in Uganda and Rwanda, pastoralists traditionally value cows less for their individual productivity than as status symbols: the wealth of a man would be measured

Kakira's knowledge was disappearing, due to the increasing use of industrial materials (paint); and so a women's association was created to maintain Kakira's work. After the 1994 genocide, most of the women, now widows, restarted their work together. Since 2001, the association has benefited from better promotion. Previously the women made no more than 20 pieces a month; now it is much more as orders have increased. Today, the Kakira Association makes 'Imigongo' art: modelled and painted tiles, panels, tables and other objects.

Working hours are Monday–Saturday, 07.30–12.30 and 14.00–18.00. Kakira products can be ordered from the workshop or via a Fair Trade registered organisation in Butare called Rwanda Arts (✆ 0252 530762; e info@rwanda-art.com; www.rwanda-art.com; ✆ S 02°16.165, E 030°41.812; 1,609m).

RUSUMO FALLS The Rusumo border with Tanzania, 60km southeast of Kibungo (✆ S 02°22.798, E 030°46.999, 1,320m), is also the site of Rwanda's most impressive waterfall. Rusumo Falls isn't particularly tall, and it couldn't be

by the size and quality of his herd, and the worth of an individual cow by its horn size and, to a lesser extent, its coloration. In Rwanda, the noblest cow is the *inyambo*, which has an even deep blackish- or brownish-red hide, large lyre-shaped horns, and long hooves. Other long-horned cows of any coloration are called *ibigarama*, while stockier short-horned cows are referred to as *inkuku* – which may or may not be a pejorative derived from the widespread Bantu word for chicken!

Traditionally, the closely related pastoralist cultures of Rwanda and Uganda were as deeply bound up with a quasi-mystical relationship to cattle as the Maasai are today. Like Eskimos and their physical landscape, this abiding mental preoccupation is reflected in the 30 variations in hide coloration that are recognised linguistically by the Bahima of Ankole, along with at least a dozen peculiarities of horn shape and size. The Bahima day is traditionally divided up into 20 periods, of which all but one of the daylight phases is named after an associated cattle-related activity. And, like the Maasai, Rwandan and Ugandan pastoralists traditionally looked down on any lifestyle based around fishing or agriculture – and they also declined to hunt game for meat, with the exception of buffalo and eland, which were sufficiently bovine in appearance to make for acceptable eating.

In times past, the diet of the pastoralists of Uganda and Rwanda did not, as might be expected, centre on meat, but rather on blood tapped from the vein of a living cow, combined with the relatively meagre yield of milk from the small udders that characterise the Ankole breed. Slaughtering a fertile cow for meat was regarded as akin to cannibalism, but it was customary for infertile cows and surplus bullocks to be killed for meat on special occasions, while the flesh of any cow that died of natural causes would be eaten, or bartered for millet beer and other fresh produce. No part of the cow would go to waste: the hide would be used to make clothing, mats and drums, the dung to plaster huts and dried to light fires, while the horns could be customised as musical instruments.

Today, neither Rwanda nor Ankole is as defiantly traditionalist as, say, Ethiopia's Omo Valley or Maasailand, and most rural Bahima today supplement their herds of livestock by practising mixed agriculture of subsistence and cash crops. But the Ankole cattle and their extraordinary horns, particularly common in eastern Rwanda, pay living tribute to the region's ancestral bovine preoccupations. Meanwhile, on a more prosaic note, this hardy breed – first farmed in the USA in the 1960s, where they are most often called Watusi cattle, a name no longer used in Rwanda – is of growing interest to international stock farmers because its meat has the lowest cholesterol levels of any commercial breed.

A NEW VARIATION ON A TRADITIONAL TALE The great King Gihanga ruled a part of Rwanda in the early 12th century – or perhaps the late tenth. Some historians say that he was the first of the royal dynasty, others claim that many kings preceded him. That's the trouble with oral history – the facts are elusive, and who knows whether or not any of this story is true! Anyway, it's certain that Gihanga had many wives and many children.

One day, his favourite daughter Nyirarucyaba lost her temper with a wife who was not her mother, scratching at the woman's face and tearing her hair until she screamed in pain. To lose control was considered very shameful and all the courtiers had seen what happened, so the king had no choice. He banished Nyirarucyaba, sending her to the deep forest where only wild beasts live. She wept pitifully but he would not yield, although his heart was torn.

After many days alone, the girl heard a rustling in the leaves and a snapping of branches – and crouched to the ground in fear. But it was a young man who had, like her, been cast into exile. Now, together, they began to contact the animals around them. There was one that seemed friendly, despite its great size and ugly voice. By day it munched the forest grasses and by night they kept warm against its soft hide.

In time it gave birth to a young one, with wet matted skin and shaky legs, which nuzzled under its mother and sucked at her teats. They saw that it drank a white liquid and learnt that it was milk. Now they had food indeed! They shared the milk with the calf and grew strong and healthy. In time they bore children of their own and the cow had many more calves.

Meanwhile the king had fallen sick with an illness that robbed him of all strength and joy. Doctors could find no cure. Finally three of the court's wisest men, so old that their hair was white and thin upon their heads, recognised it as grief, and took it upon themselves to speak. They told him Nyirarucyaba was still alive – and at once he sprang from his couch and dispatched hunters to the forest to search for her. They found her beside a stream, her children at her side and many cattle grazing nearby. Her return to her delighted father was a time of great celebration at the court.

The cattle came too, with their rich supply of milk. The courtiers gained a taste for it, and grew fat and strong. There was great competition to own the calves, which the king presented to courtiers who had served him particularly well. Needless to say, the families of his three old advisers were given the pick of the herd. As the years and the generations passed, the people could no longer remember a time when the kingdom had been empty of cattle. And that is how it still is, in Rwanda today…

mentioned in the same breath as the Victoria or Blue Nile Falls, but it is a voluminous rush of white water nevertheless, as the Akagera River surges below the bridge between the two border posts. The Rwandan officials don't appear to have any objection to tourists wandering into No Man's Land and on to the bridge to goggle at the spectacle, though they may or may not ask to see a passport first. At present you can photograph the falls from the bridge, but nothing else in the immediate vicinity. It's best to ask permission anyway.

It's here at Rusumo that the German Count von Götzen, later to become Governor of German East Africa, entered Rwanda in 1894. He then travelled across the country to Lake Kivu, visiting the Mwami at Nyanza *en route*. Later, in 1916, when the Belgians were preparing to wrest the territory from the Germans,

Belgian troops dug a trench and mounted artillery at the spot where one can see the falls today, in order to dislodge the German troops ensconced on the other bank who were guarding the only negotiable crossing. More recently, in 1994, Rusumo Bridge served as the funnel through which an estimated 500,000 Rwandans – half of them within one 24-hour period – fled from their home country to refugee camps around Ngala and elsewhere in northwest Tanzania. Journalists reporting on the exodus described standing on the bridge and counting the bloated bodies of genocide victims tumbling over the waterfall at a rate of one or two per minute.

Practicalities So far as travel practicalities go, the surfaced road between Kibungo and Rusumo is in reasonable condition, and can be covered in an hour. Regular minibus-taxis service the route. About 200m back from the Rusumo border, the basic **Amarembo Hotel** (m *078 3234911*) has a total of 11 double rooms at Rfr4,000, a decent restaurant serving a tasty buffet lunch and dinner, and a great balcony offering a view across the facing rooftops to the Akagera River and surrounding papyrus beds. It gets busy with cross-border traffic. There's also an 'Amarembo Taxi Express' running between the hotel and Kigali: Rfr2,100 one way.

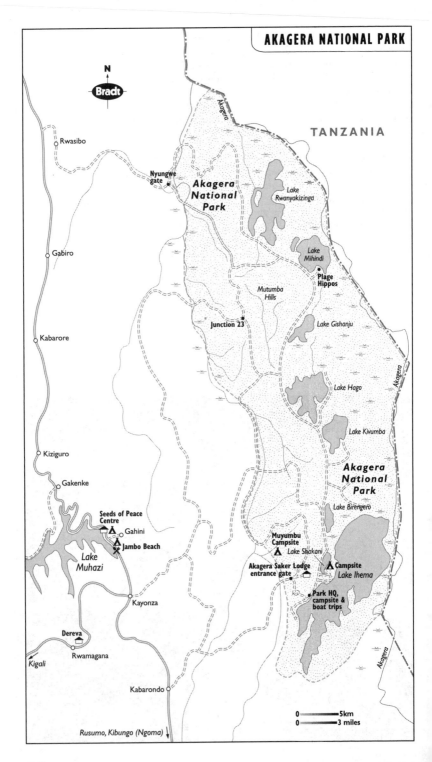

AKAGERA NATIONAL PARK

N

Bradt

Rwasibo

Gabiro

Kabarore

Kiziguro

Gakenke

Seeds of Peace
Centre

Gahini

Jambo Beach

Lake
Muhazi

Kayonza

Dereva

Rwamagana

Kigali

Kabarondo

Rusumo, Kibungo (Ngoma)

TANZANIA

Akagera

Nyungwe
gate

Akagera
National
Park

Lake
Rwanyakizinga

Lake
Mihindi

Plage
Hippos

Mutumba
Hills

Lake Gishanju

Junction 23

Lake Hago

Akagera

Lake Kivumba

Akagera
National
Park

Lake Birengero

Muyumbu
Campsite

Lake Shakani

Akagera Saker Lodge
entrance gate

Campsite
Lake Ihema

Park HQ,
campsite &
boat trips

Akagera

0   5km
0   3 miles

12

Akagera National Park

Named after the river that runs along its eastern boundary, Akagera National Park is Rwanda's answer to the famous savanna reserves of Kenya, Tanzania and the like. In contrast to the rest of the country, the area is relatively warm and low-lying, and its undulating plains support a cover of dense, broad-leafed woodland interspersed with lighter acacia woodland and patches of rolling grassland studded evocatively with stands of the superficially cactus-like *Euphorbia candelabra* shrub. To the west of the plains lies a chain of low mountains, reaching elevations of between 1,600m and 1,800m. The eastern part of the park supports an extensive wetland: a complex of a dozen lakes linked by extensive papyrus swamps and winding water channels fed by the mighty Akagera (sometimes called Kagera) River.

In terms of game-viewing, it would be misleading to compare Akagera to East Africa's finest savanna reserves. Poaching has greatly reduced wildlife populations in recent years, and what was formerly the north of the park has been settled by returned refugees. The intense human pressure on Akagera is reflected in the fact that much of the northern and western territory (together with the adjoining 300km² Mutara Wildlife Reserve) was de-gazetted in 1997, reducing its total area by almost two-thirds from around 2,500km² to 1,085km². Even after this concession to local land requirements, the lakes that remain within the national park are routinely used to water domestic cattle – indeed, the long-horned Ankole cow is far and away the most commonly seen large mammal in Akagera.

For all that, Akagera is emphatically worth visiting. There are plenty of animals around, with the likes of buffalo, elephant, zebra, giraffe, hippo and various antelope all reasonably visible, and they aren't as skittish as one might expect. The lakes support some of the highest concentrations of hippo you'll find anywhere in Africa, as well as numerous large crocodiles, while lion and leopard are still present in small numbers, and there are plans to restock the park with black rhinos after the last one died in 2006. What's more, the birdlife is phenomenal – the checklist of 550 species includes the sort of rarities that will have ardent birdwatchers in raptures, alongside a surprising density of raptors and some of Africa's most impressive concentrations of big waterbirds.

As big an attraction as the animal life is the sensation of being in a genuinely off-the-beaten-track chunk of bush: this is one African game reserve where you can still drive for hours without passing another vehicle, never knowing what wildlife encounter might lie around the next corner. Akagera is also among the most scenic of savanna reserves, with its sumptuous forest-fringed lakes, tall mountains and constantly changing vegetation.

Akagera is a good game reserve. It could, with improved management and a bit of time, once again become a truly great one. Equally, it could well be that Akagera will simply not be able to withstand the clamour for land from outside its already reduced boundaries. Which way it goes, one senses, will depend largely on its ability to generate serious tourist dollars and employment opportunities in a country whose population is doubling every 20 years. The pressure on Akagera will only increase with time; yet in the context of this rapid population growth, forsaking a vast tract of not particularly arable game reserve to grazing will not address the heart of the land issue but merely alleviate a short-term problem.

The survival of Akagera is not simply an esoteric conservation concern, but one that has implications for the country's development as a whole. Prior to 1994, Rwanda's fledgling tourist industry was one of its three main sources of foreign revenue. To a large extent, Rwanda has rebuilt that industry over the past few years, but it now consists mainly of pit-stop or cross-border gorilla tracking by tourists who spend one or two nights in one small part of the country as an extension of a safari elsewhere in East Africa. If the country is to develop a self-contained countrywide tourist circuit, then it desperately needs a savanna reserve to make it work.

The good news is that, after years of marginalisation, Akagera finally looks set to realise its potential as a safari destination and one of the lynchpins of Rwanda's tourist circuit. The neglected and once poorly managed Akagera Safari Lodge has been bought by Dubai World, and is to be managed as part of the Mantis Collection, a highly regarded South African conservation portfolio whose five-star properties include the legendary Shamwari Game Reserve. The lodge will be staffed with experienced trained rangers to take guided game drives in open 4x4 vehicles, and there is also talk of building a couple of satellite tented camps on the lakes.

Furthermore, plans exist to fence the reserve in its entirety, which will help keep out cattle and poachers, and to implement an extensive restocking program to ensure that the Big Five are all present in significant numbers. This process is scheduled to start towards the end of 2009, and will be implemented as part of a new collaborative wildlife management plan involving Mantis's wildlife department and their government counterparts.

NATURAL HISTORY

Akagera is notable for protecting an unusually wide diversity of habitats within a relatively small area. Prior to the civil war, it was regarded as one of the few African

AKAGERA'S HISTORY

The Belgian colonisers were concerned about nature conservation. From 1920 onwards (and earlier, in the Congo) conservation measures were put into practice and became the object of various legislative and administrative decrees. It was the decree of 26 November 1934 that created the Parc National de la Kagera, on about 250,000ha. The park included – which was extremely rare before 1960 – a Strict Natural Reserve and an adjoining area where certain human activities were tolerated. It came under the jurisdiction of the Institut des Parcs Nationaux du Congo Belge et du Ruanda-Urundi, which was also responsible for the three parks (Albert, Garamba and Upemba) in the Belgian Congo. (In fact 8% of the Albert Park was also in Rwanda; now representing the Volcanoes Park in the northwest.) Kagera was renamed Akagera after independence, when the new Republic's leaders announced their intention of maintaining the park (and the Volcanoes Park) despite population pressure. Akagera's borders were altered – a few thousand hectares were retroceded to local communities while almost 20,000ha of the lacustrine zone to the south were incorporated. In 1975, 26 elephants were transported, first by helicopter and then by truck, from Bugesera, which was to be developed for agriculture. In November 1984, Rwanda held an official celebration of the park's 50th anniversary.

The villages of Humure and Ramiro lie on the inhospitably dry plains south of Akagera National Park, some 40 minutes' drive from the main entrance gate. The villages were created to accommodate repatriated Rwandans who were thrown out of neighbouring Tanzania, where they had long lived as refugees, in November 2006. Some 220 houses have been built here with funding from the German government, and another 150 are in the pipeline. Organised tours to the well-organised village of Humure can be arranged through New Dawn Associates (m 078 8513652; www.newdawnassociates.com), either as a stand-alone activity or in combination with a safari to Akagera, and include visits to milk, honey and batik co-operatives, a theatrical introduction to the problems faced by refugee communities, and dancing and local cooking. Visitors are invited to participate in several activities, and home stays will become available soon. Rates range from US$50 to US$80 per person, depending on group size (minimum three) and 70% of this goes straight to the community.

savanna reserves to form a self-sustaining ecological unit, meaning that its resident large mammals had no need to migrate seasonally outside of the park boundaries. Whether that is still the case today is an open question: roughly two-thirds of the original park was de-gazetted in 1997, and, while some of this discarded territory is still virgin bush, it is probably only a matter of time before it will all be settled, putting further pressure on Akagera's diminished wildlife populations.

The modern boundaries of the park protect an area of 1,085km², stretching along the Tanzania border for approximately 60km from north to south, and nowhere wider than 30km. The eastern third of the park consists of an extensive network of wetlands, fed by the Akagera River, and dominated by a series of small-to-medium-sized lakes. Lake Ihema, the most southerly of the lakes to lie within the revised park boundaries, is also the largest body of open water, covering about 100km². The lakes are connected by narrow channels of flowing water and large expanses of seasonal and perennial papyrus swamps. The eastern wetlands are undoubtedly the most important of the habitats protected within the park: not only do they provide a permanent source of drinking water for the large mammals, they also form an important waterbird sanctuary while harbouring a number of localised swamp dwellers.

Akagera's dominant terrestrial habitat is dense broad-leafed woodland, though pockets of acacia woodland also exist within the park, while some of the lake fringes support a thin belt of lush riparian woodland. Ecologically, the savanna of Akagera is in several respects unique, a product of its isolation from similar habitats by the wetlands to the east and mountainous highlands of central Rwanda to the west. The flora shows strong affinities with the semi-arid zones of northern Uganda and Kenya, but the fauna is more typical of the Mara–Serengeti ecosystem east of Lake Victoria. Akagera's geographical isolation from similar habitats is emphasised by the natural absence of widespread plains animals such as rhino and giraffe, both of which were subsequently introduced and thrived in their adopted home (though rhino are no longer present). Much of the bush in Akagera is very dense, but there are also areas of light acacia woodland and open grassland, notably on the Mutumba Hills and to the northeast of Lake Rwanyakizinga.

MAMMALS While Akagera's considerable scenic qualities and superb birdlife are largely unaffected by the recent years of turmoil, the large mammal populations have suffered badly at the hands of poachers. Having said that, I am always pleasantly surprised at how much wildlife does remain. It is the classic 'bad news, good news' scenario. The populations of all large mammals (except perhaps hippo) are severely depleted in comparison with the pre-1994 levels, while a few high-profile species, if not already locally extinct, appear to be heading that way. The good news, however, is that most large mammals are still sufficiently numerous to form a viable breeding population; furthermore, with adequate protection, these numbers are likely to be supplemented by animals crossing into the park from unprotected parts of neighbouring Tanzania which still support plenty of big game. Akagera, in short, is a damaged but salvageable game reserve.

Extirpated species include the **African wild dog**, probably a victim not of poaching but, in common with many other African reserves, of a canine plague which would have been introduced into the population through contact with domestic dogs. Of the larger predators, **spotted hyena** and **leopard** are still around, but infrequently observed (though you might well come across hyena spoor, particularly the characteristic white dung).

The future of the park's **lion** hangs in the balance. Prior to 1994, the park supported an estimated 250 individuals, including a couple of prides that were uniquely adapted to foraging in the swamps, and others specialised in climbing

ANTELOPE OF AKAGERA

The 11 antelope species in Akagera range from the eland, the world's largest antelope, through to the diminutive common duiker. The most common, however, is the **impala** *Aepeceros melampus*, a slim handsome antelope which bears a superficial similarity to the gazelles, but belongs to a separate family. Chestnut in colour, the impala has diagnostic black and white stripes running down its rump and tail, and the male has large lyre-shaped horns. It is one of the most widespread antelope species in East and southern Africa, normally seen in large herds in woodland habitats, and common in the woodland around and between the lakes of Akagera.

The **Defassa waterbuck** *Kobus ellipsiprymnus defassa* is a large, shaggy brown antelope with a distinctive white rump. The male has large lyre-shaped horns, thicker than those of the impala. The waterbuck inhabits practically any type of woodland or grassland provided that it is close to water, and it is probably the most common large antelope after impala in the far south of Akagera.

Very common in the north of the park and in the Mutumba Hills, the **topi** or **tsessebe** *Damaliscus lunatus* is a large, slender dark-brown antelope with striking yellow lower legs. It has a rather ungainly appearance, reminiscent of the hartebeest and wildebeest, to which it is closely related, and is often seen using an anthill as a sentry point. Oddly, the herds of topi in northern Akagera seem to be far larger than those found in the Serengeti ecosystem.

Similar in size to a topi, but far more handsome, the **roan antelope** *Hippotragus equinus* has, as the Latin name suggests, a horse-like bearing. The uniform fawn-grey coat is offset by a pale belly, and it has short decurved horns and a light mane. After the civil war, roan were thought to be very rare in Akagera (a 1998 estimate puts their number at below 20) but they are now on the recovery, with some sources placing the population at around 150.

Much larger still is the **common** or **Cape eland** *Taurotragus oryx*, which attains a height of up to 1.75m and can weigh as much as 900kg. The common eland is light-brown in colour, with faint white vertical stripes, and a somewhat bovine appearance accentuated by the relatively short horns and large dewlap. In Akagera, small herds are most likely to be seen on the open grassland of the Mutumba Hills, where the population is thought to exceed 50.

trees. During the civil war, large numbers of lion were hunted out by the army to protect the presidential cattle herds; more recently they have been poisoned by cattle herders living outside the park. The situation today is open to conjecture. After a few years without any confirmed sightings, a female with three cubs was observed in the north of the park in the year 2000. More recent published estimates have placed the population at anywhere from 15 to 60 individuals, but local sources are less optimistic, placing the total number of resident lions at fewer than 10. That said, given the tenacity of this regal feline, and its tendency to wander long distances, it is one species that could naturally replenish itself through individuals crossing over from Tanzania once the park is fenced.

Smaller predators are well represented. Most likely to be encountered by day are dwarf, banded and black-tailed **mongoose**, while at night there is a chance of coming across viverrids such as the lithe, heavily spotted and somewhat cat-like **genet**, and the bulkier black-masked **civet**. Also present, but rarely seen, are the handsome spotted **serval cat** and the dog-like **side-striped jackal**.

One of the most common terrestrial mammals is the **buffalo** and, while the population is nowhere near the estimated 8,000 that roamed the park in the 1980s, it is probably still measurable in thousands. **Hippo**, too, are present in impressive

A trio of smaller antelope are also mainly confined to the Mutumba Hills. The largest of these is the **Bohor reedbuck** Redunca redunca, a light-fawn animal with moderately sized rounded horns; reedbucks are almost always seen in pairs, and in Akagera are rather skittish.

The smaller **oribi** Ourebia ourebi is a tan grassland antelope with short straight horns and a small but clearly visible circular black glandular patch below its ear. It is the commonest antelope on the Mutumba Hills, typically seen in parties of two or three, and has a distinctive sneezing alarm call.

The **klipspringer** Oreotragus oreotragus is a goat-like antelope, normally seen in pairs, and easily identified by its dark, bristly grey-yellow coat, slightly speckled appearance and unique habitat preference. Klipspringer means 'rock jumper' in Afrikaans and it is an apt name for an antelope which occurs exclusively in mountainous areas and rocky outcrops. It is often seen from the road between the entrance gate and Lake Ihema.

The only small antelope found in thicker bush is the **common duiker** Sylvicapra grimmia, an anomalous savanna representative of a family of 20-plus small hunchbacked antelopes associated with true forests. Generally grey in colour, the common duiker has a distinctive black tuft of hair sticking up between its small straight horns. It is common in all bush areas, though it tends to be very skittish.

A widespread resident of thick woodland and forest, the pretty **bushbuck** Tragelaphus scriptus is a medium-sized, rather deer-like antelope. The male is dark brown or chestnut, while the much smaller female is generally pale red-brown. The male has relatively small, straight horns, while both sexes have pale throat patches, white spots and sometimes stripes. The bushbuck tends to be secretive, but might be seen anywhere in Akagera except for open grassland.

Similar in appearance to the bushbuck, and a close relation, the semi-aquatic **sitatunga** Tragelaphus spekei is a widespread but infrequently observed inhabitant of west and central African swamps. The male, with a shoulder height of up to 125cm (much taller than a bushbuck) and a shaggy fawn coat, is unmistakable, while the smaller female might be mistaken for a bushbuck except for its more clearly defined stripes. The status of the sitatunga within Akagera is uncertain; it is certainly still present, but mostly restricted to inaccessible swampy areas.

12

numbers: on some of the lakes there must be at least a dozen pods of up to 50 animals, and the total population probably exceeds 1,000. The handsome **impala** is probably the most common and habitat-tolerant large mammal in the park, and of the 11 antelope species which occur in Akagera (see box *Antelope of Akagera* on pages 252–3), only the aquatic **sitatunga** is immediately endangered and unlikely to be seen by visitors. Small herds of **Burchell's zebra** are regularly encountered in open areas.

Also very common are three savanna primates: the dark, heavily built **olive baboon** (boldly resident around the safari lodge), the smaller and more agile **vervet monkey**, and the tiny wide-eyed **bushbaby** (the latter a nocturnal species likely to be seen only after dusk). The forest-dwelling **silver monkey**, although listed for Akagera, is probably now very rare, due to habitat loss following the reduction in the park's area, although Callan Cohen of Birding Africa reported a sighting in the trees where Lakes Ihema and Birengero meet in July 2009. For the same reason, it is debatable whether Africa's largest swine, the **giant forest hog**, still occurs in Akagera. The smaller **bushpig**, a secretive nocturnal species, is present but rarely encountered, while the diurnal **warthog** is very common and often seen trotting off in family parties, stiff tail held high.

Two large mammal species that don't occur there naturally were introduced to the park prior to the civil war. The first of these is the **Maasai giraffe**, which was introduced from the Magadi region of southern Kenya in January 1986. The original herd of two males and four females produced its first offspring in 1988 and has since multiplied to a population of around 60 head, which tends to stick to patches of acacia woodland close to the park headquarters and safari lodge.

In 1957, Akagera became the recipient of Africa's first **black rhino** translocation, when a herd comprising five females and one male was flown across from the bordering Karagwe region of Tanzania, to be supplemented by another male a year later. The rhino prospered in the dense bush and by the early 1970s had colonised most of the park – one individual is known to have strayed south almost as far as the Rusumo Falls – and by the end of that decade the population comfortably exceeded the half-century mark. Then came the wholesale rhino poaching of the 1980s: by the end of that decade no more than a dozen individuals survived, and it was long thought that the remainder were shot in the civil war. The occasional unverified rhino sighting was reported by visitors in the years that followed, but it was only in early 2004 that veterinary surgeon Claudia Schoene was able to confirm the presence of a nine-year old female she named Patricia in the north. Patricia died in July 2006, probably of natural causes, but plans are under way for fresh rhino stock to be translocated from South Africa.

Although the **African elephant** used to occur naturally in Akagera, the last recorded sighting of the original population was on the shores of Lake Mihindi in 1961. The present-day herd is descended from a group of 26 youngsters that was translocated to Akagera in 1975, part of an operation to clear all the elephants from the increasingly densely populated Bugesera Plains to the south of Kigali. Up to 100 adult elephants were shot in the process, while the young American filmmaker Lee Lyon was killed by one of the survivors upon its release into Akagera. By the late 1980s an estimated 45 individuals roamed Akagera and, although population growth was stunted by poaching during the civil war, the current population of around 80 is probably the largest the park has supported in 50 years.

BIRDS Akagera is, after Nyungwe, the most important ornithological site in Rwanda, with a checklist of 550 species recorded before its area was reduced in 1997 (now probably closer to 525 species). What's more, these two fine birding destinations complement each other to such an extent that very few birds recorded in Rwanda aren't found at one or other site. In addition to being the best place in Rwanda to see a good selection of savanna birds and raptors, Akagera is as rich in waterbirds as anywhere in East Africa, and one of the few places where papyrus endemics can be observed.

Among the more colourful and common of the savanna birds are the gorgeous lilac-breasted roller, black-headed gonolek (easily picked up by its jarring duets), little bee-eater, Heuglin's robin-chat, Meyer's parrot, spot-flanked barbet and double-toothed barbet. Less colourful, but very impressive, are the comical grey hornbill and noisy bare-faced go-away bird. The riparian woodland around the lakes hosts a number of specialised species, of which Ross's turaco, a bright-purple, jay-sized bird with a distinctive yellow mask, is the most striking.

A notable feature of Akagera's avifauna is the presence of species such as the crested barbet, Arnot's (white-headed black) chat and Souza's shrike, all of which are associated with the *brachystegia* woodland of southern Tanzania and further south, but have colonised the mixed woodland of Akagera at the northernmost extent of their range. More noteworthy still, the red-faced barbet, a localised endemic of savannas between Lake Victoria and the Albertine Rift, is quite easily seen in Akagera (indeed, a pair was recently seen nesting in the dead branch of a ficus tree at the entrance to the car park at Akagera Safari Lodge). A localised species associated with broken grassland in Akagera is the long-tailed cistocola.

Finally, the savanna of Akagera is one of the last places in Rwanda where a wide range of large raptors is resident: white-backed and Rüppell's griffon vultures soar high on the thermals, the beautiful bateleur eagle can be recognised by its wavering flight pattern and red wing markings, while brown snake eagles and hooded vultures are often seen perching on bare branches.

Most of the savanna birds are primarily of interest to the dedicated birder, but it is difficult to imagine that anybody would be unmoved by the immense concentrations of water-associated birds that can be found on the lakes. Pelicans are common, as is the garishly decorated crowned crane, the odd little open-bill stork and the much larger and singularly grotesque marabou stork. Herons and egrets are particularly visible and well-represented, ranging from the immense goliath heron to the secretive black-capped night heron and reed-dwelling purple heron. The lakes also support a variety of smaller kingfishers and shorebirds, and a prodigious number of fish eagles, whose shrill duet ranks as one of the most evocative sounds of Africa.

On a more esoteric note, the papyrus swamps are an excellent place to look for a handful of birds restricted to this specific habitat: the stunning and highly vocal papyrus gonolek, as well as the more secretive and nondescript Caruthers's cisticola and white-winged warbler. Akagera is also one of the best places in Africa to see the shoebill, an enormous and unmistakable slate-grey swamp-dweller whose outsized bill is fixed in a permanent Cheshire-cat smirk (see box on page 256). A useful birding report on Akagera can be sourced online at www.worldtwitch.com/rwanda_uganda_des.htm.

REPTILES The **Nile crocodile**, the world's largest reptile and a survivor from the age of the dinosaurs, is abundant in the lakes. Some of the largest wild specimens you'll encounter anywhere are to be found sunning themselves on the mud-banks of Akagera, their impressive mouths wide open until they slither menacingly into the water at the approach of human intruders. Not unlike a miniature crocodile in appearance, the **water monitor** is a type of lizard which often grows to be more than a metre long and is common around the lakes, tending to crash noisily into the bush or water when disturbed. Smaller lizards are to be seen all over, notably the colourful rock agama, and a variety of snakes are present but, as ever, very secretive.

DANGEROUS ANIMALS Although it is technically forbidden to leave your vehicle except at designated lookout points, the guides in Akagera seem to enforce this rule somewhat whimsically, so it is worth emphasising the folly of disembarking from your vehicle in the presence of elephant, buffalo or lion.

Hippo and crocodile are potentially dangerous, and claim far more human lives than any terrestrial African animal. For this reason, you should be reasonably cautious when you leave the car next to a lake, particularly at dusk or dawn or in overcast conditions, when hippos are most likely to come out of the water to graze. The danger with hippos is getting *between* them and the water; you have nothing to worry about when they are actually in the water. Special caution should be exercised if you camp next to a lake – don't wander too far from your site after dark, and take a good look around should you need to leave your tent during the night (if there are hippo close by, you'll almost certainly hear them chomping at the grass). Crocs are a real threat only if you are daft enough to wade into one of the lakes.

The most dangerous animal in Akagera is the malaria-carrying anopheles mosquito. Cover up after dark – long trousers and thick socks – and smear any exposed parts of your body with insect repellent. Many tents come with built-in mosquito netting. This will protect you when you sleep, provided that you don't hang a light at the entrance to your tent, which will ensure that a swarm of insects enter it with you. Incidentally, never leave any food in your tent: fruit might

the shoebill has occasionally been observed hunting co-operatively in small flocks, which splash about flapping their wings to drive a school of fish into a confined area.

Although the shoebill is an elusive bird, this is less a function of scarcity than of the inaccessibility of its swampy haunts. Nevertheless, *BirdLife International* recently classified it as near-globally threatened, and it is classed as CITES Appendix 2, which means that trade in shoebills, or their capture for any harmful activity, is forbidden by international law. Estimates of the global population vary wildly. In the 1970s, only 1,500 shoebills were thought to persist in the wild, but this estimate has subsequently been revised to 10,000–15,000 individuals concentrated in five countries – Sudan, Uganda, Tanzania, Congo and Zambia. Small breeding populations also occur in Rwanda and Ethiopia, and vagrants have been recorded in Malawi and Kenya.

The most important shoebill stronghold is the Sudd Floodplain on the Sudanese Nile, where 6,400 individuals were counted during an aerial survey undertaken over 1979–82, followed by the inaccessible Moyowosi-Kigosi Swamp in western Tanzania, whose population was thought to amount to a few hundred prior to a 1990 survey that estimated it to be greater than 2,000. Ironically, although Uganda is the easiest place to see the shoebill in the wild, the national population probably amounts to fewer than 1,000 birds.

Outside of Uganda, Akagera National Park is potentially one of the most accessible shoebill haunts anywhere in Africa. In the 1980s, the local shoebill population was estimated at around 15–20 pairs, and there is no particular reason to think this has changed greatly in the interim – shoebills are not hunted as food, they pose no threat to cattle herders, and the inaccessible swamps they inhabit were largely unaffected by the 1997 reduction in Akagera's area. Certainly, at least one pair is resident in the papyrus beds fringing the eastern shore of Lake Birengero, and they are regularly seen by visitors, though lack of road access means you need decent binoculars to pick them out from the distant western shore. We have also had unverified reports of sightings on Lake Ihema. That aside, little effort has been made to establish the current status of shoebills in Akagera, or to make the bird's habitat accessible to tourists by boat.

The major threat to the survival of the shoebill is habitat destruction. The construction of several dams along the lower Nile means that the water levels of the Sudd are open to artificial manipulation. Elsewhere, swamp clearance and rice farming pose a localised threat to suitable wetland habitats. Lake Opeta, an important shoebill stronghold in eastern Uganda, has been earmarked as a source of irrigation for a new agricultural scheme. A lesser concern in some areas is that shoebills are hunted for food or illegal trade, while in others local fishermen often kill the shoebills in the belief that seeing one before a fishing expedition is a bad omen. As is so often the case, tourism can play a major role in preserving the shoebill and its habitat: a classic example being Uganda's Mabamba Swamp, where the local community has already seen financial benefits from ornithological visits from nearby Entebbe.

attract the attention of monkeys and elephants, while meat could arouse the interest of large predators.

Not so much a danger as a nuisance are tsetse flies, which are quite common in dense bush and can give a painful bite. Fortunately, the pain isn't enduring (though people who tend to react badly to insect bites might want to douse any tsetse bite in antihistamine cream) and there is no risk of contracting sleeping sickness during a short stay in Akagera. Insect repellents have little effect on these robust little creatures, but it's worth noting that they are attracted to dark clothing (especially blue).

FURTHER INFORMATION An accurate useful fold-out colour map is sold at the ORTPN office in Kigali, as well as at the gate. The numbered junctions shown on the map help with navigation, though not all junctions are still numbered on the ground. Also for sale at the gate, the coffee-table book *Akagera: Land of Water, Grass and Fire* by Jean-Pierre Vande Weghe, first published in 1990 and subsequently reprinted but never updated, presents an alluring picture of Akagera as it must once have been – it's historically fascinating, but likely to create false expectations of a visit to the park today, and is ultimately a rather depressing testament to human destructivity.

GETTING THERE AND AWAY

The main gate to Akagera lies in the south of the park about 500m from the new Akagera Safari Lodge. It is reached via a 27km dirt road that branches east from the main surfaced road between Kigali and Rusumo at Kabarondo, about 15km north of Kibungo. This dirt road is in fair condition, and should be passable in any vehicle except perhaps after heavy rain, when 4x4 may be necessary (in any case, 4x4 is advisable for roads within the park, though any vehicle with good clearance should be OK in the dry season). In a private vehicle, the main gate is about two hours' drive from Kigali, or one hour from Kibungo or Rwamagana.

In the north of the park, an alternative entry point, Nyungwe Gate (not to be confused with the eponymous national park on the other side of the country), is accessible on a rough dirt track that branches east from the Kigali–Nyagatare road at the village of Kizarakome about 70km north of Rwamagana. This route requires a 4x4 and it may be impassable after rain. For those heading to Akagera Safari Lodge, it is a far longer drive than the one via the main gate, but it does allow you to explore the park from north to south in one go. Driving without stops, bank on five hours from Kigali to the lodge via Nyungwe Gate, and allow the best part of a day to make a game drive of the section within the national park.

Reaching Akagera on public transport is problematic. Any minibus-taxi travelling between Kayonza and Kibungo can drop you at the junction, from where the only realistic option is a motorbike-taxi (assuming that you can find one). Inside the park, unless you're staying at the safari lodge, no walking is permitted with or without a guide, and no vehicle is available for game drives. A good place to arrange relatively affordable 4x4 hire for a day safari is the Dereva Hotel in Rwamagana (see page 236).

PARK FEES

The fee structure for Akagera is rather confusing so bear with us! First up, a one-off entrance fee of US$10 (non-residents), US$5 (foreign residents) or Rfr1,000 (Rwandans) is charged to all visitors and covers the full duration of their stay. In addition, the park levies a one-off vehicle fee of Rfr2,000–4,000 (locally registered vehicles) or US$10–25 (foreign registered vehicles), depending on the size and type of vehicle, with the highest fees applying to trucks and buses. To this must be added a game-viewing fee of US$20/30/50 (non-residents), US$15/20/25 (foreign residents) or Rfr2,500/3,000/5,000 (Rwandans) for one/two/three days. Note that this fee is charged per calendar day (as opposed to per 24 hours, so you pay for two days if you do an afternoon and morning game drive either side of an overnight stay) but visits of longer than three days are treated as a three-day visit (in other words, you pay nothing more to stay on for a fourth day or longer). No fees are levied simply for staying at the safari lodge. Regular visitors can buy annual permits – for foreigners these cost US$60 (one person), US$100 (couple), US$150 (family).

WHERE TO STAY

Akagera Safari lodge (24 rooms) \ 0252 504330; m 078 8351000; www.akagerasafarilodge.com; ✪ S 01°52.314, E 030°42.911, 1,610m. Re-opened in 2003 on the site of the former Akagera Hotel, this smart lodge lies in wooded hilltop grounds that host a rich bird life & offer superb views over Lake Ihema into the hills of Tanzania. It has changed hands several times since it reopened, but was bought by Dubai World in 2008 & is now under the management of the Mantis Collection. As things stand, the lodge is dated somewhat by the rather monolithic & angular 1970s architecture, but it is otherwise very pleasantly decorated & the en-suite twin or dbl rooms are very comfortable & presentable. Facilities include a good & surprisingly affordable à la carte restaurant, a swimming pool, conference facilities & tennis courts, & the overall level of service is impressively professional given the remote locale. For those wanting to do an early-morning game drive (recommended), the filling b/fast normally starts at 06.00 & can be served at 05.30 by request. Major renovations under the new management regime will upgrade the lodge to 4-star level & are likely to be completed by mid-2010. This will include the creation of much larger suites comprising 2 of the existing rooms. The new management will most likely offer packages inclusive of guided game drives in open 4x4s, as well as guided walks & boat trips on the lake. Be aware that the baboons that loiter around the lodge grounds occasionally enter & raid rooms, so avoid leaving your door open, especially if you have any food inside. *Expect rates to be in the ballpark of US$300 dbl B&B.*

CAMPING For the self-sufficient, this is allowed at various locations in the park, and costs US$10 per person per night for non-residents, US$5 for foreign residents, or Rfr2,000 for Rwandans. Contact ORTPN (see page 84) or ask at the gate for further details.

ACTIVITIES

BOAT TRIPS Boat trips are available on Lake Ihema, and are worthwhile. Close encounters with outsized crocodiles and large pods of hippo are all but guaranteed, and you'll also pass substantial breeding colonies of African darter, cormorant and open-bill stork. Other waterbirds are abundant: the delicate and colourful African jacana can be seen trotting on floating vegetation, fish eagles are posted in the trees at regular intervals, jewel-like malachite kingfishers hawk from the reeds, while pied kingfishers hover high above the water to swoop down on their fishy prey. Of greater interest to enthusiasts will be the opportunity to spot marsh specialists such as blue-headed coucal and marsh flycatcher. Two boats are available. The small roofless boat operated by ORTPN seats up to six and costs US$20 per hour. The larger boat operated by Akagera Safari Lodge has a canopy, seats up to 18, and costs US$400 per party for a trip of unspecified duration.

GAME DRIVES Unless you're staying in the safari lodge, game drives are available only if you have a private vehicle, ideally a 4x4. Guides are provided at no extra charge (though a tip will be expected) to help you to find your way around, spot wildlife in the thick bush, and identify birds.

The main game-viewing circuit is in the south and is essentially limited to two main roads that form an excellent loop game drive out of Akagera Safari Lodge. One road runs from the entrance gate to **Lake Ihema** and then continues northwards, passing most of the lakes before it exits the park at the northern Nyungwe Gate. The other road (signposted 'Giraffe Viewing Area') forks left from the lake road about 100m past the entrance gate and then follows a long circuit through the hills before descending back to meet the lakes road on the west shore of **Lake Birengero**. Turn back south here, and the full loop will usually take 3–5 hours, depending on how often you stop.

Game drive options further north are restricted by the fact that the only accommodation is in the far south. However, north of Lake Hago, the road once again branches into two main forks, one heading west into the **Mutumba Hills**, the other continuing along the lakes, and they reconnect at **Lake Rwanyakizinga**.

WEAVERS

Placed by some authorities in the same family as the closely related sparrows, the weavers of the family Ploceidae are a quintessential part of Africa's natural landscape, common and highly visible in virtually every habitat from rainforest to desert. The name of the family derives from the intricate and elaborate nests – typically but not always a roughly oval ball of dried grass, reeds and twigs – that are built by the dextrous males of most species.

It can be fascinating to watch a male weaver at work. First, a nest site is chosen, usually at the end of a thin hanging branch or frond, which is immediately stripped of leaves to protect against snakes. The weaver then flies back and forth to the site, carrying the building material blade by blade in its heavy beak, first using a few thick strands to hang a skeletal nest from the end of a branch, then gradually completing the structure by interweaving numerous thinner blades of grass into the main frame. Once completed, the nest is subjected to the attention of his chosen partner, who will tear it apart if the result is less than satisfactory, and so the process starts all over again.

All but 12 of the 113 described weaver species are resident on the African mainland or associated islands, with some 21 represented within Rwanda alone. All but five of the Rwandan species are placed in the genus Ploceus (true weavers), which is among the most characteristic of all African bird genera. Most of the Ploceus weavers are slightly larger than a sparrow, and display a strong sexual dimorphism. Females are with few exceptions drab buff or olive-brown birds, with some streaking on the back, and perhaps a hint of yellow on the belly.

Most male Ploceus weavers conform to the basic colour pattern of the 'masked weaver' – predominantly yellow, with streaky back and wings, and a distinct black facial mask, often bordered orange. Five Rwandan weaver species fit this masked weaver prototype more-or-less absolutely, and a similar number approximate it rather less exactly, for instance by having a chestnut-brown mask, or a full black head, or a black back, or being more chestnut than yellow on the belly. Identification of the masked weavers can be tricky without experience – useful clues are the exact shape of the mask, the presence and extent of the fringing orange, and the colour of the eye and the back.

The golden weavers, of which only one species is present in Rwanda, are also brilliant yellow and/or light orange with some light streaking on the back, but they lack a mask or any other strong distinguishing features. The handful of forest-associated Ploceus weavers, by contrast, tend to have quite different and very striking colour patterns; and, although sexually dimorphic, the female is often as boldly marked as the male. The most aberrant among these is Vieillot's black weaver, the males of which are totally black

In a long half-day, you could realistically travel from the lodge as far north as the Mutumba Hills and back. To head further north requires the best part of a day, with the option of using the Nyungwe Gate to exit the park north of Lake Rwanyakizinga. The tracks in the far north are very indistinct, and should be attempted only in the company of a guide. If you exit at Nyungwe Gate, the guide can be dropped at Kayonza or Kabarondo junctions with enough money to make his way back to the headquarters by motorbike-taxi.

Starting from the entrance gate, a hilly road through very thick scrub (where klipspringer and buffalo are often seen) leads over about 5km to **Lake Ihema**. It is on a humid and mosquito-plagued island near the eastern shore of Ihema that Henry Stanley, the first European to enter modern-day Rwanda, set up camp on the night of 11 March 1876, only to turn back into what is now Tanzania the next day after he was repulsed from the lake's western shore. Today, Defassa waterbuck

except for their eyes, while the black-billed weaver reverses the prototype by being all black with a yellow facemask.

Among the more conspicuous Ploceus species in Rwanda are the black-headed, Baglafecht, slender-billed, yellow-backed and Vieillot's black weavers – for the most part gregarious breeders forming single- or mixed-species colonies of hundreds, sometimes thousands, of pairs. The most extensive weaver colonies are often found in reed beds and waterside vegetation, such as can be seen around the lakes of Akagera. Few weavers have a distinctive song, but they compensate with a rowdy jumble of harsh swizzles, rattles and nasal notes that can reach deafening proportions near large colonies. One more cohesive song you will often hear seasonally around weaver colonies is a cyclic 'dee-dee-dee-Diederik', often accelerating to a hysterical crescendo when several birds call at once. This is the call of the Diederik cuckoo, a handsome green-and-white cuckoo that lays its eggs in weaver nests.

Oddly, while most East African Ploceus weavers are common, even abundant, in suitable habitats, seven highly localised species are listed as range-restricted, and four of these – one Kenyan, one Ugandan and two Tanzanian endemics – are regarded to be of global conservation concern. Of the other three, the strange weaver Ploceus alienus – black head, plain olive back, yellow belly with chestnut bib – is an Albertine Rift endemic restricted to a handful of sites in Rwanda and Uganda, notably Nyungwe National Park.

Most of the colonial weavers, perhaps relying on safety in numbers, build relatively plain nests with a roughly oval shape and an unadorned entrance hole. The nests of more solitary weavers are often more elaborate. Several weavers, for instance, protect their nests from egg-eating invaders by attaching tubular entrance tunnels to the base – in the case of the spectacled weaver, which inhabits riverine woodland in Akagera, this tunnel is sometimes twice as long as the nest itself. The Grosbeak weaver (a peculiar larger-than-average brown-and-white weaver of reed beds, distinguished by its outsized bill and placed in the monospecific genus Amblyospiza) constructs a large and distinctive domed nest, which is supported by a pair of reeds, and woven as precisely as the finest basketwork, with a neat raised entrance hole at the front. By contrast, the scruffiest nests are built by the various species of sparrow- and buffalo-weaver, relatively drab but highly gregarious dry-country birds which are poorly represented in Rwanda.

are common residents around Ihema, as are some reportedly aggressive buffaloes. It's worth stopping to look for hippos, crocodiles, scraggly marabou storks and waterbirds; also a resident pair of the localised Arnot's chat is resident. This is also where boat trips can be arranged.

About 4km north of Lake Ihema, a road forks through more thick scrub to the small **Lake Shakani**, a scenic camping spot and home to large numbers of hippo. The bush here is rattling with birdlife (look out for the brilliant scarlet chest of the black-headed gonolek) and impala are rather common. A rough track along the marshy western lake shore is a good place to pick up the likes of African jacana, long-toed lapwing, open-billed stork, squacco heron and common moorhen. Unfortunately the lake is also a popular place to water cattle. About 8km north of this, **Lake Birengero** is a shallow, muddy body of palm-fringed water which supports huge numbers of waterbirds, notably pelicans, storks, and at least one pair of shoebill. To look for the shoebill, park at one of the open areas on the western shore and scan the papyrus beds opposite for a large static grey shape.

From here, you can follow the track into the hills through the so-called '**Giraffe-viewing Area**' back to the entrance gate. This more open country can be good for antelope, especially topi and oribi, and giraffe and buffalo are also seen with some frequency. It's worth stopping at the Rwisirabo ranger post to look for Arnot's chat and long-tailed cisticola. Better still is the birdlife at **Muyumbu Campsite**, where fruiting trees often host various barbets along with green woodhoopoe, Meyer's parrot and many smaller acacia-associated species

The best of the lakes for general game viewing is **Lake Hago**, which lies about 15km north of Birengero and is encircled by a decent track. This is where elephant are most likely to be seen, as well as small herds of buffalo and zebra, and it must support several hundred hippo. Away from the lakeshore, the vegetation here is mostly very dense, and animals are difficult to spot, though you can be reasonably confident of seeing baboons, vervet monkeys and impala.

This all changes when you ascend to the **Mutumba Hills** through an area of park-like woodland whose large acacias are favoured by giraffe. Eventually the woodland gives way to open grassland and easily the best game viewing in the park. Here, you can be certain of seeing the delicate oribi and reedbuck, as well as the larger topi. With luck, you'll also encounter eland, zebra and (in the wet season) large herds of buffalo.

North of the Mutumba Hills, the vegetation is again very thick, and animals can be difficult to spot, though impala, buffalo and zebra all seem to be present in significant numbers. The papyrus beds around **Lakes Gishanju** and **Mihindi** form the most accessible marshy areas in the park, and are worth taking slowly by anybody who hopes to see papyrus-dwellers. The **Plage Hippos** (Hippo Beach) on Lake Mihindi was, oddly, about the one place in Akagera where we stopped next to open water and *didn't* see any hippos, but it's a pretty spot, and would make for an ideal picnic site.

Heading further north, **Lake Rwanyakizinga** is another favoured spot with elephants, and the open plains to the west of the lake are excellent for plains animals such as warthog, zebra and herds of 50-plus topi. This little-visited part of Akagera is one that is inhabited by lion – and, until recently, a solitary and secretive rhino. Having looked around this area, your options are either to head back the way you came, or (more popular) to head cross-country out of the park along the route mentioned earlier in this section.

Appendix I

LANGUAGE

Words in Kinyarwanda are spelt phonetically here, to make their pronunciation easy. The letters 'r' and 'l' (and their sounds) are often interchanged, also sometimes 'b', 'v' and 'w'. When a word ends in 'e', pronounce it as the French 'é'. Pronounce 'i' as 'ee' rather than 'eye'.

English	French	Kinyarwanda
COURTESIES		
good day/hello	*bonjour*	*muraho*
good morning	*bonjour*	*mwaramutse*
good afternoon	*bonjour*	*mwiriwe*
good evening	*bonsoir*	*mwiriwe*
sir	*monsieur*	*bwana*
madam	*madame*	*mubyeyi*
how are you?	*ça va?*	*amakuru?/bitese?*
I'm fine, thank you	*ça va bien, merci*	*amakuru/meza/égo*
please	*s'il vous plaît*	*mubishoboye*
thank you	*merci*	*murakoze*
excuse me	*excusez-moi*	*imbabazi*
goodbye (morning)	*au revoir*	*mwiliwe*
goodbye (afternoon)	*au revoir*	*mwilirwe*
goodbye (evening)	*au revoir*	*muramukeho*
goodbye (for ever)	*au revoir/adieu*	*murabeho*
BASIC WORDS		
yes	*oui*	*yégo*
no	*non*	*oya*
that's right	*c'est ça*	*ni byo*
maybe	*peut-être*	*ahali*
good	*bon*	*byiza*
hot	*chaud*	*ubushyuhe*
cold	*froid*	*ubukonje*
and	*et*	*na*
QUESTIONS		
how?	*comment?*	*bite?*
how much?	*combien?*	*angahe?*
what's your name?	*quel est votre nom?*	*witwande?*
when?	*quand?*	*ryali?*
where?	*où?*	*hehe?*
who?	*qui?*	*nde?/bande?*

English	French	Kinyarwanda

FOOD/DRINK

beans	*haricots*	*ibihyimbo*
beer	*bière*	*byeri*
butter	*beurre*	*amavuta*
bread	*pain*	*umugati*
coffee	*café*	*ikawa*
eggs	*œufs*	*amagi*
fish	*poisson*	*amafi*
meat	*viande*	*inyama*
milk	*lait*	*amata*
potatoes	*pommes de terre*	*ibirayi*
rice	*riz*	*umuceli*
salad	*salade*	*salade*
soup	*potage*	*isupu*
sugar	*sucre*	*isukali*
tea	*thé*	*icyayi (chai)*
tomatoes	*tomates*	*inyanya*
drinks	*boissons*	*ibinyobura*
water	*eau*	*amazi*

SHOPPING

bank	*banque*	*ibanki*
bookshop	*librairie*	*isomero*
chemist	*pharmacie*	*farumasi*
shop	*magasin*	*iduka*
market	*marché*	*isoko*
battery	*pile/batterie*	*bateri*
film	*filme*	*filime*
map	*carte*	*ikarita*
money	*argent*	*amafaranga*
soap	*savon*	*isabuni*
toothpaste	*dentifrice*	*umuti w'amenyo*

POST

post office	*poste (PTT)*	*iposta*
envelope	*enveloppe*	*ibahasha*
letter	*lettre*	*urwandiko*
paper	*papier*	*urupapuro*
postcard	*carte postale*	
stamp	*timbre*	*tembri*

GETTING AROUND

bus	*bus*	*bisi*
bus station	*gare routière*	*aho bisi ihagarara*
taxi	*taxi*	*tagisi*
car	*voiture*	*imodoka*
petrol station	*station d'essence*	*aho kunywesbereza essence*
plane	*avion*	*indege*
far	*loin*	*kure*
near	*près*	*hafi*
to the right	*à droite*	*i buryo*

English	French	Kinyarwanda
to the left	*à gauche*	*i bumoso*
straight ahead	*tout droit*	*imbere*
bridge	*pont*	*ikiraro*
hill	*colline*	*agasozi*
lake	*lac*	*ikiyaga*
mountain	*montagne*	*umusozi*
river	*fleuve*	*uruzi*
road	*route*	*umuhanda*
street	*rue*	*inzira*
town	*ville*	*umudugudu*
valley	*vallée*	*umubanda*
village	*village*	*akadugudu*
waterfall	*chute*	*isumo*

HOTEL

bed	*lit*	*igitanda*
room	*chambre*	*icyumba*
key	*clef/clé*	*urufunguzo*
shower	*douche*	*urwiyu hagiriro*
bath	*baignoire*	*urwogero*
toilet/WC	*toilette*	*umusarane*
hot water	*l'eau chaude*	*amazi ashushye*
cold water	*l'eau froide*	*amazi akonje*

MISCELLANEOUS

dentist	*dentiste*	*umuganga w'amenyo*
doctor	*médecin*	*umuganga*
embassy	*ambassade*	*ambasade*
tourist office	*bureau de tourisme*	*ibiro by ubukererarugendo*

TIME

minute	*minute*	*idakika*
hour	*heure*	*isaaha*
day	*jour*	*umunsi*
week	*semaine*	*icyumweru*
month	*mois*	*ukwezi*
year	*an/année*	*umwaka*
now	*maintenant*	*ubu/nonaha*
soon	*bientôt*	*vuba*
today	*aujourd'hui*	*none*
yesterday	*hier*	*ejo hashize*
tomorrow	*demain*	*ejo hazaza*
this week	*cette semaine*	*iki cyumweru*
next week	*semaine prochaine*	*icyumweru gitaha*
morning	*matin*	*igitondo*
afternoon	*après-midi*	*ni munsi*
evening	*soir*	*umugoroba*
night	*nuit*	*ijoro*
Monday	*lundi*	*ku wa mbere*
Tuesday	*mardi*	*ku wa kabili*
Wednesday	*mercredi*	*ku wa gatatu*

English	French	Kinyarwanda
Thursday	jeudi	ku wa kane
Friday	vendredi	ku wa gatanu
Saturday	samedi	ku wa gatandatu
Sunday	dimanche	ku cyumweru
January	janvier	Mutarama
February	février	Gashyantare
March	mars	Werurwe
April	avril	Mata
May	mai	Gicuransi
June	juin	Kamena
July	juillet	Nyakanga
August	août	Kanama
September	septembre	Nzeli
October	octobre	Ukwakira
November	novembre	Ugushyingo
December	décembre	Ukuboza

NUMBERS

1	un/une	rimwe
2	deux	kabili
3	trois	gatatu
4	quatre	kane
5	cinq	gatanu
6	six	gatandatu
7	sept	kalindwi
8	huit	umunani
9	neuf	icyenda
10	dix	icumi
100	cent	ijana
1,000	mille	igihumbi
2,000	deux mille	ibihumbi bibili
3,000	trois mille	ibihumbi bitatu
4,000	quatre mille	ibihumbi bikane
5,000	cinq mille	ibihumbi bitanu
6,000	six mille	ibihumbi bitandatu
7,000	sept mille	ibihumbi bilindwi
8,000	huit mille	ibihumbi bimunani
9,000	neuf mille	ibihumbi bicyenda

AFRICAN ENGLISH Philip Briggs

Although a high proportion of Rwandans were raised in Kenya, Uganda or Tanzania and so speak English as a second language, not all get the opportunity to use it regularly, and as a result they will not be as fluent as they could be. Furthermore, as is often the case in Africa and elsewhere, an individual's pronunciation of a second language often tends to retain the vocal inflections of their first language, or it falls somewhere between that and a more standard pronunciation. It is also the case that many people tend to structure sentences in a second language similar to how they would in their home tongue. As a result, most Rwandans, to a greater or lesser extent, speak English with Bantu inflections and grammar. The above considerations aside, I would venture that African English – like American or Australian English – is over-due recognition as a distinct linguistic entity, possessed of a unique rhythm and pronunciation, as well as an idiomatic quality quite distinct from any form of English spoken elsewhere. And learning to communicate in this idiom is perhaps the most important linguistic skill that the visitor to any African country where English is spoken can acquire. If this sounds patronising, so be it. There are regional accents in the UK and US that I find far more difficult to follow than the English spoken in Africa, simply because I am more familiar with the latter. And precisely the same adjustment might be required were, for instance, an Australian to travel in the American south, a Geordie to wash up in my home town of Johannesburg, or vice versa.

The following points should prove useful when you speak English to Africans:

- Greet simply, using phrases likely to be understood locally: the ubiquitous sing-song 'How-are-you! – I am fine', or if that draws a blank try the pidgin Swahili 'Jambo!' It is important always to greet a stranger before you plough ahead and ask directions or any other question. Firstly, it is rude to do otherwise; secondly, most Westerners feel uncomfortable asking a stranger a straight question. If you have already greeted the person, you'll feel less need to preface a question with phrases like 'I'm terribly sorry' or 'Would you mind telling me' which will confuse someone who speaks limited English.

- Speak slowly and clearly. There is no need, as some travellers do, to take this too far, as if you are talking to a three-year-old. Speak naturally, but try not to rush or clip phrases.

- Phrase questions simply, with an ear towards Bantu inflections. 'This bus goes to Huye?' might be more easily understood than 'Could you tell me whether this bus is going to Huye?' and 'You have a room?' is better than 'Is there a vacant room?' If you are not understood, don't keep repeating the same question more loudly. Try a different and ideally simpler phrasing, giving consideration to whether any specific word(s) – in the last case, most likely 'vacant' – might particularly obstruct easy understanding.

- Listen to how people talk to you, and learn from it. Vowel sounds are often pronounced as in the local language (see Kinyarwanda pronunciation above), so that 'bin', for instance, might sound more like 'been'. Many words, too, will be pronounced with the customary Bantu stress on the second-last syllable.

- African languages generally contain few words with compound consonant sounds or ending in consonants. This can result in the clipping of soft consonant sounds such as 'r' (important as eem-POT-ant) or the insertion of a random vowel sound between running consonants (so that pen-pal becomes pen-I-pal and sounds almost indistinguishable from pineapple). It is commonplace, as well, to append a random vowel to the end of a word, in the process shifting the stress to what would ordinarily be the last syllable eg: pen-i-PAL-i.

- The 'l' and 'r' sounds are sometimes used interchangeably (hence Lake Burera/Bulera and Rue Karisimbi/Kalisimbi), which can sometimes cause confusion, in particular when your guide points out a lilac-breasted roller! The same is to a lesser extent true of 'b' and 'v' (Virunga versus Birunga), 'k' and 'ch' (the Rwandan capital, spelt Kigali, is more often pronounced 'Chigari') and, very occasionally, 'f' and 'p'.

- Some English words are in wide use. Other similar words are not. Some examples: a request for a 'lodging' or 'guesthouse', is more likely to be understood than one for 'accommodation', as is a request for a 'taxi' (or better 'special hire') over a 'taxi-cab' or 'cab', or for 'the balance' rather than 'change'.

- Avoid the use of dialect-specific expressions, slang and jargon! Few Africans will be familiar with terms such as 'feeling crook', 'pear-shaped' or 'user-friendly'.

- Avoid meaningless interjections. If somebody is struggling to follow you, appending a word such as 'mate' to every other phrase is only likely to further confuse them.

- We've all embarrassed ourselves at some point by mutilating the pronunciation of a word we've read but not heard. Likewise, guides working in national parks and other reserves often come up with innovative pronunciations for bird and mammal names they come across in field guides, and any word with an idiosyncratic spelling (eg: yacht, lamb, knot).

- Make sure the person you are talking to understands you. Try to avoid asking questions that can be answered with a yes or no. People may well agree with you simply to be polite or to avoid embarrassment.
- Keep calm. No-one is at their best when they arrive at a crowded bus station after an all-day bus ride. It is easy to be short tempered when someone cannot understand you. Be patient and polite; it's you who doesn't speak the language.
- Last but not least, do gauge the extent to which the above rules might apply to any given individual. It would be patently ridiculous to address a university lecturer or an experienced tour guide in broken English, equally inappropriate to babble away without making any allowances when talking to a villager who clearly has a limited English vocabulary. Generally, I start off talking normally to anybody I meet, and only start to refine my usage as and when it becomes clear it will aid communication.

Appendix 2

BOOKS
Historical background

Fegley, Randall (compiler) *Rwanda – World Bibliographical Series volume 154* Clio Press, 1993. This selective, annotated bibliography contains over 500 entries covering a wide range of subjects including Rwanda's history, geography, politics, literature, travellers' accounts, flora and fauna. Its preface and introduction give a condensed but useful (although somewhat dated) overview of Rwanda from early times until just before the genocide.

Kagame, Alexis *Un abrégé de l'ethno-histoire du Rwanda* and *Un abrégé de l'histoire du Rwanda de 1853 à 1972*, Editions Universitaires du Rwanda, Butare, 1972 and 1975. These works are now out of print (and there are no English translations) but the seriously interested should try to track down secondhand copies. Drawing on oral tradition, Kagame describes the country and its people from several centuries before the arrival of the Europeans (in the first book) through to the first decade of colonisation (in the second).

Reader, John *Africa: A Biography of the Continent* Hamish Hamilton, 1997. This award-winning book, available as a Penguin paperback, provides a compulsively readable introduction to Africa's past, from the formation of the continent to post-independence politics – the ideal starting point for anybody seeking to place their Rwandan experience in a broader African context.

Natural history

Briggs, Philip *East African Wildlife* Bradt, 2008. This is a handy and lavishly illustrated one-stop handbook to the fauna of East Africa, with detailed sections on the region's main habitats, varied mammals, birds, reptiles and insects. It's the ideal companion for first-time visitors whose interest in wildlife extends beyond the Big Five but who don't want to carry a library of reference books.

Field guides (mammals)

Dorst, J & Dandelot, P *Field Guide to the Larger Mammals of Africa* Collins, 1983 and Haltenorth, T & Diller, H *Field Guide to the Mammals of Africa including Madagascar* Collins, 1984. Formerly the standard field guides to the region, these books are still recommended in many travel guides. In my opinion, they have largely been superseded by subsequent publications, and now come across as very dated and badly structured – with mediocre illustrations to boot.

Estes, Richard *The Safari Companion* Green Books (UK), Russell Friedman Books (SA), Chelsea Green (USA). This unconventional book might succinctly be described as a field guide to mammal behaviour. It's probably a bit esoteric for most one-off visitors to Africa, but a must for anybody with a serious interest in wildlife.

Kingdon, Jonathan *The Kingdon Field Guide to African Mammals* Academic Press, 1997. This is my first choice: the most detailed, thorough and up to date of several field guides covering the mammals of the region. The author, a highly respected biologist, supplements detailed descriptions and good illustrations of all the continent's large mammals with an ecological overview of each species. Essential for anybody with a serious interest in mammal identification.

Stuart, Chris & Tilde *The Larger Mammals of Africa* Struik, 1997. This useful field guide doesn't quite match up to Kingdon's, but it's the best of the rest, and arguably more appropriate to readers with a relatively casual interest in African wildlife. It's also a lot cheaper and lighter!

Stuart, Chris & Tilde *Southern, Central and East African Mammals* Struik, 1995. This excellent mini-guide, compact enough to slip into a pocket, is remarkably thorough within its inherent space restrictions. Highly recommended for one-off safari-goers, but not so good on forest primates, which limits its usefulness in Rwanda.

Field guides (birds)

Stevenson, Terry & Fanshawe, John *Field Guide to the Birds of East Africa* T & A D Poyser, 2002. The best bird field guide, with useful field descriptions and accurate plates and distribution maps. It covers every species found in Rwanda as well as in Uganda, Kenya, Tanzania and Burundi. For serious birdwatchers, this is *the* book to take.

Van Perlo, Ber *Illustrated Checklist to the Birds of Eastern Africa* Collins, 1995. This is the next best thing to the above (and is cheaper and lighter), since it illustrates and provides a brief description of every species recorded in Uganda and Tanzania, along with a distribution map. I don't know of any bird found in Rwanda but not in Tanzania or Uganda, and I found that distribution details can normally be extrapolated from the maps of neighbouring countries. Be aware that the descriptive detail is succinct and many of the illustrations are misleading

Williams, J & Arlott, N *Field Guide to the Birds of East Africa* Collins, 1980. As with the older Collins mammal field guides, Williams' was for years the standard field guide to the region, and is still widely mentioned in travel literature. Unfortunately, it feels rather dated today: less than half the birds in the region are illustrated, several are not even described, and the bias is strongly towards common Kenyan birds.

Zimmerman et al *Birds of Kenya and Northern Tanzania* Russell Friedman Books, 1996. This monumentally handsome hardback tome is arguably the finest field guide to any African territory. The geographical limitations with regard to Rwanda are obvious, but its wealth of descriptive and ecological detail and superb illustrations make it an excellent secondary source. A lighter and cheaper but less detailed paperback version was published in 1999.

Others

Fossey, Dian *Gorillas in the Mist* Hodder & Stoughton, 1983. Enjoyable and massively informative, Fossey's landmark book is recommended without reservation to anybody going gorilla tracking in the Parc des Volcans.

Goodall, Jane *Through A Window* Houghton Mifflin, 1991. Subtitled *My Thirty Years with the Chimpanzees of Gombe*, this is one of several highly readable books by Jane Goodall about the longest ongoing study of wild primates in the world. Set in Tanzania, this is nevertheless obvious pre-trip reading for anybody intending to track chimps in Nyungwe.

Kingdon, Jonathan *Island Africa* Collins, 1990. This highly readable and award-winning tome about evolution in ecological 'islands' such as deserts and montane forests is recommended to anybody who wants to place the natural history of Nyungwe and the Virungas in a continental context.

Mowat, Farley *Woman in the Mists* Futura, 1987. An excellent biography of the controversial Dian Fossey, one which leans so heavily on her own journals that parts are almost autobiography.

Stuart, Chris & Tilde *Africa's Vanishing Wildlife* Southern Books, 1996. An informative and pictorially strong introduction to the endangered and vulnerable mammals of Africa, this book combines coffee-table production with impassioned and erudite text.

Weber, Bill & Vedder, Amy *In the Kingdom of Gorillas* Simon & Schuster, 2002. This superb and immensely readable account of the authors' pioneering conservation work in Volcanoes and Nyungwe National Parks featured as one of *BBC Wildlife*'s 'most influential books from the past 40 years of wildlife publishing' in 2003.

Background to the genocide

Barnett, Michael *Eyewitness to a Genocide: The United Nations and Rwanda* Cornell University, 2002. Tracing the history of the UN's involvement with Rwanda, Barnett argues that it did bear some moral responsibility for the genocide. A clear and factual study, also covering the warnings raised by the genocide and the question of whether it is possible to build wholly moral institutions.

Dallaire, Lt Gen Roméo *Shake Hands with the Devil: the failure of humanity in Rwanda* Arrow Books, 2004. Dallaire was force commander of the UN Assistance Mission for Rwanda at the time of the genocide. This angry, moving and deeply human book describes the impossible situation he faced, caught up in a nightmare of killing and terror and yet denied the men and the operational freedom he needed in order to quell it. We see the unfolding of the genocide, in all its aspects, from the perspective of probably the one man who, had he been better heeded and supported, could have lessened its effects.

Gourevitch, Philip *We wish to inform you that tomorrow we will be killed with our families* Picador, 1998. Subtitled 'Stories from Rwanda', this winner of the *Guardian* First Book Award is war reporting of the highest order. Blending starkly factual narrative with human anecdotes and observations, Gourevitch paints on a broad canvas and the picture he creates is unforgettable. He shows us 'little people' caught up in unstoppable horrors – and reaching great heights of heroism.

Keane, Fergal *Season of Blood – a Rwandan Journey* Penguin, 1995. Keane's prose – sometimes so precisely balanced that it verges on poetry – is always impeccable. Here he blends factual narrative and analysis with spontaneous emotion in such a way that the reader is both moved and informed in a single phrase. As a BBC correspondent, he was travelling around Rwanda – among the killers and among the victims – as the genocide spread countrywide. His reports at the time brought home the extent of the human tragedy and their essence is preserved in this book, which won the 1995 Orwell Prize.

Kinzer, Stephen *A Thousand Hills: Rwanda's Rebirth and the Man Who Dreamed it* John Wiley & Sons 2008. This is one of the few books to deal with post-genocide Rwanda, focussing primarily on and quoting heavily from President Paul Kagame (who granted the author several exclusive interviews), and while it inevitably has the slightly partisan flavour endemic to authorised biographies, it also provides a worthwhile and insightful overview of Rwanda's recovery over the past 15 years.

Leave None to Tell the Story African Rights Watch, 1999. Another painfully comprehensive account, full of personal testimonies based on Rwandan government records, this shows how ordinary administrative structures and practices were turned into mechanisms of murder. It describes the opposition to the killing and how it was crushed, while survivors relate how they resisted and escaped. Using diplomatic and court documents, the survey shows what might have been the result had the international reaction been swifter and more determined.

Melvern, L R *A People Betrayed – the Role of the West in Rwanda's Genocide* Zed Books, 2000, 2nd edition 2009; and *Conspiracy to Murder: The Rwandan Genocide* Verso 2004. Linda Melvern's investigative study of the international background to Rwanda's genocide, *A People Betrayed*, contains a full account of how the tragedy unfolded. Documents held in Kigali, and previously unpublished accounts of secret UN Security council deliberations in New York, reveal a shocking sequence of events, and the failure of governments, organisations and individuals who could – had they opted to do so – have prevented the genocide. Melvern's equally powerful sequel, *Conspiracy to Murder*, continues the investigation, drawing on a vast amount of new material including documents abandoned by the *génocidaires* when they fled from Rwanda. A revised second edition of *A People Betrayed* was published in July 2009.

Prunier, Gérard *The Rwanda Crisis – History of a Genocide* Hurst & Company, 1998. This painstakingly researched history of the Rwandan genocide, full of personal anecdotes and individual stories, describes with icy clarity the composition of the time bomb that began ticking long before its explosion in 1994. Prunier presents the genocide as part of a deadly logic, a plan hatched for political and economic motives, rather than the result of ancient hatred. He helps the reader to understand not only Rwanda's genocide but also the complexities of modern conflict in general.

Rusesabagina, Paul *An Ordinary Man: The True Story Behind Hotel Rwanda* Bloomsbury, 2007. This is a powerful and readable, but very controversial, autobiographical account of the genocide, written by the manager of the Hotel des Mille Collines who provided shelter to more than a thousand refuges at the height of the killing.

Rwanda – Death, Despair and Defiance African Rights, London, 1995. This 1,200-page compilation by the UK organisation African Rights is a painfully thorough and detailed account of the genocide and its effect on Rwanda's people – the careful preparations, the identities of the killers and their accomplices, the massacres, the attacks on churches, schools and hospitals, and the aftermath. Victims tell their own stories and those of their families, and the horror and immensity of the slaughter are highlighted by the simplicity of their narratives. The impact is powerful, sometimes overwhelming. The index enables the reader to discover easily what happened in any particular area or village.

Sibomana, André *Hope for Rwanda* Pluto Press, 1999. In this very personal account, subtitled *Conversations with Laure Guilbert and Hervé Deguine*, the speaker describes the unfolding of the genocide, and his own experiences, with impressive fairness, clarity and lack of accusation. A touching and informative book by a remarkable man.

Miscellaneous

Halsey Carr, R & Howard Halsey, *A Land of a Thousand Hills* Viking, 1999. Rosamond Halsey Carr moved to Rwanda as a young bride in 1949 and has stayed for over 50 years. She watched the decline of colonialism, the problems of independence and the growing violence. When the genocide started she was evacuated by the American Embassy but returned four months later, and began turning an old pyrethrum drying-house on her flower plantation into a home for genocide orphans, which still functions today. This very readable and moving book chronicles the extraordinary life of an extraordinary woman, in the country she loved and made her home.

Lewis, Jerome & Knight, Judy *The Twa of Rwanda* World Rainforest Movement (UK), 1996. The Twa are the smallest 'ethnic' group in Rwanda. This report, published by the World Rainforest Movement in co-operation with the International Work Group for Indigenous Affairs (Denmark) and Survival International (France), traces their history, highlights their current impoverished situation, quotes their opinions about their past and future, and allows them to express their fears and aspirations. It also shows the dilemma faced by African governments as they try to build national unity while still respecting cultural diversity.

Stassen, Jean-Philippe *Déogratias* Aire Libre, Dupuis (Belgium) 2000. If you can read at least some French, this 80-page *bande dessinée* (graphic novel) tells the story of a young Hutu who killed during the genocide and how this, together with drink, destroyed him. With skill and humanity, the creator succeeds in 'telling the untellable' and producing a powerful document.

WEBSITES For up-to-the-minute news reports from Rwanda and elsewhere in Africa the most comprehensive site is probably **www.allafrica.com**. Follow links to Rwanda. The website of the Rwandan newspaper *The New Times* has a range of local news items not picked up elsewhere: **www.newtimes.co.rw**.

For regular updates and reader feedback covering all aspects of travel to Rwanda, visit **http://updates.bradtguides.com/rwanda**, overseen by Philip Briggs as an interactive update service for travellers, volunteers and service providers in Rwanda.

A good site for checking the latest currency exchange rate (not all include the Rwandan franc) is **www.xe.com**. Conditions in Rwanda – as elsewhere in Africa – may change, so as a precaution, before travelling, always check the Foreign Office website **www.fco.gov.uk/travel**, or that of the US State Department: **www.travel.state.gov**. For up-to-date visa requirements (and online application) visit **www.migration.gov.rw**.

Four comprehensive websites on Rwanda are **www.rwandaembassy.org** (set up by the Rwandan Embassy in Washington, DC); the well organised **www.rwandagateway.org**; that of the Rwandan Embassy in London, **www.ambarwanda.org.uk**; and that of ORTPN (the Rwanda Tourist Board), **www.rwandatourism.com**, which provides impressive 'virtual tours' of many of the country's attractions. All have numerous links and between them cover a wide range of topics, including Rwanda's history, geography, politics, development, genocide trials, economy, business potential and tourism. On the whole the essentials are up to date although some sections haven't been touched for a while at the time of writing. Another (self-explanatory) tourism site is **www.rwanda-golf.com**.

For more-or-less current phone numbers (and sometimes addresses) of hotels and other businesses in Rwanda, try **www.rwandaphonebook.com**; it's a kind of condensed Yellow Pages.

The website of KIST (Kigali Institute of Science and Technology) generally has some interesting details of small-scale development and appropriate technology: **www.kist.ac.rw**. The site of the UN International Criminal Tribunal for Rwanda, **www.ictr.org**, has details of the current status of genocide criminals and the trials in progress. Human Rights Watch on **www.hrw.org** carries news of Rwanda, as does the Amnesty International site **www.amnesty.org**.

For regular reports relating to birding in Rwanda (and other wildlife), visit Ruhengeri resident Marcell Claassen's blog **http://rwandabirdingguide.blogspot.com/**.

For specific out-of-print books on Rwanda (and any other subject under the sun), try the unmatchable **www.usedbooksearch.co.uk**.

Fly with me...

Johannesburg

Bujumbura　　Dubai

　　　　　　　London

Kilimanjaro

　　　　　　Addis Ababa

Kamembe

　　　　　　　Brussels

Nairobi

　　　　　Amsterdam

Entebbe

　　Kigali

RwandAir
Fly our dream to the heart of Africa.

www.rwandair.com

Index

Page numbers in **bold** refer to major entries; those in *italics* indicate maps

accommodation 53–4
Akagera National Park *248*, **249–62**
    accommodation 259
    activities 259–62
    antelope 252
    birds 254–5
    fees 258–9
    getting there and away 258
    history 250
    natural history 250–7
    reptiles 255
    shoebill 255, 256–7
    wildlife 251–7
Amahoro Island 174
Ankole cattle 244–5

background information 3–32
Bagenge's Rock 196–7
banana 118–19, 136
Banda 150, 153
bargaining 43
bark cloth 125
Batwa *see* Twa
Baudouin II, King 135, 169
becoming involved 60–3
begging 43
Belgian colonisation 12–15
bicycle taxis 52
bilharzia 70–1
binoculars 46
Bisesero 175
Bizimungu, President Pasteur 18, 19
bookshops 103
border crossings 38–40, 47
bribery 44
budgeting 49–50
Bugarama hot springs 158–9, **168–9**
Bugesera District 112–14
Buhanga Eco-Park 200–1, 202
bureaucracy 44
Burton, Richard 4, 5
buses 52–3

Butare **129–38**, *128*, *132*
    accommodation 130–3
    banks 134
    cathedral 136
    genocide 130
    getting there and away 129–30
    history 129
    internet 134
    national museum 135–6
    nightlife 134
    restaurants 133–4
    security 130
    shopping 134
    university 135
Byumba 235–6

Cameroon 162–3
camping 54
camping equipment 45
Carr, Rosamond Halsey 127, 183, 184–5, 272
chameleons 148–9
charities 60–3
chimpanzees 144–5, 153, 158–9
Classe, Bishop Léon 13
clothes 45
credit cards 48
cricket 101
crime 40–2
cultural etiquette 60
culture 29–32
currency 2, 50
Cyamudongo Forest 158–9
Cyangugu 162–8, *164*
Cyarumbo 137

dance 29–30
Dancing Pots 183
deep vein thrombosis 71
dengue fever 69
diarrhoea 68–9
disabled travellers 40–1
distance chart 50

drinks 55–6
driving 50–2
DSTV 59

eastern Rwanda 233–47, *234*
eating 54–5
ebola 73
education 26–8
electricity 2
embassies 36–7

fauna 5–6
field guides 269–70
first aid kit *see* medical kit
flights to Rwanda 37–8
flights, domestic 50
football 31, 100
foreign exchange 47, 48–9
Fossey, Dian ix, x, 211, 213, 214, 221, 222,
    227, 228, 231, 270
further reading 269–72

Gacaca 20
Gakenke 190
Gashora 114
Gatagara, Poterie locale de 121
genocide 18–19, 20, 23, 30, 60, 77, 106–8,
    113–14, 115, 120, 130, 135, 137, 138,
    165, 171, 174, 175, 183, 184, 198, 200,
    215, 247, 271–2
genocide memorials 106–8, 113–14, 120,
    137, 138, 171, 174, 175
Genocide Memorial Day 57
geography 2, 3
German colonisation 9–11
getting around 50–3
Gicimbi *see* Byumba
Gihaya Island 168–9
Gikongoro 138
Gisakura Tea Estate 151, 157
Gisenyi 174–81, *176–7*
Gishwati Forest 186–7
Gitarama 115–21, *116*
glasses 47
Goma (Congo) 183–5, 186
Gorilla-naming ceremony *see* Kwita Izina
gorillas 49, 211, 212–16, 220–6

Habyarimana, President Juvenal 16, 17,
    108, 168
handicrafts 31
health 64–74
history 6–23

hitching 52
human statistics 2
Humure Refugee Village 251
Huye *see* Butare
Huye Tinnery 136–7

Iby'Iwacu Cultural Village 230
Imbabazi Orphanage 183, 184–5
immunisations 64–5
independence from Belgium 14–16
Ingoboka Coffee Cooperative 183
insect bites 69–70
interahamwe 17, 18, 19, 108, 113, 138, 175
internet 58–9
investing in Rwanda 63
itinerary planning 33–4

Kabgayi 120
Kabuye, Mount 190–1
Kagame, President Paul 2, 15, 16, 17, 18,
    19, 21, 31, 271
Kamageri's Rock 123
Kamembe *see* Cyangugu
Karisimbi, Mount 211, 213, 221, 227, 228,
    230–1
Karongi *see* Kibuye
Kayibanda, President Grégoire 14, 15, 16, 115
Kayonza 237
Kiaka Cooperative 183
Kibeho 137
Kibungo 241–3, *242*
Kibuye 169–74, *170*
Kigali **77–114**, *78–9*, *82–3*, *86*, *89*
    accommodation 85–93
    airport 80
    arts 98–9, 102–3
    ATMs 106
    bookshops 103
    buses to/from 80–1
    Camp Kigali Memorial 108
    cinema 98
    cycling 111
    dance 99
    excursions further afield 112–14
    foreign exchange 105–6
    getting around 81–2
    getting there and away 80
    Gisozi Genocide Memorial 106–8
    handicrafts 102–3, 104
    history 77
    internet 105
    Kandt House 109–10
    markets 103–4

Kigali *continued*
   medical facilities 105
   minibuses to/from 80–1
   Museum of Natural History 109–10
   nightlife 98
   Nyabugogo 110
   Nyamirambo 110
   Nyanza Genocide Memorial 108
   Nyarutarama Lake 110
   Remera Heroes Cemetery 108
   restaurants 93–8
   shopping 100–4
   sport 99–100
   State House Museum 108
   telephone 105
   tour operators 84–5
   tourist information 84
   Union Trade Centre (UTC) 100
   walking 110–11
   what to see and do 106–11
Kinyarwanda 262–6
Kitabi College of Conservation &
   Environmental Management 151
Kumbya 166
Kwita Izina 216

Lake Burera 203–9, *206*
Lake Karago 202–3
Lake Kivu 161–87
Lake Mirayi 114
Lake Muhazi 235, 237–8, 239
Lake Ruhondo 209–10, *206*
Lake Rumira 114
Lake Rweru 114
language 23–4, 262–8
limnic eruptions 162–3
literature 29
Livingstone, Dr David 5
Logiest, Colonel Guy 15, 115
luggage 44–7

malaria 65–6
Maraba Coffee Cooperative 137, 138
Mecklenburg, Duke Adolphus Frederick of
   10, 44, 178
media and communications 58–9
medical facilities in Kigali 74
medical kit 47, 68
meningitis 73
Millennium Village 113–14
minibuses 52–3
money 47–50
monkeys 143–7

mountain biking 52
Muhanga *see* Gitarama
Murambi Genocide Memorial 138
Musanze Cave 203–4
Musanze *see* Ruhengeri
museums 108–10, 120, 124–6, 135–6
music 29
Musinga, Mwami (King) 13, 121, 124
mwami 8, 9

Napoleon's Island 174
National Museum of Rwanda 135–6
National University of Rwanda 135
natural history 3–6
Ndaba Falls 174
newspapers 58
Ngoma *see* Kibungo
Nile River 156–7
Nile, Source of the 4–5, 154, *155*
Nkombo Island 168–9
Ntarama 113–14
Nyabarongo Bridge 112–13
Nyabarongo Wetlands 114
Nyabingi cult 208–9
Nyabisindu National Dairy 127
Nyagatare 238–41, *240*
Nyakabuye 158–9
Nyakarimbi 243
Nyamagabe *see* Gikongoro
Nyamata 113–14
Nyanza 121–7, *122*
Nyiragongo, Mount 186
Nyungwe Forest National Park **139–59**, *140*
   accommodation 150–1
   birds 147–9
   canopy walkway 152
   chimpanzee 144–5, 153, 158–9
   Congo-Nile Divide Trail 154–5
   Cyamudongo Forest 158–9
   fauna 143–50
   fees 147, 150
   flora 141–2
   getting there and away 150
   Gisakura Tea Estate 151, 157
   Kamiranzovu Marsh 155–6
   mangabey tracking 153
   monkeys 143–7
   new tourist developments 141
   proposed fee structure 147
   reception centre 152
   Source of the Nile 154, 155
   trails 151–7
   Waterfall Trail 165–7

oral history 7–8
ORTPN 34, 49, 80, 81, 84
overcharging 43
overland to Rwanda 38–40

packing 44–7
padlock 46
photography 56–7
place names 22, 24
politics 2
post 59
practical information 33–63
prickly heat 72
public holidays 57–8
public transport 52–3
Pygmies *see* Batwa

rabies 73
radio 59
red tape 36
religion 24–6
restaurants 54
road to Butare 114–27
Rubavu *see* Gisenyi
Rubona 182
Rudahigwa Mutara III, Mwami (King) 13,
    14, 15, 124, 125, 126, 127
Ruhango 120–1
Ruhengeri **189–210**, *194–5*
    accommodation 192–6
    birding 200–1
    excursions 199–209
    foreign exchange 199
    getting there and away 189–91
    gorilla permits 191
    internet 199
    restaurants 196–7
    shopping 197–9
    swimming pool 199
    tour operators 192, 198
    tourist information 191
Rukali Palace Museum 124–6
Rusizi Falls 167
Rusizi *see* Cyangugu
Rusomo Falls 243, 245–7
Rwabugiri, Mwami (King) 9
Rwamagana 236–7
Rwanda Na Gasabo 233–4
Rwesero Palace Art Museum 126–7
Rwigyema, Major General Fred 16, 17, 108

safety 40–2
Schaller, George 213, 222

sexually transmitted disease 73
shopping 58
skin infections 72
sleeping bag 46
snakebite 74
Speke, John Hanning 4, 5, 125, 157
sport 31–2
Stanley, Henry 5, 9
sun exposure 72

Tanzania 243
taxis 53
telephone 59
television 59
theft 40–1
ticks 70
time 2
toilet bag 46
tour operators 34–6, 84–5
tourist information 34
travel clinics 66–8
travel insurance 68
travellers' cheques 48
Twa 7, 30, 121, 183, 186, 204–5, 232

Ubushobozi Project 199
Umuganda Day 58
Uwilingiyimana, Agathe 108
Uwinka 151, 152, 153

vegetation 3–4
Virunga Mountains 228–9
visas 36
Vision 2020 21
Volcanoes National Park **211–32**, *212*
    accommodation 218–20
    getting there and away 217–18, 223–5
    golden monkey tracking 227
    gorilla tracking 214–15, 220–6
    gorilla-tracking permits 49, 220–1
    hikes 227–32
    history 213–17
    what to wear and take 224
von Beringe, Oscar 10–11, 214
von Götzen, Count Gustav Adolf 9–10

weavers 260–1
websites 272–3
when to visit 33
women travellers 42